MONOGRAPH SERIES
UNITED STATES CATHOLIC HISTORICAL SOCIETY

Volume 35

x Benedict Rh. Bm

MEMOIRS
TO SERVE FOR THE FUTURE
Ecclesiastical History of the Diocess of Boston

by
Benedict Joseph Fenwick, S.J.
second bishop of Boston

**Edited, with an Introduction, by
Joseph M. McCarthy**

Associate Professor
Suffolk University

Yonkers, N.Y.

U.S. Catholic Historical Society

Office of the Executive Secretary
U.S. Catholic Historical Society
St. Joseph's Seminary, Dunwoodie, Yonkers, New York 10704

TABLE OF CONTENTS

INTRODUCTION

Had Benedict Joseph Fenwick died in 1825 before becoming the second Roman Catholic Bishop of Boston, his career would still merit attention from historians. Scion of a Catholic family which had been established in Maryland since the time of Charles I, he was born on September 3, 1782, and, after schooling, entered the Jesuit order and was ordained priest on March 12, 1808. Sent to New York City in 1809, he was, in effect, administrator of the diocese by 1815. After a term as President of Georgetown College in 1817-18, he was sent to Charleston, S.C., where his tact and firmness healed a rebellion against ecclesiastical authority and led to his appointment as Vicar General for the two Carolinas and Georgia. Between 1822 and 1825 he was successively procurator of Georgetown College and chaplain of the Carmelite Monastery at Port Tobacco, Maryland. He had only just taken up again the presidency of Georgetown College when the call to the episcopacy came.

The choice of Fenwick was fully justified by his accomplishments. Robust, energetic and healthy despite his corpulence (he is said to have weighed in the vicinity of 300 pounds in his latter years), buoyant, optimistic and practical, Fenwick set to work to transform his diocese which, though it compassed all of the New England States, had but one strong parish, eight other small churches, and only three priests in addition to himself. Immediately upon his arrival he built a new convent in Charlestown, Massachusetts, for the Ursuline nuns, and enlarged Holy Cross Cathedral. The building never ceased, and by the time he died, he had built over thirty churches. To provide more priests for his diocese, he first established a house seminary at his residence, then made arrangements with the Sulpicians in Canada for educating his seminarians. For the instruction of his people, he founded in 1829 a newspaper, **The Jesuit** (now **The Pilot**), and in 1842 Holy Cross College in Worcester, Massachusetts. Appalled by the conditions in which the growing number of Irish immigrants in Boston were living, he set up a Catholic farming community, Benedicta, in Aroostook County, Maine. All the while, he worked diligently at perfecting the organization of his diocese. When he died in 1846, he had wrought much, and the most careful and insightful history of his episcopacy limns his achievement thus:

He was exactly the man for the situation, and he made the most of it. He did transform one of the feeblest of dioceses into one of the strongest in the American Church at that time. He brought Catholicism into wellnigh every part of New England. He built up, for the first time here, a large body of clergy, and labored hard to instill into them proper standards of discipline and high priestly ideals. He vigorously opposed and in the main stamped out "Trusteeism," which had wrought such havoc elsewhere. He first fixed the conditions of church life and parochial organization and the methods of handling diocesan business. In his zeal for Catholic education in all forms, for Catholic charities, for high standards in preaching and public worship, for proper Church music, for spreading Catholic literature, for Catholic journalism, for organizing the laity for what would nowadays be called "Catholic Action," he did all that was possible in his circumstances and marked out paths for the future. He gave us our first Catholic college, our first permanent religious orders, our first permanent Catholic newspaper. If Father Matignon and Bishop Cheverus were the true founders of the Diocese of Boston, Bishop Fenwick deserves to be called its organizer. More even than those two illustrious predecessors, he stamped his character upon this Diocese. In face of the gravest difficulties, he accomplished a magnificent and enduring work.[1]

Eminently practical though he was, Fenwick was also something of an intellectual. Orestes Brownson wrote in a memorial piece that

> he seemed to have read everything, and to have retained all he read. We never, in our intercourse with him, knew a subject to be broached of which he was ignorant...No matter what the subject, however obscure or remote from his professional studies, on which you sought information, he could either give it to you or direct you at once to the source whence you could obtain it...Upon the whole, he left on us the impression of a man of rare natural powers, of varied and profound learning, and of being the best informed man we have ever had the honor of meeting.[2]

Certainly Fenwick tried to express his intellectual interests by writing and publishing, but because he was busy about many things, his efforts often came to naught. Apart from some brief apologetic pieces, some items of journalism, and a book of church music, he was unable to publish during his episcopacy, although he did a fair amount of writing. The greater portion of this writing was the diocesan journal he kept, "Memoranda of the Diocess of Boston." The lesser part was a considerable enough project in itself, his "Memoirs to Serve for the Future Ecclesiastical History of the Diocess of Boston." From internal evidence it appears that this history was completed by 1836. The day before it was to have gone to the printer in 1842, Fenwick decided he needed the money allotted for its publication for another venture, the building of Holy Cross College,[3] and the manuscript was left unpublished. The notes for it and drafts of certain sections remain in the Archives of the Archdiocese of Boston, along with the complete final manuscript, written in Fenwick's clear and unmistakable hand in a leather-bound account book. About forty years ago, the authors of the **History of the Archdiocese of Boston** prepared a typescript of the "Memoirs" and one of them, John E. Sexton, made a variety of notations and emendations which seem to indicate an intent to publish them at last. Father Sexton died in 1949 without carrying out his design, and I found the typescript in 1961 at the former Creagh Research Library of St. John's Seminary, Brighton, Massachusetts, when I was assigned the task of organizing the Sexton Papers.

Robert Howard Lord described this work as "this voluminous and precious manuscript—an original source of unique importance for the early history of the organized Church in New England,"[4] and it is difficult to fault his judgement. Certainly Fenwick's history has many weaknesses. He omitted much, as, for example, de La Poterie's resolute troublemaking after his ouster, Father Thayer's clash with Father Rousselet, and the deliberations of the Provicial Council of 1829. Often he misplaced his emphasis, as in devoting so much space to Thayer and so little to Matignon and Cheverus. And he was given to copying items which had previously been published, such as the lengthy extracts from Thayer's controversial works. Yet the very omissions and oddities of emphasis are indices of his own personality, habits of mind and judgement. Indeed, the greatest value of the "Memoirs" is the light they cast upon the bishop's personality and outlook, and it will be the rare reader indeed who does not find Benedict Fenwick an engaging and fascinating person. It is this quality of the "Memoirs" more than any other that made me resolve to carry out his wishes at last and see his work into print.

The "Memoirs" have presented few of the problems that often bedevil editors. Fenwick had prepared his own manuscript for publication and had done a fine job of it. His handwriting is difficult only in the rarest instances, his intent always clear. Some time after completing the work, he went back and made a few corrections in pencil. From the nature of the material and the deterioration of his handwriting, these were made some years later, but in only one instance did they present any difficulty. Fenwick's account being so straightforward and the ground in any case having been pretty well traversed by later historians (most notably and successfully by Robert Howard Lord, John E. Sexton and Edward T. Harrington in the **History of the Archdiocese of Boston**), no elaborate critical apparatus is required. Some few bibliographical and biographical notes seemed unavoidable, but I have preferred to allow Bishop Fenwick to tell his story without my continually jingling the small change of historical scholarship in the background. Fenwick's own notes to his text are keyed by an asterisk, a cross, or a double cross and are placed at the bottom of the page; editor's notes are keyed by arabic numeral and are found at the end of the text. To ease the task of the reader, I've adopted the suggestion of Rev. Thomas F. Shelley, Editor of Publications for the U.S. Catholic Historical Society and divided the text into topical chapters, and have modernized or spelled out abbreviations as necessary. Where Fenwick's pen slipped without obscuring his intent, I've added a word or phrase in brackets to assist the reader. Fenwick's spelling, like that of so many persons of his time, was occasionally eccentric, and the reader may trust, therefore, that orthographical solecisms are not the result of incompetent proofreading. In a few instances in which confusion seemed inevitable or the slip was in material quoted by Fenwick, I've resorted to "[sic]." In the case of names, Fenwick's spelling was very often erratic, and these I have also let stand: for different reasons, neither the casual reader nor the scholar will require corrections. To facilitate comparison with the original, I have inserted in brackets the page numbers of the manuscript.

I am indebted to no-one more than the Rev. Thomas F. Shelley and Mr. James J. Mahoney of the U.S. Catholic Historical Society, whose interest, suggestions, and, above all, patience have been crucial to the project. Six years ago, when I began the task, Rev. Laurence W. McGrath, Librarian of St. John's Seminary, Brighton, Massachusetts, allowed me to borrow one of the typescript copies for photocopying, a much appreciated favor. In the final stages of the project, I called frequently upon Mr. James M. O'Toole, Archivist of the Archdiocese of Boston, for advice and assistance, all of which proved valuable. I must also acknowledge the impact upon my work of the late Rev. John E. Sexton, a historian of extraordinary ability and insight, upon whose efforts I was able to build, and the impact upon my formation of Rev. Msgr. Shawn G. Sheehan, who shared with me his memories of Father Sexton and guided me some years ago in my first successful attempt at researching and writing history. Finally, I am especially grateful for the continual support and encouragement of my wife and children, who bear uncomplainingly the intrusion of scholarship upon our time together.

J.M.M.
Suffolk University
Boston, Massachusetts
July 15, 1978

CHAPTER I

THE BEGINNINGS OF
CATHOLICISM IN BOSTON

Before we commence with the Diocess of Boston it may not be improper to present the Reader with a succinct account of the establishment of Episcopacy in the U[nited] States of North America.

The Roman Catholic religion was introduced into this country with the first settlers of Maryland in the reign of Charles I. who granted that Province to Lord Baltimore, a Catholic Nobleman, as a refuge for persons of his religion, from the severity of the penal laws, which that unfortunate Monarch wanted either the power or the fortitude to restrain. A number of Catholic gentlemen, and others, emigrated from England and Ireland, in the hope of enjoying that repose in the new settlement, which was denied them in their native country. The unrelenting spirit of persecution pursued them over the Atlantic. It deprived them of the just fruits of their labour; it debarred them from every post of trust and profit in the colony which they had settled; it compelled them to maintain Protestant Ministers; and finally, it enforced against them many of the British penal laws, from the cruelty of which they had fled. B. F. Andrew White, an English Jesuit of eminent piety and zeal, accompanied the first colonists in 1632; and, from that date till the period of the revolution, the American Catholics in Maryland and Virginia, were constantly served by Jesuit Missionaries successively sent from England. About the year 1720, the Rev. Father Grayton, and others, introduced Catholicity into Pennsylvania, where in a short time it received a remarkable increase. Since the peace of 1783, and the settlement of the American Constitution, penal laws are no longer known: and Catholics enjoy an equal participation of the rights of human nature with their neigh-[2]bours, of every other religious denomination. The very term of **Toleration** is exploded: because it imports a power in one predominant Sect, to indulge that religious liberty to others, which all claim as an inherent right. Catholic Clergymen of various orders and nations, have resorted to America; and they everywhere find an ample

1

vineyard to cultivate. In this state of religious freedom, the clergymen judged it expedient to give stability and dignity to the Catholic religion by the establishment of a regular hierarchy: and they, therefore, petitioned from the Pope, the creation of an Episcopal See, and the appointment of a Diocesan bishop. The Pope applauding their zeal, graciously admitted their request, and allowed them to elect their first Bishop. The Rev. Dr. John Carroll, who had been for some years the Superior of the Mission, was the object of their choice: and this Reverend Gentleman was accordingly appointed first Bishop of Baltimore.

The following is an extract from the Bull of Pius VI. constituting the above mentioned See. After the preamble, the Bull thus continues:

"Wherefore, it having reached our ears, that in the flourishing commonwealth of the thirteen American States, many faithful Christians, united in communion with the Chair of Peter, in which the centre of Catholic unity is fixed, and governed in their Spiritual concerns by their own Priests having care of souls, earnestly desire, that a Bishop may be appointed over them to exercise the functions of Episcopal order, to feed them more largely with the food of salutary doctrine and to guard more carefully that portion of the Catholic flock; we willingly embraced this opportunity, which the grace of Almighty God has afforded us, to provide those distant regions with the comfort and ministry of a Catholic Bishop. And that this might be effected more successfully, and according to the rules of the sacred Canons, we comission our venerable Brethren, the Cardinals of the Holy Roman Church, directors of the Congregation **De propaganda fide**, to manage this business with the greatest care, and to make a report to us. It was, therefore, appointed by their decree, approved by us, and [3] published the 12th day of July of the last year, that the Priests who lawfully exercise the sacred ministry and have care of souls, in the United States of America should be empowered to advise together and to determine, first, in what town the Episcopal See ought to be erected: and, next, who of the aforesaid Priests, exercising the cure of Souls appeared the most worthy and proper to be promoted to this important charge, whom we, for the first time only, and by special grace, permitted the said Priests to elect and to present to this Apostolic See. In obedience to this decree, the aforesaid Priests, exercising the cure of souls in the U[nited] Sates of America, unanimously agreed that a Bishop with ordinary jurisdiction, ought to be established in the town of Baltimore: because this town, situated in Maryland, which Province the greater part of the Priests and of the faithful inhabit, appeared the most conveniently placed for intercourse with the other states, and because from this province, Catholic religion and faith had been propagated into the others. And, at the time appointed for the election, they being assembled together, the sacrifice of Holy Mass being celebrated, and the grace and assistance of the Holy Ghost being implored, the votes of all present were taken, and of twenty six Priests who were assembled, twenty four gave their votes for our beloved Son John Carroll, whom they judged the most proper to support the burden of episcopacy; and sent an authentic instrument of the whole transaction to the aforesaid congregation of Cardinals. Now, all things being maturely weighed and considered in this congregation, it was easily agreed, that the interest and increase of the Cath[olic] religion, would be greatly promoted, if an Episcopal See were erected at Baltimore, and the said John Carroll was appointed the Bishop of it. We, therefore, (to whom this opinion has been reported by our beloved Son Cardinal Antonelli, Prefect of the said congregation, having nothing more at heart, than to insure success [4] to whatever tends to the propagation of true religion, and the honor and increase of the Cath[olic] Church) by the plenitude of our apostolical power, and by the tenor of those presents, do establish and erect the aforesaid town of Baltimore into an Episcopal See forever, for one Bishop to be chosen by us in all future vacancies; and **we, therefore, by the Apostolical authority aforesaid, do allow, grant and permit, to the Bishop of the said City, and to his successors in all future** times, to exercise episcopal power and jurisdiction, and of every other episcopal function, which Bishops constituted in other places are empowered to hold and enjoy in their respective churches, cities and dioceses by right, custom, or other means, by general priviledges, graces, indults, and Episcopal dispensations, together with all preeminencies, honours, immunities, graces and favours, which other Cathedral Churches, by right or custom, or in any other sort, have, hold, and enjoy. We, moreover, decree and declare the said Episcopal See thus created, to be subject or suffragan to no metropolitan right or jurisdiction, but to be forever immediately subject to us, and to our successors the Roman Pontiffs, and to this Apostolical See. And till another opportunity shall be presented to us, of establishing other Bishops in the U[nited] States of America, and till other dispositions shall be made by this Apostolical See, we declare by our Apostolical authority, all the faithful of it, living in Catholic communion, as well ecclesiastics as seculars, and all the Clergy and people dwelling in the United States of America, though hitherto they may have been subject to other Bishops of other Dioceses, to be henceforward subject to the Bishop of Baltimore in all future times; and to this Bishop and to his successors, we impart power to curb and check, without appeal, all persons who may contradict or oppose their orders, to visit personally or by deputies all catholic churches, to remove abuses, to correct the manners of the faithful: and to perform all things which other Bishops in their respective

Diocesses are accustomed to do and to perform, saving in all things our own authority, and that of this Apostolic See. And wherever by special grant, and for the time only, we have allowed the Priests. ex-[5]ercising the care of souls in the United States of America. to elect a person to be appointed Bishop by us, and almost all their votes having been given to our beloved Son John Carroll, priest; we being otherwise certified of his faith. prudence, piety and zeal, for as much. and by our mandate. he hath during the late years, directed the spiritual government of souls, do, therefore, by the plenitude of our authority, declare, create, appoint and constitute the said John Carroll, Bishop and Pastor of the said Church of Baltimore, granting to him the faculty of receiving the rite of consecration from any Cath[olic] Bishop holding communion with the Apostolical See. assisted by two Ecclesiastics, vested with some dignity in case that two Bishops cannot be had, first having taken the usual oath. according to the Roman Pontifical."

Dr. Carroll, upon the receipt of his Bull from Rome. immediately repaired to England, where his person and merits were already well known, and presented himself for consecration to the Right Rev. Dr. Charles Walmesley, Bishop of Rama. Senior Vicar Apostolic of the Cath[olic] religion in that Kingdom. By the invitation of Thomas Weld, Esq. the consecration of the new Bishop was performed during a solemn High Mass, in the elegant Chapel of Lulworth Castle. on Sunday. the 15th Day of August 1790, being the Feast of the Assumption of the B[lessed] V[irgin] Mary: and the munificence of that gentleman omitted no circumstance, which could possibly add dignity to so venerable a ceremony. The two Prelates were attended by their respective assistant Priests and Acolytes, according to the rubric of the Roman Pontifical. The richness of their vestments, the music of the Choir, the multitude of wax-lights. and the ornaments of the Altar concurred to increase the splendor of the ceremony which made a lasting impression upon every beholder.

Dr. Carroll, after his consecration by Bishop Walmesly. immediately returned to the United States, and entered upon the important duties of his high office. It is unnecessary to state in this brief account. how faithfully, and [6] with how abundant increase to his flock he discharged his Pastoral duties. Suffice it to say, that in the short period of twenty years after the establishment of the first Episcopal See of Baltimore. the venerable Pontiff (Pius VII.) Successor to Pius VI. who, in the midst of tribulations most trying to human nature, but equally glorious to his Divine Master was chosen to fill the pontifical chair, thought proper to erect Baltimore into a Metropolitan or Archi-episcopal See, and to establish four new suffragan Diocesses, viz: Boston, New-York, Philadelphia. and Bardstown in Kentucky. The first Pastors appointed for the new Sees were: For Boston, the Right Rev. John Cheverus; for New-York, the Rt. Rev. Dr. Luke Concannon, who unfortunately died at Naples a short time after his consecration, on the point of embarking for the U[nited] States; for Philadelphia, the Rt. Rev. John Egan; for Bardstown, Kentucky, the Rt. Rev. Benedict Joseph Flaget, characters (Dr. Concannon alone excepted, who, when appointed resided at Rome, and had never been in this country) already long known to, and revered by the Catholics of the U[nited] States, and whose promotion was considered less as a reward of their apostolic virtues, than as a common blessing upon the flocks committed to their care.

The consecration of these highly respectable Reverend Gentlemen took place in Baltimore, the most Reverend Arch Bishop Carroll being Consecrator: Dr. Egan was consecrated at St. Peter's on Sunday, the 28th of October, 1810; Dr. Cheverus, at the same Church on All Saint's Day; and Dr. Flaget, at St. Patrick's at Fell's Point, on the 4th of November of the same year. The ceremony was conducted with great pomp and solemnity, amidst an immense concourse of people of every denomination of Christians.

It will not be improper here to add, that in consequence of the advanced age of the Most Reverend Archbishop Carroll, previously to the establishment of the above mentioned Bishopricks, the great extent of his Diocess (comprising at the time the whole of the United States as they then stood) and the immense load of duty devolving upon him, the Holy See was pleased to give him a Co-adjutor. This was the Rt. Rev. [7] Dr. Leonard Neale, who was chosen to succeed him in the Diocess of Baltimore, and was consecrated Bishop of Gortyna on the 7th day of December, 1800.

New Orleans had already been erected into a Bishoprick by Pius VI. But on the death of the worthy Prelate who governed that Diocess under the Spanish administration, and, on its accession to the United States, the Holy See was pleased to appoint to it an administrator-general. Dr. William Dubourg, a clergyman of distinguished talents and eminent piety, a member of the learned congregation of St. Sulpice, and President of St. Mary's College at Baltimore, was the gentleman named to fill that office. He shortly after repaired to Europe, to make the wants of his extensive mission known, when he was immediately acknowledged Titular of the See he administered. He was consecrated on Sunday, Sept. 24th, in the Church of St. Louis at Rome, by Cardinal Joseph Doria, Sub-Dean of the Sacred College, assisted by the Bishop of St. Malo, the French ambassador, and M. Pereira, Bishop of Terracina.

In looking back to the period of the first introduction of Catholicity into this country, under Lord Baltimore in the settlement of Maryland and contrasting the state of the Church then with what it shortly became, the hand-ful of individuals then composing the flock of Jesus Christ, confined to a small Province with the numbers afterwards spread over every part of this union, we are at once struck at the astonishing rapidity of the increase: we cannot but see in it the fostering hand of the Almighty, who was pleased to bless in so extraordinary a manner the labours of his Servants; and from the judicious arrangements, combined with other operating causes, made by the Holy-See for establishing new Diocesses in the different states, in proportion to the diffusion of Catholicity among them, we are led to hope for a still more abundant harvest, a still greater increase of Faithful: and that **the Lord** will continue **to add daily to his society such as shall be saved.**

[8] DIOCESS OF BOSTON

The Diocess of Boston comprehends all the New-England States; viz: Massachusetts, New Hampshire, Vermont, Rhode-Island, Connecticut and Maine, with a population, agreably to the census of 1830, of one million, nine hundred and fifty four thousand, six hundred and nine souls. Of these Massachusetts contains 610,014; New-Hampshire 269,533; Vermont 280,679; Rhode-Island 97,210; Connecticut 297,711; Maine 399,462; the entire com-prising an Area of 65,310 square miles. It is bounded on the north and north East by Lower Canada and New Brunswick; on the East by the Atlantick Ocean; on the South and South East by Long Island Sound and the Atlantic Ocean; and on the West by the State of New York. The following table will shew the population of the New England States according to five official enumerations:

New England States	1st Census Pop. 1790	2d Census Pop. 1800	3d Census Pop. 1810	4th Census Pop. 1820	5th Census Pop. 1830	Per Cent in ten years.
Maine	96,540	151,719	228,705	298,335	399,462	33.9
New Hampshire	141,885	183,858	214,460	244,161	269,533	10.4
Vermont	85,539	154,465	217,895	235,764	280,679	19.0
Massachu-setts	378,787	422,845	472,040	523,287	610,014	16.6
Rhode I[s]land	68,825	69,122	76,931	83,059	97,210	17.0
Connect-icut	237,946	251,002	261,942	275,248	297,711	8.2
Total	1009,522	1233,011	1471,973	1659,854	1954,609	105.1

The New England States, like all the other states of the present Union, with the exception of Louisiana and the Floridas, originally formed a part of the immense Diocess of Baltimore, as already observed, created by Pius VI. and of which the Rt. Rev. John Carroll, an Ex Jesuit of the State of Maryland, was consecreated First Bishop, in the year 1790. The few Catholics who had begun to settle in them, especially in the town of Boston, the Capital of Massachusetts, towards the close and after the American revolutionary war, were served by Priests sent by him until the year 1810, when, at the solicitation of the above mentioned venerable Prelate, Pius VII. was pleased [9]   to erect Boston into a new and separate Diocess, and to assign for its First Bishop, the Rt. Rev. John Cheverus, extending his jurisdiction over all the New England States.

In consequence of the severe laws and penal statutes which had been enacted against Roman Catholics in the New England States, from the earliest period of their settlement and which had been kept in full force and vigour until the breaking out of the American Revolution, a Catholic was scarcely to be found in any one of these States before the war. The bitterest animosity had all along prevailed, which was carefully kept alive by the Puritan or Congregational Clergy whose sway over the minds of the People was at all times very considerable. The most defamatory publications were regularly imported from Great Britain, which they published anew as soon as received, and which exhibited the religion of Catholics at one time in the most ridiculous, and at another in the most odious light;—and these were industriously circulated among all classes of society. No opportunity was omitted to stigmatize the professors of it, and to inoculate the children of New-England with the venom of their prejudices. Every year, on the 5th of November, the Effigy of the Pope was regularly paraded through the towns and villages, in a mock procession: nor was any attempt made to check this offensive proceeding until the arrival of General Washington to take command of the army, at Cambridge, in the summer of 1775. Having observed the preparations which were making, even in the camp, for the celebration of the above day, he took the earliest opportunity to express his condemnation of it in the following order, extracted from his **orderly book**:

"November 5th—As the Commander-in-chief has been apprised of a design, formed for the observance of that ridiculous and childish custom of burning the Effigy of the Pope, he cannot help expressing his surprise, that there should be Officers and soldiers in this army so void of common sense, as not to see the impropriety of such a step at this juncture; at a time when **we are soliciting, and have [10] really obtained the friendship and alliance of the people of Canada, whom we ought to consider as Brethren embarked** in the same cause, the defense of the general liberty of America. At such a juncture and in such circumstances, to be insulting their religion is so monstrous, as not to be suffered or excused; indeed, instead of offering the most remote insult, it is our duty to address public thanks to these our brethren, as to them we are so much indebted for every late happy success over the common enemy in Canada." (Washington's writings Vol. 3. page 144.)

Although the order here issued by the illustrious Washington had the effect of preventing this absurd and insulting procession in the camp, the day continued to be still celebrated at Boston and other towns of N[ew] England; nor was a final stop put to it till the arrival of the fleet of Count Destaing in the port of Boston in 1778.

This fleet was ordered to Boston to assist the Americans in their struggle for independance. At this period the most blind among the Puritanick Fanaticks could not but perceive that it would be highly impolitick to renew a custom which would have the effect to scandalise as well as alienate the affections of those generous allies who had come hither to advocate the cause of the revolution, by countenancing a parade which would justly shock their religious feelings. A final stop was accordingly put to it.

In addition to this, while the French fleet remained in the harbour of Boston, which was from the 25th of August 1778, until the 3d of November of the same year, a constant intercourse was kept up between the Officers on board, and the inhabitants of the town. Frequent visits were paid on both sides. The French were pleased with their reception on shore, and with the marked attention paid them by the respectable inhabitants of Boston;—and these, on the other hand, began to entertain a more favourable opinion of their Roman Catholic allies. As Mass was regularly celebrated on board the fleet, it frequently happened that some of the most respectable Citizens were sometimes present at the divine office, who returned home favourably impressed with [11] the Catholic worship, as well as edified by the general piety of those on board, who had assisted at it. Thus a kind of intercourse was kept up which operated in some degree in favour of religion. In a short time after the departure of the French fleet, individuals professing the Catholic faith began to take up their residence in Boston. These consisted chiefly of the lower order of people, viz; some few french, a few Spaniards, and some dozzens of Irish, mostly labourers. They were soon followed by others during, and after the conclusion of the war.

The first Catholic Priest who appeared in Boston, clothed with powers to preach and administer the sacraments, was L'abbé Poterie. This Clergyman, who was a Frenchman by birth, was a perfect stranger in the United States, and nevertheless, some how or other, had the address to impose upon Dr. Carroll so far, as to obtain faculties of him for the mission of

Boston, and its vicinity. These were signed by the above Reverend Gentleman, (who, previous to his consecration as Bishop, acted as Superior of the various missions in the United States,) on the 24th of December, 1788. Shortly after he presented himself to the Catholics of Boston in quality of Pastor, and commenced by taking an apartment in the western part of the City, where he celebrated Mass, and officiated on Sundays. In a few weeks he removed from this apartment, as not being sufficiently convenient, to the small Huguenot Church in S[c]hool Street, of which he had obtained possession, where he continued to officiate. At this time a Mr. John Magner from Ireland, and a Mr. Baury, a respectable Emigrant from St. Domingo[1] were the principal Lay-members, besides the French Consul, of the Catholic Church, and his chief support. L'abbe Poterie, not having all the vestments and other ornaments requisite for the decency of divine worship in the new Chapel he had taken, requested of these to write and procure them from Paris. They complied with his [12] request, and dispatched a letter to the Archbishop of Paris to this effect praying him to assist them with his credit, as they had no acquaintance with any of the merchants in that City. They at the same time gave him an account of their infant Church, and of their endeavours to establish the true faith in this part of the country where it had been wholly unknown until now. The venerable Archbishop immediately caused the articles which they wanted to be procured, and sent to them; but at the same time gave them to understand, in his reply to their letter, that the Abbé Poterie was not a Clergyman proper for the ministry;—that he had known him at Paris, and, in consequence of impropriety of conduct, had been under the painful necessity of withdrawing his **faculties** from him. This intelligence, as it may well be imagined, greatly surprised the Catholics of Boston, especially as he had come to them with letters of approbation, as well as of recommendation, from the Superior general of the American missions. It was also the more disagreable, as they knew the scarcity of Priests in this country, and how difficult it would be for them to obtain another, at this time, if La Poterie were to be withdrawn from them. They concluded, therefore, to say nothing of the contents of the Archbishop's letter, and to wait till something should transpire, which might render the publication thereof necessary. In the meantime La Poterie, elate with the apointment he had received, continued to act as Pastor of the little Flock of Boston. His Church was generally well attended by all the Catholics, except by Monsieur L'Etombe the French Consul of that day, who would not countenance by his presence a Priest, of whom he had received so unfavourable an account, from so respectable a quarter. He could now view him in no other light, than that of an adventurer, who had imposed upon and deceived, probably by counterfeit letters, his Ecclesiastical Superior; and accordingly, knowing that a man of this character could not be relied on, and sooner or later would commit himself by his misconduct, he chose on all occasions to absent himself from his Church.

Scarcely had a month elapsed after receiving his faculties for Boston, [13] when he began to exhibit himself in his true character, and to show what he really was. Not content with serving his flock in the capacity of a simple Priest, he must also affect the Bishop, and address them, at the outset, a formal **Pastoral** letter after the manner of Prelates, who exercise ordinary jurisdiction; and in doing so, vainly to assume to himself the loftiest titles. The following document, which we copy from one published under his own eye, will show how far a man inflated with vanity will suffer himself to be carried. It is dated the 22d February, 1789. As far, however, as doctrine or morals are concerned, it is in all respects correct and proper.

"A

"Pastoral Letter from

"The Apostolic Vice-Prefect, Curate of

"the Holy Cross at Boston."

"Claudius Florent Bouchard de la Poterie, Doctor of Divinity, Prothonotary of the Holy Church and of the Holy See of Rome, Apostolic Vice-Prefect and Missionary, Curate of the Catholic Church of the Holy Cross at Boston, in North America—to all faithful Christians entrusted to our care, and of our spiritual jurisdiction, salvation and blessing in Jesus Christ, the Shepherd and Bishop of our souls.

We make known unto you, our dearly beloved Brethren, the wonderful designs of Divine Providence towards us, which by a course of unheard of events, has brought us to this city, here to open the first public exercise, and here to lay the foundation, perhaps even here to erect the edifice of our holy religion. Since the American revolution, this Divine Providence has brought about a revolution still more extraordinary in the method of grace; and being designated to be one of its instruments in the hand of God, with what sentiments of profound gratitude to the Father of mercies ought we not to be penetrated! But at the same time we look with awe upon the immensity of the duties, to which our office subjects us. The entire knowledge of their extent, and of our own insufficiency, the more powerfully engages us, and ought to incline you also, by the interest you have in the [14] success of the ministry, to implore for us assistance from Him, with whom we can do all things, as without him we can do nothing."

"My Lord Carroll, the ecclesiastic Superior of the Roman Hierarchy in the United States of America, did, on the 24th of December last, communicate to me very ample powers, for which we have requested in quality of french missionary, to be registered in the French Consuls Chancery-Office at Boston, to spend our time in this City, here to exercise our cares and vigilance, and to give you all the spiritual assistance in our power. It is for this reason we esteem ourselves, in the truest sense, the servant of you all since we are indebted to you for our appointment to carry you to God by our exhortations, by our counsels, by our examples, by our life itself, if it is necessary, to save you all. We do not place our happiness in commanding you with authority, but in serving you with charity; being full of candour and mildness towards every one, to gain your hearts to the grace of Jesus Christ, we ought to be to all a model of works, having always before our eyes the account we are to give to God for you. We beseech you, our very dear Brethren, to bring down upon us, by your fervent prayers, the spirit of wisdom and understanding, the spirit of meekness and resolution, in order that this double spirit, presiding over all our steps, over all our actions may support us against our weakness, may defend us against all kinds of danger, and be an abundant supply to our own impotency.

After having solicited your charity to obtain from heaven for us the succours we need, worthily to fulfil the functions of our charge. it is our duty to exhort you, our very dear Brethren, to renew yourselves in that same spirit of faith, and of the love of the primitive Christians towards our Saints and valiant martyrs, we invite you all, ye Christians in general. and we ardently press them in the bowels of the immense love of Jesus Christ very fervently to assist in the divine service of our Church. ye Frenchmen especially, our dear fellow countrymen, and you Americans their faithful allies. **What consolation for you [15] in these happy days, the admirable fruits of a peace so glorious to your own bravery, and to our august and** most Christian Monarch; (Louis XVI.) what consolation. I say. to be able freely here to signalize your faith, your zeal, and your religion. by the most inviolable fidelity to the holy and religious observances of our country, although in a foreign land. It is the part of your greatness of soul to draw down, by the multiplied examples of your good works. upon this happy country, and upon yourselves, the most plentiful blessings of heaven. Then shall we, all together, shed tears of joy, in singing here below the hymns of our God, and calling to mind the ineffable delights which one enjoys. after a life filled up with virtuous deeds, in our true country. that continuing City, the peaceful abode of immortality."

"Oh! how august is the sacrifice of our Altar. our dear Brethren: how worthy is it of our most profound adorations, and of our sincerest homage! But how proper is it, at the same time, for us to be penetrated with fear and dread, if we duly consider the honour we have to approach it. being taken from the sublime Altar of God. Moses, to whom the Lord spoke so familiarly, was himself intimidated, as well as the people, when he saw the fearful precautions which he required to make his holiness reverenced. Yet the sight which terrified the Mediator of the ancient law. was only a shadow of our mysteries; it was only a very imperfect figure of what passes at the Altar, where the Priest and the Faithful, who, with him. compose but one single mystery, are admitted into heaven; united to the immortal spirits, who live only by gratitude and love; being associated with the righteous already glorified; presented before the throne of the judge of all; and before the Lamb whose blood is then sprinkled upon their heads, and offered by their hands. "You are not come", says St. Paul. "unto the mountain that might be touched and that burned with fire. nor unto blackness and darkness and tempest; but ye are come unto Mount Zion, and unto the **City of the living [16] God, the heavenly Jerusalem, and to an innumerable company of angels, to the general assembly and church of the first-born** which are written in heaven, and to God the judge of all. and to spirits of just men made perfect, and to Jesus the Mediator of the new covenant, and to 'the blood of sprinkling, that speaketh better things than that of Abel.' "

"But who can tremble before that which he sees not." if faith does not go through all veils, and if it does not resemble that of Moses, of whom it is written that "he was before God, as seeing him who was invisible?" In a word, Jesus Christ covers everything with a veil, he conceals everything, he shews himself to be unknown by Infidels, and to be despised by those who have but little faith. Let us respect him, our very dear Brethren, for what he is and for what he appears not to be; let us, by gratitude, descend lower than he descended by humility; let us restore to him everything which he leaves to come to you; let us find the greatest the most majestic, the most worthy of supreme worship in the simplicity and abasement, to which his love for you reduced him; let us prostrate ourselves before him, in proportion as he inclines towards you; let us be in admiration of the humiliating mysteries, of which the Eucharist is a continuation; let us give thanks to him with the saints who are in heaven; let us not cease to say with those, "Worthy is the Lamb that was slain, to receive power. and riches, and wisdom, and strength, and honour and glory, and blessing."

"These, my dear Brethren, is [sic] what we thought proper to set before your eyes, and what we expect from your fervour. We pray the Father of mercies, and the God of all consolation, that he would enrich you with his graces, that he would grant you the light of his countenance. that he would defend you from all kinds of danger, that he would shed his salutary influences upon our Apostolical labours, that he would inspire you with great zeal for your own salvation, and for our sanctification. that we may the one and the other, be able hereafter to say, as the Apostle. "I have fought a **good fight, I have finished** [17] **my course, I have kept the faith, henceforth there is laid up for me a crown of righteousness, which the** Lord, the righteous judge, shall give me at that day; and not to me only, but unto all them also that love his appearing."

"In fine, our very dear brethren, may Jesus Christ the God of peace, who through the blood of the everlasting covenant, is become the great shepherd of our souls, dispose you to every good work, that you may do his will, he himself working in you that which is well pleasing in his sight, through Jesus Christ, to whom be glory forever and ever. Amen."

This Pastoral was accompanied by the following publication, in which the Abbé Poterie takes upon himself, as if he were already Bishop of the Diocess, to regulate the Fast of Lent and to grant dispensations even for it!

"Ash Wednesday happens this year the 25th of February next; we invite all the Faithful to come to Church, to receive the **blessed** ashes, in the spirit of repentance, there to attend afterwards to the Holy Sacrifice of the Mass, which will be said at 11 O'clock, and to enter into the sentiments of compunction which the Church endeavours to inspire into her children in the ceremony of this day. It enjoins, under pain of mortal sin, fasting and abstinence every Wednesday, Friday and Saturday, during Lent time upon all those who have completed the twenty first year of their age, unless they should have some lawful reason which excuses them, and they have asked our permission for it. We permit the use of Eggs and milk diet on these three days of abstinence, and that of fat and flesh on sundays, tuesdays and thursdays, once a day only, after the first sunday of Lent inclusively, till Palm Sunday exclusively. We permit also fat to those who are at a distance from rivers. During the whole of Holy-Week, we forbid Eggs and flesh. The rigours of the ancient discipline of the first ages of the Church, our very **dear Brethren, by** [18] **being much softened, has diminished nothing of its spirit, and the Holy Fathers have always looked upon the holy time of Lent** as a time proper to purify and renew themselves; as a time of harvest, when Christians ought, with ardour, to gather in the graces and virtues, of which they have need, to spend the year in a holy manner, to exercise repentance for our sins, by fasts and mortifications, by generous almsgiving, and all kinds of good works; that we may be disposed for the celebration of the passion of Jesus Christ, and for the feast of Easter; and to imitate in some degree, the Son of God, who fasted forty days and forty nights in the wilderness, without eating or drinking."

"We announce to you, our very dear Brethren and well beloved in Jesus Christ, that our holy father, Pope Pius the sixth, hath granted to all the faithful Catholicks, in the United States of America, plenary indulgence and remission of all sins, once every month, to all those. who. having been contrite, made confession and holy Communion. shall pray for the propagation of our holy faith."

"Given at Boston, in North America, under our hand. and the seal of our arms, the 22d of February, Quinquagesima Sunday. anno salutis 1789. (Signed.) La Poterie. Vice Prefect and Apostolick Missionary, curate of the Holy-Cross at Boston."

L'abbé de la Poterie was unquestionably a man of talents, and as far as ecclesiastical learning would go, was in every respect qualified to fill the station which he at this time occupied. He was also a man of letters—and happy would it have been for the Catholic Society in Boston had his conduct in all points been conformable to the doctrine which he taught. As he was the first Catholick Priest who had ever settled in Boston, all eyes were naturally turned upon him and his little flock, we may well imagine, therefore, how painful it was to them to see him transgressing the bounds of propriety and thereby entailing upon them and their holy religion the ridicule of their enemies. But God was [19] pleased to permit it so, for his own wise purposes.

In addition to the above, La Poterie at the same time drew up a regulation for Holy-Week, which he appended to his Pastoral, together with an abridged Formula of a Discourse, which was to be recited by the officiating Priest on every Sunday. We shall also transcribe these for the satisfaction of our readers, who may desire to see everything connected with the early establishment of our religion in this section of our Country.

"The Solemnity of the Holy Time of Easter."

"The order of the public offices, and of the divine service, during the fortnight of Easter, in the Catholic Church of the Holy Cross, at Boston."

"Palm Sunday, which happens this year the 5th of April next, the office will begin precisely at ten o'clock. The Benediction of the water, that of the Branches, the procession round the inside of the Church, in singing the Hymn, **Vexilla regis prodeunt;** the pause and reading the holy Gospel in the nave of the Church; the throwing of boughs and branches before the cross, in singing the **Ave Rex Noster,** and the strophe, **O Crux ave spes unica;** then the **Gloria, Laus, Hosanna filio David,** at the door of the Choir, and the entrance into the Sanctuary after the **Attollite portas principes vestras, et elevamini, portae aeternales, et introibit rex gloriae,** in memory of, and to honour the triumphant entry into Jerusalem by our divine Redeemer, amidst the acclamations of the Jewish people, some days before he was crucified there. Afterwards at the **grand-Mass,** will be sung the Passion of Jesus Christ, according to St. Matthew, and the Priest and the Faithful will prostrate themselves, and kiss the ground at these words, **Jesus exclamans**

voce magna emisit spiritum. A sermon and prayer as usual. Vespers at 3 O'clock in the afternoon according to custom, and a discourse upon the dispositions proper for the holy communion and the paschal duty."

"During the whole fortnight, there will be a low-Mass at eleven O'clock every day; before and after which [20] equally as during the whole of Lent time, the Priest will hear the confessions of all good Christians, who shall be pleased to comply with the Paschal duty, and have the happiness to receive at Easter, in the Holy Communion, their Saviour and Redeemer, as the Church makes it a precept to all her children."

"On Holy Thursday, the Feast of the institution of the most holy Sacrament of the Altar, the Eve of the Passion of Jesus Christ, an ever-memorable day, and peculiarly consecrated by the Church, that tender Mother, to remind her children of the ineffable mysteries of her divine Spouse, the solemn grand-Mass, at 10 O'Clock A.M. at the end of which, will be sung the **Pange lingua gloriosi corporis mysterium.** The holy sacrament will be exposed and adored all the day in the Church, which will be open till nine O'Clock in the evening."

"After having chanted the Gospel according to St. John, Chap. 13. ver. 1-16. Mr. the Abbé will wash the feet of twelve Lads, between 10 and 14 years of age; the poorest will have the preference: he will distribute to every one of them a loaf of bread and a phial of wine, blessed: any person, no matter who, with the consent of their parents, may present themselves to Mr. the Abbé the first days of the Holy-Week, he will give them a title of admission, till the fixed number is completed. During this moving and truly affecting ceremony, and the usual prayers, there will be a particular collection, which will also be all shared among those twelve Boys, representing the twelve Apostles."

"In this same day all crowned heads, being Christians and Catholics, princes in Europe, the sovereign Pontiff, our holy Father the Pope; all the Bishops, Prelates, Superiors and Pastors of the holy Catholic Church, hold in great honour the practice of washing the feet, and the ceremony of the last supper which they after the example of Jesus Christ, regard as a symbol the most expressive of humility, of love and of truly tender and paternal charity, with which we ought to love one another, and of which this divine Saviour gave us an express command before his Passion, in the text cited above, from St. John, Chap. 13."

[21] "In the afternoon, etc. at 5 O'Clock, the washing of the sacred stone of the Altar, the lamentations of Jeremiah sung, **Jerusalem, Jerusalem, convertere, convertere ad Dominum Deum tuum.** The **stabat mater dolorosa;** some prayers and proper songs; afterwards a discourse and conversation with Jesus Christ, upon the great sacrifice, which he exemplified

on the cross; and then the benediction of the most blessed Sacrament which will be reserved in the Tabernacle for the communion of the Priest the next day."

"On holy-friday, divine service will begin precisely at half after nine O'Clock, with a discourse on the death and passion of Jesus Christ, which the Priest will pronounce, with a Crucifix in his hand; the Passion, according to St. John, will afterwards be sung; prayers for the whole Church universal, spread over the whole earth, particular prayers for the Jewish nation, and all those who have separated themselves from the bosom of the Catholic Church; the solemn adoration of the Cross, and the Communion of the Priest, clothed in black, the Altar in mourning, and without ornaments."

"On Holy Friday, at 3 O'Clock in the afternoon, the **Miserere del Pergolese,** and some other Lamentations of Jeremiah, will be sung; after which it is necessary that all those who have children to be baptized, and Adult or grown persons, who would receive this sacrament, should present themselves to the Priest in the Vestry, who will first write down their Christian names and surnames. It is necessary also to see him and acquaint him with their intentions at an early period, in the beginning of Lent time, that he may have time to instruct and dispose those who shall be susceptible of it. Every person to be baptized, must have a God-Father and a God-Mother of the Catholic faith, who cannot either be the Father or Mother, the wife or husband of those who are baptized, who ought always to be clothed and dressed in white during the whole eight days of their baptism, and to have in the hand, or in that of their God-Father or God-Mother, during this ceremony, and the divine service following, a white wax-candle, which [22] **they ought likewise to have on Easter Holy-day, at Vespers, then of the procession to the sacred baptismal fonts, both on that day, and on Sundays, while the Te Deum shall be sung."**

"On holy Saturday, at 9 O'Clock, precisely, the benediction of new fire; the solemn benediction of the Paschal wax candle, and the joyful singing of the **Exultet jam angelica turba coelorum—O felix culpa quae tantum meruit habere Redemptorem!** the reading of the prophecies; the litanies of the saints; the solemn benediction of the new baptismal Fonts, the sprinkling of the Holy-water; ceremonies of holy baptism, and the very public and most solemn administration of this first of sacraments of the law of grace, to more than forty persons, as well infants as adults. Afterwards the grand-Mass, at which the instructed grown persons, newly baptised, will hold communion. The **Gloria in Excelsis** at the sound of little bells and in harmony, with the joyful proclamation of the holy time of Easter."

"On Holy Saturday, at 5 O'Clock in the afternoon, the **Alleluia** the Canticle **Magnificat, the Regina Coeli laetare,** in music with the benediction of the Blessed Sacrament."

"On the Holy-day of Easter, the grand-Mass solemnly sung at ten O'Clock: The Prose, **Victimae paschali laudes immolent Christiani,** with music: The offering and distribution of the holy bread: a general communion for all those, who, being well disposed for it, are prayed to reserve it for the great day of the resurrection of the Saviour, the foundation of our hope, and the solemnity of all solemnities. The benediction of the most holy sacrament at the end of the Mass."

"At half after 3 O'Clock, in the afternoon, the exposing of the most holy sacrament, Vespers with music, procession to the Baptismal fonts, a discourse upon the resurrection of the Saviour."

"The **Regina Coeli laetare** as in the evening; and the canticle "**O filii & filiae, rex coelestis, rex gloriae, morte surrexit hodie, Alleluia,** in musick, with the benediction of the most holy Sacrament."

"On Low-Sunday, **the grand-Mass and vespers at the usual hour, with a discourse on the grace and sacred engagements of** [23] **Baptism; the Te Deum** in musick, to give thanks to God for all the favours which he hath done us during this holy fortnight: the Canticle **O Filii & Filiae** of the Holy-day of Easter, and the benediction of the holy Sacrament."

"Mr. L'Abbé invites all those who shall have been regenerated, washed and purified in the sacred waters of baptism, very preciously to preserve the grace of their baptismal innocence, and in all their outward appearance to bear the sweet odour of Jesus Christ, by the examples of a holy life, and to exhort them always to remember that they are become the temples of the Holy Ghost, the members of Jesus Christ, the fellow Heirs of his glory and of his kingdom; and that all their conduct ought to inspire charity, that inestimable virtue, with the most profound respect for our holy religion, and to be an open book to all those to whom the Lord, even the Father of Mercies, shall do the favour to call them to it."

"There will be prayers as usual, with the Benediction of the Holy Sacrament, every thursday in the year, at 5 O'Clock in the evening, precisely, where they will alternately chant in music the Litanies of the holy name of Jesus, and that of the most holy Virgin Mary."

"The gentlemen Musicians of this City are earnestly requested to continue to give testimony of their goodness and of their generosity, the congregation reserving themselves for more happy times to prove to them their gratitude and good wishes."

"In the mean time, the congregation assembled, upon the representation of Mr. L'abbé, has fixed upon and chosen two days, when it is probable there will be a concourse of Christians, and by consequence the contribution will be greater, and when they will be pleased to receive, as a pledge of his satisfaction and of his gratitude, the whole sum and product of the collection which shall be made on Holy-Saturday, and the day of Easter, in supposing that they will have the goodness to be present morning and evening, as was said above, and that they will be pleased to exercise and prepare themselves to give some Anthem, or moving Symphony during the ceremonies of holy Baptism, the Church, that tender Mother, not being able sufficiently to manifest her joy and her consolation, in admitting Infants into her bosom: The first Sunday in May, and the second Sunday in September, days of the finding and raising the Holy-Cross, and the anniversaries of the first class in the Church of the Holy-Cross; [24] there will likewise be some feast-days for all the gentlemen musicians of this City, in supposing that they will have the goodness to be punctually present, the contribution will be offered to them, and this musick which they shall give in these four days, will be to their own profit."

"After Easter, Mr. L'abbé will exercise himself, every Sunday after Vespers, publickly to give some instructions and exhortations in English, in form of catechising. The hour fixed and constantly established, for every Sunday in the year, for the Holy-Mass, will be at 11 O'Clock in the forenoon, precisely, and, in the afternoon, Vespers at three O'Clock. If any Christian desires the holy sacrifice to be offered and celebrated, on any day of the week, for himself or for his parents deceased, he will have the goodness to indicate to Mr. L'abbé him whom he shall have chosen, and his hour and communicate to him his intentions, which he will write down upon a little book, destined for that purpose. As to the holy Mass of all the Sundays, and feasts, the intention of them is specially reserved for all spiritual and temporal needs of the Catholic Christians then present at the holy sacrifice. The Baptistry (the place where Baptism is performed) is a place solely destined, on holy saturday, and the saturday eve of Pentecost, for those who receive holy Baptism, and who are proper to participate in this ceremony. All other persons are earnestly requested not to place themselves there; as also the Ladies are desired never to enter into the Sanctuary, that place being forbidden them. All other Catholic gentlemen, or others, being always permitted to place themselves there, provided always, that in coming in there, they are resolved to kneel down during the consecration and benediction of the most holy Sacrament, without which they will have notice that they are requested to retire, and place themselves anywhere in the Church but in the Sanctuary."

The abridged formula of the Discourse, to be made on every Sunday, in the Church of the Holy-Cross, as drawn up by him, and which he also published with his Pastoral, is as follows:

"In the name of the Father, the Son and the Holy-Ghost. Amen."

"Christian People"

"Though we are obliged to serve God, our Creator, every day of our life, Sunday is, nevertheless, called the Lord's day, be-[25]cause we ought to abstain from all servile labour, on this holy day, that we may solely spend it in praising and honouring our sovereign Lord, and in instructing ourselves in the means of serving him with fidelity."

"It is for this reason, we are assembled in this holy place, where, being present at the same sacrifice of the Mass, in which Jesus Christ offers himself, in our stead, to his Father, by the hands of the Priest, under the appearance of bread and wine; first, we adore God, and render him the supreme worship which is due to him. Secondly, we thank his divine goodness for all the blessings with which he loads us every day. Thirdly, we beseech him to pardon all our sins. Fourthly and Lastly, we pray of him for ourselves and for our brethren, all the graces which we stand in need of, and particularly those of serving him with fidelity during this week, and to walk all the remainder of our life in the way of his holy commandments."

"You ought, my Brethren, to approach this Altar, with reverence and with confidence, there to present, by our hands, this divine host, and there to be offered with it, yourselves, and with the whole Church; for it is Jesus Christ entire, that is, the Head and the members, who offers it to his Father, as the sovereign Priest, and who is there offered as a victim with the faithful who are still militant upon earth, and with all the Saints who now reign in heaven."

"Let us, therefore, unite our hearts, and, during this Holy Sacrifice, let us pray God for the holy, apostolick and Roman Church, that he would be pleased to preserve it, give it peace, maintain it in union, to govern it through all the earth."

"We pray for our holy Father the Pope, for the Right Rev. Dr. John Carroll, the Catholic Superior in the United States of America; for all Prelates and Pastors of the Church, that being filled with the spirit of God, they may edify and lead the flock which Providence has entrusted them with."

"We pray for the prosperity of the Congress, for the happy establishment of the Federal government of the United States; in particular for the state of Massachusetts, Governor and its Magistrates; for the King of France [26] and the other friends and allies of America; for all those who respect the interest of his most Christian Majesty in foreign countries."

"We pray for the union and concord of Christians, for the peace and tranquility of this country, for the inhabitants of this City; we pray for the benefactors and founders of our congregation, (for those who have this day made an offering of the blessed bread) for the tranquility of families, for wants of widows, of orphans, of captives, of travellers, and of all those who are in poverty, in oppression, and in suffering."

"We pray for the perseverance of the righteous, for the conversion of sinners, for the comfort and the healing of the sick, and for the happy deliverance of all pregnant women; we pray God their fruit may receive holy baptism."

"We pray God, that of his goodness, he would be pleased to give to his people, and preserve to them, the blessing and the fruits of the earth, make them grow, multiply and ripen in their season, and preserve them from all accidents."

"We ask of the Lord, the ordering of weather necessary for the health of the body; and that he would be pleased, of his mercy, to preserve us from all contagious sickness."

"In fine, we pray, in general, for all those who make profession of the faith of the Catholic, Apostolick and Roman Church, and for all their spiritual and temporal wants."

"For all those things and others for which the Church hath been wont to pray, we are going to offer the Holy Sacrifice of the Body and of the Blood of our Lord Jesus Christ: but in the meantime, before we begin, unite in the prayers which we are going to make.

Here the Priest rises up, uncovers his head, and turns towards the altar, and the People throw themselves upon their knees.

Psalm 122

Ad te Levavi occulos meos etc.

Gloria Patri etc.. Pater noster etc.

V. Salvos fac servos tuos.

R. Deus meus sperantes in te.

V. Esto nobis Domine turris fortitudinis.

R. A facie inimici. [27]

V. Fiat pax in virtute tua.

R. Et abundantia in turribus tuis.

V. Domine exaudi etc.

R. Et clamor etc.

V. Dominus vobiscum.

R. Et cum spiritu tuo.

Oremus.

Deus refugium nostrum et virtus, adesto piis ecclesiae tuae precibus auctor ipse pietatis; et praesta, ut quod fideliter petimus efficaciter consequamur. Per Christum etc.

"The holy sacrifice of the Mass is offered, not only for the living, but also for the dead, according to the tradition of the Apostles, and the perpetual usage of the whole Church; it is therefore for them also that we are going to offer it. We ask of God, that he would be pleased to give a place of refreshment, of light and of peace to all those who have preceded us with signs of the faith, and particularly to the founders and benefactors of this Church; to our fathers and our mothers, to all our parents, and for all those whose bodies rest in the burial ground, or in the Church of this Parish."

"And you will remember N. who departed (on such a day,) who made a legacy to this Church); upon his account, unite in the prayers which we are going to make."

Psalm 124.

De Profundis etc.

Oremus.

Fidelium Deus etc.

"By the authority of God Almighty, and, of the Catholic Church, we cannot admit to our communion, all those who have a profession of faith and belief different from ours; all Simoniacs, magicians, sorcerers, soothsayers, all those who, by witchcraft, hinder the use of holy marriage; all those who injure persons through malice, abuse cattle, destroy the fruits of the earth, and exercise other mischief to the people; all those who are guilty of the crime of rape, who have given counsel and assistance to ravishers; all those of both sexes, who, without permission, marry out of the Church, without the presence of the lawful [28] Pastor, and proper witnesses; all usurers; all those who sell by false weights and by false measures; all those who lay violent hands on the Priests and the anointed of the Lord; all those who maliciously usurp and retain the goods of the holy Church, who hinder its jurisdiction, suppress, turn away, or conceal titles, papers and instruments which belong to it; and also, all those who, during the divine service, cause any scandal, or turn away the people, in any manner whatever from discharging their duty towards God; Commedians of either sex; all those who fight at Duel, who make challenge, who carry billets of defiance, who accept them, even though fighting should not ensue; all those persons, of both sexes, who continue under the curse of God, and are out of the communion of the Church, till, sincerely repenting, they are absolved and reconciled by the minister of the Church. And because we must not communicate holy things to those, who are unworthy of them, we request all persons, present in this holy place, at least to behave themselves there during this divine sacrifice with all the respect due to the majesty of God."

"We notify you, on the part of the Ecclesiastick Superior, that agreably to the holy Council of Trent, and the holy Canons, all the faithful are obliged to be punctually present, Sundays and Feast-Days, at Mass, at the lectures and instructions which are made there, unless they have some lawful hindrance. You ought also to know, that besides this attendance at the Parochial Mass, you ought to keep the rest of the time holy, in being present at the vespers, and the instructions which are performed in this Church; and in order to form your children to so holy a practice, you ought to carry them into the holy place, or at least to send them to the holy mass, and to the catechisings. This obligation is for masters also with regard to their domestics."

"You are notified that (_____) will be the feast of N. It is of obligation, and the Church orders to celebrate it the holy Sunday in attending that day at the holy Mass, the divine service in abstaining from all servile labour, and sanctifying that day by works of piety."

"Such a day (_____) is the fast of obligation for the Vigil [29] of the Feast, which I have just mentioned to you. All those who are of age, ought to fast, under pain of mortal sin, if they have not some lawful hindrance."

"There will be this week no commanded Feast, which hinders you from attending to your temporal affairs. I exhort you nevertheless, to come to Church as often as you can, to hear mass, and say your prayers there, that God may give you **his grace** and bless all your labours."

"On the 17th of March next, there will be sung, at 11 O'Clock A.M. a High-Mass in music, to the honor of St. Patrick, Apostle of Ireland. All persons, particularly the Catholics, are desired to attend, and join to our prayers for the propagation of the faith."

"All persons who wish to testify their benevolence towards the laudable and good intentions of Mr. L'abbé, may deposite their contributions at Col. Hurd's Insurance Office, State Street. The same will be carefully and religiously employed to discharge what is already due, to repair the roof, the windows etc. and the making of commodious benches. The names of the benefactors and donors will be carefully recorded; and should any persons be disposed to conceal their names, the generosity of their donations only will be mentioned."

Such were the regulations as drawn up by the Abbé Poterie for the little congregation that assembled regularly at his Church; and such was the mode in which the divine Office was conducted by him on Sundays and other days of devotion. We have been particular in recording them, that our readers may be in full possession of everything relating to the Catholic Church at its commencement in Boston.

The stay, however, of La Poterie was very short in this City. The news of his conduct in France, and the consequent withdrawal of his **faculties** by the Archbishop of Paris, had reached the ecclesiastical superior in Maryland very soon after he had entered upon his mission. In addition to this, the French Consul and others, had made some communications to him of a nature not very creditable to this Reverend Gentleman, and which convinced him at once of the impropriety of his choice in having selected him for so im-[30]portant a mission. **The following letter, written by the Rev. William O'Brien, Pastor of St. Peter's in New-York, only two months after** the date of the above **Pastoral,** will throw some additional light upon the subject. It was addressed to the French Consul residing in Boston:

"New-York, April 19-1789."

"Sir"

"As our very Reverend Superior has delegated his authority to me and sent me a special commission to inquire into the conduct of Mr. La Poterie, and as it is brought principally in charge against him, the unbecoming manner in which he made use of your name in Church, by recommending your conversion to the prayers of the Congregation, I make bold to trouble you with these few lines."

"It is needless to inform a gentleman of your good sense and education, that some more proof is necessary to substantiate the charges against him, besides your own, as you are the party aggrieved."

"The accusations made are as follows: the one I have already mentioned;—that he admits profane music in the Church;—that he causes some people to pay for admittance;—that he behaves at the altar and in Church with levity and even licentiousness;—that he drinks to excess, and that when in company he amuses his associates with tawdry and obscene songs. As for his extraordinary printed Pastoral letter I have seen it. I wrote this Post to M. La Potterie, and request of him to make his defence. I hope that you will be so kind as to give me what information you can, and procure what testimonials are requisite to judge in this disagreable affair; and by inclosing them either to Mr. La Forest or to Mr. Crevoquier they will be handed to, Sir, Your Most Obedient Humble Servant"

"Rev. Wm. O'Brien, rector of
St. Peter's Church, New York."

In a short time after the receipt of the Rev. Wm. O'Brien's letter, mentioned above, the Abbé Potterie left Boston, and repaired to Baltimore, to see the ecclesiastical Superior, Dr. Carroll, on the subject of the charges **alledged against him, [31] and to stand upon his defence. In this, however, he completely failed, as proofs of most of the charges had already reached** the Superior, sufficient to convince him of his guilt. He would not suspend him, however, in Baltimore, for some particular reasons: but committed the instrument containing his suspension to the Rev. Wm. O'Brien who was directed to hand it to him, on his way to Boston, in his return. This he was unable to do, as the Abbé Poterie, having suspected the commission with which he was intrusted, constantly avoided him whilst he remained in New York; so that, he was obliged to forward the suspension to Monsieur L'Etombe, the French Consul, to be served upon him on his arrival in Boston, as the following letter will shew:

"New-York, May 20th 1789."²

"Sir,"

"The scandalous conduct of M. La Poterie since he arrived in this city, the infamous falsehoods he has uttered, afford me sufficient grounds to believe that all the charges alledged against him at Boston are unhappily too well founded........ These matters came too late to my knowledge to have it in my power to inform Dr. Carroll of them. M. La Potterie was already in Baltimore, and for this reason Dr. Carroll did not deem it proper to suspend him there: but, he has since given me orders to do so, while La Potterie was at Philadelphia on his return to New-York. Having arrived in this City, he suspected my commission, concealed himself from me and came not to see me."

"Not being acquainted with any one in Boston in whom I can place confidence, and having been informed of your politeness to M. Barrett, of your zeal for your country and the welfare of our holy religion: I take the liberty to inclose to you his suspension and interdict which I pray you to communicate to him by some person in whom you can confide, and so as he may not suspect that you were charged with it. I send you the letter unsealed that [32] you may see the sentance and read it, and you are desired to communicate it to him in the same condition, in order that he may not pretend to be ignorant of it."

"I am persuaded your zeal for the cause of religion will excuse the liberty I take, and that I have no other motive, nor do I stand in need of any other to justify my conduct."

"If he should presume to say Mass and officiate in any manner after this, I pray you will inform the congregation of his having been interdicted, and that they cannot assist at his prayers under the penalty of excommunication."

"I have the honour to remain,
Sir, Your Obedient Humble Servant
Rev. Wm. O'Brien, Rector
of St. Peter's Church, New-York."

As soon as the above letter was received by the French Consul. the sentance was served upon La Poterie by a confidential person:—and he ceased to be the Pastor of the Infant Church in Boston. He continued. however. to reside in the City, as a private individual, until the 19th of January 1790. when he left it for the West Indies.[3]

The Abbé Poterie was succeeded by l'abbé Louis Rousselet. another French Clergyman, who continued to do duty in the little Church for a short time, when he also left Boston for the West Indies. not. however. until after the arrival of the Rev. John Thayer, and for some months afterwards.[1]

CHAPTER II

THE CONVERSION OF JOHN THAYER

The Rev. John Thayer arrived in Boston on the 4th of January 1790. This excellent Clergyman was a native of this City. He had been a Congregational Minister, and had officiated as such in Boston during two years when he felt a great desire to visit Europe, to learn some of the languages spoken there, and to make himself acquainted with the constitution of the different governments, their laws, the manners and customs of the people, in order that he might be more highly considered in his country, [33] and render himself more useful to it.[5] With this view he left Boston and sailed for France at the end of the year 1781. He immediately on his arrival set himself to read the best authors, and to study the principles of government. He was shortly after taken sick; and fearing that it might prove fatal, gave orders that no Catholic Priest should be admitted into his room, so strongly was he attached to his Sect. Upon his recovery he passed over into England where he spent three months. He was here asked to preach, which invitation he accepted; but his doctrine was found not to be conformable to that of the country where he was. He remarked, in reply, that he had drawn it from the Holy Scriptures. It is here that all Protestants find their different doctrines. He returned to France for the purpose of travelling to Rome, having his mind bent on the same objects and greatly prepossessed against the Cath[olic] religion and the people of Italy who had been always represented to him under the most odious light. He had, however, during his stay in france conceived a somewhat more favourable opinion of Cath[olic] Doctrine, and his intercourse with the Italians tended also much to correct his former preventions against them. In his passage from Marseils to Rome, he was obliged, for want of wind, to remain several days in a small harbour, called Port Ercolé. The Marquis

D'Elmoro, a respectable old Gentleman, Mayor of the place, without his having any recommendation to him received him politely and treated him with paternal affection and kindness. His house, his table, his library, all were at his service. On his departure he made him promise to keep up a correspondence with him by letter. He had every where, he tells us in the account which he afterwards published of his conversion, the happiness to meet with Italians of the same character; and all those with whom he had any conversation testified the same readiness to oblige him, especially in the decent and virtuous house in which he took up his lodgings at Rome, and in which he was treated as in the bosom of his own family. So much kindness and cordiality towards a stranger, and a Protestant known as such, both moved and surprised him. "This religion then," said he to himself, "**is not so unsociable, as it has been re[34]represented to me; nor does it inspire sentiments of intolerance and hatred towards those who are out of its pale.**" Thus was he led to condemn from day to day those unjust prejudices with which his mind had been filled against it, and thus did God prepare things from afar to lead him insensibly to the happy term at which he at length arrived. As soon as he entered Rome, his first desire was to go and visit some of the principal Monuments of Antiquity which are **so attractive to strangers, especiale [sic] the Rotunda or the Pantheon, a temple formerly consecrated to the worship of heathen Divinities, but now** dedicated to the honour of the Blessed Virgin and the Saints.

At the sight of this superb edifice, he was struck with an idea which seemed to him lofty, and which would be very proper, said he to himself, to furnish matter for a fine discourse, if the Catholic religion were the true one. The following is the substance of what suggested itself to his mind: This temple formerly consecrated to the worship of false Gods, become now a Temple of the only true God, the cross of Jesus Christ elevated upon the ruins of all the Idols united, in order to form, as it were, a more beautiful trophy, and thence exhibited to the whole world; this City, formerly mistress of the Universe and Capital of the pagan World, become now the Capital of the Christian world; here are speaking and ever subsisting monuments of the triumph of Jesus Christ over the **Strong one armed,** and the establishment of his Empire upon the ruins of the empire of Satan; it was worthy of God to make the centre of Idolatry the centre of the true religion; the first city of the world the Capital of his kingdom; in fine, of that great school of the arts, of that celebrated City, which attracts all eyes and which draws the curious to it, and strangers from all parts of the world, the School of truth and the common centre of Union among all the faithful who believe in Jesus Christ. Then nothing would be wanting to the external glory of his religion and the visibility of his Church, which he doubtless wished to place under the eyes of all his people, then she would prove to be that City truly built on a mountain and exposed to the sight of all nations, in such a manner as not to be concealed. — "This idea pleased me much," said he, "and as I was fond of Pulpit [35] eloquence, I almost wished that she was the true Church in order that I might handle so beautiful a subject. This first ray of light was calculated to lead him farther; but as yet it was only a Chimera abounding in pleasant thoughts, and he left it there to occupy himself with matters which he had first proposed to himself.

He acquired the Italian, in a much shorter time, and more easily, than the French, and was soon able to read the best authors in that language. He studied, at the same time, agreeably to his project, the constitution and actual state of Rome.

Nevertheless, the Cath[olic] religion came frequently into his mind; although it did not enter into the plan of his studies, still he wished to study it profoundly, as long as he remained in the city, as he would have wished to know the Mahometan religion, had he been at Constantinople; besides, he was far from suspecting that his own was false, or at least of thinking to embrace another; his only object was to learn the Catholic doctrine from the mouths of Catholics, that he might not impute to them what they would disavow. He addressed himself for this purpose to several Ecclesiasticks, and, according to his usual manner, to cause each one to speak of his particular profession, he put them upon the topick of religion; but they had more piety than light. Beholding a determined Protestant, they condemned without enlightening him, and they separated mutually discontented, they with his attachment to his errors, and he with their zeal which did not appear to him conformable to science; besides, he wished to know only their opinions and not to be undeceived with regard to his own; he did not experience the necessity of being enlightened, but only desired to satisfy his curiosity. Thanks, however, to that admirable Providence that makes all things serve for a good end, as the desire of travelling had conducted him to the centre of light, without his knowing it, so the desire of being informed equally carried him on to the knowledge of truth without his thinking of it.

After having often sought occasion to have conversation with a well informed man who should be able to acquaint him with the Catholick doctrine and at the same [time] [36] who should be willing to undertake to give him his knowledge, he met with two ecclesiastics in a place he was in the habit of frequenting: he there entered into conversation with them, declaring at the same time what he was and what he desired. His ideas, at that time of the Jesuits, corresponded with the opinion which Protestants generally entertained of them; nevertheless, he was anxious to become acquainted with some of them,—"I am not ignorant," said he to himself, of their cunning, and political craft, but they are considered by all as men of great learning; I shall know how to profit by their learning and at the same time to be on my guard against their subtilties": It was precisely to two Jesuits he was at this time conversing; his candour was not displeasing to them; they acknowledged that they belonged to the Society; but would not undertake to give him the information he required, themselves, but promised to introduce him to one who was in every respect qualified to satisfy him. They accordingly introduced him to one of their lecturers, well known at Rome, and highly considered both for his learning and virtue. "Sir," said he to him, "it may be that I entertain false notions of your religion, having had no opportunity to ascertain it except from its enemies. If that be the fact, my intention is to undeceive myself, for I have no wish to entertain prejudices against any denomination. Do not, however, believe, that you will convert me; for, surely you will not succeed." This abrupt manner of addressing him, did not prevent him from receiving M. Thayer, with a mildness and affability which could only be the effect of charity: he consented to his request to be allowed to have conversation with him on the subject of religion. He began by expounding to him, one by one, all the articles of catholic faith. This exposition lasted many days. He listened to him attentively, and without ever interrupting him. But on his return to his lodgings, he took care to commit to writing the objections which occurred to his mind and the arguments which seemed to combat each of these articles and dogmas. Although many difficulties presented themselves to him, he could not forbear, nevertheless, remarking that wonderful agreement **which was to be found in the whole body of catholic doc[37]trine, and which seemed to bespeak a wisdom nearly divine. After he had ended his** exposition, M. Thayer propounded his difficulties and doubts: in this way three months were spent in discussing all the different articles. He found himself often at fault and without having anything to reply, because he saw the fairness with which the discussion had been conducted, and he was sincerely disposed to be instructed and not to waste time in mere chicanery. Nevertheless, his mind was still greatly clouded, and he felt much embarrassed about several things upon which he was anxious to be informed; and as this respectable gentleman could not spare from his other avocations more than a few hours, at a time, and this at intervals on some days, he sought to fill up the space that intervened, by having recourse to another Jesuit equally learned and zealous. This gentleman's manner, at his first interview, appeared to him not a little singular: "We shall not enter, said he, "upon the matter today, go, and first recite the **Lord's Prayer** three times, and return on such a day." He could not help smiling at this commencement. "What," said M. Thayer, I am not yet a member of your Church, and already you impose a penance on me." He left him after this: however, on his return home, he reflected that prayer far from leading him astray, could not but be useful to him, and that a religion which teaches to begin with prayer, before examining into it, was, to all appearances very sure of itself. He executed, accordingly what had been prescribed him, and on the day appointed he went to see him. He already was in possession of what the Catholic doctrine was; he now only wished to have certain points cleared up upon which he still entertained some doubts. In proportion as he proposed these points to him with his objections, he pointed out to him the places in the works of the best Theologians and Controversial writers, in which they were treated at great length, and at the same time procured them for him. M. Thayer studied them attentively; this study led him to examine at bottom each of the articles contested between Protestants and Catholics, and to weigh the reasons which these **adduce in support of their sentiments. He de-[38]rived also considerable assistance from an Augustinian Friar, to whom he addressed himself at the** same time. He confined himself altogether to the pointing out to him the necessary distinction to be drawn between what is of faith among Catholics, and the private opinions which the Church allows to be treated in schools, without either adopting or rejecting them. This distinction threw much light upon the matter, and contributed to give him a clearer conception of things; for Protestants are in the habit of confounding these two objects, and thus of throwing every thing into confusion. There exists a perfect unity in things belonging to faith, the difference relates only to opinion; by blending these two things together, they take occasion to ascribe to faith what appertains solely to free and indifferent opinions.

The care which he took to consult in this manner different learned men, was doubly useful to him; he always profited by their particular lights, and was thereby enabled to observe their perfect agreement in faith, which, in fact, should be but one, as truth is one. This uniformity of sentiments, which has prevailed, in all ages among Catholics, caused a sensible impression in him, because he had never seen any thing like it among Protestants......

M. Thayer had been on terms of intimacy with the leading Ministers of the different Protestant Sects; he had often conversed with them: he knew well their sentiments; there never were two of them that agreed even upon the most essential articles; and what is more there never was one of them that had not himself varied in his doctrine. He called to mind that one of the most celebrated Preachers, with whom he was acquainted, had made on a particular day this acknowledgement to him: "When I preached," said he, "in such a place I passed for Heterodox; I was so indeed at the time; I had their very erroneous opinions; but I have changed them since; and were I [to] **preach there now, my doctrine would be deemed pure and correct; besides,"** he added, **"this thing is common to all our Preachers; I do not know one who has not, like me, varied in his doctrine." This acknowledgement made [39]** no impression upon him at that time, but it recurred to him afterwards and caused many reflections; an additional proof of what is commonly said, that good or bad principles, received in youth, produce sooner or later their effect.

This instability on the part of the leading Ministers of his communion gave him uneasiness. He saw in it a necessary consequence of the fundamental principle of Protestants, according to which each one is to be judge of his faith; according to this principle, there is no fixed rule of faith;—hence, that everlasting contradiction of Ministers among themselves;—hence, the frequent variation of each of them in his doctrine. M. Thayer had often tried to bring them to an agreement, and he had found that it could be only done by adopting the principle, that it was sufficient to believe in Jesus Christ, and to have the intention of honouring his Divinity; but with this system, which pleased him much, he would have united all Sects, even the most opposite; thus he went on, proceeding farther and **farther daily, and at len[g]th set no bounds to his liberty of thinking. He had friends among the Quakers, and Anabaptists, the Arminians and** others; he, in a short time, would have adopted toleration in its most extended sense. It is idle for Protestants to say, that they admit the Scripture as their rule of faith; as soon as they acknowledge no living authority to determine the sense; as soon as they leave the interpretation of it to every particular individual, there exists no longer any means of convincing them of error; and, if it should please the Socinian, for example, to say that he finds nothing in the Scripture which proves the Divinity of Jesus Christ, no one has any right to require of him the belief of this dogma or to condemn him, if he reject it. This principle leads still farther: it conducts a man, **who reasons justly, on to indifference [with] respect [to] all religion, and** it overthrows the very foundation of Christianity, by allowing the reason of each individual, as supreme judge of his belief. This reflection, and a thousand others which occured to his [40] mind, had not, at that time, all the effect which they might have produced, but they disposed and prepared him to open one day his eyes to the truth. Already had his researches conducted him much farther than he had thought; he had, at first, only intended to obtain an exact knowledge of the Catholic Doctrine. and he was insensibly led on to discover nothing in it but what was perfectly reasonable. He had, at the commencement of this examination, entertained no suspicion that his particular Sect was wrong: and now he perceived distinctly all the weak points in it, and even entertained serious doubts: but he was nevertheless far from having made up his mind to renounce it.

The prejudices of his education had yet a strong hold upon his mind; neither was his heart disposed as yet for such a sacrifice as this change would require of him; he thought it much to have taken the resolution to bring with him, on his return to America, the best controversial works, composed by Catholic writers, and to read them at his leisure. determined then to change his religion, when he should be no longer able to answer the arguments contained in them, after due reflection: for, he had made up his mind, whatever proofs might be adduced him, not, by any means, to make his abjuration at Rome, lest he might take an over-hasty step: but Divine Providence, which watched continually over him, would not allow him to use a delay, which might have proved fatal to him: it made different events serve to hasten his conversion. There fell into his hand a work of Father Seignery upon Guardian Angels. This pious belief, that each one of us has a tutelar angel as a witness to all his actions, was not new to him: he had been taught it from his childhood; but it had not had until then any effect upon him, or very inconsiderable. The reading of this work awakened in his breast those early impressions of piety which he had received from his p rents. He relected upon his life past,—he reproached himself with having often failed in the respect which he owed to his Angel-Guardian. and he took the resolution to watch henceforth over himself with the [41] view of avoiding whatever could displease him. This attention to keep himself from sin, contributed without doubt, to his conversion to the faith: it was, at least, one obstacle less to the grace which God wished to bestow upon him. Such was the state of things when the death of the Venerable **Labre** and the miracles reported to have been wrought through his intercession began to make a noise at Rome, and to become the subject of almost every conversation. In spite of the instructions he had received. and the lights which these instructions had procured him, he was by no means disposed to believe all that was said of them. Of all his prejudices against Catholics, the most deeply rooted was a formal incredulity in regard to the miraculous events said to have happened among them. He had been broght up in this belief like all Protestants. who far from admitting the gift of miracles, disdain it, and take upon themselves to deny it positively. He not only denied absolutely those which were published at this time, he went so far as to turn them into ridicule; he even allowed himself to utter indecent jokes in the different Coffy-Houses, upon the Servant of God, whose poverty and apparent filth had disgusted him, and upon this subject he went even much farther than his friends who were also Protestants. However, the number and weight of testimony increasing daily, he thought it was incumbent on him to examine into the thing himself; he held frequent conversations with the Confessor of the deceased from whom he was made acquainted with a part of his life. He went to see four of the persons said to have been miraculously cured; he became assured of their actual state, and of that in which they had been before; he took information of the kind and duration of the disease with which they had been attacked, and of the circumstances of their cure which had been wrought in an instant; he collected the testimony of those who knew them, and after all this information taken with the greatest care, he became quite convinced that the reality of each of these miracles had been better proved than the best established facts ordinarily are. One of these persons, [42] a **religious** of the Convent of St. Appollonia, had a bloodvessel broken in her breast; for the period of eighteen months she had fallen into a state of languor which had daily increased; her weakness had been such, that she could with difficulty endure the slightest nourishment; she invoked the Venerable **Labre**, she took, with faith, a little liquor into which had been dipped one of his Relicks, and she found herself in an instant perfectly cured. The same day she went down to the Choir with the other **Religious,** she eat [sic] with them without being in the least incommoded, and performed with great ease the most irksome labours of the house. This was attested by the Superiour of the house and six of the religious of the same Community. He himself saw repeatedly the religious Lady who had been healed, spoke to her and found her in the enjoyment of the best of health. He did not stop here; he paid a visit to the Physican who had attended her during the whole time of her illness; he confirmed all that the Community had stated in her regard, and he added, moreover, that he was ready to swear upon the holy Gospel that the infirmity she laboured under was naturally incurable. M. Thayer continued his visits to the good Lady during the whole time he remained at Rome, that is to say, during the space of six months; he accordingly had abundance of time to satisfy himself that her cure was effectual, and at his departure left her in perfect health. Persuaded, as he was, that these cures had something supernatural in them, he could [not] help reflecting within himself upon the danger he exposed himself to by remaining in a false religion. These reflections threw him into a strange perplexity; it would be difficult to express the violent situation in which he then found himself. Truth displayed herself to him on every side, but she was combatted by all the prejudices which he had sucked in with the milk of his mother. He felt the force of the reasons which were opposed to the doctrine of Protestants; he had not, however, the courage to yield; he saw clearly into the truth of the Catholic Church—that it was founded upon proofs innumerable and unanswerable; he saw [43] that the answers which it gave to all that Protestants could object to it, were solid and satisfactory; but it was necessary that he should abjure the errors in which he had been educated, and which he had himself preached to others; he was a minister among the Congregationalists, and must renounce his profession and fortune; he was tenderly attached to his family connections, and must incur their hatred; interests so dear to his heart still retained him; in a word, his understanding was perfectly convinced, but his heart was not changed. It was while he was thus wavering and irresolute, that a small book was put into his hands, intitled: **Manifesto d'un Cavaliere Christiano convertico alla religione Catholica,** a book, which should be translated into many languages, and circulated wherever hereticks are to be found. The author gives historically an account of his conversion and briefly discusses all the points which are controverted between Catholics and Protestants. He places at the beginning a Prayer which was communicated to him by a Catholic, to implore light of the Holy-Ghost, which will be seen below:

"God of bounty, almighty and eternal, Father of mercy, Saviour of mankind I intreat thee humbly, through thy infinite goodness, to enlighten my mind and to move my heart, in order that by the means of true Faith, Hope and Charity, I may live and die in the true religion of Jesus Christ; I am certain, that, as there is but one only God, so there can be but one only Faith, one only religion, and one only way to salvation, and that all the ways which are opposed to this, can only lead to hell. It is this Faith, O my God, that I seek with eagerness, in order to embrace it and obtain salvation. I protest, therefore, before the throne of thy Majesty, and swear by all thy divine attributes, that I will follow the religion which thou shalt have pointed out to me as the true one, and will renounce, whatever it may cost me, that in which I shall discover error and falsehood. I do not deserve, it is true, this favour of thee on account of the multitude and enormity of my sins of which I have a sincere grief, since they are displeasing to thee, a God so good, so great, so holy, [44] and so worthy of being loved; but what I do not deserve, I yet hope to obtain of thy infinite mercy; and I conjure thee to grant me this favour through the merits of the precious blood which has been shed for us, poor sinners, by thy only Son Jesus Christ. Amen."

He felt, on receiving this book, a kind of presentiment that it was to give him the finishing stroke; consequently it was with extreme difficulty that he could resolve to read it; his soul was, as it were, torn by two contrary movements: what combats, what terrible assaults had he not to sustain at this time! He ran his eyes over this prayer, but could not prevail upon himself to utter it; he desired to be enlightened, and yet feared to be too much so; his temporal interests and a thousand other motives presented themselves, in crowds, to his mind, and kept in balance the salutary impressions of grace; in short, the interest of eternal salvation at last triumphed. He threw himself upon his knees, and endeavoured to recite this prayer with all the sincerity he was able; and the violent agitation of his soul, added to the struggle which he had just experienced, produced an abundance of tears; he then set about reading this book, which was a short exposition of the principal proofs of the Catholic religion. The united collection of these different proofs, which until then he had only seen separately; so many rays of light brought, as it were, into a focus, struck him sensibly. He now no longer offered the same resistance to grace: God spoke to his heart at the same time that he enlightened his understanding, and gave him strength to surmount the obstacles which had stopped him until then. He had not yet finished reading the book when he cried out: My God, I promise thee to become a Catholic. The same day, he announced his determination to the family with whom he lived, they were overjoyed at it, because they were truly and sincerely pious. He went the same evening to the Coffee-house, where he communicated to all his friends his change of religion, the most of whom were Protestants; and, to repair, as far as he was able, the scandal which he had given, he boldly defended the sanctity of the venerable **Labre,** and furthermore declared that he had found more proofs of the truth [45] of his miracles than he would have required for any fact whatever. Moreover, not to be ashamed of Jesus Christ, he invited a great number of friends to assist at his abjuration; many of them pitied his weakness, while others mocked; but God, who had called him to the faith, supported him, and he had the firmest confidence that he would support him until death. It must be mentioned, that previous to his abjuration he had yet had many conflicts with his imagination on the subject of the honour paid to the blessed Virgin and the Saints. He was, however, well instructed on this article, and could not doubt but that it was highly useful to employ the intercession of the Mother with her Son; and, so far from doing him an injury by loving and honouring her whom he himself so tenderly

loved, it would be to honour him the more; nevertheless, his ancient prejudices returned continually upon him, and disturbed him in spite of
himself. The reproach of Idolatry, which he had so often heard repeated to
Catholics on this subject, terrified him, yet, although he was perfectly convinced of their being unfounded. He might be said to resemble those
persons, who, having, in their youth, had their imaginations strangely
worked upon by ridiculous ghost-stories, could not help shuddering, in advanced life, involuntarily, when the same ideas were brought anew to their
minds, in spite of reason which could not but blush at them: he was obliged
to do violence to himself; and when he began to invoke the Blessed Virgin,
he could do it but by trembling. He began by addressing himself to Jesus
Christ and protesting to him that he had no other view than to honour him,
and that he only desired to do it more perfectly, by having recourse to his
holy Mother, begging him not to impute any idolatrous intentions to him
which he disavowed from the bottom of his heart. Then addressing himself
to the B[lessed] Virgin herself: "Tender Mother," said he, "if it be lawful
to implore thy aid, assist me in the miserable state in which I find myself,
it is through thee that the saviour has come to us, it is, also, through thee
that I desire to go to him; the Scriptures teach me that it is through thy
means that the first miracle was wrought in the order of grace (the sanctification of St. John the Baptist) and the first in the order of nature (the
change [46] of water into wine) behold another thou art called upon to perform; do not deny me this favour, employ thy credit in the performance. I
do not deserve it; I have too long disowned thee; but I begin now, although
trembling, to address myself to thee; intercede for me with thy divine
Son." Then, returning to God: "Lord, added he, I demand thy light, thou
hast promised to hear those who invoke thee; I do it now with all my heart;
I am in quest of truth at whatever price it may be obtained: Thou art my
witness, O my God, I cannot be deceived in addressing myself to thy
Mother." Confidence and peace of soul were the fruits of this prayer. From
that time, he always had recourse to the Blessed Virgin and was sure to obtain, through her intercession, and receive particular graces. Gratitude
obliged him to make this acknowledgement; he sought to enter into all
those intentions which have her honour in view; and he entered into a
solemn engagement to labour, to the full extent of his ability, to induce all
others to do the same. A natural reflection here presents itself to the mind:
Can God permit a man to be deceived in the choice of his religion, who after
a diligent inquiry, an exact vigilence over his conduct, and after having addressed him many fervent prayers, is resolved to embrace it at the expense
of all that he has most dear in the world, family, profession, fortune,
reputation? If this religion were false, would he not have it in his power to

say to God, with a celebrated Theologian: "Lord it is thou who hast deceived me." "This reflection will acquire a new degree of force." M. Thayer, observes in the account he had given of his conversion, "if I be allowed to add the prodigious change which I myself experienced on my conversion: I hesitate to proclaim it; but it appears to me that I ought to do it for the glory of the divine mercy and to pay a just homage to the Catholic religion which I have now the happiness to profess. How different is my condition from what it then was! My thoughts, my inclinations, my pursuits, all are changed; I do not know myself any longer; from the moment that I took my determination I renounced all profane studies which had until this time occupied my attention; I left my books half read; I distrusted those which belonged to me: from that time the passions have had but little **influence over me; my views of ambition and worldly promotion have [47] entirely left me; I have bid adieu to them; I have now no other pleasure** than what is derived from the service of God; I experience in my soul a peace which I had never known before. It is no longer now the deceitful security of a slumbering conscience that presumes upon the mercy of God, and sees not the danger to which she is exposed; it is the sweet confidence of a child, who finds himself in the arms of his Father, and who has reason to hope that nothing will ever sever him from him in spite of the dangers which encompass him; Yes, this religion is made for the heart; however, strong, however solid the proofs are, which have convinced me of the truth of the Catholic religion, the content of mind, the pure joy which follows it, is, as it were, a new proof equally persuasive. The truths, which gave me most trouble to believe, are those which afford me now most consolation. The mystery of the Eucharist which had appeared to me so incredible, is now become a perenial source of spiritual delights. Confession, which I had regarded as an intolerable burden, appears now to me infinitely attractive in consequence of the tranquility which it produces in my soul. Ah! if hereticks and unbelievers could only experience the delights, which are experienced at the foot of the altar, they would soon cease to [be] either one or the other! Oh! that I could make myself heard by all! I would cry out to them: taste and see by your own experience, how sweet is the Lord, how good he is to those who serve him in the holy society which he himself has formed, and which he vivifies by his Spirit. Behold the predominant desire, the only desire of my heart, that of extending, as far as I am able the empire of the true faith, which constitutes now all my happiness; I have no other ambition; it is for this I wish to return to my own country, hoping to be, notwithstanding my unworthiness, the instrument of the conversion of my countrymen;—and such is the conviction I have of the truth of the Catholic Church, and my gratitude for the signal grace which God has conferred upon me, by calling me to the true faith, that I would seal it with my very blood, if God would but give me this grace; I doubt not, he would give me sufficient strength. I conjure those, who [48] may read what I have written on this subject, to pray with fervour that the God of light, and Father of mercy, may accomplish his will towards his servant, may open an easy access to the faith in my country, may cause it to spring up and fructify in a land in which it has never been professed. Perhaps—(I dwell with pleasure upon this consoling thought) perhaps, he who builds up Empires and destroys them at pleasure, who does all things for his Elect, and the interest of his Church, has he permitted, and conducted to a glorious end that astonishing revolution* we have just witnessed, but to accomplish some great design, and a revolution far more happy still in the order of grace. Amen."

M. Thayer pronounced his abjuration, at Rome, on the 25th of May, 1783. This is he publickly, and in a solemn manner, before many Protestants, and a large concourse of friends and others whom he had invited specially to assist at it. He shortly after concluded to embrace the ecclesiastical state, being fully persuaded that he was called to it by God for his greater glory and the sanctification of his own soul as well as that of his neighbour. In order to prepare himself the better for this holy state, he returned to France and entered the Seminary of St. Sulpice, in Paris, as a Theological Student. While there he received a letter from his brother in America, in which he expressed his grief and surprise, at his having renounced his religion, to embrace one so full of bigotry and superstition. He stated his objections fully against it, and seemed anxious to bring him back to the faith of his Fathers. The answer which M. Thayer gave to this letter is so interesting, and at the same time so well calculated to instruct the uninformed reader that we cannot forbear inserting it. It is dated 1st of May, 1787, not quite four years after he had made his abjuration.

Letter of M. Thayer to his brother.
"My dear Brother and Friend,"
"It is with the greatest satisfaction I have received your letter by M. * * *; and what has afforded me particular pleasure is, to find that you still entertain the same tender affection for me you always did. Be persuaded that mine is always [49] the same towards you; and so far from time, distance, or difference of opinion having weakend it in any manner, it has on the contrary received additional strength in the holy religion I have

*The Independance of the Thirteen States of North America.

embraced, a religion whose proper and essential character is to perfect those moral virtues which she finds in us."

"After the tender effusion of your heart, you express to me your regret at my having left the religion, in which I was brought up, to follow one, which (as far as you have any knowledge of it) abounds in bigotry and superstition. You have done well, My dear brother, to add, **as far as you have any knowledge of it;** for, give me leave to tell you, that you have no knowledge at all of it, and nothing could lead you to express yourself thus, but the false representations, and black calumnies of our enemies, who have the talent to conceal all that is reasonable in this religion, the most holy, and most worthy of our veneration. This ignorance is common to most Protestants; for, I cannot imagine there are many so malicious and wicked, as to impute errors to us, which they know, in their conscience, we do not believe. I was, like you, in the grossest ignorance in this particular, and must own to you that nothing surprised me more, than the exposition of the Catholic religion, such as I heard it from the mouth of those, who profess it, so different did I find it from that, represented to me, when I was at school. **Believe me, My Dear Brother, I have no interest in deceiving you; I desire nothing so much as your salvation, and that of all my dear relations. I** declare to you before God, who sees the sincerity of my heart, to obtain this grace, I would willingly endure death itself."

"Before you read my answers to your objections, I beseech you to retire for a few minutes into some lonely spot; and there with your whole heart, and on your knees, promise God firmly, to renounce all your passions; ask of him the grace to avoid all that the voice of your conscience shall declare to you to be sinful, and offer up to him this prayer: "God of mercy, I intreat thee," etc. (this prayer is found in page 43.) If such be your disposition, and if you really desire to cherish it, my answers, although short, and imperfect, will be sufficient to dispel all the clouds [50] which darken your mind: but if you are disposed to act otherwise, you seek not the truth with an upright mind."

I. "What you tell me of the persecutions which Catholics have raised against their enemies, shews only that at all times there have been bad Catholics, who have made religion serve to exercise the malignity of their heart: far from our religion approving of such Christians, she on the contrary highly condemns them, and never has she employed other arms in her defense than mildness, patience and charity. There have been, and perhaps there may be yet cruel and vindictive Catholics, as there have been, and there may be yet cruel and persecuting Protestants; but neither these nor those are so in consequence of their principles; it is on the contrary because they depart from them. We do not pretend to assert that all Catholics are Saints; we see unhappily how far they are from being so, and this is what grieves the good; I can notwithstanding assure you that of all those whom I have met with in several kingdoms of Europe, I have never yet seen a single one utter the least word of any thing like harshness, or shew the slightest animosity against Protestants; they pity and pray for them as for brethren who are deceived and gone astray; here is their whole crime; but see how your different Sects are affected towards us, see even how they are affected towards one another, and judge for yourself to whom the charge of persecution is more justly applicable, whether to you or to us? I leave the decision to your conscience.''

II. ''As we lay great stress upon the unity of Doctrine which has always prevailed and will always prevail among Catholics, you think to weaken the force of this argument by opposing the unity which reigns among the Mahometans; but the unity which you attribute to them is purely imaginary: for, according to the best historians, they are divided into two great Sects, the one of **Omar,** and the other of **Ali;** these last, named Shiites, form five principal Sects which, like so many trees, extend into seventy branches: their belief is extremely varied in all these different societies; some doubt of their religion, and by dint of doubting end by becoming pure Deists; others admit the Metempsycosis; many advocate absolute predestination, etc.; all apply mutually, from Sect to Sect, the well known terms of Orthodox and Heterodox; [51] their hatred of one another is carried to such an excess, that in making the pilgrimage to Mecka, they divide themselves into as many different bands as there are Sectaries, and sympathise so little with, that they will not even pray for one another. Let us then talk no more of Mahometan union, let us confine ourselves to that of Protestants. I maintain that were you all of one mind, and of one opinion it would be more the effect of chance than the result of your principles. That which serves as a foundation to all the others, is it not the liberty which each one enjoys to examine and judge for himself? Now, so far from such a principle producing union, it is sure on the contrary to prove a natural source of division. The same cannot be said of our Church: by its very constitution and doctrine, it is impossible that there should arise divisions in what regards the articles of faith; take notice of these words, **articles of faith.** In a mere matter of opinion, each one is free to adopt or to reject as he pleases; but as soon as the Church has declared that such or such a point is **of faith,** from that moment all true Catholics submit upon the spot, because they believe the Church infallible. Should any one refuse to submit on such an occasion, he would be instantly excluded from her communion, because he would reject this fundamental principle, that she is **the pillar and ground of truth.** (1. Tim. 3. 15.)''

III. "This indivisible unity of faith is evidently pointed out in Scripture; and Jesus Christ has established it as the foundation to the whole edifice, when he established his Church. **She is one body,** says St. Paul to the Ephesians (C.4. V. 4. & 5.) and we recognise but **one spirit** which animates it, but **one** and the same **Lord,** but **one** and the same **faith,** but **one baptism;** that is to say, that our faith ought to be one in the same sense that Our Lord Jesus Christ is one. Now, Our Lord Jesus Christ is absolutely and essentially one, our faith, therefore, ought to be absolutely and rigorously one. In the prayer which Jesus Christ addressed to his Father for those who believe in him, he prays that they may be united in faith, and that their union may resemble that of the three [52] Persons of the Trinity, a union which he exhibits as a mark by which the world will infallibly know that he has received his mission from his Father (St. John, c. 17. V. 20, & 21.) Without this perfect union the world would never have been able to believe that he was sent by God."

IV. "You will perhaps suppose that Jesus Christ prayed at that time that his disciples might be united in heart, and that he gives this mutual union formed and kept up by charity, as the distinctive mark of the society of Christians without any mention of a unity of faith. But this very explanation proves the necessity of being united in faith, since nothing destroys charity so much as a difference of religion. Witness all the disturbances and all the wars which the history of the different Sects records. Our Church alone can lay claim to this union; an incontestable truth; and there needs no other proof to convince every mind not prepossessed against the Catholic Church, that she alone is the true spouse of Jesus Christ."*

V. "Besides this unity of faith and of doctrine, we have three other distinctive marks of the true Church announced in the Symbols which you acknowledge as well as we, viz: holiness, catholicity and apostolicity. Examine well and see whether your Sects can boast of possessing these united marks, or even a single one of them."

VI. "What shocks you most in our doctrine, is the infallibility which we acknowledge in our Church; but after a few words on this subject, it will not appear so terrible to you. Remark, I pray you, My dear Brother, that it is in the universal Church, that is to say, in the majority of Bishops united

---

*All the Fathers of the Church unanimosly insist on the necessity of a union in faith in the Church of Jesus Christ. You believe as we do that they are Saints. Now, taking into view the time when they lived, and how near they were to the time of Jesus Christ and his Apostles, surely they could not be mistaken in this matter. I might produce in proof of what I here advance an infinity of passages from their works, but my limits prevent me.

in sentiment with the Pope that we acknowledge this infallibility to reside, and not in the Pope alone. If some Doctors and Theologians hold the Pope to be infallible, their pri-[53]vate opinion should not be imputed to the whole Church which has defined nothing on this question."[6]

"In order then to place our doctrine on the subject of infallibility in a clear light, let us go back to the time when Jesus Christ revealed all truths to his apostles, and appointed both them and the Pastors who were to succeed them, to be the depositaries of these revealed truths. In all ages, as soon as any new doctrine appeared, this body of Pastors declared it to be contrary to the deposits committed to their care by Jesus Christ. Thus, when Arius denied his divinity, the Church condemned him, by declaring that she had received a contrary doctrine from her divine Spouse: she held the same language against Pelagius; and to prove incontestably the corruption of our origin she opposed to him the practise of baptizing: a practise as ancient as the Church herself, and instituted by Jesus Christ. Her infallibility, then, consists in the public and perpetual testimony which she has constantly borne to the truths of fact which she holds in deposits: for the Christian religion is a public fact, or an assemblage and a succession of public facts. Is it not a public and incontestable fact that Jesus Christ has lived, that he has taught such a doctrine, that he has operated such miracles, that the Bible has been written by such authors? etc. all so many points which are matters of fact, and sensible facts,—facts which cannot be known or learnt otherwise than by witnesses who have seen or heard them. The Church teaching, that is to say, the major part of the Bishops with the Pope at their head, is truly this body of hereditary witnesses. You cannot, then deny them, my dear Brother, at least this species of infallibility which consists in a capacity of relating facts exactly, since you willingly allow it to every Society, civil or religious, or even composed of simple individuals."

"When the Mahometans, who consist of different nations, and consequently are influenced by different interests, unanimously attest, nevertheless, that at such an Epock, they received such a doctrine from Mahomet, [54] would common sense dare to question a fact of such public notoriety? Why then will you refuse the unanimous testimony of the Catholic Church, composed of different nations, influenced by different interests, and often at war with one another, when all the Pastors, at least as unanimous as the Mahometans, declare openly that they have received such a doctrine from Jesus Christ and his apostles, when they agree upon the exposition of all the articles of faith, when they affirm and declare that they have never experienced any change in their society? Besides, how can such a change be supposed?"

VII. "For there is, in the first place, as I have already observed, a body of Pastors to prevent and reject every innovation. In the second place, in all ages days have been specially set apart for the Faithful to assemble and to hear from the mouth of their Pastors the explication of our mysteries, and to learn what they ought to practise daily in the Church. In all ages there have been, as there are yet, Christians who daily approach the holy table. Is it reasonable, is it possible to suppose that when their Pastors presented to them what appeared to be bread, they did not inquire whether what they were about to receive in this sacrament, was simply bread, or the true body of Jesus Christ? In all ages, then, the Christians ought to know what they were obliged to believe in so important a matter, in those times particularly in which they approached nearer to those of the Apostles, and when the Pastors were more faithful to instruct their flocks. Whatever their faith was on this point, such it must necessarily have been handed down to us, without the slightest alteration; for, in supposing it altered, people naturally inclined to reclaim, would not have been silent upon so important a thing."

"If you tell me that they did cry out and murmur, but that their cries did not reach us, I will answer, that nothing would be more strange, since we have contemporary historians who have related the most minutious disputes that have occurred in the different ages of the Church (I do not except even those of the greatest ignorance;) how would they have let so essential a change as this to pass under silence? It is, there-[55]fore incredible, it is, therefore impossible that such a change could have ever arrived.

Besides, what interest would the Church have in this change of doctrine? Could it be imagined that so many different nations, who compose her, with such opposite interests, would have concerted together such a revolution? What the French, for example, would have done, would not the English have opposed? Could all the nations of which she is composed, have been united, to produce a change of this kind? Would not those Hereticks, too, who at all times have been found in these different nations, have seized upon an occasion like this to reproach them with their perfidy; and would they not have taken care to hand it down to posterity? I might form the same chain of reasoning on the other articles of faith."

"You see, then, My dear Brother and friend, that common sense obliges us to receive the testimony of the Church when she declares that she has received such and such truths from the mouth of Jesus Christ and his Apostles, and has preserved them in all their purity and integrity: Now, the very moment we admit her testimony in this respect, we become Catholics, since every Christian admits the truth of all the doctrines taught by Jesus Christ and his Apostles. This **moral** infallibility, of which I have just

spoken, which you are obliged to allow to the Church as to every other considerable and extensive Society, becomes **divine** in virtue of the promises
of Jesus Christ, who has expressly communicated to her his own im-
mutability."

VIII. "This second species of infallibility far superior to the other, since
it is entirely supernatural and founded upon the promises of God, appears
in the most striking manner, if we consider only these words of Jesus
Christ to his Apostles: **Go and teach, I am with you to the end of the world;**
that is to say, with you teaching: Now, a Church which is assured of the
presence of Jesus Christ, during the whole time she is teaching, must certainly be infallible, and this infallibility is found incontestably promised to
the successors of the Apostles; for it is to the successors of the Apostles, as
to the Apostles themselves, [56] that these words of the Saviour refer: **to
the end of the world,** unless it were proper to confine them to the very age
of the Apostles, **usque ad consummationem seculi (hujus);** but nothing
could be more absurd, since all the Apostles, except St. John, had died
before the end of the first age of the Church; besides, Jesus Christ had
promised his Apostles that **the spirit of truth should abide with them
forever;** (St. John c. 14. V. 16 & 19.) that is to say, again, to the end of the
world, words which include again necessarily, as well as the preceding
ones, the successors of the Apostles. If they have the spirit of truth for their
guide, they assuredly cannot, united among themselves and with their
head, the successor of St. Peter, the Vicar of Our Lord Jesus Christ, teach
error, in matters of faith;—therefore they are infallible."

IX. "It was, therefore, upon reason, upon the Holy Scripture I rested, and
not simply upon the fabulous legends of my Church, as you have been
pleased to reproach me with having done, when I told you, in my last letter,
that the Pope, united with the majority of the Bishops, was guided by the
spirit of truth, in his decisions of what we ought to believe; for, this
proposition, the Pope is the successor of St. Peter, and the Bishops are the
successors of the other Apostles, is it not a fact as publick, and as incontestable, as this other: Lewis the 16th is the Successor of St. Lewis?"

X. "All these arguments which I have just offered, prove evidently the infallibility of the Church. Our Lord furnishes a new proof of it when he says,
that he who hears the Church hears himself; and when he commands every
Christian to obey his Church under the penalty of being treated as a heathen
and a publican. Would God command us to obey a Church capable of
teaching errors which would infallibly lead us to an eternal death? Would it
not be himself, in such a case, that would lead us into error, and to death
which would be a necessary consequence of it? Why has God established his
Church? St. Paul tells us, it was, that we might not be tossed to and fro, and

carried about with every wind of doctrine; (Ephes. c. 4. V. 14.) that is to say, that we might not be placed in any doubt or uncertainty respecting what we ought to believe; but can you Protestants ever be otherwise than in a state of doubt and uncertainty? It is a thing which [57] is impossible, since you possess no infallible authority capable of freeing you from error, and upon which you can rest your belief."

XI. "Besides the Holy Scripture, which is the law, there must necessarily be an infallible authority to terminate the disputes and contentions which may arise among Christians, respecting the sense of this law. If such an authority be not recognized, there cannot be any fixed rule of faith, nor any invariable articles of faith. The prodigious multitude of your Sects, which increase every day, and which end by becoming Socinians, Deists etc. is an incontestable proof of it, and one that admits of no reply: a proof which we have a sensible example of, and quite recent in the change which has just taken place among you in the articles of faith anciently drawn up by the members of the English Church."

XII. "Let me ask you my dear Brother, what is your idea of an article of faith? Is it not a doctrine revealed by God and founded upon his veracity? As then the divine veracity is unchangeable, the truths which depend upon it ought equally to be so. For, heaven and earth shall pass away, but the word of God shall never pass away. It would consequently be absurd and impious to pretend to alter any thing in these truths, since it would make God capable of a lie; whence I conclude always that an infallible judge is necessary for you."

XIII. "How can you be persuaded to believe that the Bible is itself this judge? It is the book of the law, but a dumb book, a book upon which contestations and disputes arise daily. There ought to be a visible judge to decide the point in dispute, and to decide it sovereignly and in the last resort, and to point out who is in the right. Now, the Bible can never do this; for, to abide by the Bible alone, and not to have recourse to the decision of the Church, one will always be stopped by the following doubts. 1st Is the Bible a Canonical book, is it truly the work of the Holy Ghost? 2ly Is it entire, and has it not been altered? A doubt, the better founded, as there are an infinity of variations. 3ly Is it faithfully translated? And what is more important to know, 4ly have the Translaters given the true sense of it? In the midst of so many uncertainties, how [58] shall I be assured of my faith? Nevertheless, it ought to be so firm and unshaken, that we should be ready with the martyrs to seal it with our blood; without this disposition, one cannot be said to belong to Jesus Christ, and merits not to bear the name of Christian. We, Catholics, are protected from all these perplexities, because we submit to the Church which we believe to be infallible. Besides, that which proves the necessity of an infallible Church, is that she alone can be brought to the level of every one, of the little as well as of the great. Is not Jesus Christ, according to St. Paul, the Saviour of all men? Does he not shew the most tender solicitude for the salvation of all men? Can Mechanicks, Labourers and so many others burthened with the different cares of life, study the Scriptures? Are they capable of those eternal disputes which the principle you assume entails upon them? Alas! the longest life of the most learned men would not suffice for it; After all, with such a principle, that every one is free and capable of examining for himself, I do not see of what great use your Ministers can be to you.''

XIV. ''The infallibility of the Church once established, every doubt which a Christian might entertain will instantly vanish; for, if it be true that Jesus Christ cannot suffer his Church to deceive me, from that moment I am obliged in conscience to receive all her decisions, even those which appear incredible to my reason. This infallibility once established, the first consequence which should be drawn from it, is that the Church has never at any time taught any error, as Luther and Calvin have pretended, an assertion which they could not make without blasphemy, that is to say, without making a liar of Jesus Christ when he said, that the gates of hell should never prevail against his Church; for, if the Church here erred, the gates of hell have prevailed against her, and the promise of Jesus Christ is false. The second consequence is, that all those, who voluntarily and knowingly attach themselves to these pretended reformers, and follow their doctrine, are evidently in the way of perdition; for, what reply can they give to the following argument? In the time of Luther and Calvin [59] either the Roman Catholic Church was the true Church, or this title belonged to some other society, or in fine the Church of Jesus Christ was extinct; if the Roman Catholic Church was at that time the Church of Jesus Christ, no one could separate from her without renouncing salvation, since there is no salvation for those who separate themselves from Jesus Christ; if it was some other society, they were obliged to unite with it under the pain of eternal damnation: this is nevertheless what Luther and Calvin did not do. If the Church of Jesus Christ has ceased to exist, Jesus Christ must necessarily be an impostor, since he provided that she should always subsist, in spite of all the efforts of hell and the world.''

XV. ''What I have said of infallibility will give you a just idea of what we call Tradition, a word so odious to Protestants, because they represent so badly and disfigure so strangely the thing expressed by it. Tradition is nothing more that the **general, unanimous** and **constant** testimony of the Church of **all** ages, on the subject of truths revealed by Jesus Christ and taught by his Apostles.''

XVI. ''To answer the other difficulties you object to me, I come to this

text of the Gospel, **call no man father.** If you understand these words lit-
terally, it is not lawful in any manner, to apply the name of Father even to
those who, after God, are the authors of our days. Jesus Christ speaks in
this place of the Supreme and Sovereign Father, since he adds: **for your
Father who is in heaven is one,** that is to say, of God who, according to St.
Paul, is **the author of all Paternity.** If it be allowed to draw another conclusion from these words, **call no man father,** it seems to me it may be this: do
not leave the true Pastors whom I have appointed over you, to follow innovators, who constitute themselves the fathers and authors of new Sects."

XVII. "When St. Paul says, we **exercise not dominion** over **your faith,** he
certainly does not intend to insinuate that it is lawful to examine, and still
less to reject his decisions, since he pronounces **Anathema** even against an
angel who should dare to preach a doctrine different from his. [60] (Galat.
c. 1, V. 8 & 9.) If St. Paul had held the doctrine Protestants [hold], he
would have spoken a quite different language, he would have said: If any
one shall announce to you a different doctrine from mine, examine it
without prejudice. If it shall appear to you more true than mine, embrace it
instead of mine. But, no, he declares that we must absolutely reject it for
this single reason that it is different from his. Is it possible for one to exercise a more sovereign authority, or if you wish, a more extensive dominion
over consciences? Here, then, is the true sense of this passage of the Apostle: "Although we exact from you a full and entire submission, we pretend
not to domineer over you, because we are after all but the instruments and
organs whom God makes use of to reign over your consciences." This is
then certainly not what may be called a dominion. Thus when the Church
desires that we should accept her decisions, she does not domineer,
because she acts not in her own name, but in the name of Jesus Christ.
Every power that exercises the authority which she has received, in a
limited manner, does not domineer, except it be said, that they act after
the manner of tyrants; but she governs. Now, the Church, so far from exercising her power tyrannically, conducts herself as a tender mother towards
her children; she consults all their real wants; she regulates her laws con-
formably to them,—and never does she punish until after having tried in
vain all the ways of mercy and mildness."

XVIII. "As to the Bereans of whom you speak in your letter, they were
not yet in the Church; all those who are similarly situated, we not only allow them to examine, but we exhort them, we press them to it, we conjure
them; but, nevertheless, when once we have acknowledged the infallibility
of the Church and entered into her bosom, when we have professed to
believe what she teaches, every examen which proceeds from a real doubt

of her decisions, is a crime, the Church prohibits it and cannot allow it. In this she displays a conduct teeming with wisdom and equity, since the infallibility of the Church once acknowledged, all future examen emanating from doubt is absurd; and in practise is to fall into direct contradiction with oneself. Your objection proceeds from the belief according to the prejudice [61] of your Sect, that we keep the Bible shut up, in order that it may not fall into the hands of the People. Nothing is more false nor more ridiculous. We do not hold that it is lawful for any one to explain the Bible differently from the Church; and we are obliged in conscience to explain it according to her interpretation; but this does not prove that we keep it shut up. Do the judges of the land pretend that the study of the law is prohibited, because it devolves on them to interprete it agreably to the sense received in the State? Does a Mother forbid her children the use of a knife, because she shews them how they are to use it, not to wound themselves with it?"

XIX. "In order to point out to you the necessity of a supreme authority appointed to decide all disputes which may arise among Christians I caused you to observe that there never was yet a government in the world without a superior tribunal to judge in the last resort and from which there was no appeal. You agree with me that this is necessary in civil Government to prevent anarchy and confusion; but you add that there is no comparison between Civil Societies and religious societies; I should have wished you had shewn this difference in relation to the question before us. For my part I really see none; both are composed of men, that is to say, who are governed either by their reason or by their passions; we must take men as they are, for, we must not reason after an order of imaginary things. Now, considering the constitution of all societies and the genius of all men, there is no other means of forming any kind of society than that of authority and submission. Law and subordination, these are, as it were, the two main springs which are absolutely necessary for the government of the entire body. Take them away, there exists no longer any union, concord or harmony; every one will do as he pleases; individuals will be only so many separate and divided members; there will be no longer a body. It is true that ecclesiastical laws differ from civil laws in this sense that the former regard the spiritual government, that of souls; and the latter the temporal government, the external police; the former inflict spiritual penalties, the latter punish corporally. The object [62] of each society is also very different; here, it is the good of the body which is proposed; there, it is the welfare of the soul: both nevertheless are visible, are composed of men, who live, who converse, who treat with one another; it would, therefore, be as great a folly to pretend to form a new church without imposing laws upon minds and souls, as it would be to form a state without imposing them upon bodies.

This is so true, that there has never been an ecclesiastical body among ourselves, or among any other people, which has not had some law to bind souls. Why therefore blame that which obliges us to submit our minds to the doctrine and decision of the Church?''

XX. "You say it is to God alone we are to render an account of our faith, and you would lead me to believe that all religions conduct equally to salvation; this is a necessary consequence from the principles of Protestants. Did the limits of my letter allow me, I would shew you in detail all those [evils] which follow from this monstrous doctrine; they would fill you with horror. It would be easy for me to convince you that it tends not only to introduce indifferently all Christian Sects, but that it leads even to Mahometanism, to Deism and to Atheism; that is to say, that your principle alone is the annihilation of that religion which the Son of God came in person to establish and which he has sealed with his own blood. Can it be for a moment conceived, that he came down from heaven to erect an edifice as ruinous as the one you suppose, and found a religion which would be nothing more than a frightful mixture of all religions? Would such a work be worthy of sovereign wisdom? What kind of a system would that be which would accuse the apostles and all the men who have walked in their footsteps, and all those who, like them, have shed their blood for the faith, with having adopted the most consummate, the most inconceivable of all follies, with having suffered death in order to defend a useless religion, since without it, all men could equally be saved? The slightest reflection upon so extravagant and impious a system is sufficient to fill every Christian with horror who retains the smallest attachment to the person of our adorable Saviour and the least respect for his Gospel."

"Reflect well, My dear friend, upon what I have laid [63] before you;— see the horrible precipice which is open before you in consequence of Protestant principles; and tremble lest you fall from one abyss into a greater from which you will no longer be able to extricate yourself."

XXI. "If you communicate this letter, as I hope you will, to any one of your Ministers, I pray you be not content with any kind of answer, write it down with your own objections; and after having reflected well upon them, compare them with what you have just read. In the principles and reasoning which I have brought to your mind you will find the most solid answers, the most satisfactory solutions for any man who examines and discusses with sincerity. The more you will read and meditate on the Bible, the more you will see into the truth and the harmony of our principles on the one side, and on the other the incoherence and contradiction of those of your ministers. What I desire also, My dear Brother, is that you will converse with them and deliver my sentiments to them without passion, or without exciting them against me. How rejoiced I should be could I only be there to do it myself! They would soon see that I am not actuated by passion or by any spirit of party, but only by a love of truth and a desire to make that true faith known to them which the Lord has been pleased to direct me to embrace."

XXII. "If you are convinced of the truth of the Catholic religion, by the arguments I have placed before you, do not, O my dear friend, be ashamed to confess it; it is the property of a noble soul to acknowledge its error and to retract it. Besides, yours will be not so much your error as that of your education, if after having discovered the vice and poison of it, you make it not, by a voluntary attachment and an obstinate resistance to the known truth, your own personal error. Remember these words of Jesus Christ: **that those who will not confess him before men, he will disown before assembled nations.**"

XXIII. "Here is a reflection, my dear brother, which now presents itself to my mind, and which appears to me to establish a very strong presumption in favour of our religion: This religion is the only true, the only divine one, and which [64] alone inspires sacrifices truly heroick and above the ordinary strength of nature. Now, allow me to say it, the Catholic religion affords me examples of this kind which I should look for in vain among all the Protestant Societies. I have often seen, and even now daily see persons of the most distinguished birth and of the first consideration in the world, Ladies of a feeble and delicate health, renouncing the pleasures, the riches and honours of the world in order to devote themselves, some to the service of the sick and dying, in the Hospitals, that is to say in the midst of infection, and others to the most austere penance within the narrow Cloisters of a Monastery. Among these last, Madam Louise, the Aunt of the king of France, and beloved daughter of Lewis, the fifteenth, holds the first rank; she has been seen bidding Adieu to the most brilliant Court in Europe, and at a mature age burying herself in the obscurity of a Convent of Carmelites, in which the most austere rules are observed, in order that she might there be confounded with the meanest of her religious Sisters, and exercise the lowest functions of domestic life, such as to sweep the house, the wash the dishes, etc. and all this to honour and to imitate the humble life of her divine Jesus, who though sovereign Lord of the Universe condescended **to take upon himself the form of a slave, and became obedient unto death, even the death of the cross.** She has declared to me herself, that she never enjoyed amidst all the grandour and pleasures of this world purer delights than those which she enjoyed then in the poverty, the penance, the obedience and humiliations of the Cloister."

XXIV. "I cannot conclude my letter without adding one word more upon the Catholicity, that is to say, upon the Universality of the Church. You acknowledge, equally with ourselves, this mark in the Apostles Creed, and we see it clearly expressed in the Church. (Gen. c. 18 & 22, Ps. 2 & 7, Acts c. 1. V. 8.) etc. This universality applies surely to no other Church than to ours. She is so spread over and so visible in all the most remarkable countries of the world, that she cannot be hidden from those who sincerely desire to seek and to know the truth. She has a considerable number of Bishops and Missionaries in the East Indies. There are reckoned [65] millions of Catholics in China; and even in the very inclosure of the imperial Palace of Pekin we have a spacious Church. To deny all these facts, or to call them in question would be the height of folly;—they are too public and notorious. All know, at Paris, the Seminary which is founded for the education and maintenance of foreign Missionaries; and at Rome the one called **De propaganda fide** in which I myself have seen a great number of young men of all nations who, after having received holy-Orders are sent into their respective countries to preach the Gospel to their relations and fellow countrymen. At this very time the only Son of the king of Cochinchina is in Paris brought hither by a Missionary Bishop of his country, who had been brought up here in the Seminary of the foreign Missions, etc. I leave you now to reflect upon all this before the Lord, and in the sincerity of a heart that wishes not either to deceive or to be deceived."

XXV. "My dear Brother, why can I not produce the same impressions upon you which I myself feel, since the day when the hand of God was pleased to withdraw me from the way in which we both walked owing to the misfortune of our birth and our education. I cannot see you still in it, and think without shuddering that, by being thus separated, as we now are, in religion, one or the other of us will assuredly be lost forever. When I compare this text of St. Paul, **One faith,** with this other of the same Apostle, **without faith it is impossible to please God,** and consequently to be saved, I feel the most poignant grief at the thought of this eternal separation which will take place between us, if one or the other does not change his religion, for [only] one of us can be in the right, since our faith at present is entirely opposed. If it be I who have gone astray, come, I beseech you, fly to my succour; what can you have dearer in the world after your own salvation, than the salvation of a brother who loves you and whom you love? If it be you who walk in the way of perdition, do not deny me the liberty and consolation of rendering you the greatest of all services, by recalling you in the name of the true Spouse of the [66] Saviour, the only one that can bring forth the Elect of God, to the way of truth. United in the arms of this tender mother, we shall afterwards use our exertions to obtain of God, that he will also bring back to himself him through whom he has given us life, that is to say, that we shall unite our zeal to become, in some sort, the fathers of our father, by procuring him a far more precious life than that we have received from him. This, my dear brother and my very dear friend, is what I desire most earnestly through the bowels of the charity of our heavenly Father and his Son Jesus Christ. Reflect upon it, as you would at the hour of your death, I beseech you, and give this proof of your friendship to a brother who only lives for you, for our dear father and our fellow countrymen. I embrace you with all the tenderness of a heart wholly devoted to you, &c.''

(Signed) "Thayer."

"Paris, May 1st 1787. At the Seminary of St. Sulpice. To M. Nathaniel Thayer, Boston."

CHAPTER III

THAYER'S CONTROVERSY
WITH GEORGE LESLIE

The Rev. Mr. Thayer, after due preparation, having received the order of Priesthood, and returned to America, was appointed, shortly after his arrival, to the mission of Boston by the Rev. Dr. Carroll, as already mentioned. At this time Boston contained only 18,038 souls; and the Catholic part of this population scarcely exceeded one hundred. These had been in the habit of assembling on Sundays and Holidays, under the Abbés Lapoterie and Rousselet, in the small Church in School Street, which was formerly occupied by a congregation of French Huguenots: but which since the death of Le Mercier, their Minister, had dwindled away to nothing. In order not to be molested or disturbed, under any pretense, in the exercise of his ministry, he obtained a Lease of the above Church of the family of the Perkins', to whom this property was said to belong. Here he continued to collect his little flock, who were overjoyed at the acquisition of a Pastor, who could address them in a language familiar to the generality of his hearers, and of the correctness of whose morals, and of the lawfulness of whose ministry, they could not entertain the least doubt. This reception by his former friends and acquaintances, as [67] well as by Protestants in general, was equally flattering and kind, and led him to form the most favourable anticipations of a successful ministry. The following letter written by him to a friend,[7] a few months after his arrival in Boston, will shew how cordially he was greeted by all classes of Citizens:

"My dear friend,"

"I reached Boston on the 4th of January last, and have every where been received with the most flattering attention. My own relatives expres-

53

sed the greatest joy at my return;—the governor of the State, whose Cha[p]lain I formerly was, has promised to do all in his power to forward my views, and favour the work for which I have been sent to Boston. I have received nothing but kindness, and attention, from the Ministers of the town. Many of them have visited me, and evinced a degree of cordiality, which I had little reason to expect. The officers of the Custom-house also have carried their politeness so far, as to be unwilling to take anything for the many large Boxes which I had procured from France and England, having looked upon their contents as things designed for sacred purposes. On the first sunday after my arrival, I announced the word of God, and all flocked in crouds to hear me. A great degree of curiosity is manifested to become acquainted with our belief; and the free toleration allowed here has enabled me to enter into a full exposition of it. But I was not long in a condition to satisfy the curiosity and eagerness of the people of Boston. I had been only a fortnight in the town, when it pleased almighty God to afflict me with a sickness, which kept me confined to my bed for a month. The danger appeared to me so serious on one occasion, that I was upon the point of requesting the holy Viaticum of a French Clergyman, with whom I am associated in the work of the Lord and of his Church. My health was restored by degrees; and as soon as I recovered sufficient strength I availed myself of the priviledge allowed me to celebrate Mass in my chamber. When my health was sufficiently restored I resumed my functions of preaching, of confessing, and visiting the few sheep that compose our little flock. On every occasion the Pro-[68]testants evince the same eagerness to come and hear me; but they content themselves with that. The indifference and pilosophy [sic], which prevail here as much as any where else, are an obstacle to the fruit of preaching, which it is exceedingly difficult to destroy,—an obstacle, however, which does not in the least discourage me. I have had the pleasure to receive a few recantations, and our dear Neophytes afford me great consolation by the sanctity of their life. About one hundred Catholics, consisting of Frenchmen, of Irishmen and Americans, is what constitutes at present our Church. About one dozzen of them attend mass daily. I am engaged in instructing a few Protestants, whom I hope to restore to our common Mother shortly. I recommend our Mission most earnestly to your prayers. We are in want of labourers for the cultivation of the immense field, which has been so long abandoned in these United States.''

(Signed) ''Thayer.''

''Boston, July 17th 1790.''

Our Apostolic Missionary had now laboured ten months in his mission, when, in the ardour of his zeal for the conversion of his countrymen, whose blindness and obstinacy in error he sincerely pitied, he was induced to publish, in one of the public papers, the following advertisement:[8]

"Mr. Thayer, Catholic Priest, of Boston, fully persuaded that he has found the inestimable treasure of the Gospel, is greatly desirous of imparting it to his dear countrymen. For this purpose, he offers to preach on the evenings of the week days, in any of the neighbouring towns. If any persons desire to hear the exposition of the Catholic faith, (of which the majority of Americans have so mistaken an idea) and will furnish any place for the accommodation of hearers, Mr. Thayer will be ever ready to attend them. He will also undertake to answer the objections any gentleman would wish to make, either **publickly** or **privately**, to the doctrine he preaches; and promises that if any one can convince him he is in error, he will make as **public** and **solemn** a recantation of his present belief, as he has done of the Protestant religion in which he was educated.— Free-[69]ly he received—freely he gives."

"November, 24th 1790."

Very shortly after the above advertisement had appeared in the public Prints, a Mr. George Leslie,[9] a Minister of one of the Congregational Churches, inserted in the same Paper the following notice:

"As the gauntlet is thrown by Mr. Thayer, it is taken up by George Leslie."

After this nothing more occurred or appeared before the public until the month of January following, when the Rev. Mr. Thayer sent the following communication to the Printer:

"Mr. Printer,"

"I have observed among several Protestants an air of triumph at Mr. Leslie's advertisement. In mine of the 24th of November, I only offered to preach in the towns bordering on Boston, and to answer every objection that might be made to the doctrine I deliver; yet, as Mr. Leslie takes what I then wrote for the 'gauntlet thrown,' I now invite him or any other Minister to appoint me a time and place in Boston, or any of the neighboring towns, for the combat proposed: I will punctually attend, and I engage to answer every objection against the discriminating points of Catholic Faith, and, if convinced of error, to publickly and solemnly abjure it. Let it be observed, that I do not undertake to defend all those articles which our adversaries, out of their abundant liberality, and for reasons best known to themselves, have added to our Creed, as, the Pope's infallibility, adoration of the Saints, of their images and relics, breach of faith with heretics, etc. I stand forth in defence of the genuine Popery which is taught in all the Councils, catechisms and schools of the universal Church. I not only offer this publick disputation, but I even conjure the ministers, if they have real love to souls, to accept it, that the eyes of the people who are kept in darkness may be opened to the light. I also desire them to come armed with all the arguments which Tillotson and other champions of Protestancy have ever used in its behalf."

"In expectation of some opponent, I shall open a contro-[70]versial lecture, at the Catholick Church, to begin from to-morrow evening, at half-past 6 O'Clock. All who love the truth and sincerely desire salvation, are requested to attend, and they will hear those great and important things, which have been hitherto carefully concealed from them. It is no vain presumption in my own learning or abilities that prompts me to this step; my only motive is the glory of God in the salvation of poor souls—My entire trust is in the strength of my Redeemer, and the goodness of my cause. Perhaps Mr. Leslie's desire is to dispute in the public Papers; if this be the design of his challenge, I will begin as soon as any Printer will consent to give our controversies a place. I am prepared for every honest measure, that will tend to enlarge the empire of truth and religion."

(Signed) "John Thayer, Cath[olic] Missionary of Boston."
"Boston, January 26th 1791."

The Rev. Mr. Thayer, agreably to promise, opened a controversial lecture in his little Church, in School Street, the following evening. A great crowd attended for the purpose of witnessing the expected combat: but as the Rev. Mr. Leslie did not think proper to appear, the greater part returned home much disappointed. Those, however, who had been able to get into the Church, remained during the Lecture, and afterwards went from it pleased and satisfied with the exposition of the doctrine they had heard. In this way he continued, twice every week, to expound and defend the Catholic faith before those of the citizens of Boston whom curiosity or a desire of information led to favour him with their attention. The Church was always full on these occasions, and the little Society of School Street began, even now, to look up, and to wax stronger and stronger daily.

At length a polite letter was received from the Editor of one of the Papers in Boston, offering to publish in his Gazette any thing which he (Mr. Thayer) might think proper to communicate on the subject of his religion. The offer was equally liberal and kind. He gladly availed himself of it; and in a few days afterwards sent in his first paper to the Press. By way of Preface to the controversy, which was about to commence, and to prevent all misrepresentations of the true doctrines of the Catholic [71] Church, he began by presenting the public with an abridgement of the Catholic faith. This was indeed an excellent precaution; for, in consequence of the many falsehoods and misrepresentations, which had been industriously circulated in New England for the two last Centuries, and which had always been believed as the real doctrines of the Catholic Church, it had become necessary to correct the public mind on this important head, in the first instance by laying down in a clear and concise manner, the true principles of that Church. This he did in the following communication:

BY way of preface to the controversy which I am opening, and to avoid all misrepresentations of our doctrines, I here offer to the public an abridgment of the Catholic faith. To escape the stigma of plagiarism, I now declare that I have no pretensions to originality, and that whenever I find my idea well expressed by another, I shall use his words, without the formality of a quotation.* The following are the capital articles of our religion, viz.

FIRST

WE believe in one only true and living GOD, the Lord and Creator of all things, subsisting in three persons, Father, Son, and Holy Ghost. To this God **alone** we give divine honour and adoration; and we detest, with our whole souls, all kinds of idolatry; that is, all such wickedness by which divine worship is given to any false god, or idol, or any person or thing whatever, beside the one true and living God. We honor **indeed** the BLESSED VIRGIN, the mother of our God and Saviour Jesus Christ, but not as a goddess, nor with any part of divine worship. We honor the angels and saints of God, as his servants. We honor his priests, his churches, his altars, his word, and whatever else has relation to him: but all for his sake, and by a subordinate honor that is referred to him—such also is the veneration which we have for the cross, for relics, and for the pictures of our Redeemer, and of his saints: We value them as memorials of Christ and his holy ones; as representations of our Redeemer or of our redemption; as helps to pious thoughts and affections; but we condemn and anathematize all such as would pray to them, or believe any divinity or power inherent in them, or give them divine worship—(**See the second Council of Nice, Act 7, and the Council of Trent, Sess. 25.**)

2dly. We believe in one Lord Jesus Christ, the eternal Son of God; who for us sinners, and for our salvation, was made man; that he might be the Head, the High Priest, the Advocate and Saviour of **all** mankind. We acknowledge him our **only** Redeemer, who paid our ransom by dying for us on the cross; that his death is the fountain of all our good; and that mercy,

---

*It is presumed that the above declaration will sufficiently apologize for all I have borrowed from the controversial writers of our communion.

grace and salvation can by no means be obtained but through him—We confess him to be the mediator of God and man, the only **Mediator of Redemption,** and also the only **Mediator of Intercession,** who stands in need of no other's merits to recommend his petitions—As to the saints and angels, we address ourselves, indeed, to them, to desire their prayers, as we and all other Christians do to God's servants here on earth; but we only beg them to pray for us and with us, to our common Lord, who is our God and their God, through the merits of the same Jesus Christ, who is our Mediator and their Mediator—(**See the Council of Trent, Sess. 25.**)

3d. We believe the Scriptures of the old and new Testament to be the word of God; and we have the highest veneration for their authority, and would rather die than disbelieve or doubt of one iota or tittle of them. If at any time, or in any place, the church has restrained the ignorant from reading them, it was not out of disrespect to the sacred book, much less out of sacrilegious design to keep the people in darkness, but purely because the unlearned (as the scriptures themselves inform us, 2 Pet. iii. 16) are apt to wrest them to their own destruction: And if we also receive unwritten traditions as part of the word of God, we mean no other traditions but such as are **divine,** and which we know to be divine by the same means by which we know the scriptures to be so, viz. by the testimony of the Catholic Church, to which Christ gave, in the persons of the apostles, a promise of a perpetual and **infallible** guidance in matters of faith.

4th. We believe that there are truly and properly seven sacraments of the new law, instituted by Jesus Christ our Lord, and necessary for the salvation of mankind, though not all for every one, viz. baptism, confirmation, eucharist, penance, extreme unction, order, and matrimony.

5th. We believe that in the mass there is offered to God, a true, proper and propitiatory sacrifice for the living and the dead; that in the most holy sacrament of the eucharist there is **truly, really** and **substantially,** the body and blood, together with the soul and divinity of our Lord Jesus Christ; that there is made a conversion of the whole substance of the bread into the body, and of the whole substance of the wine into the blood; which conversion we call **transubstantiation:** We also hold that under either kind **alone,** Jesus Christ is received whole and entire, and a true sacrament. In this sacrament and sacrifice we adore not the bread and wine (which would indeed be a most stupid idolatry,) but Jesus Christ, the Son of God; whom, upon the strongest grounds of the word of God, and upon the authority of his Church, we believe to be really present in the sacred mysteries—and it is to his passion and death, which we there celebrate and offer to God; that we attribute all that propitiation and grace which we expect from the holy mass.

6th. We believe that, in order to enter into life, we must keep the commandments of God, and that whoever dies in the guilt of a wilful breach of any one of these divine precepts, will be eternally lost: that no power on earth can give any man leave to break any commandment of God, or to commit any sin whatever, or to do evil that good may come of it: that neither the Pope, nor any man living, can dispense with the law of God, or make it lawful for any one to lie, to forswear himself, or to do any thing that is forbidden in the divine law.

7th. We **indeed** hold that God has given to his priests a commission to remit sins; but we believe that neither priest, bishop nor Pope, nor any power in heaven or earth, can forgive sinners, without their hearty repentance, and a serious purpose of amendment—The indulgencies granted in our church are neither a permission to commit sin, nor pardon for sins to come; but are only a release of the temporal punishment due to sins which are already pardoned; no indulgence availing any thing towards this release, until, by hearty repentance, the guilt be renounced.

8th. **Our faith teaches us to detest all massacres, treasons and murders whatever, whether committed by Protestants against Catholics, or by Catholics against Protestants. We regard them as the worst of crimes that can be committed betwixt man and man, and such as cannot be justified by any pretext of religion**—and so far are Catholics from thinking it no sin to murder heretics (which is so falsely and unjustly imputed to them) that in all kingdoms and states, which profess the Catholic religion, any such murderer of heretics must expect nothing but death, by the laws of the country, and, if he dies impenitent, eternal damnation, according to the doctrine of his church.

9th. We believe that there is a middle state called PURGATORY, where those who have not fully satisfied divine justice in this life, must be purified, before they can enter heaven, and that the souls therein detained are helped by the prayers, fasts and alms-deeds of the faithful.

10th. In fine, we believe that no man can be justified, either by the works of the law of nature, or of the law of Moses, without faith in Jesus Christ— that [72] **we cannot by any preceding works merit the grace of justification; that all the merit of our good works is the gift of God; and that every** merit and satisfaction of ours depends entirely on the merits and passion of Christ."—(See the Council of Trent, Sess. 6.)

"These are our real principles, taught by our Church in her Councils, and learned by our children in their very Catechisms.—These true Catholic principles we are ready not only to sign with our hands, but if called to it and assisted by divine grace, to seal also with our blood. We renounce, detest and anathematize all contrary doctrines imputed to us by the Father of lies, or by any of his agents, who are, and always have been busy in misrepresenting and slandering the Church of God—But what wonder?Christ our Lord, his Apostles, and the primitive Christians were thus treated. And he has foretold (Math. 9.) that his disciples should be treated in the same manner.—The tenets which are here briefly exposed. I am ready to defend against Mr. Leslie or any other Protestant, whether he produces his real name or not, provided he be fair and candid in the statement of facts, and points of faith. God the great scrutinizer of all hearts, shall be the judge of the purity of my intentions; let every reader judge of the weight of the arguments which I shall urge.

I shall take no notice of any one who shall mingle scurrility or personal reflections with his reasonings."

(Signed) "John Thayer, Cath[olic] Missionary."

In a few days after the publication of the above, the Rev. Mr. Leslie, Pastor, of a Church in Washington, New Hampshire, thought proper to redeem his pledge, came forward and entered the lists, the same who had, in the preceding year, announced in the Gazette, that as the Gauntlet had been thrown by Mr. Thayer, it should be taken up by George Leslie. We shall insert his piece, as it appeared in the papers of the day, that our readers may be put in full possession of the events as they occurred in this new field of Catholicity. The following is the notice taken of Rev. Mr. Thayer's last communication by this champion of Protestantism:

[73]**Unus apex verbi ratione valentior omni,**
Milleque decretis, conciliisque prior.

MR. Thayer having exhibited a summary of the articles of his creed, and engaged to answer every objection against the **discriminating** points of, what he calls, catholic faith, I shall proceed to offer some objections; expecting such answers as are consistent with that regard to truth and religion he professes. The properest method, in my humble opinion, is to take some one point, and go through with that, before we proceed to another. This will be the most likely way to avoid confusion, and to come at that truth we both profess to aim at. No arguments will be looked upon and treated as worthy of notice, but such as are evidently drawn from, and grounded upon, the sacred Scriptures of the Old and New Testament. Mr. Thayer will therefore save himself the trouble of bringing into view any which have no other support than the authority of his church: for, until that is undeniably established, to draw any arguments from it would be only begging the point in question. That INFALLIBILITY, which is claimed by the Romish Church, being the main pillar of its support, it may not be amiss to begin with it; for if that claim appears to be founded in truth, all disputes with her on other points will be superseded; we have then nothing to do, but to receive her infallible dictates as the rule of our faith and practice. The objections I have to offer to this doctrine are as follow:—In the first place, it does not appear to have any foundation in the word of God. Our popish adversaries, I am very sensible, have prest a number of texts of scripture into their service, in support of the pretended infallibility of their church. To take up and canvass each of these distinctly, in order to shew how little they avail to their purpose, would take too much room for this paper. I shall therefore wave the consideration of them, until Mr. Thayer calls my attention to them, by offering them in vindication of the point in question. But then, secondly, supposing, but not granting, Christ to have promised this high and singular privilege to his church: I would fain know how the church of Rome came by the monopoly of it, to the exclusion of all other Christian churches from any share in it? Mr. Thayer, I presume, will not have the confidence to say it is because there is no other Christian church on earth. Should he offer this as a reason, his assertion will not be taken as any proof, unless he can first make it appear that a sufficient quantity of this supposed infallibility is vested in himself. A third objection is, the doctors of the Romish Church have never yet settled the point, as to where, or in whom, this infallibility is lodged: So that, if we had occasion to apply to it in any case, we should be utterly at a loss where to find it. Roman Catholic writers, as far as I can learn, are all agreed that it is somewhere in their church: But then they are not all agreed as to the particular subject of it; some of them holding it to be in the Pope; others, in a general council; others, again, in such a council, in conjunction with the Pope. Strange, if this infallibility be really in their church, and is a matter of such importance as they pretend, that it has laid so long dormant, and never yet effectually exerted itself to settle a point on which its supposed usefulness does so entirely depend! Until this matter is fully determined, we may rationally and safely conclude, they themselves do not know where it is; nor is it, in my humble opinion, of any importance they ever should. For, fourthly, we have, in the scriptures of the Old and New Testament, a complete, a perfect rule both of faith and practice. It is granted, there are in them some things hard to be understood, which ignorant and depraved minds may pervert and abuse—What then? Will it thence follow, that a right knowledge of them is unattainable by gracious, humble and diligent inquirers after divine truth? By no means. As to all points which essentially concern salvation, the scriptures are clear and intelligible, level to the understanding of children. Timothy, from a child, knew the holy scriptures.

   What need is there, then, of this supposed infallibility, when we have in these inspired writings a sure word of prophecy, which even children of tolerable capacity may, by the grace of God, so understand as to become wise unto salvation, through faith in Christ Jesus?

And further; by their assistance, without the help either of Pope or council, the man of God may be perfect, thoroughly furnished unto all good works. 1 Tim. iii. 15 to 17.

Upon the whole, until the church of Rome can make out her claim to infallibility, by clear and evident scripture proof; until it can, by the same evidence, be made to appear, that she alone is invested with this high privilege, to the utter exclusion of all Christians who are not of her communion; until the subject of this infallibility is clearly and convincingly fixed and determined; and until the necessity and usefulness of it in the Christian church is clearly evinced; in a word, until each of these points is clearly proved by the word of God, and beyond all reasonable doubt—we may safely look upon and treat this pretended infallibility as a cunningly-devised fable, a mere delusion, invented and imposed on the people of that communion, not to serve our Lord Jesus Christ, but the bellies of the teachers, and spiritual guides of that church. GEORGE LESSLIE.

[74] This was bringing the question to be discussed to a single point. The Rev. Mr. Thayer hastened to meet the wishes of his Reverend Antagonist by proceeding to adopt the course suggested by him. Accordingly he laid before the public, in a few days, his answers to the Rev. Mr. Leslie's objections, and at the same time gave him the following proofs in favour of the infallibility of the Catholic Church.

"It gives me real pleasure, that the Rev. Mr. Leslie has adopted the plan of taking up one point of controversy at a time and of going through with that, before we proceed to another.—I entirely agree with him that, until the **infallible authority** be undeniably established, all arguments drawn from that authority, will be begging the point in dispute.—Nothing can be more pertinant and consonant to right reason, than his observation, "That, if the claim of our church to infallibility be founded in truth, all disputes with her on other points are at once superseded, we having nothing to do but receive her infallible dictates as the rule of our faith and practice."—I once flattered myself with possessing a considerable share in the esteem and affection of Mr. Lesslie, for whom I still retain the same regard. I hope that I shall manage the controversy with so much calmness and moderation, as never to forfeit that place in his heart which I am greatly desirous of retaining. The glory of God in the salvation of souls is my **only** aim.—Mr. Lesslie attempts to overturn the Catholic doctrine of the **infallibility** of the church by four objections, which he proposes with great confidence, and on which he seems to lay great stress.—In his **fourth** objection, he takes for granted, what all Catholics deny, viz. "That the scriptures of the Old and

New Testament are a complete and perfect rule of faith."—On the contrary, the doctrine of our church is, that the word of God is the **complete** and **perfect rule** of our faith; which word we contend is not **wholly** contained in the scriptures, but is in part transmitted to us in the tradition of the church.—But this very important question shall be treated in some future paper, where I shall show that, even if we grant the scriptures to be our **perfect** rule of faith and practice, the Protestant Bible, maimed and corrupted as it is, can never be this rule.—Mr. Lesslie's third objection has been long ago proposed and defended by Dr. Tillotson with a great deal of wit. It is, "That Catholics know not where to find that infallibility which they all assert to exist among them."—This objection appears to me to be without the least solidity, **because** all Catholics on the globe are fully agreed, that the infallibility, which we attribute to our church, resides in the majority of the Bishops (the successors of the Apostles) united with their visible head the Pope, whether they be assembled in council or not. This is so essential an article of our faith, that whoever denies it, is regarded as a heretic. There is not the least shadow of contradiction among us on this head. Some divines indeed carry their respect for the sovereign Pontiff so far as to suppose, that Christ will never suffer him to propose any thing to the church as of faith, which is contrary to divine revelation, or in other words that he is infallible.—But this is only an opinion, which every one is free to believe or reject, according as the arguments for or against it strike his mind.—The difference we make between points of **faith** and of **mere opinion** is, that the first must be believed under pain of our being regarded as heretics, while the latter may be rejected at pleasure.—We may here observe, that whoever maintains the Pope's infallibility must, **a fortiori**, admit infallibility in the union of the Pope and majority of the Bishops, it being absurd to ascribe this privilege to a part, and to refuse it to a large body including that very part.

In order to answer Mr. Lesslie's two other objections in the clearest manner, I shall shew, in the first place, that the infallibility of Christ's church is founded on the plain word of God, and secondly, that the church in communion with the See of Rome has (to use Mr. L's. expression) the monopoly of this high and singular privilege.—The infallibility of Christ's church is the most important question that can be examined by the sincere lovers of truth and peace of all parties; for if there be an infallible church, the **lovers of truth** will think it the greatest happiness to be under the direction of a guide, by whom they cannot be misled; and the **lovers of peace** will heartily rejoice to see innumerable disputes, which rather serve to perplex the truth than to clear it, cut off by the determination of this one single point.— That the vast importance of the question now under consideration may

more evidently appear, I will here set down a few of the momentous consequences which follow from the infallibility of Christ's church, if it be
proved to be real.—It follows, 1st. That they, who are members of any
church which disowns this infallibility, are not of Christ's church.—A terrible consequence! and deserves to be seriously pondered by all those who
are not wholly indifferent whether their faith be right or wrong.—2. That
the same arguments which prove the infallibility of the church, prove also
all the articles which she declares necessary to be believed, though there
be no express scriptural texts to establish them, for an infallible church
cannot propose erroneous tenets to her children.—3. That there is no salvation out of this church, for this is a part of her doctrine grounded on the
words of Christ, "He who hears you hears me, and he who despises you
despises me:" This merits the most serious reflections, since they who
despise God are not in the way of salvation.—4. If Christ's church be proved
infallible even **to the world's end,** it follows that she never fell into any error against faith, and that, as she was once the true church, she **always** has
been so, and must continue so forever.—This consequence overthrows the
whole reformation at one blow, because that reformation never had any
other pretence or plausible colour, than the supposed errors of the church
of Rome. I do not see how this fourth inference can be evaded, but by
pretending (contrary to the manifest tenor of the Gospel) that Christ's
church is sometimes **invisible,** or that at the reformation and many ages
before it, there existed a visible church which was not united to that of
Rome, and yet was the true church of Christ.—If Christ established an infallible church on earth, it follows, 5. That she alone is the interpreter of
God's word, the **only** judge of controversy, and the supreme tribunal from
which there is no appeal, either to private judgment or to any authority.—
Though all Protestants, from Luther down to those of our day, reject **in
theory,** any supreme judge of faith, yet, **in practice** (such is the evidence of
the last consequence) they have given this infallibility to their synods—
This could be demonstrated from the proceedings of the grand Synod of
Dort, held against Arminians, in 1618.—But this would lead me too far—The
few consequences which I have hinted suffice to shew how nearly the point
now in debate concerns our salvation.

I now proceed to the scriptural proof of this article of our faith. The
truths which are of the greatest importance to man, and which therefore
God has most at heart to inculcate, are commonly, I believe, if not always,
expressed in so clear a manner, that they cannot be misunderstood by the
well disposed—I will venture to assert, that the infallibility of Christ's
church is one of these truths which are clearly and obviously contained in
the sacred writings. The promises of Christ on this head are so intelligible

as to prevent all but wilful mistakes—the solemnity also of the circumstances, in which Christ made those sacred engagements to his church, is so remarkable, that it cannot but imprint an idea of some extraordinary favour bestowed upon her—His first promise of protecting his church against all the powers of darkness, was addressed to St. Peter (Matt. XVI.) in reward of that noble profession of his divinity "which neither flesh nor blood, but the heavenly Father, had revealed to him"—The other promises were made at the last supper, when all his words seemed to be the overflowings of a heart filled with concern for his future church. Then Christ unbosomed himself to his Apostles as a friend or father; comforting them in their affliction for his approaching departure, and, as a pledge of his unalterable love to his church, bequeathed to them his **spirit of truth** to be our guide and teacher to the end of time; all which he ratified again a few moments before his ascension into heaven, when he gave the Apostles their commission to teach and baptize all nations, and encouraged them to undertake it, with a promise of his almighty and perpetual assistance (Matt. xxviii.)—Let us first consider our Saviour's address to St. Peter (Matt. xvi.)—this passage contains an **absolute** promise, no condition being expressed or even hinted in it.—The occasion of this promise is also very remarkable, as I have already observed. St. Peter's name until then was **Simon;** but God having pre-ordained him to be the chief pillar of his church, gave him a distinct faith of the divinity of Christ, of which he made this solemn profession, "Thou art Christ the Son of the living God." Upon which our Saviour dignified him with a title, suitable both to the firmness of his faith, and the eminent station he was to hold, calling him Cephas or Peter; both which words signify a **rock;** and then, as a further mark of distinction, he addresses to him the promise: "Thou art Peter (i.e. a rock) and upon this rock I will build my church, and the gates of hell shall not prevail against it." These words evidently include a promise, and a promise to the church. But what is the favour which they contain? First, Christ declares that his church should be **built on a rock.** Would he, who foresaw every event, have said that his church should be **built on a rock,** if he had foreseen its future fall? Did he not design that this rock should be a firm and lasting foundation? Or did he act by chance, and without any end in view? But Christ himself has answered these questions in the following words;—"The wise man built his house upon a rock; and the rain descended, and the winds blew, and beat upon that house, and it fell not, for it was founded upon a rock." (Matt. vii. 24.) Whence it is plain that Christ, by promising that his church should be built upon a rock, intended to assure us that its foundation should be so strong, so deeply laid, that it should stand in spite of all storms, oppositions or efforts whatever. And therefore, to prevent the very possibility of all but **willful** mistakes, he explains himself by positively asserting, "That the gates of hell shall not prevail against it." These words imply a prediction of the attempts that would be made by the enemies of the church to corrupt her doctrine, and a positive assurance that all their strength, malice and stratagems (which Christ calls "the gates of hell") should be entirely ineffectual. The prediction has been fully verified by the many cruel attacks which have been made upon the church ever since its infancy, either by Jews, Gentiles, Mahometans. Heretics. etc. Is not Christ as infallible when he promises blessings, as when he foretells calamities and disasters? Without doubt—and therefore. though the powers of darkness will never cease to make war upon the church. their efforts will always be as vain as the wind and rain against a house that is built upon a rock, and her faith will remain immoveable and incorruptible to the end of ages. For if words retain their usual signification. we cannot charge the church of Christ with error, in one single article. without drawing this im-pious consequence, that he was either ignorant of the event or unfaithful to his promises, and that, after having solemnly engaged his word "that the gates of hell should not prevail against his church." he has delivered her up to Satan to be destroyed by him. This consequence will appear undeniable to those who reflect that faith is essential to the church. and that heresy destroys faith; whence it follows that if the whole church falls into heresy, she is without faith, and is no more the church she was before. than a man can continue to be a man, when his soul is departed. The church of Christ can only be that society, which believes **wholly and entirely** the doctrine which was taught by Christ, and delivered to her by the Apostles. If, therefore, she has renounced any part of that doctrine. she has turned apostate—she has ceased, from that moment, to be the chaste spouse of Christ—the gates of hell have prevailed against her; and consequently, our Saviour, in permitting that to happen which he promised should not happen, has been unfaithful to his word. Again, Christ either foresaw that the gates of hell should not prevail against his church. or he foresaw it not. If he did not foresee it, then he promised he knew not what. which is blasphemy: But, if he did foresee it, then (as his foresight was infallible in every thing) the event must infallibly take place; and so it must be infallibly true, that the gates of hell never have prevailed nor never will prevail against his church. In a word—the gates of hell, according to Christ. will never prevail against his church; but if she fall into any error against faith, the gates of hell prevail against her; therefore, she is infallible in all matters of faith. This, to me, appears demonstration [sic]—But I shall be asked, whether all men are not fallible, and whether all their united wit, learning or industry can preserve them from errors? I answer that, if Christ had made the infallibility of his church to depend on this feeble support, he would, like the foolish man, have built his edifice on the sand.—Thanks to God, his church does not lean on so feeble a basis. He has secured to her the perpetual assistance and direction of the Holy Ghost, who cannot err.—This stands plainly recorded in the holy Gospel.—Our Redeemer, addressing his Apostles, says, (John xiv.) "I will ask my Father, and he will send you another Comforter, to abide with you for ever." He then informs them who this Comforter is to be, and to what end he is to come:-"The Comforter, the Holy Ghost, whom the Father will send in my name, he will teach you all things, and bring all things to your mind, whatsoever I shall have said to you." He afterwards (John xvi.) repeats the same promise:—"I have yet many things to say to you: but you cannot bear them now. But when he, the Spirit of truth, is come, he will teach you **all** truth." From these promises, joined with that in Matt. xxviii. where Christ declares that he will ever be present with his church, it is evident that the Holy Ghost is the author of the infallibility of Christ's church.

I suppose that most Christians hold, that Christ's church was infallible, while guided by the apostles themselves. But is not infallibility as necessary to the church now, as it was under the apostles? Has she not even more need of the promised Spirit to preserve her from errors? What reason is there then to think that Christ should withdraw his Spirit when his assistance is most needed? Or that the engagement of an **unlimited** and **unconditional** promise should become void, at the very time when the **sole** end and motive of it was not only fully existing, but more pressingly called for its fulfilment than at first? Or, must we accuse Christ of inconstancy, and say, that he was less tender of his church in process of time, than when he first espoused her, and sealed the contract with his precious blood? St. Paul so little doubted of Christ's perpetual fidelity to the church, his spouse, that he calls her "the pillar and ground of the truth," (1 Tim. iii. 15) which would be flatly false, if she could ever uphold error, or bring in corruption, superstition and idolatry. For the same reason Christ himself has declared, that "he who will not hear the church shall be reputed as the heathen and the publican." (Matt. xviii) And shall a man be esteemed, with the heathens and publicans, as out of the way of salvation, for not hearing a church that can teach false doctrine? It is also for the same reason that Christ has pronounced—"He who believes shall be saved, and he who believes not shall be damned. (Mark xvi.) Believe what? Why, the doctrine of the church which he has established. Would Christ oblige mankind, under pain of eternal damnation, to believe a church which he foresaw would seduce them in process of time? Shall we be damned for not crediting a seducer? This would directly contradict the Saviour's admonition in

another text—"Beware of false prophets." (Matt.vii.) For if we are bound
to beware of false prophets, and yet the church herself may turn false
prophet, and mislead us, then we are both commanded to beware of her,
and at the same time threatened with eternal damnation if we refuse to
believe her. What strange incoherences do men run into, when they
abandon the truth! By this command **to beware of false prophets**, Christ
shows plainly that it was his intention to establish an infallible church on
earth; a **church** that should be to all her children a safe, unerring guide, to
preserve them from imposition and falsehood; a **church** that should be
taught and directed by the Spirit of truth even to the end of the world.—
These are the texts on which we fairly build the infallibility of Christ's
church. They are not "prest into our service," but spontaneously offer their
aid to establish this fundamental tenet of the Catholic church.—Now suppose the contradictories of these texts were found in the Bible: Suppose, for
instance, that the Saviour had said to Saint Peter, "I will **not** build my
church upon a rock, and the gates of hell **shall prevail** against it:"—"I will
not send the Holy Ghost to abide with you for ever. He shall **not** teach you
all things, **nor** lead you into all truth." Suppose that St. Paul had positively
asserted, that "the church of God is **not** the pillar and ground of the truth."
Would not all men of sound sense have concluded from such texts, that
there is no such thing as an **infallible church** on earth? This would certainly
have been the consequence. Now, if texts so contradictory to those which
are really found in scripture would force us to conclude against the doctrine
of infallibility, surely the texts which I have quoted must oblige us to conclude in favour of that doctrine.—Having now proved; as it appears to me,
that Christ has established an infallible church on earth, I shall **secondly**
show that the Roman Catholic church **alone** is that church.

The FIRST proof which I shall advance in favour of the church in communion with the See of Rome is, that no other society can, with any colour of
reason, lay claim to this privilege—This title cannot certainly belong to the
schismatic Greeks, who have repeatedly changed their faith on points that
are deemed important by all Christians—For the same reason, infallibility
cannot be adjudged to any Protestant sect, because their variations have
far exceeded those of the Greeks—Besides, all our dissenting brethren
frankly renounce all pretensions to this prerogative—Now, as I have
proved that infallibility is essential to Christ's church, and that no society,
except ours, can claim this high privilege, it must of course be all our own.

If it should now be boldly asserted that the Catholic church has erred as
much as any other, we might fairly desire our adversaries to assign some
public, notorious fact in proof of this injurious accusation. We might also

insist on their showing how such a charge can be urged, without impeaching the veracity or the power of the Redeemer.

SECONDLY. That the church of Rome **alone** is infallible, appears from her being the **only** one that can show a **perpetual visibility** from the apostles down to the 16th century, when the Protestant religion first made its appearance. Now Christ's church was always visible or invisible before that period. If **visible,** and if the Roman church was not this true church, then our adversaries are bound to mark out distinctly in what other visible society the church of Christ subsisted for 1500 years before the reformation. If this could be done, they would be obliged immediately to unite themselves to that external communion of the true church, it never being lawful to live a moment separated from Christ. If it be said that Christ's church was invisible for several ages, it is manifest that none of the reformed churches, at their separation from the Roman church, joined themselves to the true church; for it is inconceivable how men can receive instructions from, or join themselves to, an invisible society. Now all the reformed churches were invisible for many ages, as they themselves all fairly own.—The consequence is, that infallibility (which I have proved to be a property of Christ's church) of right belongs **exclusively** to the Catholic church, which has always been visible in a succession of Bishops and Pastors, teaching one and the same faith from the beginning of Christianity down to this very time.

THIRDLY. That the church in communion with Rome has the **only** just claim to the promised infallibility, is plain, because that church was the true one when St. Paul wrote his epistle to it.—He stiles the Romans the **"beloved of God"**—**"called to be saints,"**—and thanks God **"that their faith was spoken of throughout the whole world."**—Which he would not have done had they been tainted with any error. As the See of Rome was then free from error, it is clear that the whole Christian church in communion with her was likewise untainted; because the Apostle says, that **"their faith was spoken of (or** preached) **throughout the whole world."**—The consequence is, that the true church of Christ was then visible **only** in that society of Christians which was united in faith with the See of Rome— Hence I argue thus: The church in communion with Rome was once Christ's true church (and almost all Protestants own that she continued so for some ages): therefore, unless it be demonstratively proved that she has since forfeited her right, she must be still acknowledged the same true church to which all the promises of infallibility were made—I say, **demonstratively,** for surely nothing less than clear evidence of guilt can deprive any society of a privilege to which it once had an incontestible right.

FOURTHLY. The infallibility promised by Christ must be lodged either in the church of Rome, or in some other, from which she has separated herself; and then that church, in which it is lodged, and from which the church of Rome has separated herself, must in all ages, have had a succession of Bishops and Pastors, teaching a doctrine directly opposite to what is now called Popery. But no history informs us of a church, in which there has been a perpetual succession of Bishops and Pastors, teaching a doctrine opposite to that of the church of Rome, and from whose communion that church separated herself; nay, our greatest enemies confess, that **"Popery reigned universally and without contradiction for many hundred years."** Therefore the infallible church established by Christ can be no other than the church of Rome; which **alone** can truly show a perpetual succession of Bishops teaching the same doctrine from age to age, and from which all other churches went forth and separated themselves.

FIFTHLY. The last argument which I shall now use to prove that infallibility is peculiar to the Catholic church, is this:—At the end of the sixth century when St. Gregory Pope sent missionaries to convert England, there existed **only** the vast body of Christians which were united to the See of Rome, and some remains of Arians, Nestorians, Eutychians, Donatists, Pelagians, etc. who were no part of the true church, having been justly cut off from it for heresy (as Protestants themselves confess).—Now I ask, whether Christ had at that time a church on earth, or not? If **he had not,** then the article of the Creed; **"I believe one holy, Catholic and Apostolic Church,"** must at that period have been untrue, and Christ must have falsified his solemn promise of protecting her against all the attacks of her enemies. If, at that time, Christ **had** a church, it was the church then in communion with the See of Rome; and therefore, if the church now in communion with the See be the same in her faith as in Pope Gregory's time, it follows manifestly that, as she was **then,** so she is **now** the **only** true, and, consequently, infallible church of Christ on earth. In proof that her faith is the same **now,** as it was **then,** we have the concurring testimonies of historians, both Catholic and Protestant, who unanimously agree, that St. Augustine brought into England that religion which is now called Popery.— Some Protestants **indeed** are pleased to say that England was converted from one idolatry to another; but all own the fact—Besides, it is notorious to all who have read the homilies, that England never changed its faith for nine hundred years, i.e. from its conversion to Christianity under Pope Gregory, until the XXIII. of Henry the VIII. It is therefore demonstration [sic] that Catholics hold **now** the same faith which was planted by St. Augustin in England, when it was first converted, and consequently, that, as St. Augustin was then a member of the true church of Christ, so Catholics must be so at present.

The arguments which I have adduced, appear to me abundantly sufficient to convince all, that the infallibility, which Christ has by promise attached to his church, is found **only** in that society which is in communion with the See of Rome. The subject is by no means exhausted; but, that I may not any longer intrude on the patience of the reader, I will now leave him to seriously consider the weight of my proofs.

As a postscript to my defence of the Catholic doctrine of infallibility, I here insert the sentiments of some of the Fathers who lived in the primitive times, when Protestants themselves own that the church was in its purity. Their belief on this subject will corroborate my interpretation of the promises of Christ, and show that it is not invented at pleasure, and to serve an occasion. Those eminent Saints and illustrious Doctors died before any contest had arisen concerning this matter:—All real Christians venerate their names, and regard them as authentic witnesses of the faith of the ages in which they flourished. St. Gregory, the Great, speaks of the four first general councils which represented the Catholic church, in these terms:—"**I do profess to reverence the four first councils as I do the four books of the Gospel.** Now, it is to be presumed that this Saint believed the Gospels to be infallible: Therefore, he must have held the four above mentioned councils to be so. Saint Leo says, that "**the council of Chalcedon was assembled by the Holy Ghost.**"—St. Cyril asks, "**How it can be doubted but Christ did preside in the great and holy council of Ephesus:**"—And St. Athanasius says, "**The word of God, as declared by the Nicene council, does remain forever.**" All this is certainly the language of persons holding the church infallible, when she decides by a general council.—But let us now hear them speak concerning the church at large. St. Ireneus, who lived in the age immediately after Christ and his Apostles, says, "**You are not to seek from others the truth which you have easily from the church, with which the Apostles have deposited all truth, that whoever desires it may have it from the living waters.**" St. Cyprian, in the third century, writes thus:—"Though great numbers of such stubborn and self-willed people, as will not submit, become deserters, **yet the church will never fall from Christ;** which church is the people united to the priests, and the flock following their pastor. The spouse of Christ cannot become an adulteress: She is uncorrupt and pure." This passage surely holds up, that the church will always maintain the doctrine which Christ taught, and that she cannot be corrupted by errors.

This is just what Catholics now believe and teach, and what they mean by infallibility: I wish that this observation may be carefully retained by those who desire to enter into the merits of the question debated between Mr. Lesslie and myself. For whenever, in my hearing, the Protestants have spoken of the church's **infallibility**, they have uniformly affixed to it the idea of **impeccability**; whereas, by that term Catholics mean nothing more than the church's incapacity of teaching errors in faith.—Saint Cyril of Alexandria says, **"that the church of Christ is so settled and established, as** never to fall, **but to bear up against the gates of hell, and so to remain forever."** Here the doctrine of infallibility is as strongly asserted as words can express it.—Saint Austin, on the words, **They have gone astray from the womb and spoken lies,** remarks: "It is in the church's womb that truth remains. Whoever is separated from this womb of the church **must of necessity speak lies.** I say, he must of necessity speak lies, who refuses to be conceived, or being conceived, has been thrown out by the mother."

Again, "The holy church, the one church, the true church, the Catholic church fights against all heresies. Fight she may, but she cannot be overcome. All heresies have gone out from her, like useless branches lopt off from the vine; but **she** remains in **her root,** in **her vine,** in **her charity:** the gates of hell shall not prevail against her." I might swell my quotations to a volume; but from these few I leave it to the reader's own judgment, whether the Fathers were Protestants or Catholics on the subject of infallibility. They wrote against heretics, who all pretended that Christ's church had failed. They, on the contrary, maintained, "that it was **an abominable and accursed calumny** to say that she had failed or could fail:—That it is in the church's womb that the truth remains:—That, being the spouse of Christ, she cannot become an adulteress, but will always be pure and uncorrupt in her doctrine:—That she will remain in her root to the end of the world." Whence it follows, that their writings as fully condemn our reformed brethren, as they did the heretics of their times, and that not only the word of God but the whole current of antiquity is flatly against them; unless they call to their aid the old enemies of the church, whom they, as well as we, regard as justly expelled from her bosom. Let them look back as far as they please into primitive ages, they will find **only** heretics who pleaded for a **fallible** church; and Protestants do nothing but revive their arguments, and turn them against our church. Let then the reformed churches put the fairest glosses they please upon their separation from the church of Rome, still the antiquity of her doctrine, maintained by those eminent Doctors who certainly delivered the public faith of the church of their times, is an argument of such weight as will ever carry the cause in the judgment of those persons in whom the love of this world has not stifled all sense of a future state. (N.B. If any persons should wish to see the book and page whence I have taken the passages which I have quoted, I am ready to satisfy them. The reason why I have not marked them is, that I might not uselessly add to the bulk of my paper, knowing that the works of the Fathers, especially the genuine editions, are scarcely to be found in these States.)

I now advance to the discussion of the question, whether the Scriptures of the Old and New Testament be the **complete, perfect** and **infallible rule** of our faith.* On this head, I suppose, for principle, that the Scripture cannot be the **complete, perfect** and **infallible** rule of faith, if we have no certainty of its divine inspiration but through the church; if what Protestants call Scripture is neither entire nor pure; and if they themselves believe and practice many things which are not contained therein. All this I shall attempt to prove.

FIRST. I say, that we can have no certainty of the Divinity of the Scriptures, but through the Catholic church. I know that our adversaries, when pressed on this point, have had recourse to the internal evidence of the books, to private inspiration, etc. But at present (as far as I can discover) all those who are consistent, admit that the **grand** reason for admitting the books of Scripture as canonical, is the constant and unvarying testimony of the Catholic church. This has ever determined and still determines all Christians to receive the Bible as a divine book. If I thought that this assertion was not generally regarded as true, I should enlarge upon it; but this I believe to be unnecessary.

SECONDLY. I maintain that the Protestant Bible is neither entire nor pure. Here let me previously declare, that I have no design to lessen the credit or authority of the Holy Bible. It is a common accusation of our adversaries, that we set light by the written word of God; that we undervalue and contemn the sacred Scripture. This calumny is carefully propagated among the people, who as firmly believe it as any other part of their creed. Whereas all who know us, see plainly, that we have the highest respect and veneration for the Bible, receiving and honouring it as the pure word of God, neither rejecting, nor so much as doubting of, the least tittle

---

*Those who hold the Bible to be the **sole** rule of faith, must suppose that the Christians had no rule of faith from the death of Jesus Christ until the Apostles wrote, which was a long time after the establishment of Christianity—They must also suppose that every thing which regards religion has been written—These two suppositions cannot be supported. The **first** is destroyed by the commission given to the Apostles: "Go, teach all nations"—the **second** formally contradicts the sacred writers, who refer us to tradition on several points.—Deut. xxxii. 7-2 Thess. ii 17-2 Tim. ii. 2.

Our erring brethren vainly boast of the clearness of the Scriptures—I ask them the meaning of the text, "This is my body." Each of them explains it in a different manner. These words signify, (says Luther) **This bread is truly united to my body.** That is not the sense, (replies Zuinglius) but it means, **This bread is the sign or figure of my body, which is not present.** You are both deceived (says Calvin) here is the true explanation of the passage: **This bread which you are going to eat is not united to my body; nevertheless, when you eat it, my flesh is really united to you.** If the Scripture be so plain, why these different interpretations of so capital a text?

from Genesis to Revelations. Many Catholics carry their veneration for it so far, that they always read it on their knees with the greatest humility and reverence, not bearing to see it prophaned in any way, nor so much as a torn leaf of it put to any improper use. It is this very esteem for God's word that makes our church so jealously watch against those who attempt to corrupt it, and anxiously give the alarm.

1. The Protestant Bible is not **entire**. If it be true (as they know in conscience it is) that the only **real** reason which can be assigned for receiving the Bible as divinely inspired, is the testimony of the Catholic church, that Bible cannot surely be **entire** from which are expunged several books, which lean on that testimony equally with the others. Now, besides the books which our Protestant brethren receive in common with us, the primitive church admitted Tobias, Judith, the rest of Esther, Wisdom, Ecclesiasticus, Baruch, with the epistle of Jeremiah, the Song of the three children, the Idol, Bell and the Dragon, the story of Susannah, and the two first books of the Maccabees.

The reasons commonly assigned for rejecting these are, that they are not in the Jewish Canon, and that their inspiration was once called in doubt by the church. But if these were good reasons, a great part of the other books might also be rejected. It is not from the synagogue, but from the church that Christians receive the true Scriptures. The third council of Carthage, (held in 397) which was very numerous, and which has always been famous in the church, gives the same catalogue of the sacred books which we now receive; and the great Saint Austin, who was present at that council, and subscribed to it, makes the same enumeration. I could here make out a long list of illustrious Fathers and Doctors, who have enforced their doctrines by quotations from the above mentioned books, as well as from the others which our erring brethren esteem canonical. I could also adduce the words, of Brentius, Dr. Covel, Dr. Fulk, and other Anti-Catholic writers, to prove that the primitive church admitted all these books as of divine authority. But the bounds prescribed forbid it.

2. The Protestant Bible is not **pure**.—How indeed should it be so, since the translators profess to follow the Hebrew and Greek copies which are generally allowed to have been corrupted by the Jews and the Oriental heretics? and to despise the vulgate, which from Saint Austin down to this day, has ever been regarded as the best version by all able judges? Yes, the bitterest enemies of our church, as Mr. Whitaker, Dr. Dove, Dr. Covel, Dr. Humphrey, Molinoeus, Conrad Pellican, and even Beza himself, all commend the integrity, the learning, the fidelity and piety of Saint Jerome, its translator. The vulgate was made at a time when the Hebrew and Greek fountains were yet clear and untroubled. This, therefore, ought to have

been regarded as the original, and to have been translated by the reformers for the use of Christians; their not having done this, is a strong presumption that their translations is not wholly **pure.** That the English version is grossly defective, I prove from the petition presented to King James, which declares, that **"The book of Psalms alone differs from the Hebrew, in at least two hundred places;"**—from the words of Mr. Carlisle, who asserts, that **"the English translators have depraved the sense of Scripture, obscured the truth, and deceived the ignorant; that they show themselves to love darkness more than light, falsehood more than truth;"**—from the declaration of the Ministers of the diocess of Lincoln, who affirm, that **"the English translation takes away from, and adds to, the text, and** that **sometimes to the changing or obscuring the meaning of the Holy Ghost; that it is absurd and senseless in many places"**—and (that I may not fatigue the reader by quotations) from Mr. Broughton, who assures us, **"that the English version perverts the text of the Old Testament in eight hundred and forty-eight places, and causes millions of souls to run to eternal flames."**—These Protestant invectives against the English version, were made, it is true, before it was revised by King James; but, as the greatest part of its errors were left untouched, they equally regard, for the most part, the Protestant Bible as it now stands.

In order to set my assertion, that the **Protestant translation is neither faithful nor pure,** in a clearer light, I will now point out a few of its gross falsifications.

The first corruptions of the Protestant Bible, which I shall remark, concern the sacrifice and sacrament of the altar.—We read, (Gen. xiv. 18) that Melchisedeck king of Salem, brought forth bread and wine; "for or because he was the priest of the most high God." The word **for** assigns the reason of his bringing forth the bread and wine, viz. that he might offer them in sacrifice to God. The English translators knowing, that, as Christ is called a **Priest according to the order of Melchisedeck,** this offering which Melchisedeck made of bread and wine, must have been typical of the sacrifice of the New Testament, and, consequently, that Christ, to fulfil this type, must have established a sacrifice, and in it used the same matter by which that ancient priest characterized his ministry, and distinguished it from all others before him; they, I say, knowing this, have purposely put **and** instead of **for,** though in many other places where the sense demanded it, they have rendered the same Hebrew particle **(van) for** or **because.** They must have known that the ancient Fathers of the church, as Clement of Alexandria, St. Cyprian, Eusebius, Saint Ambrose, Saint Jerom, Saint Austin, Saint John of Damascus, Theophilactus and others, had all pointed out the conformity between Christ and Melchisedeck from this very circumstance, viz. that they both offered bread and wine in sacrifice.

It is said (1 Cor. 11. 27.) according to both Latin and Greek (vel. e) "Whoever shall eat this bread **or** drink the chalice of the Lord unworthily, shall be guilty of the body and of the blood of the Lord." The Protestant translators, that they may from this text infer the necessity of communicating under both kinds, substitute the conjunctive **and** for **or,** reading:—"**Whosoever shall eat this bread and drink,**" etc. The disjunctive **or** evidently implies that the crime of an unworthy communion may be committed in one or both kinds, and consequently that it is lawful to receive under one kind **alone.** In effect, all antiquity attests that Christians, in divers cases, did formerly communicate under a single kind. Thus infants received only the precious blood: Thus the sick, the hermits in the wilderness and others, were communicated under the appearance of bread **alone.** Even the Apostles seem to have administered the Sacrament in one kind **only;** for, in their Acts, (chap. ii. 42. xx 7.) the Christians are said to have "**continued stedfastly in the breaking of bread,**" and to have "**come together to break bread.**"—Christ himself, when sitting with his two disciples at Emmaus, is said (Luke xxiv. 30.) to have "**taken bread, to have blessed and given it to them.**" The best commentators, both Catholic and Protestant, interpret these passages of the sacramental bread. And as they make no mention of the chalice or wine, we hence justly conclude, it is lawful (in imitation of Christ and his Apostles) to communicate the faithful under a single kind. Nor can it be pretended, that, thus acting, we do them any wrong or deprive them of any grace, since Christ in his present glorified state cannot be divided, but must be whole and entire, wherever he is at all.—His **blood,** soul and divinity, must be wherever is his body, and his **body,** soul and divinity, must be wherever is his blood—This is the doctrine of all sensible Protestants, as well as ours. The text of St. Paul must then have been designedly falsified, to make the people believe, that we mangle the Sacrament when we refuse the cup to the laity, and that there is a strict obligation of receiving it in both kinds.

The next corruptions, which I shall mention, respect the continency of the Priests. Celibacy, or a single life, has been annexed to the Christian Priesthood ever since the Apostolic times. But the Protestant translators, who felt no vocation to this holy life, attempt to make many texts speak in defence of their own incontinency.

St. Paul (Phil. iv. 3.) calls a fellow-bishop his "**sincere companion**"— This text, contrary to the original word, which is masculine, is rendered in King James's version **true yoke fellow,** and **this** on purpose to sound in English **man and wife,** though St. Paul expressly declares (1 Cor. vii. 7, 8,) that he was unmarried, and that he wished others to be as he was.

It is with the same design that **they** read (Heb. 13. 4.) "Marriage is honourable in all;" thereby insinuating, that it is honourable for all persons to marry, even though they are devoted to chastity by vow, as are priests, monks and nuns. This text of the Apostle is an exhortation to married people not to abuse the sanctity of their state by any liberties or irregularities contrary to it;—which is clear from the reason that is added, **"for fornicators and adulterers God will judge."** This, as well as the preceding and following verses, contains a command, and not an affirmation, and the very same phraseology is translated as an exhortation in the next verse. **"Let your conversation** (or manners) **be without covetousness."** Could they have any good design in making the Apostle, in this one verse **alone**, speak in the indicative mood, while in the others of a similar structure, they make him speak in the imperative?

To palliate the sensuality, and to excuse the sacrilegious marriages of the first reformers, the English Bible makes our Saviour say, (Matt. xix. 11.) "all **cannot** receive this saying," i.e. all cannot become eunuchs, or lead, not merely a chaste, but a virginal life, for the kingdom of heaven. The text thus rendered, implies, that it is impossible to live continent;—whereas Christ only says, "all **do** not receive this saying," i.e. because they will not, for God is ever ready to grant this, and every other grace, to those who seriously and humbly crave it from him.

The same translation makes St. Paul say (1 Cor. vii. 9.) "If they **cannot** contain, let them marry; which is expressly contrary to the Greek, where we read, "If they **do not** contain themselves, let them marry." Here the Apostle speaks not of such as have pledged their faith, and vowed their chastity to God, but of those who are free, whom he advises to marry rather than to be burnt **with** unlawful lust here, and **for** unlawful lust hereafter.—The same advice is now frequently inculcated by Catholic divines. But as to those who have vowed to the Lord, they must not retract, lest **they have condemnation for casting off their first faith"** (1 Tim. v. 12.)—**They must use other means to prevent this burning,** particularly fasting and prayer, by which the flesh will be kept in due subjection, and the gift of continency obtained from God.

The Protestants, in order to exclude entirely from their Bible the idea of penance and satisfaction for sin, constantly render **repent,** the word (metanoeite,) which all the Doctors and Fathers of the church ever translated **do penance** (agite poenitentiam.) The word **repent** not only does not give the sense of the Greek, but is proved a false translation by the phrase, in **sackcloth and ashes,** which is added to several of the texts (Matt. xi. 21. Luke x. 13.) These additions determine the sense of the original to something more than repentance or amendment of life. All who have any acquaintance with Christian antiquity know, that there was in the church a place assigned for the penitents, who, for a time, were excluded from the Sacrament, and were condemned to fasting, prostration on the ground, sackcloth, etc. for a greater or less space of time, according to the degree of their crimes. The English translators could not have been ignorant, that when Sozomen, Socrates, St. Basil, St. Chrysostom, and others, mention persons who performed the penance enjoined them; that when the Councils of Laodicea, of Nice, etc. fix the time of penance to offenders proportionable to their faults; that when they speak of shortening or prolonging the days of penance; they could not have been ignorant, I say, that the same Greek word was employed which is used in Scripture. They must also have known that the word, which, in all those passages, so evidently implies a prescribed time of satisfaction for sin by rigorous penalties, could not be truly rendered **repentance.**

To render all images odious, and to make the word sound to the ears of the vulgar synonimous with idols, they have falsified several texts which I shall not now quote. I shall just mention two passages, into which they have thrust **image,** without any other reason than to decry the practice of our church. They say, (Rom. xi. 4.) "the seven thousand have not bowed the knee to **the image** of Baal," instead of **to Baal.**—They read (Acts xix. 35.) "the **image** which fell down from Jupiter," in place of **Jupiter's offspring.** If the translators were disposed to falsify the text, they should have added, **idol,** rather than **image;** but this would not have answered their purpose of throwing contempt on the mother church. They wished to persuade the people that image and idol were the same thing, and equally forbidden by God, and consequently, that Popery is **idolatry,** for admitting the use of images. They have but too well succeeded in their wicked design.

Protestants pretend, that there never was, from the beginning of the world, any other place, after this life, except heaven and hell. In consequence of this doctrine, they hold. that all Saints of the Old Testament went not into the third place, called Abraham's bosom. or the limbo of the Fathers, but ascended to heaven; and therefore that Christ was not the first man who entered there.—It follows also from this opinion, that the Redeemer did not descend into a third place, in the Creed called **hell,** or **hades,** to deliver the ancient Fathers, and to carry them triumphantly with him to heaven; and that, therefore, this article must be expunged from the Creed (as it was by some of the first, and is now by many latter, reformers) or refer to our Saviour's body in the grave, or else to his suffering the torments of the damned (as Calvin impiously explained it.) Jacob, (Gen. xxxvii. 35.) in grief for the death of his beloved Joseph, exclaims, **"I will go down to my son into hell, mourning;"** that is, into limbo, the place where the souls of the just were received before the death of our Redeemer. This text, in the reformed Bible, is most absurdly rendered **into the grave.** For allowing that the word **hell** is sometimes taken for the **grave,** it cannot be so taken in this passage; since Jacob did not believe his son to be in the grave, but devoured by a wild beast: he could not therefore mean to go down to him thither, but to the place of rest where he believed his soul to be. No soul ever entered heaven before the ascension of Christ, "**the way into the holies being not yet made manifest.**" (Heb. ix. 8) because he himself was "to dedicate that **new and living way,**"—(Heb. x. 20) to open it by his passion and to enter it in his person; therefore the common phrase of the Old Testament concerned holy men, when they died, was:— "They descended into hell," i.e. the general receptacle of good souls. So we say in the Creed that the Saviour himself "**descended into hell,**" according to his soul.

The Protestant version says (Ps. lxxxix. 49.) "**What man shall deliver** his **soul from the hands of the grave?**" This (besides it being nonsense to speak of delivering a soul from the grave) is directly contrary to the original, which is **hell.** I may here remark once for all, that whenever the English translators perceived the word **hell** to signify the place where reposed the ancient Patriarchs, they have rendered it **grave.**—These palpable falsifications, which are but a very small part of those which are contained in the Protestant Bible, are all I shall point out at present.

I will conclude this head by one simple question, viz.—How can Protestants adopt for the **only** rule of their faith, a book which has been so grossly adulterated by wicked and designing men?

The observations which I have here made, must, I think, cause many serious reflections in all those who are sincerely desirous of salvation.

I shall now proceed to prove in the third place, that the Bible cannot be the Protestants' **complete and perfect rule,** because they are forced to admit many points of faith and practice not contained therein.

1. All Protestants pretend, (and this is one of the fundamental articles of their faith) that nothing ought to be believed as essential to the Christian religion, which is not contained in the Bible: And yet, with the same breath that they declare this, they affirm that the Bible, and the Bible too as they have it in their translation, is their **complete and perfect rule.** But I wish to know in what text of Scripture is contained the assertion, that the Scriptures of the Old and New Testaments are the complete and perfect rule of a Christian's faith? In what part of the Bible is it affirmed, that the books, beginning with Genesis, and ending with Revelations, are divinely inspired?—Can any Protestant show us, in the Bible, a catalogue of the books which we are bound to revere as sacred? If they could even do this, we should not be obliged to believe the testimony of the Bible in its own

favour, until we had proved its divine inspiration by some other medium—And what could this medium be, but the authority of Christ's church, to which the sacred oracles were committed?—But, if our dissenting brethren can show us no declaration from the Bible, that it is the **complete and perfect rule** of Christian faith, and that such and such books are canonical, then they are obliged to confess, that the Scriptures are not the complete and perfect rule of faith, and consequently, that there are some things to be believed, which are not therein contained.

2. The Protestants believe that infant baptism is valid. Yet how can we be sure that an infant, which is just born and which has no use of reason or liberty, can receive the remission of original sin, and become the child of God? This is such a mystery to human reason, that the Anabaptists deny it, founded on the text:—**"He that believeth and is baptized, shall be saved."**—These words seem to prove that actual faith, of which infants are incapable, is a disposition necessary for baptism.—If therefore we had nothing but Scripture for our guide, this point would be **at least** doubtful; and yet it is of such importance that the salvation of millions of souls depends on its certainty.

3. It is certain from Scripture, that the Apostles administered the sacrament of baptism by immersion, or by plunging the person into the water.—This is so clear in the Bible, that I have often wondered how those who contend for infant baptism can, with any sincerity, pretend the contrary. For several ages, however, this practice has been changed, and the majority of Protestants believe with us, that baptism is valid which is performed by the effusion of a small quantity of water on the subject of it.

4. Our Protestant brethren, as well as we, hold that Christians are not obliged to observe the legal institutions prescribed by Moses, as, to abstain from blood, and from things strangled; yet the Scripture no where teaches that these things can now be lawfully eaten:—On the contrary, the Apostles expressly forbad them to Christians (Acts xv. 29.)—Could Scripture **alone** ever certify us, that this prohibition was made only out of deference to the synagogue, and that it was to last only for a time?

5. Protestants observe Sunday instead of Saturday, or the first day instead of the seventh, and I imagine that the most of them would deny the possibility of salvation to one who should do all manner of servile work on Sunday, and, with the Jews, keep Saturday in its stead. Now they cannot produce any command to sanctify Sunday, as we can to keep holy the Saturday (Exo. xx.)—The Bible, then, is not their **complete** rule on this head. The most we can derive thence respecting this practice is conjecture. St. John **indeed** speaks of the **Lord's Day** (Rev. i. 10.) but he does not tell us what day of the week this was; much less does he tell us that this day was

to take place of the Sabbath ordained in the decalogue. St. Luke also speaks of the disciples meeting together to break bread on the **first day of the week** (Acts. xx. 7.) And St. Paul (1 Cor. xvi. 2.) orders, that, on the **first day of the week,** the Corinthians should lay by in store what they designed to bestow in charity on the faithful in Judea: But neither the one, nor the other, tells us, that the first day of the week was to be henceforward the day of worship, and the Christian Sabbath. These texts can never surely afford a sufficient warrant for abolishing the express command;—"**Thou shalt keep holy the Sabbath.**"—From this short enumeration, it appears, that many points of Protestant faith and practice are not grounded on Scripture, and, consequently, that the Scriptures of the Old and New Testament, are not (as Mr. Lesslie asserts) the **complete and perfect rule** of Christian faith and practice.

JOHN THAYER, **Catholic Missionary.**

[75] The Rev. Mr. Leslie returned no answer to the above. Indeed, whoever reads the production will not find it difficult to account for his silence. He was unquestionably struck at the force of the reasoning, and felt himself wholly unable to meet it, or to offer any thing in reply which would prove satisfactory to the public. He, accordingly preferred to remain silent, rather than hasard an answer, the insufficiency of which, he was conscious, would be immediately detected, and felt by his Protestant friends, whose cause he had too rashly undertaken to defend.—Things continued in this state for more than a year, when the Rev. Mr. Thayer anxious to enlighten the public still more on the subject of the Catholic Church, and convince them of her great superiority over all other Churches from the very foundation of Christianity, addressed the following letter to the Rev. Mr. Leslie through the medium of the public prints.

To the Rev. Mr. Leslie

Reverend Sir,

I have, I think, answered all your objections against the infallibility of the Church: I have expected your reply for a full year; and, as none has appeared, I have a right to conclude that you do not [76] find the Catholic doctrine on this point totally unscriptural and absurd. Permit me, dear Sir, from the great desire I have of your salvation, to expose to you, in a summary way, those marks which so evidently distinguish the Roman church from all others, as to prove her **alone** to be the one founded by Jesus Christ. As God (according to all Christians) has imposed on men the indispensible obligation of believing, embracing and practising the religion which he has revealed, he must have rendered it so bright and visible, he must have clothed it with such **characteristic** marks of truth, that no well disposed, sincere seeker could avoid finding it. If God should permit his church to have only ambiguous marks of truth, or such as are common to other religions, and should suffer it to be, as it were, buried in darkness and obscurity, he himself would be our deceiver.—But as God can neither deceive, nor be wanting to, his creatures, the marks of **his** church must be more conspicuous than those which distinguish the sects that are separated from her. Now, as there are many religious societies in the world widely different in their faith, and all calling themselves Christians; which of all these is most distinguished by marks of truth, and, consequently, which are we bound to embrace, in order to secure our salvation? Surely, to an attentive mind, no society will appear to possess so many great, **shining, singular,** and even **divine** marks of truth, as the Roman Catholic church.

I earnestly beseech all who do not mean to sport away their souls, to weigh well the following considerations.

I. The **first** mark of truth in the Roman Church is, her invariable existence, from Jesus Christ, to the present day, by a continual succession of sovereign pontiffs and bishops, without the least interruption.—This church is the **only** one that can be called **perpetual,** for two reasons; because no one can point out her beginning or origin after Christ, and because she has an innate principle of duration.

1st. As the good grain precedes the tares, so the true church preceded all heresy: We can name the authors of all the sects, the place where and the time when they began. The Arian heresy, of which the priest Arius was author, began in Egypt in 316. The Nestorian heresy, of which the bishop Nestorius was author, began in Thrace, in 429. We know the exact time when Luther began to dogmatize in Germany, Calvin in France, and Zuinglius in Switzerland; and thus we can trace the origin of all other sects.

Before 200 years ago there were no Lutheran or Calvinist churches; but the Roman church was then reigning, and even before the times of Arius, Nestorius, Cerinthus, Ebion, and all other heresiarchs: Nor can our adversaries point to any period since the apostles, in which the Roman church was not yet in being, and did not make a conspicuous figure. The flame of this church has never been extinguished since it was lighted up by Jesus Christ, and placed by St. Peter on the candlestick at Rome. From that moment it has ever been spreading its light throughout the whole world; that is, from St. Peter, who first established his See at Rome, down to Pius the VIth. the present Pope, we find a perpetual succession of high priests, without the least interruption.

The empire has been transferred from the Latins to the Greeks; the form of government has been often changed at Rome. The city has been several times taken, pillaged and burnt, and yet, amidst such horrible tempests and furious storms, the See of St. Peter, often without any human aid, has stood firm and immoveable. We can reckon up more than 200 heresies, of which there is scarecely a trace left behind, except in the decrees of the councils by which they were condemned. How many heresies, supported by force of arms, and by the protection of princes and people, have threatened nothing less than the total extirpation of the Catholic church! yet all these formidable sects are now no more. The church of Rome **alone** continues firm and perpetual.

2d. Nor must we be surprised that the sects rise up and die away by perpetual changes; for they have not in themselves a principle of perpetuity; that is, they have not an union of all the members with one general head, by whose authority the pastors are maintained in the order of succession, and the faithful kept in the unity of faith.

Luther and Calvin, like all other sectaries, succeeded to no one; but both, despising the authority of the sovereign pontiff, established themselves heads of the church, and interpreted the Bible as they pleased, adding, diminishing, or changing, according to their fancy.

Now, as Luther and Calvin withdrew from the authority of the Pope, their followers had, each, the right to withdraw from their control. Hence it is, that all the sects are divided and subdivided, until, weakened by their divisions, they fall at last into total ruin.

The principles of the Catholics are very different. Their first and inviolable law is, to refer all controversies to the judgment of the church, and never to separate from the chair of St. Peter, in which resides the Apostolic authority, and which is the centre of unity.

According to the holy Fathers, "the Apostolic See was established at Rome, **that by this See** unity might be every where preserved, and that he might be declared schismatic, who against this See should erect another."

II. The **second** mark of the truth of our religion is, its firmness and stability. It has been attacked by all the powers of earth and hell. The heathen Emperors omitted nothing to stifle it at its birth. Several different nations have more than once pillaged Rome, massacred or banished the Popes. All the schismatics and heretics, down to the present day, have done every thing to exterminate the Catholics, and to overturn the Papal See.

Yet all these formidable attacks have not only been fruitless, but have even served to render the mother church more solid and unshaken.—This is a perpetual, a standing miracle. **"The finger of God is here;"** and in this the promise of Christ is most visibly fulfilled, that **"the gates of hell shall never prevail against his church."**

III.   The **third** sign that the truth is with our church is, that all the sects, which have attacked her and which called themselves Christ's true church, have fallen. Why? because they were not founded on the rock, but on **the sand**. We can scarcely find a few miserable remains of them in the East, and there they have adopted so many new errors that they are not now the same sects. The Roman Catholic church **alone** subsists for almost 1800 years. Who is it that supports her? If she had fallen into error (as innovators have always said, and now say) would God have so visibly protected her? Would she not have shared the fate of all other false sects? Yet God does defend her. What! would God have defended for almost 18 centuries a false religion, while he reduced the true one to ruin and destruction? This shocks and revolts all the ideas which we ought to entertain of the all-perfect Deity.

IV. The **fourth** mark of the truth of the Roman church is, that she went out from no other, whereas all the sects went out of her by an open and public rupture. History attests (and our adversaries do not deny) that there were Popes in the four first ages, the time of pure Christianity, who had succeeded to each other ever since St. Peter, the vicar of Jesus Christ. Several Fathers have given us the names of them all, and the exact time of their nomination and death. Those of the fifth age succeeded to those of the fourth; those of the sixth to those of the fifth; and thus they have gone on, in an uninterrupted line, down to the present Pope.

The Roman Christians were always Catholics and Papists (as the Protestants call us;) They were before all sects: They began under the pontificate of St. Peter, and, consequently, their religion never went out of any other.

But all heretics, before their revolt, were Catholics and Papists. Simon the magician, the first author of heresy, was certainly of the religion of St. Peter, the first Pope, and who was established by Jesus Christ. Simon was then a Papist, before his heresy, and, consequently, the Papists were before Simon, the first heretic, and therefore before all the sects. Arius was a Priest, Luther was a Monk, and Calvin was a Canon, in the Roman church, of which the Popes were the heads.

These heresiarchs, as well as all others, were, before they began their sects, Papists, that is, subject to the Popes to whom they had publickly professed submission.

They all separated, therefore, from popery, and all went out from the Roman church, which was founded by St. Peter, who was sent immediately by Jesus Christ.

V. The **fifth** mark of truth in the Roman church is, that she is the **only** one that carries the gospel to the infidels, and converts them to Jesus Christ. The sectaries exert their zeal only in making proselytes from among the Catholics. We do not see their preachers undertake to draw the idolatrous nations to their religion, and courageously expose themselves to martyrdom, for the propagation and glory of their faith. All their societies for propagating their religion are a **mere** name. Their zeal is satisfied when they have distributed a few Bibles among those whom they ought first, in charity, to teach how to spell—and yet no people on the globe has ever had a fairer opportunity, than the English nation, to spread the Christian religion both in the East and West-Indies—we hear, however, of no one heathen nation that has renounced their idols, and embraced the reformed faith—America is filled with savage tribes. While the Catholic missionaries, by their zealous and laborious exertions, have brought over to the mother church all the idolators within the French and Spanish territories; what considerable tribes have embraced the reformation? There are, indeed, a few dissenting ministers called missionaries; but none of them advance into the heart of the Indian countries. They all (as far as I am informed) fix their abode among the tribes that are partly civilized by their commerce with the whites, and that border very nearly upon them.

Is not this defect of zeal an evident proof that they have not the Spirit of God, nor of the Apostles, who preached to the whole world, according to their Lord's command—**"Preach to every creature"**? (Mark xvi. 15) On the contrary, this Apostolic zeal was always hereditary in the Roman church. For (without speaking of the five first centuries) it is certain that, in the **sixth** age, St. Augustin, a monk, who was sent by St. Gregory, Pope, converted the English nation to the Christian faith. In the **seventh** age, the Flemish were converted by preachers sent from the Popes. In the **eighth** century, the Germans were converted by popish missionaries. In the **ninth** age, the Sclavonians, the Poles, the Danes, and many other nations, were gained to the Roman church by apostolic priests. In the **eleventh** century, all Hungary, with Stephen its king, was brought to obey the faith through preachers commissioned by the Popes. In the **twelfth** age, the Norwegians, the Finlanders, the Livonians, and many other northern nations, were converted by the zeal of Pope Adrian the 4th, an Englishman. And in the same century, establishments were made at Tripoli and Algiers in Africa, by which many Mahometans were won over to Christianity. In the **thirteenth** age, God raised up in his church several religious orders, which, by their zealous preaching and labours, brought back to the Catholic faith great numbers of the Albigenses and other heretics, and also opened the eyes of many schismatics and infidels in Greece, Tartary, etc. In the fourteenth century, a great part of the Saracens were added to the church by that great apostolic man, St. Vincent Ferrier. In the two last centuries, St. Francis Xavier, and several other missioners, all sent by the Popes, have converted to the faith many idolatrous nations in the East. They formed in Japan, China, Cochin-China, etc. millions of the most fervent Christians that ever illustrated the church of God, many of whom, especially in Japan, have generously sealed their faith with their blood—St. Francis **alone** is supposed to have gained as great a number of idolators to the church, as Luther and Calvin had seduced of Catholics from her bosom. Very great is still the number of holy priests, who are yearly sent into the Indies, into China and America.

These are not cunningly devised stories to amuse: they are public facts. Several of those who were educated with me in the same ecclesiastical seminary, and who were my intimate friends, have bidden adieu to all their dearest connexions at home (and some of them were of the noblest families,) and have exiled themselves for life, to gain souls to Christ—and I call heaven to witness, that nothing but an ardent desire of the salvation of my countrymen has brought me back from Europe, to a life of poverty, contempt, persecution and labour.

VI. The **sixth** mark of truth in our church is, her unity and indivisibility of faith. This church, ever since her first establishment, has always believed, in **the first place,** all the articles revealed by Jesus Christ, by his Evangelists and Apostles; and wherever there are men of her communion, there is the same faith.

2d. She has never varied in her professions and formularies of faith; for whenever any point of doctrine has been once decided by a general council, all succeeding councils have regarded that point as an article of divine revelation; nor have our general councils ever contradicted each other in a **single point of doctrine.**

3d. She has a sure and infallible rule for preserving the unity of her faith, viz. the decisions of the general councils, confirmed by the Pope, or, when no council is assembled, the decisions of the Pope **expressly or tacitly** accepted by the body of bishops.

These councils (as was just remarked) have never varied; for since the first, which was held at Jerusalem by the Apostles, they have always begun, by approving and confirming the acts of those that preceded.

4th. In fine, the Catholic church retrenches from her bosom all those who alter, retrench, or add a single point to her faith.—Thus she preserves her unity.

Now, none of the sects have ever had this unity—for, 1st—They have believed certain articles at one time, which they have denied at another. They have increased or diminished points of faith, according to the interest of their party, or the necessity of the times. Thus the Calvinists approved the doctrine of the Lutherans, though different from their's to fortify each other, by uniting together.

2d. They have often varied in their formularies of faith; and, though they are always talking about articles **fundamentally** necessary to salvation, they could never yet agree upon their number—some say ten, some six, some four, and some **only** two. Is this unity of faith?

3d. They have no sure rule for preserving unity, since they believe their very synods subject to error. For this reason the Gomarists and the Arminians continued to hold the same doctrines, even after the judgment of the synod of Dort.

4th. Finally, we do not see them retrench from their communion those who differ from them in some articles: Thus they did not excommunicate the Gomarists nor the Arminians. They even sometimes unite with other sects, very different in faith.

It is therefore only in the Catholic church that there is a perfect unity of faith: "**One Lord, one faith, one baptism.**" (Ephes. iv. 5.)

VII. The **seventh** mark of the truth of our religion is, that it is more holy than any other—all the rest give much to flesh and blood, by retrenching the austerities, the fasts and the most difficult sacraments. It is natural to suppose, that persons, who are loosed from the restraints of **confessing and punishing their sins,** should more easily yield to all the inclinations of corrupt nature, than those who believe themselves bound in conscience to confess their most secret crimes, to perform the penance imposed on them by the priest, to restore whatever they possess unjustly, to make reparation of honour, if they have wronged their neighbour in his fame, and to avoid all the immediate occasions of relapse into sin. The Catholic religion, then, which imposes all these retraints, must necessarily be holier than all others.

I do not, however, accuse the sectaries of **directly and positively** encouraging libertinism or vice.—This would be a misrepresentation, (and we always carefully avoid misrepresenting them)—I mean, that Protestant principles, if followed, would lead to an unholy life. By reforming away the sacrament of penance, for instance, they have deprived their religion of the most powerful remedy against vice, and have broken down the strongest fence from about God's law. The restraints of **shame** and **fear,** the one of confessing the other of punishing their sins, being removed, corrupt nature set at liberty will be too powerful for the commandments left thus unguarded.

It was a full conviction of this truth, that made several of the reforming Ministers of Stratsburgh petition the Magistrates for the re-establishment of confession.

Our church does not **merely** prescribe austere maxims, but she reduces them to practice—She **alone** performs the most rigorous fasts and mortifications—She **alone** observes the evangelical counsels of poverty, chastity and obedience, and that in innumerable communities of men and women.

VIII. The **eighth** mark of truth in our church, is, its visibility.—Our adversaries grant, that the true church must be somewhere among the different **visible** societies that exist in the world—for, if "God will have all men saved, and, for this purpose, come to the knowledge of the saving truth," and if out of the true church, which ever it be, there is no salvation, this true church must be necessarily visible; otherwise men would be excuseable for not entering it. No one, surely, can be blamed for not embracing a religion, which he cannot find. It is therefore evident to reason, that the true church of Christ, which is the way to salvation, must be always **visible**. Scripture also comes in here to the aid of reason; for Jesus Christ declares, that his church is a **city**, situated on a mountain which cannot be hidden; that it is a great **candle** placed in a candlestick to enlighten all around; and indeed in an **invisible** church, the commands of Christ could neither be obeyed by the pastors or by the sheep. He enjoins on the pastors to govern and admonish their flocks, to teach and baptize them, (i.e. to administer to them the sacraments) to correct sinners, to bring back wanderers, etc.—He commands the **sheep** to hear and obey their pastors, to tell one another's faults to the church, etc. Now all these mutual duties of the teachers and the teached, evidently pre-suppose a **visible** church: indeed they could not be complied with, in an **invisible** one.—Yet our protesting brethren pretend, that the true church had disappeared ever since the fourth century, and was concealed in some corner, until about 250 years ago, when the clear-sighted Luther and Calvin found out her lurking hole, and were pleased to lead her forth in triumph, the one to Wirtemburgh, the other to Geneva. But the Roman church has always been **visible and conspicuous,** even amidst the most furious persecutions and the most horrible storms.—This **city** could never be destroyed, nor this **light** extinguished.

IX. The **ninth** mark of the truth of our church is, its catholicity or universality. It is in her **alone** that is accomplished the promise: **"I will give the Gentiles for thine inheritance, and the utmost parts of the earth for thy possession."** It is in her **alone** that is fulfilled the command given to the Apostles: **"Go, teach all nations—Go throughout the whole world, and preach the gospel to every creature;"** and, consequently, she is the **only** church to which truly and properly belongs UNIVERSALITY. So fully has God's promise of giving the nations to his church, been accomplished in ours, that almost all the inhabitants of the earth have, at different times, been under the Roman pontiffs. Though the Roman empire was amazingly extended in

Asia, Africa and Europe, yet St. Leo assures us, that, in his time, the Roman church extended still much further. Since that period she has made many acquisitions. There are few nations which have not been formerly, in whole or in part, subjected to the papal authority. Whatever space the sectaries now occupy, or formerly occupied, once belonged to the Roman church, except some thinly inhabited spots in America and the Indies, of which they first took possession. Neither the Lutherans, Calvinists, nor any others, can ever apply to themselves the promise: **"I will give the Gentiles for thine inheritance."** They cannot show that any other kingdoms or provinces were ever in their church, except those which they now possess, and which were all torn by force from ours, and **that** only a little more than 200 years ago. For before that time they did not exist, or were invisible. Therefore the Roman church **alone** can be called **catholic** or **universal.** But not to speak of a **successive** universality, (which what I have said directly tends to prove) I assert, that the Roman church is always **actually and permanently** UNIVERSAL, as to **time,** by being the standing church of all ages, and as to **place,** by having on her side "the agreement of peoples and nations."—Both these parts of UNIVERSALITY are clearly marked out in the Bible, as belonging to the true church. That of **time,** by Christ's promise, that **"the gates of hell shall never (at no time) prevail against her,"** and that he **"will be with her always (omnibus diebus) even unto the end of the world;"** and by God's declaration (Isai. lix. 20) that **"his Spirit and his words shall not depart out of her mouth, nor out of the mouth of her seed, nor out of the mouth of her seed's seed, from henceforth and forever."** The universality of **place** is clearly pointed out by God's promise to Abraham, that all nations shall be blessed in his seed; which is to be no other way accomplished than by their being brought into the church of Christ, who is the **seed** here mentioned.—The same is also evident from the commission which Christ gave to the Apostles and their successors, to **"Go and teach all nations."** The Roman church at this time as formerly, possesses this universality of **place.** We do not, however, take the term in its fullest and most extensive meaning. The claim of our church to **universality of place** is sufficiently proved, if she is known and visible to all nations, though they are not all her children; if she is more extended than any one sect, or, perhaps, than all of them joined together; and if she is actually obeyed through the principal parts of the globe. Now this is indisputably the case. For, if to Italy (where remains unshaken the Apostolic See) we add Sicily, Sardinia, the neighbouring islands, France, Spain, Portugal, half of the low countries, the greatest part of Germany, of Hungary, of Poland, and of Ireland, the Catholics in England, in South and North America, and the numberless churches founded by zealous missionaries in China, Cochin-

China, Persia, and in all the Indies; who can reasonably dispute our actual universality? who will dare to compare so many peoples and nations with the Protestants of the West and of the North, and with the heretics and schismatics of the East?—The Roman church reaches to the South and to the North, to the East and to the West. Wherever there are heretics, there are also Catholics; but there are Catholics in many regions where the names of any heretics are scarcely known.

X. The **tenth** mark of the truth of our church is, her resemblance to that of the primitive ages. 1. She has the same name. As **then,** so **now,** she is called CATHOLIC. **"She is catholic,"** says St. Austin, **"and is called catholic, not only by her own children, but, by her enemies. The heretics themselves, when with strangers, call her catholic, and, when asked where is the Catholic church, show our's, and not their own. So true is it, that they cannot appropriate to themselves the title, CATHOLIC, nor dispossess us of it."** 2. Our church resembles the primitive one in the uninterrupted succession of her pastors. St. Irenaeus, who lived in the second age, gives us a list of the Popes from St. Peter to Eleutherius; St. Optatus continues it to Siricius; and St. Austin to Anastasius; from whom all our ecclesiastical historians show a direct line down to Pius the 6th, the present ruling Pope; who acknowledges all his predecessors as the lawful vicars of Jesus Christ; who believes whatever they believed and defined; who condemns whatever they condemned, and approves whatever they approved. 3. The Roman church is similar to that of the first ages in her form of government. Now, as formerly, the believers are governed by the priests; these priests are subject to the bishops, the bishops to the metropolitans or archbishops, the metropolitans to the patriarchs, and the patriarchs to the Pope, the **visible** head of the whole church. 4. Our church is the same as the primitive one in her judiciary proceedings. If any bishop be now oppressed by a cabal of his false brethren, he may appeal from their judgment to the tribunal of the Pope, as the Saints Athanasius and Chrysostom formerly did. 5. Our church bears a perfect resemblance to that of early times, in her rites and ceremonies, and in her manner of celebrating mass, of administering the sacraments, of consecrating churches and altars, of observing fasts, vigils and festivals of saints. 6. She has also the same exterior form. She, like that, distinguishes between the secular and regular clergy. She has also her monks and nuns, who profess to follow the evangelical counsels of **poverty, chastity** and **obedience,** and who sing the praises of God night and day. 7. She is also perfectly similar in the interior spirit of holiness. Her bitterest enemies have done justice to the eminent virtue of Saints Xavier, Borromy, Francis of Sales, Vincent of Paul, and others, who in modern times have illustrated the Roman church. 8. In fine, the Roman society is entirely conformable to the first Christian church, as to the spirit of zeal which at this day animates her missionaries to carry the light of the gospel to the most barbarous nations, across the most tempestuous seas, and amidst the most horrible dangers. Many of these zealous preachers, in Japan, China, and other places, have, like the apostolic men of old, suffered martyrdom for the faith of Jesus Christ, and for the salvation of infidels.

As the Catholic church is the same in all times, so the heretical sects always resemble each other. The second were like the first, and the last like the second. I appeal to the great Scrutinizer of all hearts, that I have no wish to exasperate any person of whatever denomination. Zeal and love for the souls of my erring brethren guide my pen: I therefore earnestly beseech all well-meaning, truth-searching dissenters to appreciate my intentions, and not to be offended at what is now to follow—Though they belong **externally** to heretical societies, yet, if they sincerely seek the light, if they read, hear and pray with the resolution of acknowledging it, when it strikes their minds, however it may thwart their interests, prejudices, etc. if they constantly endeavour to purify their hearts from every vice, that they may become fit temples for the Holy Ghost; we do not regard them as guilty of heresy (in which obstinacy is a principal ingredient,) but as really belonging to **the soul** of our church. To judge, however, from the general carelessness and indifference about religious matters which now prevail, we have great reason to fear that the number of such persons is very small. But to resume my subject; I say that all the sects have ever resembled each other. 1st. They have always quitted the name, CATHOLIC, and taken that of their author. The Arians take their name from Arius, the Nestorians from Nestorius, the Lutherans from Luther, the Calvinists from Calvin, the Arminians from Arminius, etc. The different sects themselves call one another mutually by the names of their authors. The Lutherans and Calvinists do not call the followers of Arius and Nestorius **Catholics;** they call them Arians and Nestorians. The Arians and Nestorians, in their turn, do not call the disciples of Luther and Calvin **Catholics;** they call them Lutherans and Calvinists. And, what is still more extraordinary, the different sectaries do not blush to say: "I am a Calvinist; I am an Arminian, etc." though Christ has expressly forbidden us to **call any man master on earth.** Now what do such assertions mean? They mean, that they, who make them, profess a religion which is as much posterior to Christ, as is the time in which Calvin, Arminius, etc. lived, that is, above 1500 years; and, consequently, that they are not the disciples of Christ, but of men. **"Those who are called by the name of Marcion,** (and the same may be said of every other man) **are not of the church of Christ, but of the synagogue of Satan,"** says St. Jerom.—When our adversaries nickname us PAPISTS, they undesignedly do us honour; for they in effect say that we belong to that ancient society, which has never changed its name, but has always been united to the Pope, the successor of St. Peter, and prince of the Apostles, and the **visible** head of Christ's church. It would be very easy to prove, that all the Christians, martyrs, and confessors of the primitive church were, what Protestants now call, **Papists.** 2d. All the sectaries have quitted the Roman church in which they were born, have opposed her authority, and blackened her by all sorts of invectives and calumnies. The Catholic church flourished before the birth of Arius.—That audacious man declaimed against the divinity of Jesus Christ, and gained followers. The Catholics opposed the novelty; disputes arose; and the two parties had recourse to the church for the decision of their important debate. The church, assembled in council at Nice, under the authority of the Pope who presided in it by his legates, solemnly condemned the doctrine of Arius. The Arians, dissatisfied with the sentence, exclaimed against the council, declared every where that their condemnation was manifestly contrary to God's word, and that it was necessary to separate from the Roman church, which was now become the school of error. All teachers of novelty, who have sprung up since Arius, have exactly imitated his conduct. Like him, Luther and Calvin first solicited a council to terminate the controversy between them and the Catholics; but as soon as they were condemned by the council to which they had appealed, they declaimed against its decisions, as not conformable to the pure word of God, publishing every where that the Roman church had fallen into error, and that they must flee from her as from Babylon—This conformity of conduct with the Arians is a strong presumption against our protesting brethren.

From the Apostles' time down to Luther and Calvin, those who refused submission to the judgment of the church established under the Roman Pontiff and the Bishops, were always deemed heretics. The Lutherans and Calvinists refused submission to that of the council of Trent, the representative of the **universal church;** therefore, they must be placed in the same class. They can shew no difference between themselves and their predecessors.

Of the 200 different sects that have started up since the Apostles' days, there has been no one which has not protested against its condemnation, as unjust, and which has not pretended good reasons for separating from the Roman church: and yet, the greater part of them have come to an end, or have only left some miserable remains behind.—Those which now exist, must expect the same fate.

Ever since I came to the use of reason, long before I had any thoughts of becoming a Catholic, one thing among the sectaries always appeared to me very inconceivable; this was, how they dared to treat each other as heretics.

The Lutherans and Calvinists charge the Arians, Nestorians and others with heresy, while themselves are condemned at the same tribunal, and smitten by the same anathemas. Why should Arius and Nestorius be deemed heretics, if Luther be not one also? Why should Donatus be guilty of schism, if Calvin be not involved in the same crime? If it be answered that these modern sectaries see clearly in Scripture that the Arians, etc. are heretics, they can reply, in their turn, that they see evidently, in the same Scripture, that the Lutherans and Calvinists are heretics.—Here are precisely the same reasons on both sides.

The ancient sectaries, Manes, Arius, etc. said (as their modern brethren do) that their faith was pure, being drawn from Scripture, and not from human traditions, like that of the Catholics; that they had retrenched the points which had been newly introduced into the church, and had purged her from her errors. To these frivolous, though specious reasons, the holy Fathers replied as we now do: "That the true church continues **perpetual and without interruption,** while all the sects arise and die successively, one after the other: that she is universal, being spread throughout all nations, and is therefore called CATHOLIC: that she is **one** by the union of all the churches to the See of St. Peter, the centre of **unity:** that the sects, on the contrary, are obscure **conventicles,** the pastors of which have no predecessors **in the Apostolic line,** but come of their own authority: that they are divided kingdoms, which are destroyed by their subdivisions: that they are green **herbs** which soon wither and die, and **torrents,** which, for a moment, make a violent noise, but rapidly pass away."

Such, Sir, are the principal marks of truth in the Roman church. These are so plain and visible as to distinguish her from all sects; and are so many strong reasons and motives for believing her to be the true church of Christ.

I here ask our protesting brethren, with that zeal which a consciousness of truth inspires, whether they can counterbalance what I have said with as **numerous** and **strong** reasons? If they cannot, they are bound (as they wish for salvation) to renounce their errors and enter our church. No one sectary can assign a mark of truth in his sect, which is not common to all the rest, and which will not equally oblige him to embrace all other errors, or renounce his own.

1. They will say, perhaps, that they descend in a direct line from the Apostles, but that they were for some ages invisible until the time of Luther and Calvin. But cannot all sects that ever existed, or ever shall exist, assert also their descent from the Apostles, if we dispense them from showing

their succession, or permit them to tack themselves to all the ancient heretics, and when they find themselves embarrassed, to have recourse to an **invisible** church? Most certainly they can. I have already shewn, that Christ's church is always necessarily visible.

2. They will say, perhaps, that their belief is all contained in the pure word of God; that they find their religion clearly in the Scriptures; and that they have compared passage with passage, etc. But every heretic, that ever arose since the New Testament was written, has made the same assertion. All who call themselves Christians, father their opinions on Christ and the Apostles; and for this purpose cite scriptural texts. The dispute is not **often** about the existence of the words quoted, but about their sense— and as long as human minds are different, so long will texts be differently interpreted.

The way to arrive at the true meaning of Christ and the Apostles, is not to amass texts upon texts, and explain them by private judgment. Experience shows, that this method is a fertile source of error and confusion. Our aim should be, to find out how the primitive church, which received its instructions from the Apostles and their disciples, understood the texts in question. And this can never be known, but from the Catholic church, which has ever carefully preserved the whole line of tradition, as delivered by the body or majority of the holy Fathers and Doctors.

No other method than this, can ever settle the jarring pretensions of differing sects, who all see plain Scripture in their favour. Let the Lutherans, Calvinists and others, pretend as much as they please, that the Arians, Nestorians, etc. do not rightly understand the Bible, the Arians, Nestorians, etc. will always retort, that it is **they** who do not understand it. The being founded on Scripture is, therefore, the **common** plea of all sectaries.

3. Perhaps the sectaries will alledge in their defence, that they believe all the mysteries which are necessary to salvation. But this also is a reason **common** to all heretics. Was there ever one in the world, who did not pretend to believe every thing necessary to salvation? Two sects may even both believe the same mysteries, and yet be both false; either because they receive not all revealed mysteries, or admit others which are not revealed.

4. Will they say that their religion contains many good things, that it forbids blasphemy, theft, murder, adultery, etc.? But this is not only common to all heretical sects, but even to the Turks and heathens.

As this mark does not distinguish any one sect from the other, it is therefore insufficient to fix a preference on any one in particular.

5. If they say that their religion is holy, we reply, that it is, on the contrary, sensual, and favourable to flesh and blood, since it retrenches all

corporal austerities and mortifications, all fasts and abstinences, and regards the observation of Christ's counsels of **voluntary poverty, perpetual chastity, and entire obedience,** as superstition and an invention of the devil. Not only have Protestants retrenched all mortifications, but many of them have, by their principles, authorized all vices; for they hold, as an article of their faith, that no sin is imputed to those who believe: and Calvin, their great patriarch, blasphemously asserts, **"that the man who has faith, whatever be his crimes, is as sure of his salvation, as was Jesus Christ himself."** His words are: "Nobis securè spondere audemus vitam etērnam esse nostram, nec regnum caelorum posse nobis magis excidere quăm ipsi Christo."

Agreeable to this principle, he says, that baptism not only remits all **past,** but also all **future** sins, however enormous they may be. So that a baptized Calvinist may, with impunity, commit every crime, because all is forgiven him beforehand in his baptism; and, what is sovereignly impious, this abominable sinner is as sure of his salvation at last, as was Jesus Christ himself.

6. If they say, that their church is very extensive; we reply, that many of the ancient sects, which themselves regard as heretical, were much more diffused than their's. But however extended be the whole body of sects together, it is very certain, that each particular one occupies but a very small space, compared with the vast provinces and kingdoms, which profess the Catholic faith.

7. Protestants will not surely plead in favour of their religion that it was confirmed by miracles, since, according to their doctrine, miracles ceased at the death of the Apostles, as being wholly unnecessary. But, if they should use this argument, I would ask who among them could perform these wonders? God has seldom conferred this gift on any but persons of eminent holiness—Who was **their** so highly favoured saint? Was it Luther, the author of all the modern sects? But **he,** after solemnly vowing to God a life of perpetual chastity, publickly married a nun, who was also bound by the same vow: **he** permitted the land-grave of Hesse-Cassel to have two wives at once, a thing unheard-of before among Christians since the establishment of their religion, and so horrible, that the most dissolute Protestants have blushed for him, and have never dared to imitate this disorder. Such conduct was not certainly a mark of distinguished sanctity, and, consequently, very unlikely to draw upon him miraculous grace. If they should still insist, that it is a great miracle, that the reformation became so extensive in so short a time, we reply, that unluckily for their cause the Arians performed a still greater prodigy, since their partizans were in much greater number, and their heresy much more general. If

there be any miracle in the case, it is infinitely superior on the side of the Arians.—Their heresy was merely speculative. It was no way more commodious to flesh and blood, than our's. The religion of the Protestants, on the contrary, takes away all the fasts, the abstinences, and the most difficult sacraments: it frees men from the yoke of obedience to the commands of the church, and makes them independent of all jurisdiction: it gives to princes the goods of the church to buy their faith and protection: it permits priests, monks and nuns to marry, and promises them heaven, after all. So far from any thing miraculous or supernatural in the progress of such a religion, it is wholly natural, human, carnal, and agreeable to corrupt nature. The miracle is, that the reformation stopped where it did.

8. If Protestants say that they have purged the church of her errors, of her superstitions and idolatry, and have restored her to her original purity, we can shew that this was always the pretension of heretics.

They all boasted that they had brought back religion to its primitive simplicity.

This argument is then **common** to all separators. Besides, what authority had Marcion, or Luther, or Arius, to reform the universal church? Who were they? Whence came they? Who gave them their power?

There is no factious and turbulent man in the world, who may not erect himself into a reformer, and who has not as much right and authority as Luther and Calvin. He might in his turn, reform their reformation, as those two men pretended to reform the mother-church; and, as all their churches, by their own confession, are fallible, it will be absolutely necessary that new reformers arise, even to the end of the world, to reform the preceding reformations, since it wil be always impossible to tell certainly which reformation is true and genuine.

I think, Sir, I have not omitted any thing which can be urged in your behalf, and yet I do not find one **specific, peculiar reason** for preferring your religion to any heresy that ever arose. If all your brethren unite together, they cannot produce a single argument for your religion, which as those whom they call heretics could not as well produce for their's: and, therefore, you must either embrace all the sects, and become Marcionites, Donatists, Anabaptists, Arians, Nestorians, etc. as well as Lutherans and Calvinists, since the reasons for all are the same; or else you must renounce them all together, and return to the bosom of the Catholic church.

Thus having pointed out the **real** marks of truth which appear in the Roman Catholic church, and the **pretended ones** which the sects boast of in their's, I now proceed to the positive marks of falsehood that are conspicuous in the societies which dissent from our church.

I. The **first** sign of falsity that strikes every attentive mind, is their **novelty.** We know the place and the year when they all began to appear in the world; we know the names of their authors and first adherents. Every new religion must be false, because it is **new.** The true religion must mount up to Christ and his Apostles; and that which cannot show its genealogical descent from them, cannot be the church of God. Almost all the sects had their origin from dissolute Catholics. Such men joyfully throw off the shackles of a religion which condemns their disorders—Libertinage of heart easily produces libertinage of mind. New religions, which flatter the passions, have admirable charms for libertines, especially when they appear under the specious covering of reformation and severity. This is the mask which innovators have always assumed; but how fair soever their pretences, how severe soever their maxims of morality, their novelty is a standing mark of falsehood.

II. The **second** mark of the falsity of all the sects, is the manner of their establishment. They all first began by intrigues and secret cabals, and were afterwards propagated by factions, seditions and civil wars: I speak of those which have had any considerable extent. The sect of Luther, which has been the source of all the other modern heresies, has caused the death of innumerable persons in Europe. And the followers of Calvin have fought seventeen pitched battles in France against their lawful sovereigns. What a religion! what a reformation! Granting (as they pretend) that they were persecuted for conscience sake, was this a lawful cause of rebellion? Was it thus that the primitive Christians, whose doctrine they profess to follow, resisted the cruelty of Nero, of a Dioclesian, etc.? No: whole legions of the Roman troops, which were composed of Christians, laid down their arms, and suffered themselves to be butchered, like innocent lambs, without the least opposition. And when they were so numerous that they could have risen and destroyed their enemies, or else have abandoned the empire and left it almost a desart, (as Tertullian appeals to the Emperor and Senate they could have done) **even then** they used no other weapons of resistance or defence than fervent prayers to God, heroic patience, and humble, but manly, apologies presented to their persecutors.

III. A **third** mark of falsity in the sects is, their constant variation. This causes among them a horrible confusion and frightful chaos. To-day they have one formulary of faith, to-morrow another; several different ones have appeared at the same time among those of the same sect; as if what was true yesterday be false to-day, because interests are different. Whence all these their perpetual changes? They proceed from their want of a sure rule of faith, which they have never found since they have abandoned the decisions of the mother-church, and withdrawn themselves from her authority. They have followed all the wanderings of their imaginations since they have become their own judges in matters of religion.

IV. A **fourth** mark of the falsity of all the sects is, their different interpretation of the Scripture. They have a strange variety of sentiment, for instance, on the words: **"This is my body."** Luther maintained that Jesus Christ is really present in the sacrament **with the bread.** Zuinglius, on the contrary, contended that Jesus Christ was present **only in figure.** Calvin pretended to reconcile them both, by saying that Jesus Christ is really **present by faith.** Let Protestants tell us, who of the three was right, who had the Holy Spirit. They could not all have been right, since their explications were contradictory, the one denying and destroying what the other established. Two at least of these interpreters must have been necessarily deceived: and, as Protestants know not who of them was deceived, they know not whom to believe. At least the third may have been deceived as well as the two first; therefore they must believe neither of them. But perhaps one of the three was right; but (I reply) perhaps he was wrong, since he might be deceived. This incertitude reduces Protestant faith, on so important a matter, to **a mere perhaps.** The Calvinists say: they see clearly in Scripture that Calvin was right—But the Lutherans and Zuinglians affirm also, that, according to Scripture, Luther and Zuinglius were evidently in the right. Neither the one, nor the other, believe themselves infallible. Of the three sects **two** must necessarily be deceived, their opinions being contradictory. No good reason can be assigned, why the **third** is not deceived as well as the two others. The Protestants cannot, therefore, believe either the first reformers or themselves: their faith then must be always doubtful and wavering, or rather they can have no faith, because a faith which is mixed with doubts and incertitudes is imaginary and chimerical.

V. The **fifth** mark of falsity in the sects is, the form of their judgments and decisions. Among them, according to their principles, every one is judge of religion and interpreter of Scripture. Every man erects for himself a tribunal, where he decides all points of faith: And these private tribunals are subject to no **superior and sovereign one;** for they have no such.—They have indeed among them, in some places, assemblies and synods; but these decide nothing in matters of faith. They content themselves with regulating certain points of discipline, and with imposing silence on contending parties; but they leave the disputants in possession of their interior belief. This was the case at the famous synod of Dort. The reason why these synods decide nothing in matters of faith is, that, according to the fundamental principle of their religion, every man has a right to appeal to Scripture, and to his own private reason. It is true, that their synods obliged the people to acquiesce **interiorly** in their decisions; though, at the same time, they declared themselves fallible, and subject to error. What extravagant contradiction! to enjoin an **inward** submission to a tribunal which can err, and perhaps has erred! The sects have a thousand times declared, that Scripture is clear in itself, and more than sufficient to settle all controversies; and yet they are constantly exhibiting the most striking proof of its obscurity, by everlasting contentions among themselves about its true meaning. What is very clear strikes every one in the same manner. If Scripture be so abundantly **evident and sufficient,** one would think it useless to assemble their synods—This, however, they do; and, after they have examined and decided upon the point in debate, and enjoined on all an **interior** acquiescence, they say that every one is bound to compare their decisions with the word of God, and to believe what, according to his own private reason, is grounded there. Can the private judgment of illiterate mechanics, of women who do not usually apply themselves to study, and even of the most vicious characters, be more infallible in explaining Scripture than the universal church, than all the councils from the Apostles down to our time? Is God more interested to preserve from error individuals to whom he has made no such promise, than his whole church, to which he has engaged his ever present aid? Absurd! to believe that the whole errs, and that the parts are guided by the Spirit of God! But this is not the whole of their extravagance; for every individual has as much confidence in his own judgment, as if it were **infallible,** though their explications of the same texts be often diametrically opposite to each other. I wonder that men of sense and learning (and there are very many among our dissenting brethren) do not blush at these glaring contradictions, which are so disgraceful to their sects, and which so clearly demonstrate their religion to be false: for to submit religion to the interpretation of every private man is to open the door to all sorts of errors, to authorize all kinds of lies.

VI. The **sixth** mark of the falsity of the sects is, the bad use which they make of the holy Scriptures. All sectaries, ancient and modern, have explained the Bible according to their own private notions, and have mutually condemned each other's interpretation. The Lutherans and Calvinists condemn the explanation of the Arians, since they regard them as heretics; but, to be consistent, they ought also to condemn their own, because they are not more infallible than the Arians—Besides, according to the Protestant principle of private judgment, the Arians had an incontestible right of interpreting Scripture as they pleased; and, therefore, the Protestants ought to condemn their own interpretations, or approve those of the Arians; since both have the same right and the same authority. Men, if left to their own judgment, can turn and twist the Scripture as they please, and make it speak what they please. They have recourse to a Hebraism, to an ambiguous word, to a Greek or Syriac text which they understand not, or at **most** very imperfectly, and thus they make God speak in Scripture what he never meant. In fine, contrary to the design of God, they make the Bible an inexhaustible abyss of disputes and contentions.

VII. The **seventh** mark of falsity in the sects is, that they all inveigh against the church established under the authority of the Roman Pontiff. In this particular the Lutherans and Calvinists have not only copied, but far surpassed, the ancient heretics. The horrible things which their patriarchs vomited against the ROMAN CHURCH excite disgust and indignation in the breasts of all honest Protestants—So impious and immodest are many of their expressions, that, when we quote them we are suspected of having invented them, in order to render their authors hateful. But how is it that those who are ashamed of the transports of their Doctors, do not quit their doctrine? Could the Spirit of God, who is all peace, gentleness and love, animate such turbulent and even furious Apostles? To be convinced of their outrageous fury and hatred against the Pope, we have only to read their writings. By what conduct had the Vicar of Jesus Christ provoked such injurious and cruel treatment? Foreseeing that their new and false doctrine would be condemned at his tribunal, they undertook to blacken and calumniate him to the people, to prevent the impression which his sentence would have naturally made on their minds—But in doing this they only followed the footsteps of all the ancient heretics who went before them.

VIII. The **eighth** mark of falsity in the sects is, their want of mission. The reformers never had any other authority to preach the gospel and administer the sacraments, than that which they gave themselves, and which every person can assume as well as they. **"How can they preach unless they be sent?"** says St. Paul. (Rom. x. 15) There are two kinds of mission, extraordinary and ordinary. The **extraordinary** is, when God immediately sends men to declare his will, and authorizes them by the gift of miracles. Thus Moses was sent under the old law, and the Apostles under the new. The **ordinary** mission is, when God **mediately,** or by the hands of the already established pastors, ordains bishops and priests to govern his flock. Luther and Calvin had not, certainly, an **ordinary mission,** since the church, instead of deputing them for the sacred ministry, excommunicated them as devouring wolves. It is also as clear that they had not an **extraordinary mission,** since they had neither the gift of miracles, holiness of doctrine, nor sanctity of life, which always accompanied those who were extraordinarly raised up by God. They had therefore no other mission than all other heresiarchs had, that is, they sent themselves. No man can tell why Arius and Nestorius had not as lawful a mission as Luther, Calvin, or any of their followers. How deplorable then is the state of the protesting societies, being all absolutely destitute of pastors sent from God!

IX. The **ninth** mark of the falsity of the sects is, their separation from the UNIVERSAL CHURCH. Whoever will take the trouble of running through the history of past ages will see, that all Christians ever regarded as heretics those who separated themselves from the church which was governed by the Pope and the body of bishops. The Lutherans and Calvinists separated themselves from this church; they therefore merit the same title.

X. The **tenth** mark of falsity in all the sects is, their invisibility. When we ask the Arians, the Donatists, the Lutherans, Calvinists, etc. where their churches were before Arius, Donatus, Luther and Calvin had established their sects; they answer that they were invisible, and that they conserved the pure faith in the secret of their hearts until God's time for declaring it was come. But on this principle every fanatic or impostor can establish a new religion; and, when asked where it was for ages before its appearance, he can say, as the existing sectaries do, that it was invisible until God's time was come. Thus all may boast a direct descent from the Apostles, and he must be clear-sighted indeed who can discover them under their refuge of invisibility.

XI. The **eleventh** mark of falsity in the sects is, that they all went out of the Roman church; whereas she has no other origin than Christ and his Apostles. If we mount up, we shall find her constantly existing under a line of pastors directly descending from St. Peter, as I have already proved.

XII. The **twelfth** mark of the falsity of the sects is, that the authors of them, though they all pretended to be immediately raised up by God, contradicted, calumniated, blackened and excommunicated each other. They could never agree in points which they believed to be **fundamental**. The injurious things which they vented against each other were shocking, and they seemed to be enraged that they could not find terms strong enough to express their mutual hatred. Their own partizans were ashamed of their excesses. It was to unite these jarring Apostles, and to hide from the people their difference of opinions, that so many conferences were held in Germany. Yet, after all, Luther and Zuinglius could never be reconciled. They remained obstinate, each determined to be the sovereign judge of Scripture, and to make others submit to their decisions. They were, each, resolved to have the glory of being the head of a party: they were tired of being disciples, and would be masters in their turn. Luther was extremely provoked that many of his disciples became patriarchs, and had their adherents as well as himself. All this is matter of public notoriety. Now I ask every sincere Protestant, whether he can seriously believe that God raised up, in an extraordinary manner, men who contradicted, blackened and excommunicated each other; whether he can think that God spake by Luther when he said, that Christ was **really present in the sacrament**; by Zuinglius, when he said, that Christ was **present only in figure**; and by Calvin, when he said, that Christ was **really present by faith**. Could God be the author of so many contradictions? No: those men spake according to their caprice, their interest, their passions; and God permitted this strange contrariety of sentiment to show their fraud to the world. From these first reformers have sprung up the innumerable sects which are to this day spread throughout Great-Britain and America; the Episcopalians, Presbyterians, Independents, Anabaptists, Antitrinitarians, Arminians, Socinians, etc. etc. etc.—This monstrous diversity of religions resembles the confusion of Babel, where every one spake a different language, without being able to understand each other. Though all these sects are so diametrically opposite to each other, yet, strange to tell! they all agree in one point, and in this **alone,** viz. to hate the Pope most heartily, and every thing that is connected with his religion. Whence this hatred to a church, in which they **generally** allow the possibility of salvation as well as in their own? the reason is, that she is constantly reproaching them with their desertion and apostacy from her. They fear a religion which commands obedience to ecclesiastical authority, a religion which enjoins mortification of the flesh by abstinence and fasting, confession of sins and doing penance for them—In a word, our religion is too hard and difficult for them; they therefore form more commodious ones, and force the Scripture to authorize them.

XIII. The **thirteenth** mark of falsity in the sects is, that they would always be judges and parties in their own cause. Our adversaries cannot, with any propriety, retort this objection against us: because, in the **first place,** our church was always in possession of judging all controversies about religion, and no other origin of this authority can ever be pointed out, except Christ and his Apostles; and therefore it must have been derived from him. But whence had Luther, Calvin, etc. their authority? From themselves: and every individual has as much authority as they. We say, **secondly,** that our church is **only** the judge, and not a party. When Arius, Luther, etc. began to broach their novelties, several Doctors attacked them, and the dispute grew warm. In the mean while the church regarded the disputants on both sides as her children: but, when they could not settle their difference, they both appealed to her judgment, and pleaded at her tribunal. In these cases she was no more a party, than was the church at Jerusalem, when she decided the contest between the Christian and Judaizing teachers. The sentence was at last pronounced, and those who submitted to it were held as true believers, and the rebels were excommunicated as heretics. The universal church is not therefore judge and party. She raises no controversies herself, but only decides those which individuals raise. She is the **sovereign and infallible judge** established by Jesus Christ; and he orders, that all who **"will not hear her shall be regarded as heathens and publicans,"** that is, as out of the way of salvation. The Lutherans, etc. at first owned the church for the judge appointed by God, and clamoured loud for a general council; but they would have a council that should judge **according to the pure word of God,** that is, in plain English, that should judge in their favour, or else they were determined not to submit. In vain have they been told a thousand times: "The Bible is the subject of dispute; all plead it in their favour; it is a mute book, and says not, understand me in this sense or the other; and therefore a **living, speaking** and **infallible** judge is necessary to determine, in a sovereign manner, what is its genuine meaning."—Without such a judge, (and it can be no other than the church established by Christ) men may dispute about Scripture until the end of the world, without ever knowing what is its true sense.

XIV. The **fourteenth** mark of the falsity of the sects is, their speedy fall. Nothing better proves a religion to be false than its overthrow; because the true church of Christ must be immoveable, invariable, and alway visible until the end of ages. There were more than 200 different sects from Jesus Christ to Luther. They all called themselves **the true church,** and accused our's of error and prevarication. These sects, however, are **almost** all extinguished, and we know little of them but from history, which records their ruin as well as their rise. The sects of Luther and Calvin have made no progress since their first fury, but have always declined; and, without the gift of prophecy, we can foretell their certian ruin, because for many centuries all that have risen up against the Roman church have come to nothing, while she herself, like a rock, stands unshaken.

I have now proved that the Roman Catholic church **alone** has evident marks of the true religion of Jesus Christ, and that all the sects have as evident marks of falsity. The plain inference from the whole is, that we are obliged, if we have any regard for our salvation, to profess the first, and to abandon all the others. A Catholic, in the day of judgment, can boldly address his Judge in this manner: "O Lord, I have followed the religion which appeared to have the greatest marks of truth, and I have avoided all those which were marked with the seal of falsehood—If the Roman Catholic religion was false, why, O God, didst thou clothe it with so many visible marks of truth, with so many powerful and convincing motives of credibility? If since the fourth century she had fallen into error, (as her enemies asserted) why didst thou support her against such frequent and powerful attacks? Why didst thou always favour her with thy protection, while all the sects that accused her of error fell to ruin? Oughtest thou not to have crushed this church also, if it was not thine? Nevertheless, this is the **only one** which thou didst sustain without interruption: it is the **only one** that thou didst render perpetual, immoveable, eternal. If a religion, so wonderful and so visibly protected by Heaven, was false, thou thyself, O God, didst spread a snare for thy creatures, and induce them into error." On the other hand, what can a sectary reply, when God shall ask him why he quitted, or did not embrace, the religion which he knew to have been always existing and triumphant, in which there appeared so many motives of credibility, and so many marks of his protection; to follow a new religion which was full of dissentions, variations, contradictions, and other marks of falsity? Will this man be able to excuse himself by saying, that his sect justified itself by texts of scripture? But God will show him that all heretics who at any time infested his church, had the same plea, and that consequently, he ought (if this were a good reason) to have embraced all their tenets. His Judges will then reproach him for following innovators who had no authority, in preference to the **universal church** which had subsisted invariably ever since the Apostles: for embracing a religion, which, under pretence of reformation, had retrenched all austerities, as fasts, abstinences, confession, penance, etc. and, consequently, for having followed it from sensuality and a love of independence—and this will be his condemnation. May the all-merciful God avert this dreadful fate from every one of my dear countrymen."

"JOHN THAYER, **Catholic Missionary.**"

CHAPTER IV

THAYER'S OTHER CONTROVERSIES

[77] The Rev Mr. Leslie continued still silent, and offered no reply to the above. In fact, after his first attempt the public received no further communication from him. The Rev. Mr. Thayer continued, in the course of this year, to employ his pen on several other points of Catholic faith. In reply to a **query** in the **Essex Journal,** a periodical of that day, he published the following short piece in proof of the existence of a Purgatory.

"Mr. Printer,"

"To satisfy your querist, I shall, in this paper give you some of the Catholic arguments in favour of the doctrine of a Purgatory. By purgatory we understand a third place distinct from heaven and hell, where temporary punishments are inflicted on those souls, who have not fully satisfied divine justice for their offences, and who in consequence of their defilements, are unfit for the presence of God. In proof of the existence of such an intermediate state of sufferings, I shall confine myself at present only to those texts of scripture, which our Protestant Brethren admit as canonical.

[78] 1. St. Paul (1 Cor. iii. 15) makes mention of certain Christians who shall be **"saved as by fire,"** that is, like persons that escape from the midst of a conflagration, who always suffer in their cloaths, in their hair, or in the parts of the body which are most exposed to the flames. But who are those Christians who shall be saved with such difficulty?—They are those, says the Apostle, who, after having established Jesus Christ for their foundation, "build on him, wood, hay, stubble," that is, those who, though they believe in Christ, and are united to him by love, mix many imperfections and smaller sins with their good works.—This sense appears natural. For here are persons who shall not be saved until they have suffered some pain.

The whole difficulty is, to know whether this pain is to be endured in this life, or after death. The Apostle decides the question in the same passage: For after mentioning **one** who enriches his edifice with gold, silver and precious stones, and **another** who builds with wood, hay and stubble, he adds,—**The day of the Lord shall make known their works, and the fire shall try them. He whose works shall stand, shall be rewarded; and he whose work shall be burnt, shall suffer loss, but he himself shall be saved, yet so as by fire.** Now it is clear, that **this day of the Lord** can be no other than that in which the Lord shall examine and judge every one's actions; which is certainly after death; therefore the pain here mentioned cannot be understood of the afflictions of this life; therefore the imperfect Christian must suffer some pain after death: Which pain will be **only** temporary, since, after having suffered it, he **shall be saved.** The text of St. Paul speaks then of a **temporary pain,** of a pain **suffered after death,** and by those who shall be **saved at last**—It consequently fully contains our idea of a purgatory.

2. The existence of a third place is no less solidly proved from the passage, (Matt. xii. 32) where it is said, that for him who sins against the Holy Ghost there is no pardon **in this world nor in the world to come.** For to say, that there are some sins which will not be pardoned here nor hereafter, supposes that there are others which will be pardoned hereafter. Now, since Christ says, that the sin against the Holy Ghost shall not be forgiven in this nor in the future life, it follows, that some sins are pardoned in the other world, though this particular one be excepted. But these sins are not certainly forgiven in hell, where there is no remission, nor in heaven, where nothing defiled can enter; consequently, there is a third place, where the remission of some sins may be obtained. If it be said that this expression of the Saviour signifies only, that the sin against the Holy Ghost shall never be forgiven **throughout all eternity**—I answer, that a sin which will not be forgiven in this nor in the other world, will indeed never be pardoned throughout all eternity, and that a sin which will never be pardoned throughout all eternity, will not be pardoned in this nor in the other world. It will, however, by no means follow, that these two expressions are synonimous, or that they may be used indifferently on all occasions. When the Saviour was about to wash St. Peter's feet, that Apostle exclaimed, "Lord, you shall never wash my feet." This phrase is no way extraordinary; but if St. Peter had said, **"Lord, you shall not wash my feet in this world nor in the world to come,"** it would have been ridiculous. Why so? Because it would imply, that feet are washed in the future world.

3. A third text very proper to establish the reality of a purgatory, is that of St. Luke (xii. 59) where it is said—**"Thou shalt not go out thence** (that is, from the prison just before mentioned) **until thou pay the very last mite."**

The prison here mentioned cannot be a prison of this world where persons are confined for debt or crimes. For this threat of the Saviour could not be strictly true of an ordinary imprisonment, since men oftentimes can escape thence by address, or by powerful friends. Perhaps, hell is the prison here spoken of? Hell, I own, is a real prison: but Christ speaks of a prison whence the criminal may be delivered after his debts are discharged. This cannot be hell, from which there is no redemption; therefore it must be purgatory, whence we shall **indeed** be delivered, but not until after full satisfaction to divine justice. It may be objected, that the word **until** (DONEC) does not always mark the term and end of the thing specified, but sometimes its continuation and perpetuity; for example, when it is said, that "**Joseph knew not Mary** until **she had brought forth her son**," It does not thence follow, that he knew her afterwards: And when God says to his Son, "**Sit at my right hand** until **I make thine enemies thy footstool**," it does not thence follow that Christ will cease to sit at his Father's right hand after the subjection of his enemies; and thus, when it is said, "**Thou shalt not go out thence** until **thou pay the very last mite**," it does not therefore follow that the prisoner shall ever come out. This objection, which, at first sight, appears formidable, is wholly in our favour. For, as from the expression: "**Joseph knew her not** until **she had** brought forth her son," we have a right to conclude, that Mary **certainly** brought forth her son; and as from the words—"**Sit at my right hand** until **I make thine enemies thy footstool, we conclude, that the time will infallibly arrive when Christ's enemies shall be all put under his feet;**" so from the phrase—"**Thou shalt not go out thence,** until **thou pay the very last mite**," we can as justly conclude, that the debts of the prisoner shall one day be **certainly** paid, and that then he shall go out.

4. St. John (Rev. xxi. 27) declares, that nothing defiled can enter the kingdom of heaven; therefore, in order to enter there, the soul must be exempt from every spot. Now **venial** sin is a spot; for, though it does not destroy the friendship of God, it certainly displeases him, and consequently tarnishes the beauty of the soul. This spot, until it be effaced, is then an obstacle to the possession of God. Many **really** good Christians live and die sullied by these smaller sins. Nothing is more frequent with them (because they partake of human infirmity) than little impatiences, slight negligences in the service of God, sentiments of vain self-complacency, too free and hasty judgments of their neighbours, etc. "**The just man**," says Solomon, "**shall fall seven** (that is, many) **times:**" And St. James adds, that "**we all offend in many things.**" To pretend, that all these faults are **mortal**, and merit eternal damnation, is dishonourable and injurious to the divine goodness. To pretend, on the other hand, that these faults do not

retard the future felicity of the soul, shows inattention to the express declaration, that nothing defiled can enter heaven.

5. St. Peter (Acts ii. 24) says—**"God raised up Jesus Christ, he having destroyed the pains of HELL."** Now what pains of hell did the Redeemer destroy? Not those surely which the damned endured; for Jesus Christ, in his descent to hell, delivered none of the damned; and it is an article of faith common to most Christians, that **their** pains will never cease. These pains must then be those which the just suffered for some remains of sin, that is, the pains of purgatory. The word **hell,** as all know, does not always mean in Scripture the abode of the damned, but sometimes signifies, **the whole lower invisible regions.** In this sense it is used in the Apostles' Creed, when it says that **"Jesus Christ descended into HELL,"** that is, into the invisible world. I know that King James' translation, which renders the words of St. Peter according to the modern Greek, has the **pains of death** instead of the **pains of hell.** But the proof that this is a corruption is, that both the Greek and Latin Fathers quote the verse as it stands in our vulgate. Thus St. Polycarp, who lived in the Apostolic age, cites it in the beginning of his epistle—St. Austin, who speaks of this text more than once, always supposes it as we now have it—The Syriac version agrees with our's: For it says—Christ **"brake the bands of hell;"** (SOLUTIS FUNIBUS INFERNI) and the words, "Thou wilt not leave my soul in **hell,"** which St. Peter immediately after cites from the Prophet David, serve much to justify our translation. This text is then no feeble nor contemptible argument in favour of a purgatory.

6. St. Paul, in his epistle to the Philippians, (ii.10.) assures us, that **"at the name of Jesus every knee shalt bow, of those that are in heaven, on earth, and under the earth."**—Now, who are those under the earth, that bend the knee at the name of Jesus? Are they the devils or the damned souls? But surely neither the one nor the other are much inclined to give marks of veneration to this adorable name. It is more natural to suppose that they tremble, shudder, and burst into blasphemies, at the thought of a name which, far from recalling the idea of an amiable Saviour, only presents that of a pityless Judge. The good souls **only,** who are penetrated with gratitude for the benefit of redemption, can bless and respect this name, so far as to bend the knee, or give marks of veneration, at hearing it pronouced. These subterraneous places can, then, be no other than purgatory.

These are the chief texts of Scripture which we adduce in favour of our belief on this head; and these texts, we have the consolation to find, were understood in the same manner by the most illustrious Fathers and Doctors of the church. Of these I shall name the Saints, **Ambrose, Jerom, Gregory,**

Austin, Bernard, Cyprian, Bede: to whom I will add Origen and Tertullian. Let it be here observed, that, whenever I cite the Fathers, my intention is not to impose their opinions as articles of faith, but only to introduce them as the vouchers and witnesses of the public faith of their times; and surely their universally allowed erudition and excellent virtue must have rendered them competent to relate what passed under their own observation.

JOHN THAYER, **Catholic Missionary.**

The publication of this piece drew forth a new antagonist, who was not, however, candid enough to give his name to the public; but who merely signed himself, **a sincere and unbiased reader of the Holy Bible.** As there is no subject on which the adversaries of truth harp more than upon the doctrine of Purgatory, it will undoubtedly be interesting to our Readers to see the principal objections which they are in the habit of urging against this tenet of Catholicity, together with the triumphant answers of the Rev. Mr. Thayer.

Mr. PRINTER.

YOU have lately published, under the signature of Mr. THAYER, scripture proofs of the doctrine of purgatory. I own that there appears some ingenuity in his reasonings upon the several texts which he adduces. But, Sir, I have a number of strong scripture objections to make against this **popish** tenet, and which this zealous missionary must answer, if he ever expects to bring Americans to his faith.

My **first** objection is this: We read of only two sorts of persons in the holy Bible. To **the one** it will be said, "Take possession of the kingdom;" to **the other,** "Go, ye cursed, into eternal fire." This evidently excludes a middle state.

My **second** objection is taken from the words of Solomon, (Eccles. ii.3) "If the tree fall toward the South, or toward the North; in the place where the tree falleth, there it shall be." This tree is surely the dying man; and, therefore, when the man is dead, the soul is fixed, and shall forever remain where it shall have been placed by the quality of its works.

My **third** objection is founded on the words of the prophet Ezekiel, (xviii. 22) in which God declares, that he will no more remember the iniquities of the converted sinner. But does not a condemnation to purgatory prove that God remembers his crimes?

My **fourth** objection is drawn from the declaration of St. John, (Rev. xv. 13) "that they are blessed who die in the Lord: and that henceforth they rest from their labours." Hence it appears that all who die in the Lord (or in a state of grace) shall be happy **immediately** after death; that they have nothing more to suffer, and, consequently, that there is no purgatory.

My **fifth** objection is contained in St. Paul's words, (2 Cor. v. 1) "If our earthly house be dissolved, we have a building of God, a house not made with hands, eternal in heaven." The Apostle here puts no inter-[79]val between our quitting the **earthly** and our entering the **heavenly** mansion; therefore we shall pass **immediately** from the one to the other; therefore there is no purgatory.

My **sixth** objection is taken from Christ's promise of immediate heaven to the good thief. If any one ought to remain in purgatory, it should certainly be this great sinner, who was not converted until the hour of death, and who, consequently, had no time to expiate his crimes.

My **last** objection against the doctrine of purgatory is, that it appears injurious to that complete redemption which has been wrought out by the Saviour. Jesus Christ is said, in the Bible, to be our **propitiation and redemption,** and his blood purifies from all sin; therefore to seek another redemption in the alms and prayers of the living, or in the sufferings of purgatory, looks like an insult on, and contempt of, the blood of the Redeemer.

These, Sir are the difficulties that have occurred to me on this subject. I have waited some weeks, expecting that some abler hand would have written. If what I have set down will tend any way to the elucidation of the truth, I shall have gained my object.

A sincere and unbiassed Reader of the Holy Bible.

A N S W E R to the foregoing.

Mr. PRINTER,

I SHALL endeavour to answer the difficulties of your **unbiassed** correspondent with that spirit of candour and moderation with which they appear to have been dictated, being ever ready to satisfy those who ask a reason of the hope which is in me. I say, then, 1st. that the text: "**Take possession of the kingdom;—go, ye cursed, into eternal fire,**" is the final sentence of the general judgment, at which time there will **indeed** be but **two classes of men,** one destined for heaven and the other for hell; and that purgatory will then cease, those who are there now detained being united to the heavenly band.—But that day is not yet arrived, and the state of things at present is very different from what it will then be. I would ask those who deny a middle state before the final judgment, where were reserved the souls of those who were raised from the grave by the Prophets under the old law, and by Jesus Christ and his Apostles under the new? Were they detained in hell? But all Protestants (a very few innovators excepted) will reply with us, that from thence there is no redemption. Were they in heaven? But it could be no favour, but rather a punishment, to quit that delightful abode, to return to this mortal life.

2. If the tree mentioned (Eccles. xi. 3) really signifies the dying man, (as the objector asserts) Solomon probably means, that, at death, the soul is for ever fixed either a friend or an enemy of God, either in the number of the elect or of the reproved; that is, that its fate for eternity is decided, though it be not immediately received. There is not the least absurdity in supposing that a final sentence may be pronounced, the execution of which may be deferred for a time. This takes place daily at the tribunals of this world. All Christians, I think, must own, that before the resurrection of Christ, there was a **third** place which he sometimes calls **Abraham's bosom** and sometimes **paradise.** This bosom of Abraham or paradise could not be what we now call heaven, because the Apostles' Creed, which all admit, evidently insinuates that Christ did not ascend thither until after his resurrection. We believe, that, by the sin of Adam, heaven was shut against men until it was opened by Jesus Christ at his triumphant ascension, St. Paul assuring us that he entered heaven as **"the forerunner."** Now, if Jesus Christ was the first who entered heaven, (as the word forerunner implies) and if he did not enter thither until after his resurrection, as clearly appears from Scripture and the Creed, it follows that the holy souls of the old law must have been reserved in some **third** place until heaven was opened for them. This could not be hell, the pure souls of the Patriarchs and Prophets meriting better company than that of devils and damned souls.

On which side then did those holy souls fall? Was it to the South or to the North? Were they placed forever, or only for a time? As the text of Solomon makes nothing against the being of a middle state before the coming of the Redeemer, how does it now prove anything against a purgatory? This passage is therefore as difficult for a **real** Protestant to explain, as for a Catholic.

3. To the declaration of the Prophet Ezekiel, (xviii. 22) **that God will no more remember the iniquities of the true convert,** I might answer, that the sinner, who, according to the prescription of the same Prophet, does a penance proportioned to his crimes, who keeps all the commands and practises the works of justice and holiness, will so fully satisfy all his debts here as to have nothing to suffer in the other life. But I content myself with observing, that God's receiving a sinner into favour is truly to **forget** his crimes as to their principal effect, which is to render man an enemy of God and deserving of his hatred. Did not God truly pardon and (in the sense of Scripture) **forget** the adultery of David, on his sincere repentance? Yet he assures him, that his son, the fruit of his crime and whom he greatly loved,

should in punishment be taken from him. Did not God pardon and **forget** the sin which the same king committed in numbering his subjects, contrary to God's will? Nevertheless, he chastised the royal penitent by the loss of 70,000 of his subjects; so true is it that God may be said to **forget** the sin of him whom he receives to favour, though he reserve for him some temporary pain.

4. St. John, it is said, assures immediate rest and happiness to those **who die in the Lord.** But who are those who are said to **die in the Lord?** The preceding verse shows them to be those who preserve their faith in Jesus Christ by suffering martyrdom; to be those pure and innocent souls who keep exactly the commandments of God. No Catholic ever doubted of the felicity of such souls immediately after death. But this concludes nothing in favour of less pure souls, whose spots have neither been effaced by penance nor by martyrdom. These must be purified by the pains of purgatory, before they can arrive at the clear vision of God. Again; when it is said, **they shall rest henceforth** is not necessarily to be referred to the moment of death; but may as conveniently relate to the day of judgment, which is much spoken of in the chapter, and beyond which term the good cannot suffer—Or, the word **henceforth** (amodo, ἀπάρτι) may mark the difference between the Christian and Jewish dispensation—As if St. John had said: "The Christians are more peculiarly happy than the Jews; for **now,** if men are careful to be perfectly pure before their death, they can be admitted to the immediate enjoyment of God: whereas, under the law, the holiest personages were obliged to wait the coming of the Redeemer."

5. I do not see how St. Paul's assertion, (2 Cor. v. i.) **that we enter an eternal house when we die,** disproves the existence of a purgatory; since he adds, as the express condition of an immediate admission there, **"if we be found clothed, not naked,"** that is, if we are so adorned with virtues and good works that divine justice can have no claim upon us. The Apostle's design, in this chapter, is to console the suffering Christians—For this purpose he tells them, that, in order to arrive at heavenly glory, the body must be dissolved, that they must bear this dissolution and whatever sufferings precede it with patience, and that they shall be amply indemnified for the whole by the habitation which is prepared for them in heaven. This morality is frequently inculcated from Catholic pulpits, and yet no one doubts of their believing a purgatory.

6. The objection drawn from our Saviour's promise of immediate happiness to the good thief, vanishes at the thought, that all was extraordinary in that great penitent. His courage to bear testimony in favour of oppressed innocence, his belief and generous confession of the divinity of Jesus Christ at the time when he was most cruelly insulted, his confidence in the power

of a man whom he saw overwhelmed with torments, his patience in suffering his merited punishment, his humble and sincere acknowledgment of his guilt; all these were so many heroic acts of virtue: and it is not surprising, that, with God, they were accounted as a long penance, and were accepted by him in place of the temporal pains to which divine justice would have otherwise subjected the penitent, after pardoning his sins. I add, that this man, dying by the side of Christ, watered, as it were, with his blood, received a more peculiar and copious application of this blood, and that this singular example cannot be alledged for the generality of Christians. I say further, that the prayer which he was inspired by God to pronounce: **"Lord, remember me when thou comest into thy kingdom,"** marks that he believed he needed help in the other world, and that he hoped to obtain it from the Redeemer. This example, therefore, is rather in our favour, and serves to establish our doctrine.

7. The last objection, viz. that the doctrine of purgatory is injurious to the complete redemption of Jesus Christ, who is our propitiation and redemption, and whose blood cleanses from all sin, is the effect of ignorant or wilful misrepresentation. We, as well as our Protestant brethren, believe that no man could ever have satisfied either for the sin of Adam or for his own sins; that all men and angels united could never atone for one **single** mortal sin; that none but a person of infinite dignity, such as Jesus Christ, who is both God and man, could ever offer to God a price sufficient for our offences; that the smallest of **his** actions was of infinite value; that a single drop of **his** blood could redeem not only this whole world, but, millions of others a thousand times more criminal than this: nevertheless, we believe, that, however superabundant be the satisfaction of Christ, it does not operate the **full** remission of our sins, unless it be **fully** applied to us. The damned experience not the effect of this satisfaction, though it be infinitely adequate to efface all their crimes. Why? Because it is not applied to them. A person, who is baptized in adult age, receives at that moment the remission of all sin, original, actual, mortal and venial, and the remission of all pain, temporal as well as eternal. For this he is indebted to the satisfaction of Jesus Christ, which, through infinite mercy, is **fully** applied to him. This is not the case in the sacrament of penance. God, who is so gracious at baptism, is more difficult towards those who have violated their baptismal promises; he grants them a **less perfect** remission, changing the eternal pain which they deserved into a temporary one. To this he is in some measure forced by their ungrateful abuse of his goodness. The satisfaction of the Saviour is ever equally infinite; but God will not apply it so fully to those who have shamefully lost their baptismal innocence: he is master to pardon under what conditions he pleases. It is just, and even

salutary for us, that God, when he remits our sin, together with the eternal pain which is due to it, should impose some temporary pain, either in this world or in the world to come, in order to keep us to our duty, lest, being released too soon from the hands of justice, we should abuse his facility to pardon.

It is the blood of Christ, doubtless, which cleanses from all sin; for no sin could ever have been pardoned but in view of the Redeemer's merits. But every sin is not so perfectly pardoned that the sinner is dispensed from all obligation of penance. Now, if the sinner is wanting to this obligation which is annexed to his pardon, is it strange that divine justice reclaim its rights in the other life? and is this a derogation to the plenitude of Christ's redemption? By the meritorious satisfaction of Christ we are delivered from original sin, when we are regenerated by the water of baptism; this being the method ordained by God for applying the blood of his Son to this effect. Nevertheless, we see and feel that we are not freed from all the sad consequences of this sin. We are subject to death and to many corporal and spiritual infirmities, which this sin has caused. Shall we for this reason think that any thing is wanting to the fullness of the Saviour's redemption? Heaven for-bid. How many persons, after being reconciled to God, are still afflicted all their lives by sickness, losses and other adversities, and **that** in punishment for the sins of which they have obtained the pardon? Now, as these sorts of pain suffered in this life do not hinder us from believing Christ's redemption to be whole and entire, how can the temporary pains, endured in a future life, derogate from the plenitude of this redemption? We offer sacrifice and prayers for the deliverance of the souls that are suffering these pains. But what is the **sacrifice of mass** according to our belief, but Jesus Christ himself with all his merits and satisfaction, whom we present to God, for the souls in purgatory, as the price of their deliverance? and what are our prayers but a humble petition, that God would please to apply perfectly to those souls the satisfactions of his Son? To say that such a sacrifice and such prayers are an insult on the merits and satisfactions of the Redeemer, discovers **at least** a great inattention to our doctrine, and in many, I fear, a determined resolution to calumniate and blacken us.

Thus have I endeavoured, according to my ability, to remove every objection to our doctrine of Purgatory. The impartial public must decide what has been my success.

JOHN THAYER, **Catholic Missionary.**

At this time another antagonist presents himself upon the arena. This was a Quaker, or perhaps one, who assumed his style in order the better to disguise himself, and who signed himself **Simplex.** As his piece contains many other popular objections, we shall also insert it for the sake of the answers.

To the Man who styles himself C A T H O L I C   M I S S I O N A R Y.
   FRIEND,
THOU art always writing or preaching in defence of thy religion. Thou art not content with doing this in the capital, but thou ramblest from state to state to propagate thy tenets. I cannot, **indeed,** suspect thy sincerity; because thy doctrine is so unpopular, and thou makest so few proselytes, that great courage seems requisite to support thee under so many discouraging circumstances. I would not blame thy zeal, if it were according to knowledge, which I fear is not the case.

Attend to a few remarks of a plain dispassionate man. I will not stab thee in the dark, by endeavouring to wound thy fame, as some, who call themselves teachers of righteousness, have done, hereby **tacitly** acknowledging that they are unable to answer thy manly challenge, and to oppose argument to argument.

1st. In the history of thine own conversion, and in thy controversy with Mr. LESSLIE, thou talkest a great deal about **infallibility;** but I do not see that you settle the point, where this great prerogative resides.

2d. Thy church requires a blind, implicit belief of her doctrines. This to me doth not resemble the conduct of the Apostles, whose doctrine she pretends to maintain.

3d. Thou quotest as many texts in thy support, as do our Protestant neighbours; but can we, unlearned, tell whether thou understandest them right, since (as a writer somewhere says) "A long and laborious study, an accurate and extensive knowledge of profane history, a correct and intimate acquaintance with the original languages, is requisite" for this purpose?

4th. Thy church forbids to marry; and commands to abstain from meat.—This conduct St. Paul calls "a doctrine of devils."—1 Tim. iv 3.

5th. It appears to me that thy Pope is clearly pointed out as the man of sin, in 2 Thes. ii 3, 4.

6th. I am astonished, that, in the history of thy conversion, thou speakest of the miraculous cure of a Nun. Why, friend, miracles are ceased since the establishment of Christianity, and this age is too enlightened to believe such wonders.

7th. Is it not an argument against thy religion that Deism prevails most in Catholic countries? Yet this is a notorious fact.

8th. I must think, that thy Pope will be shortly thrown down from his greatness, and his religion every where destroyed. What the National Assembly has already done, affords us a happy prelude to this joyful event.

Thine in sincerity, SIMPLEX.

P.S. If thou answerest in any rational way, I shall not reply; but if thine answer appears absurd, I will send thee a few lines more, provided the Printer will correct a little my grammar and spelling, which plainly discover that I am not much used to writing.

The CATHOLIC MISSIONARY's REPLY **to** SIMPLEX.

FRIEND,

I HAVE read your plain objections, and will answer them with plainness, in the order they stand.

1. You say, Sir, that I have not yet determined where resides that infallibility which we attribute to our church. But you must have read very superficially indeed, not to have seen this **point clearly settled.**—I said in both the writings you refer to, (and I now repeat it, lest the same objection should be ever made again) that **"the privilege of infallibility resides in the body of Bishops, whether assembled or dispersed, united to the visible head, the Pope."**

2. You say, that the Apostles, whom we pretend to follow, did not, like our church, require a **blind, implicit belief of their doctrines.** I reply, in the first place, we do not require any more blindness of belief than all other professors of Christianity. We wish that every man's faith should be rational and enlightened; that he should be first fully convinced that God has established an infallible authority on earth, to which all are obliged to submit in matters of religion, and that then he should never call it in question any more than other Christians do those points which they believe divinely revealed. When once men are thoroughly convinced that infallibility is a revealed doctrine, it is not blindness, but the height of reason, to submit to it. Would not men be absurd and **blind** indeed, to believe that God has established for them an unerring guide, and commanded them to obey it, (and this is the faith of every Catholic) and then refuse to submit to it? It is no usurpation, then, on the part of the church to **exact,** nor **blindness** on the part of the faithful to **pay,** an entire submission. Protestants may accuse us, if they please, of weakness for holding an infallibility which they think not well proved; but they can never call us **blind,** with any propriety, for submitting to an authority which we think the holy Scripture holds out as an article of divine revelation. As well might the Socinian accuse us of blindness for holding the divinity of our Saviour, which we take to be divinely revealed. But if, as you say, the Apostles did not require an implicit belief of their doctrines and submission to their orders, what then means their conduct after the decision of the council of Jerusalem?—They sent Paul, who, accompanied by Silas, "went through Syria and Cilicia, confirming the churches; **commanding** them to keep the precepts of the Apos-

tles, and the ancients." (Acts xv. 41) What means that extraordinary sentence of St. Paul: (Gal. i. 8) "Though we, or an angel from heaven, preach a gospel to you besides that which we have preached to you, let him be anathema?" (or accursed) You must own, Sir, that the Roman church never required of her children a more implicit belief than this. If St. Paul had been a Protestant, he would, on the contrary, have advised the Galatians to examine any new doctrines which might be preached to them, and to receive **them** if **they** appeared better than his. So far is he from this, that he makes it a sufficient reason for rejecting them with contempt, if they varied in the least from what he had taught.

3. You acknowledge, my friend, that I cite as many Scripture texts in my support as my protesting neighbours; but the unlearned, you say, cannot tell whether I understand them right or not. This doubt, Sir, must for ever remain in the minds of those who admit no other interpreter of the Bible than their own judgment. But for us, who regard the sense which the church puts on the sacred books as infallible, we have no such doubts. That "a long and laborious study, an accurate and extensive knowledge of profane history, a correct and intimate acquaintance with the original languages, is requisite" to a complete understanding of the sacred volumes, I readily admit. But, whoever was the author of that passage, (for I know not) he admirably corroborates by it the necessity of a living authority to explain the Bible, since very few **indeed** possess all the qualifications there marked out for so great a task.

4. You say, that St. Paul calls the prohibition to marry, and the command to abstain from meat, **a doctrine of devils.** (1 Tim. iv. 3) Common sense, one would think, must suggest, that the Apostle speaks of something very different from the Catholic doctrine, which is, that, for greater mortification, it is sometimes good to abstain from those meats which most pamper the flesh; and that, from the same principle of self mortification, as well as for God's glory, and the greater advantage of men, it is good that a certain number of men and women should live unmarried. There is surely no Protestant, who, when popery is out of his mind and he forgets the interest of party, will not readily allow the propriety of both these points. Common sense, then, and charity to the largest society of Christians on the globe, would incline every candid man to look out for some other application of the words of St. Paul. This application is easily and very naturally made (and in fact was always made by the Fathers of the church) to the Gnostics, Encratites, Marcionites, Manicheans, etc. who arose in or about the time of the Apostles. Those sectaries condemned marriage, flesh-meat, etc. as, **bad in themselves, and as proceeding from an evil principle.** This doctrine, which makes Satan the author of the visible creation, and of the

marriage union, is **most certainly devilish.** But our church holds no such tenets. With us marriage is not only esteemed good and honourable, but is even a holy sacrament. Our church, indeed, judges that matrimony is incompatible with the faithful discharge of the duties of the priestly and monastic life, and therefore forbids any to embrace it, who do not find themselves able to submit to celibacy. Are there not likewise many employments in Protestant universities, colleges, families, etc. which cannot be filled by married persons? Would it be fair in us to conclude thence, that Protestants teach the **doctrine of devils,** by forbidding those persons to marry? No, surely; for they, no more than we, compel any one to accept those offices for which a single life is a necessary condition. If certain more nourishing meats are forbidden on days of fasting and humiliation, this is not done from a belief that they are bad in themselves, (as is clear from our permission of the very same meats on other days) but by way of self denial and mortification. On those days it is not the meat, but the transgression of the precept, that defiles the conscience. No Christian will dispute, I presume, whether or not there may be sometimes wise reasons for prohibiting a **good** thing; since God himself forbad our first parents, as a test of their obedience, to eat of a certain fruit; since Moses forbad swine's flesh to the Jews; and the Apostles, **"blood and things strangled,"** to their first converts. Yet all those things are **good,** in themselves, and to be used, at proper times, with thanksgiving. These observations, I think, plainly show, that the words of St. Paul are no way applicable to the Catholic church.

5. It appears to you, Sir, that our Pope is clearly pointed out in 2 Thess. ii. 3, 4—But Grotius, Dr. Hammond and many other learned Protestants thought very differently, and even refuted and ridiculed this idea. I will here add a short passage from Doctor Heylin, (a most rigid Presbyterian) to show that he applied this text to the Grand Turk, instead of the Pope. "If," says he, "his sitting in the temple of God be an assured direction to find out the Anti-Christ, we may as well look for him in the temple of St. Sophia at Constantinople, which is now a Turkish mosque, as in St. Peter's church at Rome, which is still a Christian church."

In order to remove your unjust prejudices against the Pope, be pleased to weigh the following remarks:

1. Antichrist, the **man of sin,** the **son of perdition,** the **opposer,** (ὁ ᾱntikeímenos) is, according to all the ancients, to be **one particular man,** and not a succession of men. This is evident from the Apostle's frequent repetition of the Greek article, o, which answers to the English definite article, **the.** 2. He is to come a little before the general judgment. 3. He will not

only deny the Saviour, but will pretend that himself is the Messiah, and will cause himself to be adored as God. Did any Pope ever usurp this sacrilegious honour? On the contrary, do they not call themselves the Vicars of Jesus Christ, pay adoration to him, and take the humble title of, **"servant of the servants of God."** 4. Antichrist is to reign only three years and a half; is to kill two prophets; is to be received by the Jews as their deliverer; is to set a mark on the foreheads of his followers, etc. I believe, Sir, you would find it a task to apply all these, and several other particulars, which I could mention from Scripture, to the Pope, the man whom we venerate as the **visible** head of the Christian church.

6. You express an extraordinary astonishment, that, in the history of my conversion, I should mention any miraculous cures in this enlightened age. You add, that miracles have ceased since the establishment of Christianity. On this addition, I shall only remark, that I have frequently read and heard the same objection; but never knew any one attempt to prove it. As, then, it is advanced without proof, I shall take the liberty to deny it in the same manner. However, I defy any one to prove it from Scripture, which, **alone,** you know, is the Protestants' rule of faith. You wonder that I should mention miracles in the **enlightened** age. I have nothing, Sir, to say against the age. On the contrary, I feel happy, that it is my lot to live at such an eventful period. I readily grant, that we know more than our forefathers in politics, natural philosophy, and in many of the useful arts of life. I will allow also that there is a more general diffusion of knowledge than in former times. But are there now better poets, orators, painters, sculptors, musicians, etc. than in the days of the ancients? I leave it to the learned to discuss this question; for I do not mean to enter into any debate on such subjects, to which I profess myself totally unequal. But I have always understood, that the heighth of the ambition of modern artists is, to imitate, in some degree, the masterpieces of antiquity. It is for this purpose, that they croud Rome, and other parts of Italy, where there are any fragments of the great masters. I am willing, however, to grant, that we moderns stand upon the heads of the ancients, who are but pigmies compared to us, and that our capacities are greater than theirs, in proportion to the distance that separates us from them. I grant all this, if you please, as to every thing but the science of religion. With respect to this, I should be glad to be informed what new discoveries have been made in modern times. I am sure, that the jarring opinions which distract the different sects of Dissenters, are all, with a very few exceptions, the renewal of old errors, which have been exploded in some of the early ages of Christianity.

Now, let us come to the miracles. Facts, Sir, are facts, in an **enlightened,** as well as in an ignorant age; and the proof of facts, which we have not seen ourselves, is always the same, that is, human testimony.—But, in an enlightened age, like our's false miracles are with more difficulty imposed on the world, because of the facility of detection. Yet at this very time our church proposes to the public an infinity of miracles, and at ROME, the resort of the curious and inquisitive of all nations, Protestant and Catholic; ROME, where open and hardy discussion, even in frequented coffee-houses, is as free as in any other part of the world, (for this I appeal to all persons who have been upon the spot) and she defies the most scrutinizing critics to invalidate their truth. If such facts are not to be believed, there is an end to human faith, and, consequently, all history is sapped by the foundation. I had, Sir, as much evidence of the supernatural cure of the Nun I mentioned in my conversion, as I should require for any interesting event. Half the number of witnesses I examined, would be more than sufficient, in any court of justice, to deprive a criminal of his life. But every thing of a religious kind is suspected, if it comes from Catholics.—When we see Protestants refusing credit to accumulated human testimony on public and momentous facts, we are not surprised, that some of their own writers have undertaken to prove false all the miracles of the gospel. They are, **at least,** more consistent than their brethren. They reason thus:—"The Roman church boasts of miracles as great as those recorded in the gospel, and proves them by numerous competent witnesses. We reject these; therefore, to be consistent, we must also reject those of the gospel, which **equally** lean on human testimony."

7. You urge, as an objection against my religion, that Deism prevails **most** in Catholic countries; and this, you say, is a notorious fact. On my side, Sir, I assert it, as a notorious fact, that Deism prevails **least** in Catholic countries. It is well known to every one, who is conversant in the writings of the French Deists, such as Voltaire, Rousseau, D'Alembert, etc. that they have borrowed their strongest arms, and most plausible arguments, against Christianity from the works of Shaftsbury, Hobbs, Chubb, etc. all British subjects. It is also as well known to every one, who has the least acquaintance with Europe, that France, which borders the nearest on England, is, of all Catholic countries, the most infected with deistical tenets.

8. When you speak of what the National Assembly has done to "**throw down the Pope from his greatness,**" you seem to be exceedingly rejoiced. MARTIN LUTHER also, in his day, exultingly predicted the fall of that dignified character, and was soon to see the accomplishment of his prediction. But, instead of falling, his empire increased; for while that apostate, with his adherents, was seducing the tepid and corrupted Catholics from their subjection to the holy See, zealous missionaries, in several parts of

the world, especially in Japan, were converting the heathens by thousands. What happened then, is taking place now; for almost all Cochin-China, with the King at their head, has been lately added to the Roman church; and the bishops and priests who are now in China, though pretty numerous, are unable to satisfy the eagerness with which the inhabitants demand instruction in the doctrines of our church. Even in this land, thanks to our truly enlightened **general** government, which, in every quiet subject sees a useful member of society, let his religious profession be what it may, even here, from North to South, we have made the most rapid increase since the peace. All attempts to overthrow the Pope will be vain. For he presides over that church, against which Jesus Christ, truth itself, has declared, that **"the gates of hell shall never prevail."** The Pope still retains over Catholics all that authority, with which they believe him invested by the Saviour of mankind. Temporal advantages are merely accidental, and increase or diminish according to the greater or less degree of affection borne to religion by Catholic princes. Should the Pope lose all his territories, and become a subject, as he once was, and as **most** other bishops now are, he would still be revered and obeyed as the **head of the church, the successor of St. Peter, and vicar of Jesus Christ on earth.**

JOHN THAYER, Catholic Missionary.

(Mr. THAYER begs that all printers, who may have inserted **Simplex** into their gazettes, would be impartial enough to give a place to his reply; for if their papers are only to give one side of a question, they will be vehicles of prejudice, not of light and liberality.)

[80] Thus did the Rev. Mr. Thayer continue to support the Catholic doctrine with the most convincing arguments in spite of his numerous occupations, and other official duties. His flock was, indeed, small, and the major part of them extremely poor; nevertheless, he remitted no part of his care and attention to them. He regularly said Mass every day, in his little Church, preached frequently, was constant in his attendance at the Confessional, and indefatigable in catechising the children, in visiting the sick, and administering to them the holy rites of the Church. The Lectures, which he had likewise instituted on week-days for the purpose of imparting correct information upon Catholic subjects to those, who, after the labours of the day might think proper to attend, engaged no small portion of his attention. On these occasions he frequently had the satisfaction of seeing his Church crowded almost to suffocation, and sometimes of witnessing, too, the happy effects of the grace of God upon several among them who had listened to him with the sincere desire of knowing the truth. He was in the habit also of visiting occasionally the towns and Villages in the vicinity of Boston, as well as other places more remote, with a view to afford to as

many as possible the means of salvation. It does not appear, however, that his Apostolic labours in these excursions were ever attended with any very great success. The prejudices, which the people had imbibed, at an early period, against the Catholics, and their religion, were too deeply rooted to be easily removed by such transient visits—they had, nevertheless, the good effect of allaying, in some degree, these prejudices, and of exciting a spirit of inquiry among the better informed, which of itself was highly advantageous to the true faith. But, in the town of Boston, where his labours were more constant, he had the happiness to gain over and to unite several with his little flock. Among these we may mention Mrs. Ann Bright, widow of Mr. Richard Bright. It was the good fortune of this Lady to be present at one of his first lectures in which he expounded some of the prominent doctrines of the Catholic Church. The impression which this lecture made upon her [81] induced her to go regularly afterwards to the others, until she became perfectly convinced of the insecurity of the Protestant faith, and of the necessity of looking elsewhere for the religion founded by Christ. She had before been distinguished by every virtue, which could render a woman happy in herself and amiable to others. But that which had particularly crowned all her excellent qualities was the charity which she exercised to the poor. This her attentive goodness to the needy members of Jesus Christ was, doubtless, what drew upon her in the end the signal grace of her conversion to the Catholic faith, which faith, after the maturest examination and many hard struggles with the prejudices of education she at length embraced, and continued boldly to profess to the day of her death. This event happened a year and a half after her admission into the Church. During her last illness, Rev. Mr. Thayer was absent in one of his distant excursions, until a short time before her final dissolution. On his return he repaired in all haste to her house where he was received with the liveliest joy and satisfaction. No sooner did she behold him than she declared anew her steady and unwavering belief of every article, which the Roman Catholic Church believes, and received from him the sacraments of penance, Eucharist and extreme Unction with the most edifying piety.— The reader will unquestionably be surprised to learn in addition, that notwithstanding these unequivocal proofs of the sincerity of her conversion to the Catholic Church, she had scarcely breathed her last, when a Protestant Minister, such was the bigotry of the times, and that very Parson, too, whom she had constantly refused to see in her sickness, was called in, to the exclusion of Mr. Thayer, her true and acknowledged Pastor, to perform the funeral service over her body!

After the publication of the several communications in defense of the Catholic religion which we have cited at full length, the public mind, as was naturally to be expected, became considerably excited in Boston. The thinking [82] part of the Community were indeed greatly surprised at the apathy of the Ministers. Every one naturally looked up to them for a refutation of those Catholic tenets which they had all along taught others to hate, but which, now, to the no small astonishment of all, they suffered to remain unanswered, and to wear before the publick all the appearance of truth. Yet, not one of them would venture to undertake the task. At length, with the view of exciting some one or other of them to the encounter, an anonymous writer, signing himself **Impartialis**, sent the following notice of a conversation to the Editor of one of the papers.

Mr. PRINTER,
A FEW evenings ago, conversation turning on the contests in which Mr. THAYER has been engaged since his return from **Europe**, that gentleman, who was present, expressed himself to the following purpose: "We read, says he, of an Emperor who wished that the whole city of **Rome** had but one head, that he might have the pleasure of striking it off at a single blow. What that Emperor wished in reality and from cruelty, I wish **figuratively**, from motives of charity, concerning the whole body of ministers in this country. That is, I should be glad, that in their **corporate** capacity, they would draw up and sign an exposition of what they conceive to be the errors of our church; **fairly and coolly** representing every point of Catholic faith and morality; and shewing wherein each is inimical to salvation, declaring at the same time, which articles were the lawful causes of beginning the schism from the mother church, and of continuing it at present. Such a piece, I say, would give me an opportunity of cutting off all their heads at a single stroke, or (to drop the figure) or refuting them all at once, and of thus discovering to this deluded people, on how weak a foundation their religion leans. It is not, continued the Missionary, from an overweening opinion of my own talents, natural or acquired, that I make this declaration, (for in these I acknowledge many superiors among the ministers) but from a consciousness of having truth on my side, and from my knowing how to wield the Catholic arms. "So confident am I (said he) that the victory would be adjudged to our church, that I would, myself, stand out of the contest, and would commit it to any other priest, or even to a private Catholic who understands his religion and can write; and I would leave the decision to an impartial Protestant public."—Mr. T. went on: "Mistake me not, Gentlemen; think not that I desire to excite religious war in this peaceful land, of which I glory in being a native citizen: I think I cannot better act the part of a good member of the community than by challenging to an open controversy those who have been, and still are, the instruments of blinding

the people, and filling them with unjust prejudices against the most considerable part of the civilized world: If all feel as I do, I am sure that theological questions may be canvassed with as much good temper and manners, as those of a political nature. I seek only the glory of God by enlightening the deceived: The man who takes off unjust preventions against any class of quiet citizens, and thereby promotes mutual confidence and brotherhood, is a friend to society: In all my disputes I will never use personalities or misrepresentations: I will always write with that dispassionate coolness for which the public has already rendered me full justice: Acrimonious language betrays passion rather than love of truth: I wish to live in amity with the ministers, and that public discussion may not lessen private esteem." This, I think, was the substance of the conversation. If I am wrong, let Mr. T. set me right—If, after so many repeated challenges from the Missionary, our ministers do not **publickly** take him in hand, I shall be among the many who think their cause incapable of a good defence, and that we have been for many years minister-ridden.

IMPARTIALIS.

This was succeeded by a writer signing himself, a **Protestant,** as follows:
Mr. PRINTER,
A WRITER in a late gazette, whose signature is IMPARTIALIS, after trumpeting Mr. THAYER'S "challenges" and his wishes for "an opportunity of cutting off all the heads, at a single stroke, of the whole body of Protestant ministers in this country," concludes with saying, "If, after so many **repeated challenges** from the Missionary, our ministers do not **publickly** take him in hand, I shall be among the many who think their cause incapable of a good defence, and that **we** have been for many years **minister-ridden.**" No **Protestant** could draw such a conclusion, either of the ministry or people, nor be the **rider** or the **ridden,** consistently with such principles as Mr. Thayer acknowledges to be fundamental principles of Protestants, viz. That our Bible contains the only and infallible rule of faith and eternal salvation, and that every man has the right of private judgment in matters of faith and the worship of God, or the right to search the Scriptures, to examine doctrines by the word of God, and to judge for himself, as every one must give account of himself unto God. This right of private judgment, Mr. **Thayer,** in his narrative, gives us to understand, in the exercise of it, and in the full conviction of his judgment, he abjured forever the claim of using it as the right of man, or as his own right; and so subjugated his judgment and conscience to the Popish church, by his oath of allegiance to that church, as an infallible body; that if he should only so far resume the power of examining the evidences of the infallibility of that church, or of the truth of her doctrines by Scripture or reason, he would, **ipso facto,** become an heretic!

In the same narrative, he intimates, that he was coming into his native country with strong desires, yea hopes, of bringing the people here, over to Popery; that is, to bring us to abjure, as he had done, the essential right of examining for ourselves in matters of faith, etc. and expressed a hope, that the **surprising revolution** in America would open the door for his wished-for revolution in favour of Popery by his instrumentality! In all which he writes and talks like himself, that is, like a person void of thought and judgment; for how fast Popery falls into contempt in France, since the establishment of the rights of man in their civil constitution! And the revolution in America is in fa-[83]vour of all the rights of man; and the right of private judgment in matters of faith and worship, is established by all our constitutions of civil government, as the essential right of every citizen; therefore such persons, who abjure the right of private judgment in matters of religion, abjure the constitutional right of citizens, and become the abject creatures of the Pope of Rome; and if our legislature should send the Pope's Missionary home to Rome with the Pope on his back, neither the creature nor his rider could complain of being deprived of any constitutional right—for what has our civil constitution to do in a way of protection of the Pope in his pretended claim of right to judge for and dictate to Papists as their **infallible head?** And what has our constitution to do to protect such creatures, as citizens, who disclaim the right of thinking and judging for themselves in religion? It is certain that such persons, who have no right of private judgment, have no conscience, and consequently no claim to liberty of conscience! Therefore, what Protestant minister, who claims the right of thinking, examining, and judging for himself in matters of religion, as an essential right of man, can look upon it as acting in character to accept of a challenge for a public disputation, from a creature whom he knows to have abjured the right of private judgment, and become **a sworn slave** to the Pope and church of Rome, as infallible.

A PROTESTANT.

Aug. 23, 1792

P.S. If Mr. **Thayer,** without thinking, and without resuming his absurd right of private judgment, will demonstrate, by clear reasoning, that the right of private judgment, claimed by Protestants as a fundamental principle, is not an essential right of man, and that Protestants ought, in the full exercise of this right, or from a full conviction of their own judgment, to abjure the right, and to bind themselves, by a solemn oath, to submit their judgment and conscience forever to the absolute control of the infallible church of Rome, consisting of fallible men, equally accountable to JESUS CHRIST, the great Lord of conscience, with ourselves—**he will** then at one stroke cut off all the heads of our ministers!!

This was again immediately taken up in defence of Rev. Mr. Thayer by one who signed himself **another Protestant,** thus:

Mr. PRINTER,

AS the piece signed a PROTESTANT, comes under the description of anonymous scurrility, to which the Catholic Missionary has long ago declared he will make no reply, permit another Protestant to say a few words in his defence. I shall not take up the public's time in pointing out the unintelligibility of the writer's phraseology, the inconclusiveness of his logic, or his gross misrepresentation of Mr. THAYER'S belief, concerning the Pope.* How far Mr. THAYER has hitherto shewn himself to be **"void of thought and judgment,"** the impartial public has decided: This priest has ever acted with openness; from the very time of his return from Europe, he has been uniform in declaring his intention of labouring for the conversion of his countrymen, to what he thinks the **only** true faith; and every person who knows what advantages he quitted in Italy, France and England, (and there are several in this town who do) and his conduct here, must believe him sincere in his declaration.

Catholic priests were once accused of lurking in private, and of not daring, from a consciousness of the weakness of their cause, to appear. If ever they did lurk, the true reason, as is now evident, was the rigour of the laws against them. When there is liberty of conscience, none are bolder. Your Protestant correspondent seems rather to have listened to his own prejudices, than to what Mr. T. has written; for this Missionary, in his answer to **Simplex,** acknowledges every man's right of examining for himself, until he is fully convinced that GOD has appointed for him an infallible guide; that he is to use his reason in order to find this guide; but he asserts (and common sense approves his assertion) that when a man has found this guide, it is extremely absurd to refuse his submission. If Mr. T. could fully convince my judgment, that GOD has appointed an infallible guide to regulate the articles of my creed, as well as the conduct of my life, I would join his church immediately. This appears to me so important an article, and to involve in it so many others, that I am for giving the Missionary a fair chance. Whoever hopes to attack Mr. T. with success, must first prove (it seems to me) that there is no revelation from GOD ordering a submission of private judgment to the decisions of the church. We must show him that he is deceived in this, and then the whole body of his tenets falls of course. The Rev. Mr. LESSLIE attempted this, and in the judgment of us

---

*Mr. THAYER has often declared from the press, that he believes not the Pope's infallibility; and yet this writer, who pretends to have read his writings, has the unfairness to croud this article into that gentleman's creed. If he has renounced the right of private judgment, he probably retains sense enough to tell us, what are the points of his belief.

all failed in the attempt. His brethren in the ministry, from kindness to him, and from charity to their flocks, which may be misled by the persevering efforts of the Popish priest, ought to lend him a friendly hand, to get out of his present embarrassment. It would be unreasonable, among rational sons of liberty, to require Mr. T. to renounce his present system, while unconvinced that it is erroneous. The insinuation, that the Missionary has no right to legal protection, must excite indignation in the breast of every friend to the American constitution, but more especially in those who know the peaceable disposition of that priest in private life. To refute a man by exiling him from his native country, is what is called a **knock-me-down** argument; but does not give a very advantageous idea of the cause which is thus defended. This writer is not certainly the man who will convince the public, that our **Protestant cause is capable of a good defence, and that we have not been hitherto Minister-ridden.**

ANOTHER PROTESTANT

August 26. 1792.

All these different pieces appeared in quick succession, one after another; But they did not seem to produce any effect upon the Ministers, so far at least, as to induce any of them to come forward and take up the defence of Protestantism. An anonymous writer, in the Salem Gazette, endeavoured indeed about this time to apologize for the long silence of the Rev. George Leslie by lamely saying, that the people should not be in too great haste—that they should allow him time to prepare his reply to the Rev. Mr. Thayer—as if an entire year and more was not allowing him time enough!-"because," says the writer, "he is a Protestant who claims the right of private judgment, or to examine and judge for himself, as an essential right of man; but, Mr. Thayer, in his right of private judgment, has absolutely given up that right to the Popish Church as an infallible body, and now totally disclaims all right to think, consider, examine, judge, and believe for himself in matters of faith, and eternal salvation!"

But we shall refer the reader to the piece itself, as below: **The following appeared in the** SALEM GAZETTE.

Mr. PRINTER,

IT seems, by the squibs, in one or two of your papers of late, against Mr. Lesslie as "a slow worm," and "a writer of Protestant bulls," etc. etc. that somebody is in great haste to have Mr. Lesslie's reply inserted, before you had finished Mr. Thayer's long piece in support of the infallibility of the **Roman Catholic church.** People should give Mr. Lesslie time to prepare his reply, because he is a Protestant, who claims the right of private judgment, or to examine and judge for himself, as an essential right of man;

but Mr. Thayer, in the exercise of his right of private judgment, has absolutely given up that right to the Popish church as an infallible body, and now totally disclaims all right to think, consider, examine, judge and believe for himself in matters of faith and eternal salvation!—and therefore what he writes, in such a **floundering** way, are the dictates of his infallible church. He does not dare to offer any thing to the public as the result of his own private judgment, because he would thereby become a **heretic**! He believes the church of ROME to be infallible, because she says she is infallible. He believes the **Protestant** BIBLE to be an imperfect rule of faith and holiness, because the Popish church says it is imperfect. He believes that certain texts, in the Protestant Bible, do prove the infallibility of the Popish church, because that church says they prove it, as they interpret them. He believes that no person can be saved out of that church, nor any who does not believe the infallibility of that church, because that church teaches him thus to believe. He believes whatever doctrine that church teaches, is infallibly true, because she teaches the same, even though nothing can be produced from the holy Scriptures to support the doctrine. He therefore receives every doctrine of his faith as the word of **man,** and no doctrine of the Bible as being in truth **the word of God.** And the Popish church on earth is the lord and master of his conscience. Hence what use are such persons to make of the Bible, who have no right of private judgment, no right to examine and consider what doctrines are taught them? Mr. Thayer, in **his challenge,** promises to renounce the Popish doctrines if he should be convinced that they are false; but how can a person be convinced, who disclaims the right of private judgment? In the narrative of his conversion he tells us how he renounced the right of private judgment, which he says is "a fundamental principle of Protestants;" and that he returned to his native country in hopes of prevailing with his countrymen to come into the bosom of the mother church, and be saved: But we must give up our right of examining and judging for ourselves? Is he such a simpleton, as to think of prevailing, at this day, with the citizens of these United States, to part with that fundamental right of man, to examine and judge for themselves in matters of everlasting importance! No; he who has no right to judge, has no power to think, but as the POPE dictates to him, whose Missionary he is! It is too late in the day for the Pope to send forth his Missionaries to persuade the sons of liberty to give up to him their right of judging for themselves. Tyranny in Popish governments is falling; the Pope lately was burnt in effigy at PARIS; and the **whore** of ROME is hated, and it is expected she will shortly be **made desolate and naked, and be burnt with fire.**

A PROTESTANT.

These trifling reasons in behalf of the Protestant principle of private judgment, and lame apology for the Rev. Mr. Leslie's silence, which, in fact, was never broken from that day to this, were noticed by an able writer in Philadelphia, in a letter to the Rev. Mr. Thayer. It is a triumphant reply, and worthy of the perusal of the public, as it completely puts to rest this absurd right, claimed by Protestants in general, of every man, woman and child forming their own Creed out of the Bible;—a principle which must generate in its consequence as many different religions as there are heads in the community, and in the end, sap the foundation of Christianity itself.

The following is the Letter referred to:

Philadelphia, August 26, 1792.

DEAR FRIEND,

I HAVE seen by several eastern papers that you have been deeply engaged in controversy since your return to Boston. Your polite treatment of your adversaries, joined to the cogency of your arguments, must, I think, excite attention and good will towards you, in the minds of your very adversaries. The Protestant cause, on the contrary, must naturally lose ground among the enlightened and candid, when they consider the delays, the shuffling, the bad humour and scurrilous language, of our opponents, in endeavouring to refute our tenets. All this must demonstrate to them, that Popery is not so contemptible a religion as it is affectedly represented. If the Protestant religion be so clearly established in holy writ as to be discernible by the illiterate, why are the learned Protestants so embarrassed to reply to our proofs, why so divided among themselves?

I am led to these reflections by a **Salem Gazette** of last October, No. 262, which lately fell into my hands. The person, who there signs himself **A Protestant,** seems apprehensive of Mr. Lesslie's insufficiency to answer your arguments; else, why has he stepped in between the combatants? This is not fair play. Nay, it must produce an effect diametrically opposite to the wishes of your opponents. A discerning public, seeing you attacked by **Barebones, Simplex,** the **Salemite,** and a croud of small paragraph writers, will naturally interest itself on your side, and cannot avoid suspecting that the Catholic religion must be a quite different system of belief from what it had been represented to be, before the glorious revolution of America had done away those penal laws, which violated the natural right of man to utter and defend his religious opinions.

I have been often surprised, that a people so generally eager for instruction as the Americans are, should be so little acquainted with the real doctrines of the far greatest society of Christians on earth. The sacred deposit of Christianity was handed down by the Catholic church to all the reformed societies which exist in America. Does not the imposing title of a reformation suppose a knowledge of the pre-existing corruption? Yet it is a certain fact, that the errors which are objected to the Catholic church by Protestants, are their own misconceptions. It is evident, that the Salem Protestant was more conversant with the **Emilius** of Rousseau, than with the authors who defend the Catholic church, which he reviles with so much bitterness. It would be too tedious to correct all his mistakes. Let us examine his leading principle—**A Protestant claims the right of private judgment, or to examine and judge for himself, as an essential right of man, in matters of faith and eternal salvation.**

Christianity is not a mere evolution or a declaration of the natural laws. It is moreover a revelation of mysteries, which natural reason alone could never discover, and enacts positive laws, depending entirely on the divine choice. Jesus Christ requires, as indispensable conditions of the pardon of sin and admittance into supernatural bliss, that man believe in these mysteries, and observe these precepts. When God speaks, has man a natural right to weigh his revelation, in the balance of reason, or to object to the fitness of supernatural precepts? The pretension would be absurd and impious. The inalienable right of a man, when God has not immediately spoken to him in person, is to examine by the light of natural reason, whether the revelation which is called divine be genuine. When its authenticity is once firmly established, the duty of man is to assent to the truths revealed by the God of wisdom, and to obey the precepts of the Lord of the universe. The **Protestant,** I flatter myself, will not controvert these principles.

We were not witnesses of the Christian revelation; but divine goodness intended the propagation of the benefit to us. Dare we prescribe the mode to God? **We have the inspired writings,** say the Protestants. We Catholics also receive them as the word of God: we revere them, as a code of divine laws. But are these sacred writings the only medium of information granted by God to man? I shall prove with the clearest evidence, that they are not. Did mankind enjoy no benefit from divine revelation, before Moses wrote the Pentateuch? Did the Apostles defer the preaching of the gospel, until they had written the New Testament? There was therefore a channel of information concerning the saving doctrines of revelation, independent on the sacred writings of the old and new law. Were the just men before the time of Moses, were the first Christians, therefore, deprived of the essential rights of natural reason, because they could not enjoy the boasted liberty of framing, by their private interpretation of the Bible, fourscore different religions, as our modern Protestants have done? Will the **Protes-**

tant insist, that man has an essential right to deduce contradictions from the word of God?

God requires from us the belief of mysteries and the observance of supernatural precepts. This revelation concerning both must have some determined meaning: He cannot reveal contradictories. That the meaning of the Sacred Writings is not always obvious, is evident from the many opposite sects, which divide the Protestant denomination. Could not God provide some means to decide such interesting doubts, without destroying the essential rights of human reason? Could he not, if he pleased, decide, by a new revelation, the disputes, which exist between the different Protestant societies? Could he not establish a tribunal to decide every question in which faith was interested? Did not this prerogative reside in the Apostles? They exercised it, and from them the Catholic church alone inherits it by uninterrupted succession. Let the **Protestant of Salem** refute, if he can, the proofs of **this** fundamental article, which you have produced against the Rev. Mr. Lesslie.

This essential right of man, this right to examine and judge for himself in matters of faith and eternal salvation, and many other such phrases, have a seducing effect in a country, in which the invaluable blessings of civil liberty are so deservedly admired. But, did the Apostles violate the essential rights of the first Christians, by deciding the question concerning the observance of the Mosaic rites by the Gentile converts? Did God violate the rights of natural reason in deciding by revelation many questions about the laws of nature? Let me ask the **Protestant,** whether a citizen of Salem suffers any violation in his essential rights, when in a question about property, he is bound to submit his private opinion concerning the meaning of a civil law, to the decision of a court of justice? What would become of the State of Massachusetts, if the only bond of society were a code of laws, abandoned to the supposed **essential right** of every citizen to interpret them by his **private judgment?** It might then be soon parcelled into four score, and perhaps more, independent republics.

The principles hitherto laid down, so evidently refute the fundamental doctrine of Protestants, that it is useless to enter into a particular refutation of the sophisms of the **Protestant** of Salem. They are all founded either on misrepresentations or misconceptions. Perhaps he might sooner perceive the fallacy of his reasoning, were he to suppose himself disputing with a Deist, who might easily retort all his arguments against himself, by substituting the word **Bible** for Popish Church or Church of Rome, etc.

I remain, etc.

A PHILADELPHIAN.

[84] Among other assailants of the infant Catholic Church in Boston we find the name of John Gardiner Esq. Counsellor at law.[10] This eminent Lawyer, as the accounts of the day report him, seeing that none of the Clergy were willing to undertake to refute the arguments of the Rev. Mr. Thayer, in favour of the catholic religion, came forward to try what sarcasm and ridicule could effect. He accordingly published an article in which he called the Catholic religion a compound of **ridiculous supersteiions** and **unintelligible mysteries;**—St. Jerom, **the holy, lying Father;** and St. Austin, **the impenetrable St. Austin.** He talked of **the unintelligible fables of the ecclesiastic descendants of the ancient Romans,** and of **the unintelligible nonsense of transubstantiation, purgatory, the worship of pretended saints, pretended miracles wrought by the bones,** etc. **of many a canonized villain etc.** He styled the Rev. Mr. Thayer, at one time, **the young stripling David,**—and himself, **the Philistine Goliah, alias, the Eastern Sachem,—alias J.G.—alias Barebones;** at another, **His Holiness Pope Thayer—His Holiness, friend Thayer,** and the like. —But he soon found, that whatever superiority he might claim for ability in managing a cause in a court of justice, he made but a poor figure in Polemic Theology, and was exceedingly glad to withdraw from the field after one or two attempts, and abandon the contest altogether. —"When men of sense and learning," said Rev. Mr. Thayer in his reply, substitute vain and indecent declamation in the place of solid reasoning, they give strong suspicions, that their cause is bad; for," said he, "if they were furnished with good arguments in its defence they would produce them." He then followed him step by step, and after having refuted, in the most satisfactory manner, all his hackneyed charges, he concluded with the following singular allusion: "Mr. Gardiner," said he, "disbelieves all miracles—But is there not something miraculous in his being struck with the Palsy in his right hand, at the very time he was writing all his blasphemies against God and his saints? This is a positive fact. If he will believe, perhaps he may be made whole."

[85] About this time the Rev. Dr. Belknap published his history of New Hampshire. This bigotted and prejudiced writer, like most of his Predecessors in New England thought proper to foist into his work some very illiberal and highly unjustifiable assertions of the Catholic Church as well as scandalous insinuations touching the character of one of her most distinguished missionaries, the Rev. **Sebastian Rasles.*** As this history was

*Dr. Belknap is not the only prejudiced and illiberal writer who has endeavoured to asperse the character of this great and truly good man. Frederick Butler, still more recently, in his history of the United States (Vol. 1. page 235.) thus speaks of him: "This Jesuit, (Father Rasles) practised all the arts of his order upon these savages of the forest. He taught them the doctrine of salvation, through Jesus Christ, the Son of God; but, at the same time led them to believe **that Mary the mother of Jesus Christ, was a french woman; that he was murdered by the English, and that it was lawful, right and best, for all good Christians to butcher the English!!!** How mean, how contemptible must the writer be, who could descend to re-[86]hearse so unblushing a falsehood! It is truly wonderful that such men are not afterwards ashamed to appear before the much read at the time, the Rev. Mr. Thayer thought it a duty incumbent upon him to address him a letter on the subject, and, if possible to induce him to correct his blunders in a future edition. But the only answer he received from him was: "It is put into a file entitled, "**Consideranda.**" So much for his love of historical truth! The following is the communication of Dr. Thayer to him on this subject:

"To the Rev. Dr. Belknap, Writer of the History of New Hampshire."
Sir,
I have lately read your interesting history of New Hampshire, and your discourse on the discovery of America. Though you afford much useful information, and shew liberality in many of your remarks, yet, whenever you mention the Roman Catholic Church, you totally disfigure her doctrines. What a pity that [86] a man, so well qualified as you are to instruct your countrymen, should endeavour to rivet the unjust prejudices, in which we New Englanders have all been educated! As I flatter myself that you are open to conviction, I shall take the liberty to remark on a few passages on your books, and shall presume to hope, that, in a future edition, and in the other writings which you propose to publish, you will avoid the same errors.

I take no very particular notice of the terms, **Popish, Romish, Papist,** etc. which so frequently occur; though, as they always express contempt. and are taken in a bad sense, a liberal Protestant ought to avoid them, and substitute in their place, **Catholic** or **Roman Catholic,** by which we designate those of our religion. We always call our dissenting brethren by the names which themselves adopt.

But a matter of more serious consequence, Sir, is, your putting among the Catholic tenets, that, "to break faith with hereticks is no sin."* This assertion you attempt to prove by the conduct of the Missionary Thury. But, perhaps, that gentleman had many reasons for dissuading the Sachems

---

public! How very differently does the learned and liberal Dr. Harris, of Dorchester, write of this same much injured Missionary! In a Memoir, recently published by him, [87] he thus expresses himself of him: "He was a man of superior sense, and profound learning; and particularly skilled in Latin which he wrote with classical purity. As a Missionary he was zealous; and by the Catholics his memory was cherished with veneration. Indeed to have devoted such talents to the instruction and christianizing the savages; to have consented not only to live among them all his days, in the depths of the forests, in an unrepining conformity to their customs, and upon their unpalatable food in irregular and uncertain supplies; but to have taken such long journeys through a rugged wilderness, without shelter or comfortable repose by night, and with incessant fatigue by day; and to have endured such privations, hardships and sufferings, as he did, in discharging the offices of his sacred mission, must extort the admiration of all. And yet influenced, I apprehend, by the prejudices common to the age against the Roman Catholics, and by the resentment excited against the Indians the earlier historians of our country (he might have added, as well as some of the later) have recorded some slanders against Father Rasles which later writers have copied without examining into their truth.

*Hist. of New Hamp. Vol. 1. p. 268.

from fulfilling their treaty with our forefathers; which you should see to be founded in justice, had we knowledge of all the circumstances of that affair. Granting, however, [87] that he acted an unjust and wicked part, it by no means follows that, according to the Catholic religion, it is no sin to break faith with heretics. Catholic priests are often bad men, and may therefore act contrary to the principles which they profess.

You likewise relate the history of the Missionary, Sebastian Rallé,* in a manner that tends to confirm your readers in the same unjust prevention against the Catholic religion. Yet, according to your own account, the New-Englanders did not fulfil one very express condition of their charter, viz. to attempt the conversion of the Indians; did not erect public truck-houses for their convenience, but suffered them to be cheated by private traders; were always encroaching on their hunting-grounds, etc.—while the French "taught them to pray to God;" sent them presents; abstained from seizing on their lands, etc. The good priest, Rallé, at the expense of every comfort and advantage in this life, administered consolation to those poor helpless savages, and undertook to see them righted: Therefore the Catholics hold that no faith ought to be kept with heretics! Instead of breach of faith, I see justice, humanity, and heroic generosity in such behaviour.

It is so far from being a part of our belief, **"that it is no sin to break faith with heretics,"** that in all Catholic countries such a breach of faith is as severely punished, as if it were with Catholics. This imputation is as ancient as the **pretended** reformation of England; and was invented to furnish a plea for persecuting Catholics as enemies to the State, because it was found easier to blacken them than to refute their arguments. This charge has been constantly renewed by our adversaries, though they have been always challenged to produce their proofs. Not only the ancient, but all the modern, writers of our communion have positively declared this abominable position to be no article of their creed. The famous Father O'Leary has distinguished himself on this head, in his dispute with Mr. John Westly. The whole body of English and Irish Catholics have lately expressed their detestation of this falsely imputed tenet. The English, in their petition presented to the House of Commons, "reject, reprobate and abhor the doctrine, **that faith is not to be kept with heretics,** as contrary to religion, morality and common honesty. They hold and solemnly declare, that no breach of faith with, or injury to, or hostility against any person whomsoever, can ever be justified under pretence that such person is a heretic or an infidel." The Irish Catholics, in their declaration made by their general committee, say: "We hold it as an unchristian and impious

*Vol. II. p. 46, etc.

principle, **that no faith is to be kept with heretics.** This doctrine we detest and reprobate, not only as contrary to our religion, but as destructive of morality, of society, and even of common honesty; and it is our firm belief, that an oath made to any person, not of the Catholic religion, is equally binding as if it were made to any Catholic whatsoever." These pieces, Sir, have both appeared in our public papers.

If you still insist, that this point belongs to our belief, I beg you to have the goodness to show it me in our creeds or in our general councils, where we always expect to find the dogmas of our religion. For my part, I cannot discover this article in any of our creeds, from that which is called the Apostles' down to that more particular one that was published by Pope Pius the 4th; nor can I trace it in any decree of our general councils, from that which was held at Jerusalem, a few years after the ascension of our Lord, down to that which was assembled in the city of Trent.

I pass on to your other work. In the first place, it appears somewhat singular, that, in a discourse expressly commemorative of the advantages of the discovery of America, for which the world is wholly indebted to Catholics, and in some degree to a Catholic priest,* you should take occasion to blacken the religion of the hero and heroine whom you undertake to panegyrize.[11]

You say (p. 31.) that **"the ancient imperfect system of geography became a part of the creed of the Roman church, and was defended by the court of inquisition."**† This assertion seems rather hasty; for we do not read, that either Isabella, Perez, Columbus, or the physician Paul, were ever accused, or even suspected, of heresy, though they did all they could to destroy that system. Now, considering the extreme jealousy our church has always shown in preserving the sacred depositum of the faith, those persons would certainly have been arraigned and punished, if that old system were then a part of the Catholic creed—In that case, Paul of Florence would never have been suffered to declare (as he does) that **"the voyage round the globe was honourable and glorious among all Christians."**

I do not recollect any thing in the history of our church which can afford any reasonable pretext for this accusation. Pray, Sir, when did the **"infallible chair"** decide upon geographical questions?

It would not be fair to repeat the history of Galileo or of Virgilius, since the church gave no judgment in either case. The alarm which those men occasioned in their time was **wholly** on account of the Redeemer's honour.

---

*PEREZ—Discourse, p. 22.

†Upon inquiry, you will **perhaps** find that the establishment of the inquisition was posterior to, or at most coeval with, the discovery of America.

Virgilius advanced, that **"there is another world and other men under the earth, or another sun and moon"** (quod alius mundus et alii homines sub terrâ sint, seu alius sol et luna). Pope Zachary ordered Virgilius to come to Rome that his doctrine might be examined; but he pronounced no sentence. It was not the idea of the antipodes or of the spherical figure of the earth that startled the good pontiff, but the opinion that there was on earth another race of men, not descended from Adam, nor redeemed by the blood of Christ. It is nothing to our purpose, whether the Pope was misinformed or not—But supposing that a condemnation **really** took place, and that (if you please) in support of the old imperfect system of geography, or of the non-rotundity of the earth; yet be assured, Sir, that Catholics themselves would not respect it, because they consider the Pope's decrees as binding, **only** when they concern some point of religion, and when they are received by the universal church.

I more readily make allowance for the mistakes you committed in the first volume of your History of New Hampshire, because it appeared in 1780; but that, after so many opportunities of better information, in the year 1792, you should denominate the Catholic religion "idolatry,"* and should doubt whether our Indian converts "have not changed their original superstitions for others,"* does not look very candid. You here insinuate that we are not even Christians: And that this is your idea I conclude from your saying, that "the Moravians seem to have an art of attaching savage nations to their faith—beyond any **other denomination of Christians;"*** which no man can pronounce with truth, who admits our title to Christianity, and who knows any thing of the wonders which our missioners have performed, and still perform, among the Indian tribes. This exclusion of us from the Christian name appears a little contrary to the prevailing sentiments of this land, where for salvation you require **at most** a belief of what are called the fundamentals of religion. Now which of these fundamental points to we deny? Is it the doctrine of three divine persons in one God? Is it the doctrine of the incarnation, of the redemption, of original sin, of the general resurrection and judgment, of the absolute eternity of hell torments, of the necessity of grace for beginning and ending every good work, of the free-agency of the human will, etc.? You know, or might know, Sir, that our church firmly believes and tenaciously maintains all these capital articles of divine revelation. And we have so frequently explained ourselves on the eucharist, the Saints and their images, that few, except the most ignorant among you, accuse us of idolatry on those heads.

*Discourse, p. 51,52
**P. 54

This **superstition and idolatry,** which you impute to our Indian converts, is the very same which all Christian nations once professed. It was this which formed the greatest heroes of the kingdom from which we derive our origin—an Alfred the Great, a Sir Thomas Moore, etc. It was under its influence that princes, princesses and other personages learned to practice the virtues of the gospel, such as humility, alms-deeds, contempt of the world, etc.—that the universities of Cambridge, Oxford, and many others, were founded. I could run through all the different ages, from the Apostles down to the present day, and show that no one people ever received the gospel but from preachers commissioned by the Popes: I could defy you to point out a single heathen nation that ever received its Christianity from any society separated from ours; which **alone** inspires its ministers with a pure and generous zeal for extending the reign of Jesus Christ.

It would be worth your while to inquire why the sects do not make the same exertions in the cause of their Redeemer, and why his blessing has not hitherto crowned the feeble efforts which they have made.*

Our **idolatrous, superstitious** Indians, according to the testimony of the most competent judges, Protestant as well as Catholic, show forth the Christian virtues in a much greater degree than could be expected from people of their way of life: They even put to shame civilized Christians of all denominations. They have a spirit of humility, of prayer, of self-denial, of chastity, of charity, etc.**

Could you reasonably expect to make them better, were you yourselves to be their teachers? But this is not likely to be the case. For, as you very wisely remark, "you had better first agree among yourselves, what the truths of the gospel are,"† before you begin to preach among the savages. If we are allowed to form a conjecture concerning the present dissenters from our church by those of ancient times, and by yourselves hitherto, this agreement will not speedily take place.†† It seems to me, there is an in-

---

*The reason of this unfruitfulness you will, perhaps, find in their being sects. "Ab arbore frange ramum, fractus germinare non poterit. A fonte praecide rivum, praecisus arescet."—St. Cypr. **De Unitate Ecclesiae.**

This charity they show by praying most cordially for the conversion of the **erring brethren. This is the tender name they give to all Protestants, as I am informed by a dissenting minister, who resided near them for many years. He expressed to me how much this surprised him, because he expected that they had imbibed from their instructors a spirit of hatred and persecution against those who are of our church.

†P. 52.

†† A famous artist once made a painting in which all the different nations of the earth were represented, in the peculiar dress of their country. Instead of clothing the Frenchman, he drew him in a shirt with a bundle of cloth under his arm. Being asked his reason for this singularity, he replied: "The French dress themselves in so many different ways, and change their fashions so often, that whatever dress I should have put on him, in a very short time he could not be known. Having the stuff, he may cut it to his liking."

It being impossible, likewise, to represent exactly the doctrine of the Protestants, on account of its constant variation, we leave them their Bible, that every one may form from it whatever profession of faith he pleases.

creasing division of sentiment among you. Your present appearance of union **entirely** consists in an indifference about all points of faith, in a toleration of one another for mutual ease and peace, and in a fixed hatred and
contempt for the Roman Catholic church, which **alone** has Jesus Christ for
founder.

Be pleased, Sir, to excuse these few observations on your own writings,
which I have made according to the duty of my office, in virtue of which I
am constituted a defender of the Catholic doctrines. I think that,
throughout the whole, I have treated you with Christian moderation and
politeness. At least I have not intentionally failed in either.

I have the honour, Reverend Sir, to subscribe myself

Your very Humble Servant. John Thayer, Catholic Missionary

Boston, July 26. 1793.

[88] The last piece, which attracted the notice of the Rev. Mr. Thayer,
was the printed sermon of the Rev. Dr. Lathrop. We have never seen any
Copy of this discourse, and consequently cannot furnish our readers with
any extracts from it. But it is quite evident that it contained little else than
a mere repetition of the same hackneyed charges against Catholicks which
have been more than a thousand times triumphantly refuted, as the following answer will abundantly show.

To the Rev. Dr. L A T H R O P.

SIR,

WHILE the collection of my pieces is now in the press, your Discourse falls
into my hands. As many persons, my friends at least, will expect my
remarks, I shall endeavour to gratify them, as far as the shortness of the
time will permit. Your pamphlet is called, **A Lecture on the Errors of
Popery.** A more proper title would have been, **The Errors of Dr. Lathrop,**
or of the Protestant authors whom he has servilely copied.

As you took for text, **"Being lords over God's heritage,"** (1 Pet. v. 3) you
ought, if you intended to avoid confusion of ideas, to have shown what is
meant by lording it over God's heritage: which would naturally have led
you to say, that every exercise of power is not lording it, but that this expression imports an usurpation of authority which has not been lawfully
conferred. You ought next to have shown, that the Roman Catholic church
thus lords it. And here you should have produced those **"arguments from
Scripture and reason, which** (you say, p. 30) **are the only weapons of your
warfare,"** in order to overturn the claim of our church, to regulate the faith
of Christians. You know she pretends to prove, and from the Bible too, that
she has a divine commission for this purpose. Perhaps you might have been
more successful than your brother Lesslie in disproving this our fundamen-

tal tenet. Until this is overturned, all attempts to show the usurpations of our church are extremely ridiculous. But having destroyed this our strong hold, you might then, with propriety, have pleaded for the Scripture as the only rule of faith, and have established the independency of conscience. But if our arguments for the church's infallibility are solid, the plain consequence is, that every Christian is bound to submit his conscience to her decisions, and to receive her interpretations of the Scripture. These few observations preclude the necessity of many remarks, which naturally offered themselves, while I perused your Discourse.

All your professions of esteem for the learning and piety of several members of our communion (p. 7, 28) seem only intended to give greater weight to the many groundless charges which you afterwards bring against us. At every page **almost** we meet with misconceptions and misrepresentations. On no one point have you given our real doctrine, except with respect to transubstantiation. To the Pope's supremacy you have added infallibility, (p. 16, 22) which we attribute **only** to the church. To the Saints you make us give the power which belongs to Jesus Christ: (p. 14, 15) whereas we **only** implore the aid of their prayers with our common Mediator, in the same manner as we beg those of our fellow Christians on earth. To indulgencies you make us ascribe "**the forgiveness of all sins past, present, and to come—salvation from hell—redemption from the pains of the infernal regions:**" (p. 21, 22) whereas, in our real creed, an indulgence is nothing but the releasing of the pains due to **sin already forgiven**. These, and many other, unfair representations of the Catholic belief, you might have spared yourself the trouble of writing, and the disgrace of publishing, if you had only spent a day or two in reading over our catechism. For the refutation of the absurdities and lies of Dr. Middleton and others, whom you quote, I refer you to the preface of Bishop Challoner's CATHOLIC CHRISTIAN.

The church, you say, has been guilty of usurpations over the fortunes of men. She, it is true, condemned Wicliff for asserting the possession of temporalities to be contrary to the institution of Christ. For, however dangerous riches may be to those who possess or administer them, the holding of them can be no crime. Our Saviour and his disciples had a common purse, of which Judas was the keeper: The first Christians sold their possessions, and laid the price of them at the feet of the Apostles. It cannot be sinful to copy these models. I imagine that most of you consider Wicliff as erroneous on this head; else so many of your churches would not possess estates. The desire of riches, I presume, is not peculiar to clergymen of our communion. Generally speaking, gentlemen of your cloth have an eye to this particular in the choice of their wives. They are commonly pretty assiduous in their court to the rich; and very frequently, by their attentions, obtain good legacies: And I have never heard of one who was so scrupulous or generous, as to refuse them in favour of the poor relations. There is no vanity in saying that our clergymen have exhibited as many examples of disinterestedness as those of any other society. Ever since the Apostles, the pastors of the Catholic church have always been the fathers of the poor, and, of course, the natural depositaries of the alms which were destined for their use. Instead of dissipating these alms for themselves or relations, they regarded it as a sacred duty to augment, by economy and industry, a fund which was destined for religious and charitable purposes. A great number of religious communities have increased their possessions by laboriously cultivating lands, which, when first bestowed upon them, were of very little value. The maintenance of the miserable, in former times, without any poor tax, the deliverance of entire provinces from the distresses of famine, the erection of vast numbers of noble hospitals, seminaries of learning, and temples, the establishment of missions throughout almost the whole world, are so many witnesses that the riches of the church have been **habitually** employed according to their destination. The instances of the contrary are the crimes of individuals, and not of the church, which has always condemned them. The church, far from encouraging avarice in the clergy, has, in several councils, forbidden the acceptance of donations to the prejudice of poor relations.

You make a lamentable outcry against the cruelty and persecution of our church. (p. 28) If some of her members have been persecutors, you must attribute it to human nature, and not to their religion. Men of all religions have persecuted in their turn, either to keep or to get possession. Were I, by way of recimination, to call your attention to the conduct of Luther, Calvin, and their followers on the continent of Europe, and to the state of Catholics under Protestant government in England, Ireland and Scotland, and even in North-America, from its first settlement, until our happy revolution,—it would appear that the reformers, considering they are not yet of 300 years standing, have made a laudable progress in the science of persecution. But I scorn to lay open old wounds, when no other end can be effected by it than to widen the breach which charity should incline every Christian to endeavour to close. Had this charity been your guide, Sir, we should not have seen you undertake, in these days of liberal sentiment, to rake together a few scattered transactions, performed in different ages by **in-dividual** Catholics, and charge them to the **whole church**, of which they were members:—We should not have read, in the very beginning of your Discourse, of the **"idolatry, tyranny, usurpations, damnable heresies, fatal errors, abominable superstitions, and other crying wickednesses of the**

Romish church; that she is that mystical Babylon, that man* of sin, that apostate church spoken of in the New Testament."—You would have disdained to repeat this language which was dictated in the days of religious rancour.—Instead of accepting the office, to which you were invited by the University, of blackening your fellow Christians, you would have solicited your brethren to join their efforts to your's to abolish altogether a foundation, whose object is to nourish animosity among American citizens. The Pope no longer appears at the head of your Primer, to affright your children; his effigy is no longer burnt on the fifth of November; no longer likewise should he be held up as a bugbear to terrify our collegians.

All the facts which you have heaped up, require a long explanation, and when explained, are nothing to what ought always to be the main question among candid Protestants, viz. Has the Catholic church ever taught, or does she now teach, any errors dangerous to salvation? All the rest is nothing to the purpose. We, as well as you, condemn the Popes who have usurped authority over kings. There always were a great number of Catholics who reprobated this conduct, without being excluded from our communion; which proves that the right of Popes over sovereigns was never an article of our faith. It is ever the conduct of individuals which you impute to the church. It is proper, however, to observe, that all those princes, whom the Popes have attempted to depose, were tyrannical oppressors of their subjects, and that the church alone at that time had power and credit enough to resist their vexations. This may, perhaps, entitle them to our gratitude, as the protectors of the people, and the friends of humanity.

Considering how often, from Luther to the present day, the prophecy of the Pope's speedy downfall has been repeated and turned out false, in your place, Sir, I would not have hazarded it again. (p. 30) The present commotions in Europe, on which you ground your prediction, so far from foreboding the destruction of our church, will, on the contrary, if we may judge from what has already happened, extend her empire to countries where she was scarcely known before.

The confession you make, (p. 7) that "Protestant churches still retain errors which many in their communion wish to see reformed," would afford me a fine field to prove, that they cannot be the church of Jesus Christ, which is ever the pillar and ground of the truth (1 Tim. iii. 1)—and to point out the horrible dangers to which the simple believers are exposed, surrounded as they are with so many errors. But this would lead too far.

I conclude by offering myself again as a "champion to defend the

---

*These are the words of Mr. Dudley, the founder of the lecture. They contain a bull: the Church (she) being called a man of sin.

doctrines of the church of Rome," confident that I should not "retire
without notice," (p. 31) if you, or any other of your brethren, were so abundantly provided, as you pretend, with **arguments from Scripture and reason**
to refute me. But perhaps you are so sparing of them at present, that you
may reserve them against those who may escape from the ruins of Popery
into this land, and **"attempt to seduce your children."**

I am, Rev[erend] Sir, your very humble servant,

JOHN THAYER, **Catholic Missionary.**
Boston, Sept. 27, 1793.

P.S. A Protestant, to whom I read the above, put me in mind, that I ought
to have said something of St. Peter's having been in Rome, which you in-
sinuate to be doubtful. To this I say that there is no one historical fact bet-
ter proved. The ancient Fathers who have attested it, are, St. Irenaeus,
Bishop of Lyons, St. Denys, Bishop of Corinth, Caius and Origen, quoted by
Eusebius, Tertullian, St. Cyprian, Arnobius, Lactantius, Eusebius, St.
Athanasius, St. Cyril of Jerusalem, St. Ambrose, St. Jerome, Sulpitius
Severus, St. Austin, St. John Chrysostom, Orosius, St. Peter Chrysologus,
St. Optatus, Theodoret, and many others.—St. Peter's being at Rome was
never called in question by any man, Infidel or Christian, Catholic or
Heretic, [89] "for thirteen or fourteen hundred years after Christ. Grotius,
a learned Protestant, writes, that **no Christian ever doubted but St. Peter
was at Rome.** Chamierus, another learned Protestant, tells us, that **all the
Fathers, with great accord, have asserted that Peter went to Rome and
governed that Church;** and Dr. Pearson, the Protestant Bishop of Chester,
one of the most eminent men that the reformation has produced, has
demonstrated that St. Peter was at Rome, and that the Bishops of Rome
are his successors. A little more acquaintance, therefore, with ecclesiastical history, or even with your own authors, would have induced you
to suppress the insinuation, that St. Peter was never at Rome."

"I suppose the gentlemen, to whom I addressed the above letters, instead
of answering, intend [sic] to come off by affecting to treat me with silent
contempt. This treatment may satisfy the ignorant, and perhaps a few par-
tial friends; but men of sense, an impartial public, will impute their silence
to the true reasons, viz: the hardness of their cause, and their incapacity to
defend it. And this so much the more, as I have promised to answer every
argument, when unaccompanied by scurrility and personality whether it be
subscribed by the authors name or not.

Boston, October 19. 1793.

John Thayer"

[90] Thus did the Rev. Mr. Thayer repel single handed all the attacks of the adversaries of Catholicity in the town of Boston, at this time, the most hostile of all the cities in the Union to the Mother Church. As he never suf- fered an argument from any quarter against his religion to go unanswered, he undoubtedly effected much good, and must have created a favourable opinion of the Catholic religion in the minds of many. The fact is, however enlightened, in other respects, the generality of the citizens of this Metropolis were, it is very evident, that their information, at this period, on catholic subjects was extremely limited. How, in fact, could it be otherwise when we consider that all the knowledge which they possessed of it, was wholly derived from the declamations of the Pulpit, and the mis- representations of the most embittered prejudice? The very ministers who were in the habit of inveighing most against us, had themselves never studied our principles, and only knew them from the misrepresentations of our avowed enemies. They had read the angry invectives of the Tillotsons, the Burnets, the Seckers, and a host of others, and had imbibed their spirit—with these they remained satisfied; and as it was, also, their tem- poral interest not to investigate the truth of, but rather to declaim against Catholicity, they would take no trouble to inform themselves correctly on this subject. They might be said in one sense to resemble **Demetrius, the silversmith,** as recorded in the 19th Chapter of the Acts of the Apostles, **who made silver temples for Diana, and who brought no small gain to the craftsmen, whom he calling together, with the workmen of like occupation, said: Sirs, you know that our gain is by this trade; and you see and hear, that this Paul by persuasion hath drawn away a great multitude, not only of Ephesus, but almost of all Asia, saying, they are not Gods which are made by hands. So that not only this our Craft is in danger to be set at naught, but also the temples of the great Diana shall be reputed for nothing, yea, and her majesty shall begin to be destroyed whom all Asia and the world worshipeth.** Thus it was with many of the Congregational Ministers, [91] after Rev. Mr. Thayer had begun to announce the truth of the Catholic religion in Boston. They soon took the alarm. At first they thought of repell- ing it by fair argument, by pointing out its gross idolatry, its many supersti- tions and numerous absurdities, such as they had been taught to believe of it by their forefathers; but when they discovered from the various publica- tions of the Rev. Mr. Thayer that they had grossly mistaken its real doctrines—that their own religion was in fact grounded upon a wrong basis, viz: upon a false supposition respecting the Catholic religion—and that the reformation itself could not in consequence be defended with any degree of success, they thought it best, to decline entering, at all, upon the subject in

a formal manner, and chose rather to pursue a different course. They felt indeed the weakness of the cause of protestantism; nevertheless, they were its ministers, and must live. Thus situated, their only alternative was to counteract as far as they were able, the efforts of Rev. M. Thayer and check his influence by continuing to discredit his religion in the minds of the community, by the low base mode of misrepresenting and ridiculing it as formerly, in order thereby to prevent, if possible, the people from embracing it, or even from examining and investigating its true principles;—and in every instance where any conversions should take place under the preaching of the Rev. Mr. Thayer, to use every effort to deter others from following their example, by arming their own relatives against them, by depriving them of the society and assistance of their friends, and by cutting them off even from the means of obtaining a decent maintenance, so long as they should persevere. Discouraging, as it might be, to join the catholic church under these circumstances, the little society still continued to increase and to add daily to its number such as should be saved.

Eng by S. Hollyer.

RIGHT REV. JOHN CHEVERUS.

BISHOP OF BOSTON.

CHAPTER V

THE APOSTOLATE OF

MATIGNON AND CHEVERUS

[92] Things were in this state, when the Rt. Rev. Dr. Carroll, at this time Bishop of Baltimore, thought proper to send the Rev. Francis Matignon to Boston. He arrived on the 20th of August, 1792. This truly great and good man was one of those gifted ecclesiastics whom the storms of the French revolution had thrown upon our shores. Never was there an individual better calculated than he was for the meridian of Boston. Learned, mild, amiable and pious, he was in every respect formed to convince the understanding and to gain the heart. "This excellent man," says an able writer who knew him well,[12] "was born in Paris, on the 10th of November, 1753. Devoted to letters and to religion from his earliest youth, his progress was rapid and his piety conspicuous. He attracted the notice of the learned faculty as he passed through the several grades of classical and theological studies; and having taken the degree of Bachelor of Divinity, he was ordained a Priest, on saturday, the 19th of September 1778, the very day of the month, and week, which 40 years after, was to be his last. In the year 1782, he was admitted a Licentiate, and received the degree of Doctor of Divinity from the college of the Sorbonne in 1785. At this time he was appointed **Regius** Professor of Divinity in the college of Navarre, in which seminary he performed his duties for several years, although his state of health was not good."

"His talents and piety had recommended him to the notice of a Prelate in great credit (the Cardinal de Brienne) who obtained for him the grant of an annuity from the king (Louis XVI.), which was sufficient for all his wants,

145

established him in independance and took away all anxiety for the future. But the ways of Providence are inscrutable to the wisest and best of the children of men. The revolution which dethroned his beloved Monarch, and stained the altar of his God with the blood of holy men, drove Dr. Matignon an exile from his native shores. He fled to England, where he remained several months, and then returned to France to prepare for a voyage to the United States. He landed in Baltimore, and was not long after appointed by [93] Bishop Carroll to the Catholic Church in Boston, at which place he arrived, (as already observed) August 20th 1792.''

"The talents of Dr. Matignon were of the highest order. In him were united a sound understanding, a rich and vigorous imagination, and a logical precision of thought. His learning was extensive, critical and profound, and all his productions were deeply cast, symetrically formed, and beautifully coloured. The Fathers of the Church and the great Divines of every age were his familiar friends.—His Divinity was not merely speculative, nor merely practical; it was the blended influence of thought, feeling and action. He had learned Divinity as a scholar, taught it as a Professor, felt it as a worshipper, and diffused it as a faithful Pastor. His genius and his virtues were understood; for, the wise bowed to his superior knowledge, and the humble caught the spirit of his devotions. With the unbelieving and doubtful, he reasoned with the mental strength of the Apostle St. Paul; and he charmed back the penitential wanderer with the kindness and affection of St. John the Evangelist. His love for mankind flowed in the purest current, and his piety caught a glow from the intensity of his feeling. Rigid and scrupulous to himself he was charitable and indulgent to others. To youth, in a particular manner, he was forgiving and fatherly. With him the tear of penitence washed away the stains of error; for he had gone up to the fountains of human nature, and knew all its weakness. Many retrieved from folly and vice can bear witness how deeply he was skilled in the science of parental government, that science so little understood, and for want of which so many evils arise. It is a proof of a great mind not to be soured by misfortunes, nor narrowed by any particular pursuit. Dr. Matignon, if possible, grew milder and more indulgent as he advanced in years. The storms of life had broken the heart of the man, but out of its wounds gushed the tide of sympathy and universal Christian charity. The woes of life crush the feeble, make more stupid the dull, and more vindictive the proud; [94] but the great mind and the contrite soul are expanded with pure benevolence, and warmed with brighter hopes by suffering—knowing that through tribulation and anguish, the diadem of the Saint is won.''

"In manners Dr. Matignon was an accomplished gentleman, posessing that kindness of heart and delicacy of feeling, which made him study the wants and anticipate the wishes of all he knew. He was well acquainted with the politest courtesies of society, for it must not, in accounting for his accomplishments, be forgotten, that he was born and educated in the bosom of refinement; that he was associated with Chevaliers and Nobles, and was patronized by Cardinals and Premiers. In his earlier life it was not uncommon to see Ecclesiastics mingling in society with Philosophers and Courtiers, and still preserving the most apostolic purity in their lives and conversation. The scrutinizing eye of infidel Philosophy was upon them, and these unbelievers would have hailed it as a triumph to have caught them in the slightest deviations from their professions. But no greater proof of the soundness of their faith or the ardor of their piety could be asked, than the fact, that from all the Bishops in France at the commencement of the revolution, amounting to 138, but four only were found wanting in integrity and good faith, when they were put to the test; and it was such a test, too, that it could have been supported by religion only. In passing such an ordeal, pride, fortitude, philosophy, and even insensibility would have failed. The whole strength of human nature was shrunken and blasted when opposed to the besom of the revolution. Then the bravest bowed in terror, or fled in afright; but then these disciples of the lovely Jesus, taught mankind how they could suffer for his sake."

"When Dr. Matignon came to Boston new trials awaited him. He found the people of New England more than suspicious on the subject of his success; they were suspicious of the Catholic doctrines,—Their ancestors from the settlement of the country, had been preaching against the Church of Rome, and their descendants, even the most enlightened, felt a strong impression of undefined and undefineable [95] dislike, if not hatred towards every Papal relation. Absurd and foolish legends of the Pope and his religion were in common circulation, and the prejudice was too deeply rooted, to be suddenly eradicated. It required a thorough acquaintance with the world to know precisely how to meet these sentiments of a whole people. Violence and indiscretion would have destroyed all hopes of success: Ignorance would have exposed the cause to sarcasm and contempt, and enthusiasm, too manifest, would have produced a reaction, that would have plunged the infant establishment in absolute ruin. Dr. Matignon was exactly fitted to encounter all these difficulties. And he saw them and knew his task. With meekness and humility he disarmed the proud; with prudence and learning and wisdom he met the captious and slanderous; and so gentle and so just was his course, that even the censorious forgot to watch him, and the malicious were too cunning to attack one armed so strong in honesty."

The Rev. Mr. Thayer rejoiced at the acquisition of a co-operator of so great merit, and already began to anticipate from his superior learning and piety the most favourable results to the rising Church in Boston. He received him, in his humble mansion, as an Angel from heaven sent expressly to promote the great cause of the Redeemer in this new section by extending his Church which already began to attract considerable notice. Dr. Matignon applied himself during the first months of his residence with all diligence to the study of the English language, sensible that until he should attain a competent knowledge of this, his usefulness would be greatly circumscribed in New England. He accordingly laboured at it without intermission; and in a short time, such was his progeess, that he was able not only to converse in it freely, but likewise to exhort in it publickly, and even to write it correctly. The Rev. Mr. Thayer was now at liberty to give greater scope to his zeal by taking a wider range [96] and extending his visits to all parts of New England. His excursions were more frequent, and he was able to tarry longer in particular places where his services were more required. In this way he continued to labour announcing the gospel through every considerable town and village and gaining in many places souls to God by reclaiming them from the errors of protestantism and attaching them to the one fold and one shepherd, until the year 1799, when the venerable Bishop of Baltimore anxious to provide for the spiritual necessities of all under his pastoral care withdrew him from the New England mission, and sent him to labour on that of Kentucky, whose vast extent and increasing population seemed to require one of his activity and great zeal.[13]

During the absence of Rev. M. Thayer, which frequently occurred after the arrival of Dr. Matignon, this excellent Priest had to sustain alone the whole weight of the burden of the ministry in Boston, although his constitution was far from being the strongest. This lasted until the 3d of October, 1796, when the Rev. John Cheverus arrived to take part in his labours. This great and distinguished man, says the able writer of his memoir, from whom I quote,[14] "was born at Mayenne, in the province of the same name, on the 28th of january, 1768. His family were highly respectable. At an early age he entered into the ecclesiastical state, and in two or three years afterwards, when thirteen or fourteen years of age, was preferred to a benefice, by the late King of France, Louis XVIII., then Monsieur. It being required of those who applied to the University for the degree of D.D., to bring forward some young gentleman they had instructed, to show by the progress of the pupil, the knowledge and skill of the instructer—once a salutary provision, then a mere fiction of the schools—M. Cheverus was selected by three or four of the candidates for the doctorates, to support a thesis on some given subject, on their behalf; and on these occasions, he acquitted himself with honor.

At this period, he was on terms of intimacy and friendship with Abbe McCarthy, now one of the most celebrated preachers in France. The Abbe McCarthy, whose parents were obliged to leave Ireland on account of their religion, often proposed to M. Cheverus, to teach him the English language, but the latter declined the task, thinking the acquisition would not be of much service to him as an ecclesiastic, and that his time would be more profitably spent in Oriental literature.

M. Cheverus was ordained December 18th, 1790, at the last public ordination in Paris, before the revolution. The canons of the Catholic church, requiring a candidate for orders to be, at least, twenty five years of age, a special dispensation from the Holy See became necessary for this ordination, Mr. Cheverus being at that time, not quite twenty three. The Bishop of Mans, to whose Diocess M. Cheverus belonged, had, noticing his superior talents and acquirements, applied for this dispensation, in order to have, at this threatening and perilous period, the advantage of his support in the church. M. Cheverus soon after entering into priest's orders, was appointed pastor of the church in his native parish, and vicar-general of the Diocess. These early distinctions gave him a celebrity not acquired by many, venerable for their age and virtues, among the ecclesiastics of that time. He had not long resided at Mayenne, when the persecutions of the clergy commenced. The storm of the revolution grew fiercer and darker every hour, and the infuriated spirit of Paris, was then pervading every village and hamlet in France, particularly those in the vicinity of the great city. In some places however, the clergy had a strong hold on the affections of the people; this was strikingly the case at Mayenne. The municipal authorities attempted to persuade M. Cheverus to take the constitutional oath, but on account of his popularity and extensive influence, were fearful of proceeding, at first, to acts of violence. On one occasion, they entered the church with a military force, while he was at the altar offering up the holy sacrifice of the mass. In the midst of this solemn service, he turned and asked what they wanted? The reply was, we come to make you take the constitutional oath, or go with us to prison. He requested them to wait till he had gone through the service, and he would give them an answer. But the excitement among the congregation was such, at this outrage, the military thought it prudent to retire, for the time, and press the subject no further. The situation of M. Cheverus at this period, was alarming; for several months, he thought each day was the last of his life; and at one time, it was rumored that he was to be carried away, or assassinated. As this report spread, the inhabitants armed themselves in the best manner they could, and assembled before day-light around his father's house, to prevent any violence from being done to their beloved pastor, exhibiting a disposition to proceed to extremities in avenging any insults offered him. After his surprize was over, he exhorted them to abstain from any rash act on his account and dismissed them with an entreaty to return peaceably to their homes; and they did so. The municipal authorities urged him to quit the town, but he was unwilling to leave his flock, for he considered his charge a sacred one, although he was well aware that his life was in continual danger. At length however, being apprehensive of some injury happening to his father and friends on his account, he told the Prefect he would not resist the civil authorities, in temporal matters, but that he should not leave the city unless he was taken by the shoulder and driven away; upon which he was immediately conducted out of the city, and was concealed for some time among his friends. In the summer of 1792, he, with the Bishop of Dol, and several other clergymen, were ordered to repair to a certain place, the name of which is not recollected, and report themselves every day to a civil officer. A month elapsed in this manner, when they were ordered to retire to a monastery or convent, the inmates of which, had been driven out of doors by the fanatical spirit of the times. In this place, they were confined for a fortnight, momentarily expecting to hear the doors grate upon their hinges, and to see the murderer with his dagger at their breasts. The place was destitute of furniture or provisions, and their distresses were great, until partially relieved by a few courageous friends to humanity and religion. Delivered from this confinement, M. Cheverus repaired to Paris, and was concealed in that city on the second and third of September, the memorable days of the massacre of the clergy. In a few days after this bloody scene, on the ninth or tenth, he left Paris, disguised in a military dress, having a passport bearing the name of his brother, whom, though much younger, he greatly resembled. He never spoke of his sufferings, during his two last years in France, or his difficulties or privations in England, without being so much affected as to distress his friends; and they forbore to make those inquiries, or to learn those details, which would now be so deeply interesting to the community.

On his arrival at Dover, he could not speak a word of English. He then regretted not having followed the advice of his friend McCarthy. He was in a strange land, without being able to tell his common wants to those around, in any language they understood. In the commencement of October, his father succeeded in making a remittance for his immediate support, which he repeated for some time, so that M. Cheverus was never under the necessity of receiving any portion of that bounty the British government so promptly afforded to the suffering French clergy, but was at times able to assist some of his brethren.

In January, 1793, he took up his residence in the house of a Protestant clergyman, who, in addition to his pastoral duties, had five or six young men with him, preparing for the university. M. Cheverus was employed in giving these scholars lessons in the languages and mathematics. He found the conversation of these youths the best instructer in the English language. Finding in the neighborhood a few Catholic families, who had no pastor or place of worship, he applied to Dr. Douglass, R.C. Bishop of the London District, and obtained permission to officiate for them. A house was procured, and part of it converted into a chapel, while the other part he appropriated for his own use as a dwelling house; and from this arrangement he was enabled to invite a few clergymen to reside with him.

While in England, he was invited and strongly solicited to take charge of a college at Cayenne. This he declined; for he then cherished the strongest hopes of soon returning to France; but the hour of return was not at hand.

In 1795, he was invited by Doctor Matignon, with whom he had been slightly acquainted in Paris, to join him in Boston. Having informed the Bishop of Mans of his intention of crossing the Atlantic, M. Cheverus received an affectionate letter from the aged Prelate, then an exile as well as himself; praising the zeal, still expressing fears that his young friend would undertake too much, and the loss, if he should not return, would be irreparable to his Diocess; but nothing could alter his determination, and he arrived in Boston, October 3d, 1796. Shortly after he came to Boston, Bishop Carroll offered him the pastoral charge of St. Mary's church in Philadelphia, and of other places, but his attachment had become so strong for Doctor Matignon, that he could not think of leaving him. The services of M. Cheverus could not, without great injury to the Catholic cause in Boston, at that time, have been dispensed with. Doctor Matignon, a name ever dear to religion and learning, was truly a great man, content with doing good; but at this time, he required the best assistance. The germ of a church was starting amidst a thousand difficulties, and liable at every moment to be crushed by prejudice and suspicion. There had been several Catholic priests in Boston, before him, and they were very good men; but being over zealous, or not understanding the genius of the people among whom they lived, had fallen into many errors of policy, which the prudent, pious Matignon was redeeming by slow and sure degrees. It was fortunate for the cause, that such a coadjutor should have been found. Their tastes, their pursuits, their dispositions, were kindred, and they became inseparable. Those who witnessed the manner in which they lived together, will never forget the refinement and elevation of their friendship;—it surpassed those attachments which delight us in classical story, and equally the lovely union of the son of Saul and the minstrel of Israel.

Learning and virtue will have weight even among those of a different faith. A pious Protestant clergyman, considered it his duty, to go and talk to these Catholics, and see if it were not possible to convince them of the errors of their belief; but after an interval of some length, he returned to his friends, who were waiting to hear of the success of the mission, exclaiming **"these men are so learned there is no doing anything with them in argument; so pure and evangelical in their lives, there is no reproaching them; and I fear it will give us much trouble to check their influence."** The enlightened part of the community, however, indulged no fears from the establishment of a Catholic Church in Boston; on the contrary, made no small exertions to assist in building up one.They saw the United States was extending her arms to embrace emigrants from all nations, and knew these foreigners would be better governed by their own creeds than ours, which but few could understand, who were not educated in this republican country. The Catholics were increasing at this time in Boston, and many gentlemen subscribed liberally, to assist in erecting a church for them. At the head of the subscribers was the President of the United States, at that time, the venerable John Adams. This gentleman has, during a long and eventful life, professed the most liberal sentiments on religious subjects, and has often, amidst bigotry and fanaticism, most fearlessly avowed them. At length, by the efforts of many, a convenient church was erected, and was consecrated by Bishop Carroll, on the 29th of September, 1803, and named THE CHURCH OF THE HOLY CROSS IN BOSTON. This might be considered by all as prosperity; and it was so; but still their resources were scanty, and many privations were felt by these divines. Both Doctor Matignon and his colleague were well connected in France; but had no opportunity at the time of their escape to gathermuch for future support; and most of their flock were exiles too, and were struggling for themselves. It was not always that the necessaries of life were at the command of Matignon and his colleague were well connected in France; but had no opportunity at the time of their escape to gather much for future support; and menced his journey, by day and night, like the primitive missionaries of the church, not to disturb the faith of others, nor to combat heresy, but to shrive some humble Catholic who was dying among strangers, and whose soul was panting to catch the last consolations of the religion he professed. Often he continued his travels to the wilds of Maine, to instruct and comfort a few Catholics scattered through that country; but the great object of his visit was to enlighten and cherish the sons of the forest in that region—and at each visit he spent two or three months with the Passamaquoddy and

Penobscot tribes of Indians. Numerous instances of their affection for their spiritual guide were frequently mentioned by him, and he always thought the aborigines of this country had more character than the early historians had been willing to allow them.

After the Concordat of 1801, the friends of M. Cheverus were anxious to have him return to France, and the letters of his father and friends were affectionate, and almost unanswerable. They detailed their claims to his society with such minuteness and force as to stagger him. At one moment he was nearly yielding to their entreaties; but the distress of the Catholics in every part of the country, at the thought of losing him, was so great, and the reasons offered by Bishop Carroll,* with his love of Doctor Matignon, were superior to all his friends in France could say. On the Sunday after Easter, in 1803, he announced to his flock, that the conflict in his mind was over, and he should stay with them to share their good and ill fortune. In the year 1808, it was thought by the most enlightened of the Catholics, with Bishops Carroll and Neale, then the only R.C. Prelates in the United States, that the cause required a See in New England. Of course, it was proposed to Doctor Matignon to take this office; but without letting his colleague know any thing definitively on the subject, he, with Bishop Carroll, prevailed on the Holy See to appoint M. Cheverus to the office. This was done in the year 1808. But from the troubles of that period in Europe, and particularly from the afflictions of the Sovereign Pontiff, the bulls were not forwarded until the year 1810. On the first of November, in that year, he was consecrated at Baltimore, and returned to Boston to receive the congratulations of his friends. He was happy with his people and those around; but felt at times some strong emotions for his kindred and his native land. This was natural: but he had learned to quiet the throbbings of his heart by the application of principles of duty. The maxims he taught, he had learned to practise.

*Note

Baltimore, April 9, 1803.

Rev. SIR:—After reading your letter of March 31st, received yesterday, I am not surprised that you are agitated with doubts, trouble and anxiety. Perhaps I am too much interested in the welfare of the faithful committed to my pastoral care, to decide your doubts, and remove your perplexity. However, you are entitled to my opinion on a subject, in which both of us, and many besides us, are deeply concerned.

I take it for granted, that you were, by the usual and regular law of the church, attached to your native Diocess, and subject to its bishop; and, therefore, that you were bound not to abandon it, and enter into the service of any other Diocess, without obtaining license for that purpose, as prescribed by the canons; which canons likewise subject those prelates to the censures of the church, who shall employ clergymen abandoning their own Diocess without proper authority.

Such is the **usual and regular law of the church:** but this law supposes, evidently, that the clergyman, who becomes subject to it, shall have employment assigned to him in his Diocess, and that he may be supported in its services and exercise his ministry, at least as long as he does not forfeit the confidence of his Ordinary Diocesan Bishop, by his own misconduct. But if events take place, even much less violent than those produced by the late revolution, so that a clergyman cannot hope for support, protection or safety; if his bishop can no longer employ him; and the clergyman, in consequence of the necessities pressing on him, be induced to seek for safety, and undertake elsewhere the care of souls; it appears clear to me, that he is no

While most men do little more in life, than to labor for themselves or their dependants, there are some in every age and country, who seem born for mankind, and whose habits, reasonings and feelings separate them from the rest of the world, and whose actions prove, that the true christian philanthropist is not an ideal character, created in the dreams of fancy and fiction. I speak not of high minded statesmen or patriot warriors; they live on the rolls of honor, and the world is ready to do them justice; they are the

longer bound in justice to the service of his former Diocess—what claims of charity may remain, shall be considered afterwards.

That the general and usual obligation of ecclesiastical institutions was dissolved with respect to the persecuted clergy of France, so that they were at liberty to enter into other engagements, incompatible with their primitive connection with their native Diocess, or former parish, appears evident from various considerations. 1st. If persecuted priests, expelled from their benefices, having annexed to them the care of souls, should have been nominated to valuable prebends or professorships in foreign countries, with this express condition, that they should hold their places for a certain term of years; might they not have accepted such appointments, though it was possible, that before the expiration of the stipulated term of years, peace would be restored to their country? 2d. In the same manner, when French clergymen, wandering in want through the world, and victims of persecution, accepted offers of employment, made to them by Catholic prelates, and obtained the respect, confidence and veneration of the faithful placed under their care, is it not to be thought, that these have acquired to themselves that right of service, for the rendering of which, their former parishoners could not afford sufficient protection? 3d. Clergymen persecuted at home, crossed dangerous seas, and travelled to a vast distance to seek the occasions of rendering that service, which they were not allowed to render in their own country: but a change happening in this their country, is it to be thought that the clergymen are obliged to measure back the same seas, and abandon those who received them in their distress, and profited by their instructions?

These are some of the many reasons, which persuade me, that your original connexion with your native Diocess was so far dissolved, as to leave you at liberty, by the law of self preservation, to seek elsewhere that necessary protection which you could not find in your own country. Moreover, the changes made in your own Diocess and parish, render them no longer the same. The pope, in his bull, for the concordat, expressly suppresses and totally extinguishes all the pre-existing Diocesses of France. Their extinction necessarily drew with it the extinction of all claims founded on their existence, and consequently the new Diocess and Parish are foreign to you, and without any rights extending to your person or services.

To make an examination of this matter, as satisfactory to you as possible, I divested myself as much as I could, of every personal consideration, and endeavored to view it solely in itself; and the result of my reflections has been more satisfactory to my mind, than when I first began them. I am fully persuaded, that you are not obliged, by your previous engagements to, or connexion with your former Diocess or parish, to return to them.

But do not the claims of charity compel you to resume the spiritual care of those, whose attachment to you has been so durable, and who perhaps, after the sacrifices of the revolution, are much in need of your zealous and charitable services?

In determining this, there is not much difficulty. Considering the number of excellent clergymen in France, the resources of that populous country, the numerous ecclesiastical seminaries already, and the many more, soon to be established, there is but little danger of the faithful remaining destitute of the bread of christian doctrine, and the graces annexed to the sacraments. But what resources will remain for those, whom you have begun to train here in the principles and duties of true religion, if you quit your present station? none at all. The labor you have bestowed, will be lost to them, and the claims of charity are assuredly stronger in their behalf, than in behalf of those, who are not, and probably will never be in the same extreme necessity. With regard to the solicitations of your respectable father, and your other near relations, it becomes me not to interfere by offering my advice. You must decide on them: and I ought to say only, that I flatter myself with the hope, that the service of God, the extension of the kingdom of Jesus Christ, the salvation of souls purchased by his death, will speak more forcibly than the voice of flesh and blood. I received with yours a very respectable letter from some of the chiefs of the congregation of Boston, and to-day another from the much respected Doctor Matignon. I will send an answer to both in a few days, and promise myself, that you will at all events remain till I have the pleasure of seeing you, when the business may be discussed farther, if you should still have any doubts in your mind.

I am, with the highest esteem, Rev[erend] Sir, your most obedient servant,

†J., BISHOP OF BALTIMORE.

theme of every pen, and their praise is in every mouth. But I mean the quiet, pious man, who asks nothing of human glory, and who does good, and blushes to find it fame. These men pursue their journey in making the world wiser and better, looking only for their reward in an approving conscience and the hopes of heaven. They think nothing of all their sacrifices; for in them the ordinary passions are subdued, and ambition, "**the last infirmity of noble minds,**" through piety, yields to the love of humble duties. In contemplating them, who can doubt that human nature is permitted to approach perfection, and assume a near and sweet resemblance to the MAN DIVINE. The Pagan world was full of instances of lofty and virtuous conduct, which dignified and exalted human nature. History and fable have preserved the fact. The Orphean lyre was but a type of the union of genius and virtue, struggling to recover the long lost happiness of man; but at the same time, it clearly shadowed out his inability to retain it when apparently secured. The **day spring from on high** had not visited man. Jesus of Nazareth, who **was the light and the way,** had not come to share our natures and to develop our destinies. The hero, the seer and the sage, had existed before christianity was known—but the saint is a character which has been added to the catalogue since. Socrates, the wise and the good, had not, like St. John, a master's bosom on which to lean his head, where all was purity and love. Far be it from me to say, that the lawgivers, psalmists and prophets of the early ages, and from the **chosen people,** should be passed without reverence and admiration; for some of them **walked with God and were not,** and to others were vouchsafed the horses and the chariot of fire; but it was not until the birth of Immanuel, that it was found that man was made **but little lower than the angels,** and **that the second Adam, had restored the ruins of the first.** When human nature was not so refined and pure, the traits of character were, perhaps, more readily discovered, as the primary rays of light show their distinct colors on the rain drop and the passing cloud; but in the fulness of day, and in serene skies, the sun-beams are commingled, and assume a common appearance. The humility of our Great Teacher is diffused through every action of his followers. The man of God does not now call down the fire of heaven to consume his enemies, but wrestles with his Maker that they may be forgiven. He does not now send to watch the new-born cloud when he has prayed for rain, and gaze upon it until it has spread over the land; but rests in humble resignation, in the belief that his communion with heaven will at some time spread over the moral world, as the gentle dews of the night fall on the rose whose fragrance is to be thrown upon the breath of the morning.

If there is not so much awe and majesty in the character of the legate of heaven now, as when he was protected, and the authenticity of his mission

proved, by the thunders of Sinai, or some other special interposition of Om-
nipotence, still the advantage is with the present day. We can now approach
the man who instructs us in the laws of God, and dare analyze his claims to
distinction and reverence. There is nothing so sanctified in crape, or sacred
in lawn, that we should not examine the wearer and judge him like other
men.

In delineating the character of M. Cheverus, I fear that I shall not give
satisfaction to any one; for those who know him well, know also that many
things might be added to those found in this sketch; and those who are not
acquainted with him, will wonder, so much in truth could be said of one who
never laid any claim to superiority, but held the peaceful tenor of his way in
the discharge of his duties. I shall speak of him as I knew him.

The literary and scientific acquirements of Bishop Cheverus were of a
high order. He read Greek and Hebrew with great readiness;—he spoke
and wrote Latin as a vernacular tongue, and has often been heard to say,
that if he were to make an argument for his life, he should prefer, before
competent judges, to use the Latin, believing that his thoughts would flow
more readily in that language than in French or English. He was well acquainted with the philosophy of universal grammar, and had made himself
master of the difficulties of the English in its arrangement, construction
and etymology; but he began the study of it too late in life to get rid entirely
of his French accent—this, however, did not diminish the sweetness of his
elocution in reading English.

His eloquence was of the most persuasive order; his manner was sincere
and devotional; his style pure and refined; his voice was clear and
melodious—and every thing he said, seemed to flow from pure and elevated
feelings, and reached every fibre of affection in the breast of his hearers.
With a sound judgment, he suited his arguments and course of reasoning to
his subject, and no one went from his presence without acknowledging the
delight he felt in being in the society of such a man, nor without believing
himself made better by holding communion with such a spirit.

The sermons of M. Cheverus were for the most part extemporaneous,
and in the form of moral and religious lectures. They were succinct and
sweet effusions of piety and affection; at times, however, he poured out his
feelings and reasonings in all the graces of composition and the charms of
eloquence. The seraphim seemed to have touched his lips with a coal from
the altar of the Most High. Whoever heard him, will never forget his address to his flock on the news of the Sovereign Pontiff's release from confinement and return to his ancient dominion. Other joys at the same moment crowded upon his mind, and he indulged his feelings to the full tide of
his delight. These effusions of pulpit eloquence were without effort, for his

heart was full of sympathy for mankind, and he suffered and enjoyed with those near or remote. This feeling had nothing of weakness in it. He was always severe upon those who gave up to a sickly sensibility, which enervates the mind instead of purifying the heart; and always strove to impress upon his friends the necessity of intellectual courage in every vicissitude. He considered life a succession of duties, and a place of preparation for higher employments. At no moment did he ever lose the dignity of his character or the command of himself. The distressed saw his heart like the pure diamond, ready, as it were, to become liquid as water, while he was engraving his own sentiments and feelings, as with the power of the same precious stone, upon the minds of those he came to comfort and instruct.

His variety of talent was remarkable. He could accommodate himself with perfect ease to all grades of society, and understood the business and habits of all. He never checked innocent mirth with austerity, nor suppressed a smile at what was playful or witty, made in its proper time. His remarks always enlivened, illumined and instructed every circle he entered. He never permitted his social feelings to interfere with his professional duties, but he considered them in a good measure united. He was prepared for every occasion and every accident. I have seen him in the morning administering the vows of chastity to the vestal virgin, and exalting her soul to higher and sublimer views, and fanning and raising the flame of devotion in her breast, whose purity and loveliness were already such as to create a wish in the beholder, that in **her orisons all his sins would be remembered.** At noon, I have heard him conversing with politicians, thoroughbred in the ways of the world, and they were watching to catch every principle, fact, or illustration, which fell from his lips—and turning from them to play with some sportive child, and by some kind thing said or done by him, would make infancy happier; or he would start from the social board at a call from the sick, to give the last seal of religion to the penitent's hopes.

To those who made a serious inquiry of him in regard to his doctrines and faith, he returned a solemn and decided answer; but when assailed by croaking bigotry or assuming ignorance, he replied by putting some questions far beyond the depth of the interrogator; or if crowded by good natured curiosity, he got rid of the subject by some adroit evasion which gave no offence. He was not fond of mixed company or large circles, but thrown into them, his conversation was easy and pleasant, and the kindness of his manner threw a charm over every thing he said.

He was accessible at his house at all times; and after the church increased, and his own finances would admit of it, he kept a most hospitable table—it was plain and frugal, but bountiful, and every thing in the house was free as air to his guests, and amongst them were found persons of almost all countries.

His industrious habits gave him time for a great variety of duties. He arose at all seasons of the year at the dawn of the day, or before, and continued his avocations, with unceasing assiduity, until nine in the evening. He seldom, at home or on a journey, suffered a day to go over him, without refreshing his mind by the [97] perusal of some classic; and he seemed to pass from business, and from the altar to the groves of the academy, by a private and short path of his own, and then return to his duties with new vigor, from drinking at the fountains and culling the undying flowers of the muse.''

''Women are often the best judges of the characters of men; for they do not view them through the medium of rivalry, envy or party spirit, as men often do each other; but weigh with accuracy their merits, both of heart and head, when they have an opportunity or right to judge. A priest of the Roman Catholic Church with the vows of celibacy on him, if his reputation be good, is the proper confessor, friend and adviser of women. M. Cheverus numbered among his most intimate friends, a large circle of intellectual females of the Protestant faith, and many of them moving in the higher walks of life. In his judgment and friendship they reposed implicit confidence; and not only consulted him themselves, but taught their children that in every painful or delicate exigency of their lives, to call on him for counsel and direction. They knew his bosom would be a safe repository of their secrets and their griefs, and that his wisdom would suggest the most honorable course of duty. In truth it may be said, that he had as many confidential communications out of the confessional as in it.''[15]

These two truly pious and apostolical men laboured together in the same vineyard ''blessing and being blessed'' for more than twenty years. By their exemplary piety, their care of and unwearied attendance upon the poor, the sick and the infirm, the faithful distribution of the word of God on Sundays and holidays, regular catechetical instructions, the clear and masterly exposition [98] of the doctrines of the Catholic Church joined to their amiable manners and gentlemanly deportment they won by degrees the hearts and gained the affections of every denomination of Christians; prejudices began to disappear, inquiries after truth to be made, and numbers successively to join the Church.

A comparative view of the state of the Church during the first ten years of its existence in Boston, that is from the year 1790 to the year 1800 will enable our readers to form an accurate judgment of the progress of things at this early period.

Anno Dom.	Baptisms	Marriages	Deaths
1790	30	1	4
1791	23	3	4
1792	15	4	2
1793	28	12	11
1794	42	5	18
1795	40	5	9
1796	47	11	6
1797	60	11	10
1798	59	26	34
1799	77	18	8

In the above table, which estimates solely the baptisms, marriages and deaths which were performed, and which occurred solely in Boston, no notice is taken of those which occurred in remote or even in adjacent places. As new Churches arose new Registers were kept of baptisms marriages and deaths in them. Dr. Cheverus was in the habit of visiting annually those Catholics, who were scattered in the various towns of this, and even of some of the adjacent States, in which they were constantly increasing, such as Salem, Newburyport, Portsmouth, Damariscotta, Bristol, Waldoboro, Penobscot and Passamaquoddy (two Indian settlements entirely catholic) Plymouth, New Bedford, Newport etc. In all of these and other places, many of which he annually visited and some others frequently through the year, he never failed to preach, to baptize and administer the other sacraments, to the great delight of his hearers, protestant as well as Catholic, to the great increase of the faith and to the edification and improvement of all.

[99] Hitherto the Catholics had always assembled, for divine worship, in the small Church in School-Street, of which a lease had been taken, as already observed. That lease had now nearly expired. It was all important, therefore, for them to look out for some other place; and as their number had already multiplied considerably beyond what it was when the congregation was first formed, the greater part preferred to purchase at once a Lot of land, and proceed to erect, with as little delay as possible, a Church which should be at once decent and capacious.

Accordingly, on sunday the 31st of March, 1799, a meeting of the whole congregation was held at their usual place of worship, in order to take this matter into consideration. It was there proposed and determined to use every exertion to raise sufficient funds to carry the above object into effect. A Committee was, at the same time, appointed for this purpose, consisting of the following persons, all members of the Church, viz:

The Honourable Don Juan Stoughton, Consul of his Catholic Majesty.

John Magner   Patrick Campbell

Michael Burns   Owen Callaghan

John Duggan   Edmund Connor

And on the following Sunday (April 7th) in conformity with a report of the same Committee, it was unanimously resolved:

"1st That a subscription be immediately opened for the purchase of a piece of ground, as above mentioned; and that half of the money subscribed be paid either immediately, or within three months from this day, and the other half within six months."

2ly That the monies thus paid shall be deposited into the hands of the Treasurer, appointed for that purpose, who shall faithfully lodge the sums, thus raised, in one of the Banks of Boston within seven days after each term of payment, as above specified, or employ them in the purchase of some of the public stocks, bearing interest, according to the advice of the Committee."

3ly That the Deposites so made shall be considered as [100] money belonging to the subscribers, as heretofore annexed, until the same is invested and laid out in or towards the purchase of a piece of ground, and materials for erecting the new contemplated Church."

"4ly That the Rev. Dr. Matignon is and shall be considered as the Treasurer for the receipt of said monies together with his Reverend Colleague M. John Cheverus."

(Signed)

"Don Juan Stoughton, Consul of Spain,

John Magner

Edmund Connor

Michael Burns."

On the same day books were opened for subscription with the following heading or preamble.

"We the Subscribers feeling the necessity of, and earnestly desiring to procure, as soon as possible, the erection of a Church or place of worship, belonging to us, where we, our children, relations, friends, and all persons professing our holy religion, may have the inestimable happiness of worshipping God, hearing his word, and enjoying all the benefits of the free and public exercise of our religion, to which we have a right by the free constitution of this State and of the Federal Government, promise and pledge ourselves punctually to pay, for the purpose of purchasing a Lot of ground for the erection of said Church the sums respectively affixed to our names, to wit: half of said sum, either at the time of subscription, or within ninety days from it, and the other half within six months from the said subscription."

This was signed, within a very few days by two hundred and twelve persons, of whom Two subscribed, each $250

One subscribed $333
One Ditto...$200
Eight Ditto (each) $100
One Ditto...$60
Seven Ditto (each) $50
Two Ditto (each) $40
One Ditto...$35
Two Ditto (each) $30
Two Ditto (each) $26
Two Ditto (each) $25
Nineteen Ditto (each)..$20
One Ditto...$15
Fifty one Ditto (each) $10

[101] And others from $ eight down to one Dollar; the whole of whose subscriptions amounted to the round sum, notwithstanding the poverty of this little community, of $3,202. This was indeed an excellent beginning, which evinced the great zeal and truly exemplary piety of these first members of the Catholic Church, and their determined resolution to accomplish the great object which they had so near and dear to their heart. The very poorest among them came forward with a generosity truly characteristic of the best ages of Christianity, and laid at the feet of their Pastors the whole of what they possessed in the world, and pledged themselves, moreover, to contribute the half of their earnings, in monthly payments, till the Church should be completed.

After this the Committee were requested to look for a proper and convenient piece of land, and to report thereon as soon as possible.

Accordingly, "on the 28th of october of the same year at a meeting of the whole congregation, called on purpose to hear the report of the Committee, the Reverend Pastor in the name of the Committee informed them, that, after several inquiries, and the matter having been fully examined by them, no spot appeared more eligible for the erection of a Church, out of the few which had been offered for sale, since their appointment for that purpose, than one lying at the end of Franklin Square; that it appeared to unite the advantages of cleanliness and decent neighbourhood, with a central and airy situation, was remote from noise, especially upon Sundays;—that it was offered at the moderate price of $2,500, while as much as $10,000 had been asked for other grounds not much preferable;— that the owners, who are the Proprietors of the Boston Theatre, were very willing to let it go at the above mentioned price, though the price they had expected till now, was $4000, and that it was reported, and even certainly known to some of the Committee, that they might have a higher price, than that which they ask, did they consent to have a tavern, or other public house erected on [102] it; that therefore it is their opinion that it ought to be purchased, after the usual inquiries concerning the validity of the purchase, the form of it, upon which subject it is their intention to have the advice of some of the most respectable Lawyers in the town."

The Congregation expressed their full approbation of the purchase proposed, desired the Committee to proceed to the bargain, and voted the thanks of the society to the gentlemen of the Committee.

In consequence of the note above mentioned, and after having agreed, that the Deed be passed under the names of the Rt. Rev. Dr. John Carroll, Bishop of the Diocess, and of the Rev. Francis Anthony Matignon, Pastor of the Congregation, and naturalized citizen of America, and having, concerning the drawing of the same Deed taken the advice in writing of Dr. James Sullivan, Attorney General, and of Dr. Rufus Emery, two very eminent Lawyers of the town of Boston, the said land was bought, and paid for, out of the monies deposited in the hands of the Treasurer, as appears by the Deed signed by Elisha Sigourney in behalf of the Proprietors, bearing date the 24th day of December 1799, and recorded July 3d 1801. Lib. 198. fol. ƒ6.

The next object was to obtain a proper plan of a Church. This was generously furnished them by James Bulfinch, Esq. who kindly offered at the same time to superintend **gratis** the execution of it, for which he received the thanks of the Congregation together with an elegant Silver Urn valued at 165 Dollars, which was unanimously voted him by the Congregation.

Another subscription was, in the mean time, opened and at the suggestion of several Protestant gentlemen of liberal minds, an appeal was also made to the liberality of other denominations of Christians, who, with a generosity deserving a grateful recollection evinced the most friendly feelings when called upon. Dr. Matignon, at the same time, with a view to forward the undertaking, took a journey to the South, and solicited the aid of his Catholic friends, in New-York, Philadelphia, Baltimore, Washington, George Town, D.C., [103] Conewago, Burlington, N.J. and Elizabeth Town. The amount of the sums collected, both at home and abroad, stood finally thus:

From members of the Congregation $10,771.69
From other Catholics $1,948.83
From Gentlemen of other persuasions.............................. $3,433.00
Whole amount of subscription $16,153.52

The Church, agreably to the plan of James Bulfinch, Esq., was erected, measuring eighty feet in length, and sixty in width. It is of the Ionick Order, and stands with its front on Franklin Street, leaving a space of six feet for steps to the three entrances, without incommoding passengers on the side walk. It has two spacious Side-Galleries, and another for the Organ and Choir. There is, besides, a Basement story, nine feet in the clear, and of equal length and breadth with the Church. The entire cost of the Building, including the purchase of the ground was $20,000. The Basement is of stone, and the superstructure of brick. It was consecrated by the Rt. Rev. Dr. Carroll, on the 29th of September, 1803, with great splendor, and was called, the Church of the HOLY CROSS. An elegant Altar-Piece, representing the Crucifixion, was placed over the High Altar, executed by Mr. Sargeant, Junior for which he was allowed by the Congregation $200. For the purpose of liquidating the debt, and thereby freeing the Church from every incumbrance one half of the Pews were sold, which yielded the sum of $3,325, which, with the sum of money in hand, at the time of opening the second subscription, was sufficient to cover the whole expence, and still leave a balance in favour of the Church.

Thus by the prudence, zeal and indefatigable exertion of the Rev. Dr. Matignon, and his worthy Colleague Dr. Cheverus, with the co-operation of the members of the Congregation of the HOLY CROSS, was this great undertaking happily concluded. We have been more particular in recording the proceedings as they occurred, as this was the first Catholic Church ever erected [104] in Massachusetts, sensible that they will not be unacceptable to our readers.

About this time two other Priests arrived in Boston. These were the Rev. J.S. Tisserant and the Rev. Jas. Romagné, both pious and zealous Clergymen whose enlightened conversation, polite and edifying demeanor contributed also much to allay the unjust prejudices of other denominations and elicit the respect of their own. The former aided in the ministry occasionally in Boston and in Newport, R[hode] Island, but his feeble and extremely delicate constitution soon compelled him to return to his native country, (France) where he still lives (1834) beloved and respected. But the latter, enjoying more health, found ample field for the exercise of his zeal among the Indians in Maine. During eighteen years he laboured in this arduous mission dividing his time equally between the tribe residing at Passamaquoddy and that residing at Old Town on the Penobscot and suffering all the privations incident to the wandering life and precarious subsistence of these Aborigines.

These two Tribes with another near St. John's, N.B. are all that now remain of that once powerful and numerous nation, the **Abenakis,** that once principally peopled the large district of country now called the State of Maine. They were converted by the Jesuit Missionaries as early as the 17th Century and were afterwards regularly served by them from their house in Quebec until the 23d of August 1724, when the last of them, the pious, the zealous, the learned and justly celebrated F[ather] Sebastian Rasles was barbarously murdered by a horde of New Englanders, at the shameful instigation of the Government, at their principal village on the Kennebeck, called **Nanrantsouack,** now Norridgewock.* As the history of this bloody deed has been greatly distorted by Protestant historians, we shall here present our readers with a true and faithful account of it, as given by a contemporary writer, who had every means of being correctly informed on the subject. It is principally taken from the **Lettres Edifiantes,** 7th Vol. Paris Ed. published in 1809.[16]

[105] "Father Rasles, the Missionary among the Abenakis had become extremely odious to the English (the New Englanders.) Persuaded, that his zeal in fortifying the Indians in the faith, presented the greatest obstacle to the design which they had formed, of seizing upon their lands, they offered a reward for his head, and, more than once made an attempt to carry him off, or to take his life. At length they succeeded in satisfying their hatred and ridding themselves of this Apostolic man; but at the same time they procured him a glorious death which had ever been the object of his ardent desire; for we know that he for a long time aspired after the happiness of laying down his life for his flock. I shall give you a short account of the circumstances of this tragical event."

"After repeated hostilities between the two nations, a small band of Englishmen and of Indians, their allies, to the number of about Eleven hundred men, surprised and fell upon the village of **Nanrantsouak.** The thick brushwood by which the village is surrounded aided in covering their march; and as besides it was unprotected by Pallisades, the Indians, taken by surprise, had no notice of the approach of the enemy till after a general discharge of their muskets, which perforated every hut. There were at this time only fifty warriors in the village. On the report of the first discharge they tumultuously snatched up their arms and sallied out of their huts to meet the enemy. Their intention was not to sustain rashly the shock of so

* A beautiful monument (see page   )[37] has since been raised on the spot where this distinguished missionary fell and was interred, by Bishop Fenwick, with a Latin inscription commemorative of the event.

superior a force, but to favour the escape of their wives and children, and to give themselves time to pass the river, the opposite side of which was not yet in possession of the English."

"Father Rasles, warned by the shouts and general confusion, of the danger which threatened his Neophites, instantly left his house, and presented himself fearlessly to his enemies. This object was either to check their first assault by his presence, or to draw their whole attention upon [106] himself, and to procure the safety of his flock at the expense of his own life."

"As soon as they perceived the Missionary, they raised a general shout which was succeeded by the discharge of a multitude of pieces fired at him. He fell dead at the foot of the large Cross which he had erected in the middle of the village, to signify the public profession which they made in that village, of adoring a crucified God. Seven of the Indians who endeavoured to cover his body, and who exposed their own lives to save that of their Father, were killed at his side."

"The death of the Pastor threw consternation among the flock. The Indians took to flight, and crossed over the river, some, where it was fordable, and others, by swimming. They had to encounter all the fury of the enemy until they reached the forest on the other side of the river, where they were enabled to assemble again to the number of one hundred and fifty. After more than two thousand discharges of muskets, only thirty individuals were killed, including women and children, and fourteen wounded. The English did not pursue those that fled; they contented themselves with pillaging and burning the village. Before they set fire to the Church, they impiously profaned the sacred vessels, and the adorable body of our Lord."

"The precipitate retreat of the enemy allowed the Nanrantsouakians to return to the village. The following morning they visited the smoking remains of their Cabins, while the women were employed in gathering medicinal herbs and plants proper for the wounded. Their first care was to weep over the body of their holy Missionary which they found mangled in a shocking manner, with his scalp taken off, his scull fractured from the blows of an axe, his mouth and eyes filled with mud, the bones of his thighs and legs broken in pieces, and all his limbs mutilated. Such wanton barbarity inflicted on a body deprived of life can with difficulty be imputed to any others than to the savages (not yet Christians) who had accompanied the English as their allies."

"After these fervent Christians had washed, and respectfully and repeatedly kissed the venerated remains of their Father, they buried them in the very spot where, the day before, [107] he had celebrated the holy sacrifice of Mass, that is to say, in the place where the altar had stood, before the Church was burnt.''

"Such was the glorious end of this truly apostolic man, who was martyred on the 23d of August after having spent thirty seven years and over in the arduous duties of this mission. He was in the 67th year of his age.''

"Father Rasles united to the talents of an excellent missionary all those virtues which are required for a successful evangelical ministry among savages. He possessed a robust constitution, and with the exception of the accident,* of which I have spoken elsewhere, I know not whether he had ever experienced the slightest indisposition. We have been surprised at his facility and application in acquiring the different Indian languages. Scarcely was there one of them in this northern section with which he was not somewhat acquainted. Besides the **Abenakis,** which he spoke for the most part, he knew also the **Huron,** the **Ottowa,** and the **Illionois** languages; and he used them to some advantage in the different missions where they were spoken. From the time of his arrival in Canada, he was never seen acting a part inconsistent with his character,—always firm and intrepid, severe towards himself, tender and compassionate with others.''

"Three years ago, by the orders of our Governor, I made the tour of Acadia; conversing with Father Rasles, I observed to him that in case war should be declared against the Indians, he would run great risk of his life; that his village being only five leagues [108] from the English Forts, he would be exposed to their first incursions; that his preservation was necessary to his Flock, and that he ought to take some precautions for his personal safety. "My precautions are already taken," said he with a firm tone of voice,—"God has confided this flock to my pastoral care; I shall follow its fortunes, and happy shall I be to have it in my power to lay down my life for it."—He repeated the same thing several times to his Neophytes to strengthen their faith. "We have, alas! too sadly experienced," they have often since declared to me, "what our good Father spoke from the abundance of his heart;—we have seen him facing death, with a serene and tranquil air, and exposing himself, alone, to the fury of the enemy, and retarding their first assault, in order to afford us time to flee from the danger and save our lives.''

---

* The accident here alluded to, was the fracture of his right thigh and left leg occasioned by a fall. Father De la Chappe speaking of this fracture states, that the bones had been so badly united that the surgeons deemed it necessary to break the leg a second time to restore its straitness. At the time when the most violence was used in this operation, he endured the pain with extraordinary firmness and admirable composure. Our Physician, M. Sarrazin, who was present, was so astonished that he could not refrain from saying to him: "Ah! my Father, let some groans escape, you have occasion enough for them.''

"As a price had been set upon his head, and various attempts had been made to carry him off, the Indians offered to conduct him farther into the interior of the country in the direction of Quebec, where he would be sheltered from the dangers that threatened him. "What opinion have you formed of me," he would reply, with an air of indignation, "do you take me for a base deserter? Alas! what would become of your faith, should I abandon you? Your salvation is far dearer to me than life."

He was indefatigable in the exercise of his zeal; ever employed in exhorting the Indians to the practice of virtue, his whole mind was bent upon making them good Christians. His manner of preaching, which was vehement and pathetic, produced the liveliest impressions upon their hearts. Several families of the **Wolf** nation, lately arrived from **Orange,** have declared to me, with tears in their eyes, that they were indebted wholly to him for their conversion to Christianity, and that having received Baptism at his hands, about thirty years ago, they still retained the instruction which he gave them on that solemn occasion, so efficacious were his words, and so deep the impression which they made upon all those who had heard him."

He not only instructed the Indians in his Church almost every day, he also visited them in their Wigwams; his familiar [109] discourse charmed them; as he knew how to season his conversation with a holy sprightliness, which takes better with the Indian Character, than a grave and gloomy air, so also he possessed the art of persuading them to every thing he wished;—he was in the midst of them like a School master surrounded by his scholars."

"Notwithstanding his continual occupations in the ministry, he never omitted the holy exercises which are practised in our houses; he rose in the morning and performed his prayer at the hour, which is there laid down; he never omitted his Eight-days annual retreat; he selected for this retirement the first days of lent, when the Saviour went into the desert. "If one do not appoint," said he to me, "a particular time of the year for these holy exercises, the occupations of life succeed one another, and after many delays, he will not find time to acquit himself of them."

"Religious poverty appeared throughout his whole person;—in his furniture, his manner of living and in his dress. He deprived himself, from a spirit of mortification, of the use of wine, even when he was with his own countrymen. A mess, prepared with Indian Corn boiled, was his ordinary nourishment. During certain winters in which the Indians suffered a great want of provision, he was often reduced to the necessity of making his meals upon acorns; so far from complaining on these occasions, he appeared more than usually cheerful. In the three last years of his life, as the war prevented the Indians from hunting with their usual freedom and cultivating their grounds, the distress of their poor people became extreme, and the good Missionary had his share in it; provisions had to be sent him on this occasion from Quebec for the support of life. "I feel ashamed," he wrote to me at this time, "of the care which you take of me; a Missionary, born to suffer, ought not to be so well treated."

He would never suffer any one to lend him a hand to assist him in his ordinary wants. It was always himself that cultivated his garden, prepared his fuel, [10] swept his room, and cooked his food, that mended, in short, his clothes when torn, endeavouring out of a spirit of poverty to make them last as long as possible."

"Rigidly as he treated himself, he was always compassionate and charitable towards others; he possessed nothing of his own; and what he received he took always care to distribute immediately among his poor Neophytes; and never was grief more poignantly felt, or expressed by any, than by them at his death. It could not have been greater had it been for their own parent."

"He took always great care to adorn and embellish his Church, persuaded that this external show is calculated to strike the senses, to animate the devotion of the Indians, and inspire them with a still greater veneration for our holy mysteries. As he had some knowledge of painting, and could also manage the Lathe with sufficient dexterity, he employed, sometimes in its decoration, the work of his own hands."

"You judge right, my Dear Father, when you say that these were the virtues, of which New France was witness so many years, that gained him the respect and love, both of the French and of the Indian."

"Hence we see him so universally regretted; all are perfectly convinced that he was sacrificed out of hatred of his ministry, and of his great zeal in establishing the true faith in the hearts of the Indians. It is the opinion of M. De Belmont, Superior of the Seminary of St. Sulpice, at Montreal; for, having requested of him the usual suffrages for the deceased, in consequence of the communication of prayers which subsists between us, he replied in the words of the great St. Austin, which are so well known: that it is doing an injury to a martyr to pray for him. **"injuriam facit martyri qui orat pro eo."**

"May the Lord grant that his blood, shed in so just a cause, may fertilize these infidel countries which are so often watered with the blood of the Evangelical labourers, who have preceded us! May he render them fruitful in fervent Christians! And may he animate the zeal of Apos-[111]tolical men to come and gather in the abundant harvest which so many nations, still buried in the shades of death hold out to them!"

"However, as it belongs only to the Church to declare who are Saints, I recommend him to your holy sacrifices and to those of our Fathers."

It was to succeed this holy and zealous Jesuit Missionary and to continue the work which he had so happily begun, that the Rev. M. Romagné left Boston in 1799, just 75 years after the death of this great man, to enter upon the same missionary field, and among the descendants of this very same people. They no longer retain the same name as when Father Rasles laboured among them; nor do they possess any longer the same district of country, or even the same village where this bloody scene was enacted. Driven back by the continual encroachments of the Whites from the land of their Progenitors, and where repose the ashes of their spiritual Father, they are now divided into three distinct Tribes, of about 450 souls each, and are, exclusive of the Tribe in New Brunswick, confined to a small limited territory which has been guaranteed to them and to their posterity by the State, and which by treaty they have consented to take, in lieu of that immense tract of country owned by their Predecessors, the Abenakis nation. But their faith, cemented by the blood of their Apostle, they have always retained. In a small Church erected at each of the Villages where they abide, they assemble every Sunday, with, or without a Priest, accordingly as they may be provided or unprovided;—here they chaunt the divine service, partly in Latin, and partly in their mother tongue, and perform their other prayers. The children are carefully instructed by their Parents in the great truths of religion at an early age; and nothing is more common [112] than to see them at eight and ten years old, leave on a sudden their childish amusements, even at this day, and retire for a while to the Church to offer up their prayers to God, and invoke his blessing.

In the absence of a Priest, it has frequently happened that a Minister of other Denominations would pay them a visit in the hope of seducing them from the faith and of inocculating them with their various errors; but their efforts have, in every instance, proved abortive. Their invariable answer to them on these occasions, was: "We know our religion and cherish it;—we know nothing of you or of yours."

"The Rev. M. Romagné took up his residence, for a part of the year with the tribe at Passamaquoddy; and, for the other part, with the tribe on the Penobscot, thus dividing his time equally between them. Like his great Predecessor, he applied himself first to learn their language which he soon acquired. His next care was to accommodate himself as nearly as possible, to their diet and mode of living, the better to win their affections and prove his disinterestedness. In which he succeeded to the full extent of his wishes. He became their spiritual Father, their adviser, their friend and companion; and they obeyed him as dutiful children, and were never more happy

than when he was with them. He continued among them for 18 years instructing and edifying them by his example, when finally the bad state of
his health compelled him to withdraw and return to France, to their very
great loss and regret, in 1818.

In the year 1808, the new Diocess of Boston was created by Pius VII. But
in consequence of the great troubles in Europe at that period, the Bulls did
not reach America until 1810. By these it soon appeared that the Rev. John
Cheverus was appointed by his Holiness its first Bishop. This appointment
had been effected at the solicitation of the Rev. Dr. Matignon with the con-
currence and approbation of Dr. Carroll. Shortly after the arrival of the
Bulls from Rome Dr. Cheverus repaired to Baltimore and was there consecrated Bishop by Dr. Carroll [113] in the Church of St. Peter on the 1st of
November in the same year, on the feast of ALL SAINTS. The ceremony was
performed with great pomp and solemnity and in the midst of an immense
concourse of people who had assembled from all parts to witness the imposing scene. The new dignity, however, now conferred upon him, made no
alteration either in his simple mode of life, or in his former occupations. He
returned soon after to Boston, where he continued to occupy the same humble dwelling, in the rear of the Church, now become an Episcopal Palace,
and to share with his esteemed friend his frugal fare, as well as the
minutest duties of the ministry.

His first care on his arrival was to visit his Diocess for the purpose of administering the holy sacrament of confirmation, which had not been conferred since the visit of Dr. Carroll in 1803. In the course of this first visitation he confirmed three hundred and forty eight persons, of whom one
hundred and twenty two belonged to the Indian tribe on the Penobscot,
already mentioned. The following year he repeated his visit; and this he
continued to do, year after year, every where unfolding, in his peculiarly
happy manner, the glad tidings of salvation to his widely separated flock,
and gathering in at every visit a new and increased harvest of souls. A few
Churches now began successively to spring up in different places for the accommodation of Catholics, newly formed into congregations, as in Salem,
New Castle, Whitefield, New Bedford, South-Boston and Claremont; all of
them, however, extremely small—and in proportion as these Churches
arose clergymen became necessary. How to provide these in sufficient
number to supply the wants of a growing Diocess, was a matter that filled
the good Bishop with many anxious thoughts. To found an Ecclesiastical
Seminary, in his destitute circumstances, was impossible;—and even had
he the means he could not, at this time have spared from the laborious
duties of the ministry any of the extremely limited number of Priests he
now possessed, to superintend and conduct the studies of those who might

feel disposed to devote themselves to God, and the service of his holy Church. In this extremity he cast his eyes upon the two Colleges [114] at George Town, District of Columbia and Baltimore, Md. and indulged the hope, that these might serve as nurseries for the Diocess, till such time as he should have it in his power to have one of his own. In the mean time Providence enabled him to provide partially and to a certain extent, for the immediate wants of the Faithful in those places where he had established Churches. Several Catholic Clergymen successively offered themselves during this time from other parts whose services he accepted. These were the Rev. F.X. Brosius, the Rev. Matthew O'Brien, the Rev. Philip Laressey and the Rev. Paul McQuade. Besides these, there were five others on whom he conferred holy orders at different periods. These were, The Rev. Dennis Ryan, on the 31st of May, 1817; the Rev. Stephen Caillan, on the 5th of June, 1819; the Rev. Patrick Byrne, on the 18th of March, 1820; the Rev. John Loughnan, on the 31st of January 1821; and the Rev. Virgil Horace Barber, on the 1st of December 1822. Of these, the Rev. V.H. Barber, being a Scholastic of the Society of Jesus, was ordained at the request, and with the approbation of his Superior, residing in Maryland, and subject at any time to his recall; and the Rev. John Loughnan was ordained, for the British Province of Nova Scotia, and consequently not subject to his jurisdiction. Notwithstanding this increase in the ministry, the duties of it were principally discharged in Boston by the Rt. Rev. Dr. Cheverus himself and by his worthy Vicar General, the great and good Dr. Matignon; for most of the Clergymen named, who had entered the Diocess at different periods, as the Rev. Matthew O'Brien in 1812, the Rev. M. Brosius in 1814, or thereabouts, the Rev. M. Laressey in 1818, and the Rev. Paul McQuade in the same year, soon left it again, and but a short time after their respective arrivals.

The Rev. Dr. Matignon, after having edified the Church of Boston during twenty six years, died this year, (1818) on the 19th of September, deeply regretted by the whole Diocess. For some time past his health had been greatly impaired by the constant discharge of the duties of the ministry— yet, such was the ardor of his zeal he would by no means spare himself on its decline or remit any portion of those which devolved on him to perform, especially during the absence of his Right Reverend friend in the frequent visitations of his Diocess. He died as he had lived, a faithful servant of God, an exemplary Pastor, a sincere friend and a true pattern of a good Christian. His remains were con-[115]veyed, with all due ceremony, attended by a multitude of mourners, to the old burying ground in Boston, and there deposited in a tomb; but were removed, after three months, to the new Cath[olic] Cemetary in South Boston, followed again by an immense concourse of people of all denominations, by whom he was equally beloved and respected, where they were deposited in a Vault immediately fronting the principal entrance into St. Augustine's Church.*

[116] "Thus, far from the sepulchre of his Fathers," to repeat the language of his Epitaph, "repose the ashes of the good and great Dr. Matignon; but his grave is not as among strangers, for it was watered by the tears of an affectionate flock, and his memory is cherished by all who value learning, honor, genius, or love devotion." The following stands on the record of his interment in the hand writing of Bishop Cheverus:— "September, 21st"—"Francis Anthony Matignon D.D. and for twenty six years Pastor of this congregation (HOLY CROSS.)—On Saturday, the 19th he died as he had lived—a saint. AEt: 65."

In 1820, on the 16th of June two professed Nuns and two Sisters of the Ursuline Order, arrived in Boston, at the invitation of Bishop Cheverus, to take possession of the Convent recently established by him, adjoining his Cathedral. The origin of this establishment is as follows: The Rev. M. Thayer, after his departure from Boston, well knowing how important it was in a religious point of view, to have the female Catholic Youth well educated, conceived the laudable design of establishing a Convent in Boston for this laudable purpose;—and to carry the same into effect, he left Kentucky, where he had been recently appointed, and set out with the approbation of the Bishop upon a European tour, with the view of raising by eleemosinary contributions, sufficient funds for its establishment. The plan was, at this time ridiculed by some, and laughed at by others; and even those most friendly to the undertaking, thought it a desperate one. Rev. Mr. Thayer, notwithstanding, persevered in his pious project, and after making a collection of eight or ten thousand Dollars, this excellent Priest died, leaving his funds and the completion of his scheme to the great

*This Church has since been considerably enlarged in the direction of Dr. Matignon's tomb, so as to cover it completely, and to bring it immediately in front of the High-Altar, at the distance of about sixteen feet from the same. The white marble slab which formerly covered the tomb is now affixed to the wall on the Epistle side of the Altar and corresponds with the door of entrance into the sanctuary from the sacristy. The following is the Epitaph originally inscribed, and which is still left on the marble in gilt letters:

Dr. Matignon's Epitaph

Here lie the mortal remains of Francis Anthony Matignon, D.D. and for 25 years Pastor of the Church of the **Holy Cross** in this town: Ob. Sept. 19th 1818, AEt. 65.

"Beloved of God and men whose memory is in benediction"
Eccl. C. 45.V. 1.

"The law of truth was in his mouth and iniquity was not found in his lips: he walked with me in peace and equity and turned many away from iniquity; for the lips of the Priest shall keep knowledge, and they shall seek the law at his mouth: because he is the Angel of the Lord of Hosts."
Malachy, C. 2. V. 6. 7.

Far from the sepulchre of his Fathers repose the ashes of the good and great Dr. Matignon; but his grave is not as among strangers, for it was and will often be watered by the tears of an affectionate flock, and his memory is cherished by all who value learning, honor, genius, or love devotion. The Bishop and congregation in tears have erected this Monument of their veneration and gratitude.

R.I.P.

and good Dr. Matignon. These funds were wisely and prudently managed by him until the sum had nearly or quite doubled itself. At the death of Dr. Matignon, Bishop Cheverus became sole Trustee, and set about carrying the intentions of his Predecessors into effect, as far as he could. A piece of ground next to the Church of the HOLY [117] CROSS, was purchased, and buildings were erected for the purpose, and taken possession of by the above mentioned Ursuline Ladies, and the Order regularly established by the Rt. Rev. Bishop of Boston. In a short time, a school for the female Catholic Children was opened in it, which soon proved its advantages by diffusing a degree of piety and intelligence among the pupils highly creditable to the establishment.

In this year (1820) Bishop Cheverus was left with only the following Clergymen in the Diocess; viz: the Rev. Philip Laressey and the Rev. Paul McQuade in Boston; The Rev. Dennis Ryan in Whitefield; and the Rev. Stephen Caillan at Passamaquoddy; the Rev. Matthew O'Brien had withdrawn from it some time previous to the year 1815, and died in Baltimore, Md. that year; the Rev. Mr. Brosius had returned to Europe in 1816; and the Rev. M. Romagne had returned to France in 1818, to the Diocess of Mans, his native place.[17]

The following table will shew the increase of Catholics in Boston during the last twenty years.

A.D	Baptisms	Marriages	Deaths
1800	54	9	7
1805	94	20	32
1810	151	15	18
1815		26	25
1820	112	44	17

In the spring of 1821, the Rev. William Taylor arrived in Boston, and was shortly after constituted by Bishop Cheverus his Vicar General. In the same year the Rev. Philip Laressey left it to repair to St. Augustines Church in Philadelphia, where he shortly after died. The Rev. Paul McQuade continued in Boston till 1823, when he returned to Europe. About the same time the Rev. Stephen Caillan left the Diocess to repair to the West Indies. Thus the good Bishop was reduced, at a time when he most needed them, to four Clergymen for the entire Diocess, viz: to two in Boston, and two out of it. Notwithstanding his duties became every day more and more arduous,—and he laboured indefatigably. [118] The small number of his Priests compelled him almost incessantly to discharge even the ordinary functions of a Priest, besides his other weighty employments. Compelled to travel unaccompanied through the different missions. he had to sustain alone the entire burden of the ministry in every town and village through which he passed, preaching, baptising and confessing. It was plainly seen by his friends that his health was sinking under his exertions.[18] No complaints, however, escaped his lips, for he had made up his mind, that God would soon call him to follow his departed friend. and he viewed such an event without emotion. It was, however, otherwise ordered by Providence. In 1822, on the return of Baron De Neuville to France. who had been residing in this country, as Minister from the Court of St. Cloud, the state of the Bishop's health was represented to Louis XVIII., and the talents of the Prelate, as also his attachment to the Royal family of France, being well known, he was nominated by an ordinance, dated january the 13th 1823, to the Bishoprick of Montauban. In April following his appointment, he received a letter from the Minister of the Interior, naming this ordinance, and requesting him to come immediately to France. The Prince de Croij, Grand Almoner of France, likewise pressed him to return, and many others of distinction were equally urgent. His own family seemed to place their own happiness on the event; but after the first emotions of pleasure were over, in knowing that he was remembered in the land of his birth, and among the friends of his youth; he looked around upon his flock, and deeply felt how hard it would be, to part with them forever. If for a moment he thought of home, the duties and attachments here, tugged at his heart strings, and brought him back to our shores. Not only his flock were in distress at losing him, but the influential people of the Protestant faith, joined with his own to detain him. He, too, flattered himself that his cough was less severe than it had been, and he should shortly be restored to perfect health; and after a short struggle with himself, he came to the determination, of declining the offer of the translation to the see of Montauban.

The Memorial, signed by more than 200 gentlemen, of the first distinction in Boston, was sent to the Prince de Croii, which fully evinced the respect in which he was held in this country, and the importance of his services among us. In justice to the subject and the City, we have taken the liberty to insert it.

MEMORIAL
United States of America. Boston, April 22, 1823
To His Serene Highness the Prince of Croij,
Grand Almoner of France, and Bishop of Strasburg.

We have taken upon ourselves a painful and a responsible duty. We rejoice that the exalted merit of Monseigneur L'Eveque Cheverus, is so justly appreciated by your highness, and by his sovereign, and the evidence of his worth is found in the distinguished favor of a nomination to the Bishopric of Montauban. That we should interfere in the hope of preventing his translation to this higher scene of social and pious usefulness, demands an entire justification.

It is found in this: the Catholics of this place, and of the New England States, are generally a description of persons, who need not only instruction as to their great duties as Christians, but also advice, consolation, encouragement or correction in their temporal concerns.

To accomplish objects, so important to them, and so necessary to the good order of society, the most commanding confidence is indispensable in their ecclesiastical rulers.

It is impossible for us to make known to you, by any words, how entire, grateful and beneficent, is the dominion of Bishop Cheverus over all to whom he ministers in his apostolic authority. We hold him to be a blessing and a treasure in our social community, which we cannot part with, and which, without injustice to any man, we may affirm, if withdrawn from us, can never be replaced.

If the removal to the proposed Diocess, would be conformable to his wishes, we should mourn over this in silence.

If it proceed from your own wishes, and those of his sovereign, to have this truly estimable prelate associated in the immediate Church of France, it would not become us, to attempt to oppose those wishes. But if the removal can be referred to the principle of usefulness, we may safely assume that in no place, nor under any circumstances, can Bishop Cheverus be situated where his influence, whether spiritual, moral or social, can be so extensive, as where he now is.

In the sincere hope, that this excellent divine, and amiable gentleman, may consistently with the wishes and views of your highness, and of the worthy sovereign of France, remain to ornament and bless our community,

We have the honor to be,

With the highest consideration,

And the most entire respect.

(Signed by 226 Gentlemen.)

After these communications were sent to France, he appeared relieved from the agitation attending a decision of a point so important to himself and others. He thought the question of his translation at an end; but it was not so. The solicitations were renewed from such high authority, that they came to him in the nature of a summons, which could not be refused; and he commenced the preparations for an early departure. A few days previous to his leaving Boston, his flock presented him the following address. It was a grievous calamity to lose him; but he had taught them to submit to the dispensations of Providence without repining. He left them prosperous, and in the care of men deep in the affections and confidence of every member of the congregation, and highly respected by the whole community.

ADDRESS

DEAR FATHER:—Permit your flock, penetrated and subdued by grief, to place before you an humble offering of gratitude and affection. Your departure, which has now become certain, is to us a most afflicting dispensation of Providence; and the event has inflicted a wound, whose anguish time may assuage, but can never heal. The thought of this separation brings with it a thousand recollections which labor for a tongue to reveal themselves; but perhaps it were better they should not be freely spoken; for we know by long experience, that your delicacy would shrink at once from even such a bare recital as the coldest and most careless of us would make in sincerity and truth.

As a religious community, we were connected and consolidated under your auspices; and by your watchings and your prayers we have enjoyed the smiles of an indulgent Heaven; but at this solemn moment of parting, probably forever, the memory of the dead crowds upon us, in the loved form of him, who gathered us as a flock, and who with you walked hand in hand, laboring for our good; but this kind pastor to us, this coadjutor and friend to you, the ever lamented Matignon, had passed to a better world, to receive the reward of the faithful and the just. The living and the dead together possess our hearts.

At this crisis, when the agony of separation is fast coming upon us, we cannot entirely stifle our feelings, and we must, and we will, amidst our tears and lamentations, catch hold of your garments as you turn to leave us, and utter some faint cry of your services and our attachment.

You have fed the hungry and clothed the naked; brought back the wandering; reclaimed the vicious; shared the joys of the happy; softened the pains of the suffering; held the medicinal cup to the sick and parched lip; and taught the dying that, through faith and repentance, he might repose his hopes on the bosom of redeeming love.

Most spiritual guides go no farther than to instruct in spiritual matters; but you have not stopped there, nor there considered your work as finished; for you have come down, as it were, from the altar of God, to the common offices of mankind, to give us council and direction in our temporal concerns. We believe it seldom happens, that one so devoted to things divine, should be so wise in the business of the world; but this wisdom has not been shown by collecting perishable riches for yourself; but in striving to increase intelligence, comfort and respectability, among the people of your charge.

At your approach, discord fled from among us; for in every lecture, in every strain of devotion, you have breathed the mild and holy spirit of the new commandment, to calm the irritations and quiet the heart burnings incident to frail humanity; and we trust in grace that this example, and these instructions, will have a salutary influence on our lives, when you are not longer with us to advise and direct us in the paths of duty, virtue and religion.

You are going, dear father, to a distant country, where honor waits your coming, and where new duties are to thicken upon you; but we entreat you, that even in the joy of beholding your native land,—in the transports of embracing kindred and friends, and in the fresh activity of ecclesiastical engagements, that you will remember us, who can never forget you.

May the mild climate of Montauban restore and confirm your health, and awaken your spirits to life and happiness; and may God in his mercy and goodness, continue you for many years, a name and a praise in the church. And when you shall sleep with your fathers, and be numbered with the great and the good of other times, may our descendants here, learn that your blessing fell upon your first, as on your second love; and that Boston and Montauban were remembered together in your dying benediction.

> WILLIAM TAYLOR, **Rector,**
> T. WALLEY,
> JOHN McNAMARA,　　　　　　**Committee**
> JOHN WARD,　　　　　　　　　**of the**
> WILLIAM L. CAZNEAU,　　　　**Congregation.**
> FRANCIS McKENNA,

Boston, September 16th, 1823.

ANSWER.

MY DEAR CHILDREN IN JESUS CHRIST:—Your kind address has been presented to me, and is wet with my tears. How unwilling I am to leave you, I hope you all know, and have seen how cheerfully I refused, last May, the appointment which I **must** now accept.

Since it becomes a necessity, it behoves you and myself to submit.

My services, so gratefully noticed by you, have been at least, prompted by a sincere heart, entirely devoted to your spiritual and even temporal welfare.

It was as it were, at the school of the regretted and sainted Doctor Matignon, that I learnt how to love and serve you. Remember him always as the founder of this church.

I expected my mortal remains to be deposited with his, and never can you honor or gratify me more than by uniting our names in your blessing and remembrance.

Remembered and cherished you will be, as long as I breathe. Never shall I cease to watch over my dear flock with paternal anxiety. Happy if I can at any time do any thing for you. Excuse my faults in the exercise of my ministry; pray that they may be forgiven by the Supreme Pastor. I feel consolation in leaving you under the direction of the Rev. William Taylor, Rector of this Church, whose talents and piety are already known to you, and who has been for more than two years my faithful co-operator.

My beloved children, I press you all to my paternal bosom. I wish, and still have some hopes, to come to you again, and indulge the comforting hope that we shall be united in the kingdom of our Heavenly Father.

JOHN CHEVERUS.

"He left Boston," says the writer of his memoir, "in September, 1825, for New York, to embark from that place for France. The parting scene I never shall forget. At a very early hour in the morning, the vestry was filled with Protestants and Catholics, dissolved in tears to think they should never see him again. It required all his firmness to support himself in bidding them farewell. As he left the house for the carriage, lisping infancy and silver-haired age rushed forward to pluck **his gown** and **share the good man's smile;** and the last accents of his blessing were mingled with the moans of grief at his departure."

"He embarked from New York, on board the Paris, bound to Havre; and on the 31st of October, suffered shipwreck in a violent tempest on the coast of France. Thus, after an absence of more than thirty years, he was thrown upon his native shores. The storms of the political world, as well as the winds and the waves, have borne testimony to his fortitude and his confidence in God. Like the wanderer of Ithaca, he found many changes had taken place in his country and family; but unlike him, he was known by all, and received with affectionate enthusiasm."[19]

[119] This great and good Prelate was in the 55th year of his age, when he took his departure from Boston, and leave of the Church of America. He had the consolation, on withdrawing from the United States, to see that por-

tion of his Flock which had been committed to his own immediate care, spread in almost every State of New England. He repaired shortly after his arrival in France, to the Diocess of Montauban, which he governed only for a few years, when he was translated on the death of the venerable M. Davian to the Archdiocess of Bordeaux, where he still lives (1834) esteemed, respected and beloved by all.

CHAPTER VI

THE ARRIVAL OF BISHOP FENWICK

The very Rev. William Taylor, his Vicar General, succeeded to the administration of the Diocess after the departure of Bishop Cheverus and during the vacancy created by it. He was assisted in the ministry by the Rev. Patrick Byrne. Besides these, there were at this time but two other Priests in the entire Diocess, viz: the Rev. Dennis Ryan, stationed at Whitefield, Maine; and the Rev. Virgil H. Barber, S.J. who officiated at Claremont, New Hampshire. Things continued in this state until the year 1825, when his Holiness Pope Leo XII was pleased to appoint a new Bishop to the See of Boston. This was the Rev. Benedict Fenwick, a native of the State of Maryland, and a member of the Society of Jesus.

He was born on the 3d of September, 1782, at his Father's Plantation, on Beaverdam Manor, in St. Mary's County, Maryland; and was leneally [sic] descended from one of the 200 families that originally came over from England, under the Charter of Lord Baltimore, and settled in that State. He was educated in the College of George-Town, District of Columbia, and afterwards taught **Humanities** in the same College, during three years. In 1805, he left the College, and repaired to Baltimore to commence the study of Theology in the Seminary of the Sulpicians at that time under the direction of the venerable Nagot. The Jesuit Order being at this time reestablished in the United States by a **Rescript** of his Holiness Pius VII., and some of the Fathers of that Society having arrived in the [120] fall of 1806, in George Town, and opened a Noviciate in the College, he returned to it, after an absence of one year, and was among the six first, who entered it, after the restoration of the Society in the United States. He continued the study of Theology during this term, and at the conclusion of the course, was received into the Order, and ordained a Priest by the Rt. Rev. Leonard Neale, Bishop of Gortyna, and Co-adjutor to the Bishop of Baltimore, in the Church of Holy Trinity, in George Town, on the 11th of june, 1808. In the fall of the same year, he was sent with the Rev. Anthony Kohlmann, of the same Society, upon the mission of New-York, where he continued until the Spring of 1817, when he was recalled by his Superior, and shortly after appointed Rector of the College of Georgetown.

In consequence of some troubles in the Church in Charleston, South Carolina, he was sent thither by the Archbishop of Baltimore, as his Vicar General, in the fall of 1818, to restore peace to that distracted portion of his Diocess, and take charge of the congregation there. It was while he was employed on this mission, that Charleston was formed into a new Diocess, and Dr. John England was appointed its first Bishop. He continued, however, there, after the arrival of the Bishop, until May, 1822, when he returned to the College of George Town—and was appointed to the double office of Minister of the College and Procurator of the Society. In 1824, he was again nominated Rector of the College; and it was while discharging this office, he received in july, 1825, the Bulls of Leo XII. appointing him to the vacant See of Boston. They were dated the 10th of May in the same year.

After preparing himself by an Eight-day's retreat for the great and awfully responsable charge which he was now about to assume, he repaired to Baltimore, and was consecrated Bishop by the Most Rev. Ambrose Marechal, archbishop of Baltimore in the Cathedral of St. Mary, assisted by the Rt. Rev. Dr. England, Bishop of Charleston, and the Rt. Rev. Henry [121] Conwell, Bishop of Philadelphia, on the 1st of November (All-Saints) 1825, just fifteen years after the consecration of his venerable Predecessor, Dr. Cheverus. After a short visit to the beautiful College, which had been the Seat of his youth, and in which he had spent so many happy years of his life, he set out for Boston, accompanied by the Bishop of Charleston, and the Rev. Virgil H. Barber, S.J., and reached it on the 3d of December of the same year. He was met by the Very Rev. William Taylor, V.G. and the other Reverend Clergy of the Diocess, who had repaired to Boston to await his arrival. The following Sunday he entered the Cathedral of the Holy Cross, amidst a large concourse of people who had come to witness his inauguration, and was there received by the very Rev. William Taylor, who welcomed him at his entrance and exposed to him in a brief manner the state of the Diocess, and especially of the Catholic congregation of Boston. He concluded his discourse with giving in his resignation, and making known his determination to leave America and return to Europe. Mass was then celebrated. After the first Gospel, the Rt. Rev. Dr. England ascended the Pulpit, and addressed an able discourse to the people, who were delighted with his eloquence. The service being over, Bishop Fenwick returned to the Sacristy, and received the congratulation of the principal members of the Congregation. In the afternoon, at Vespers, he officiated again, when the Bishop of Charleston addressed another discourse to the people, which was equally well received. In a few days he returned to New York, where he embarked for his Diocess. The following sunday the Very Rev. William Taylor * also took his departure for the same City, in order to [122] avail himself of the Packet for Havre, with a view to join his ancient friend and benefactor, Dr. Cheverus, at this time Archbishop of Bordeaux.

Bishop Fenwick, on the departure of the Rev. William Taylor, had many serious difficulties to encounter. He saw himself in a situation far from being enviable—in a section of the country to which he was a perfect stranger, without a single confidential friend of ancient acquaintance, and in the midst of a congregation wholly unknown to him and particularly devoted and attached to their late Pastor. He found at his disposal only one Clergyman at Boston, and two at the distance of one hundred miles from it, who had each his own congregation to attend to. He had no other Priests for the various calls which might be made upon him from other parts of the Diocess—nor had he any means of increasing his Clergy, or even a prospect of being able to add to their number in his present emergency. At this time there were nine Churches in the Diocess, the greater part of them, however, scarcely deserved the name. These were the Cathedral of the HOLY CROSS St. Mary's Church in Salem, Mass; St. Patrack's [sic] at New Castle, Maine; the Church at Whitefield, Maine; a very small Church in South Boston, called St. Augustine's; another equally small, at Claremont, N.H.; an unfinished one at New Bedford; and two small wooden churches, quite decayed and no longer fit for divine service belonging to the Indians at Old Town and at Passamaquoddy. These Churches were all destitute of Pastors with the exception of the Cathedral of the HOLY CROSS, and those at Claremont and Whitefield. The Bishop, however, did not yield to despondence—he had put his whole confidence in God, who was the strength of the weak, and who could out of the very stones raise up children to Levi as well as to Abraham. He did not take the honor to himself, but was called of God, through his Vicar Leo, as Aaron was,—and he knew that he who had called him, could impart to him sufficient strength and grace to

*This Reverend Gentleman on leaving Boston went to New York, where at the solicitation of friends he sojourned awhile; but finally sailed for France and fixed himself at Bordeaux where he was made an honorary Canon by the ArchBishop. On his going to Paris to take his seat in the house of Peers, Rev. Mr. Taylor was requested to accompany him thither. He was there taken sick and died in the Irish College, in August 1828.

accomplish his end, and could also furnish him, in due time, with all the means requisite for its full accomplishment.

His first care was to visit the good Ursulines, who inhabited the house adjoining the Cathedral, and who had been esta-[123]blished in this City since the year 1820, as has been already remarked. He found the situation of it extremely confined. Cooped up within four narrow walls, these good Ladies were unable to take any exercise, or even to enjoy the pure air. In fact, during the short space of little more than four years, since they had first taken possession of this house, the little Community had already been deprived of two of its most efficient members, and the few that remained were reduced to a very sickly and infirm state. "As to health," said the good Superior to the Bishop, "that has long since taken leave of our abode." In this contracted place, (for the entire Lot, on which the Convent was built, did not contain much over 3500 square feet of ground) a s[c]hool-house was also erected which was frequented by 50 or 60 female children of the congregation. Here these highly talented and accomplished Ladies were exerting themselves in the cause of science and religion; but in the mean time were wasting away for the want of exercise and air.

The Bishop, after viewing the premises, and seeing the impractibility of improving them to any advantage, resolved at once in his mind, to remove the good Ladies, at a convenient time, to some situation better adapted to the establishment of an Ursuline Convent, and which should afford ample space for the erection of buildings calculated to embrace the whole scope contemplated by their Institute, as well as for a garden, and for spacious and airy walks.

On retiring from the convent he took the matter into serious consideration. The more he reflected upon the confined situation of these good Ladies, and their declining health, the more he became convinced, that some agreable spot in the vicinity of Boston, consisting of a few acres of choice land with a suitable house, provided it were not too remote from the City, would be far better adapted to their holy secluded State, than their present confined abode, situated in the heart of a noisy and populous City, with a Theatre in their front, and a range of Buildings in their rear, which [124] completely overlooked their premises, and where it would never be in their power, either to enlarge their sphere of usefulness, or act in accordance with the main objects contemplated by the Institute of their Order.

Accordingly having made all the necessary inquiries respecting the price of land in the vicinity of Boston, in the course of the following year, he finally made choice of what he deemed a proper location in the town of Charlestown, about two and a half miles from the centre of the City, and having ascertained that the same was for sale, as well as the price demanded for it, he repaired to the Convent, and made this proposition to the Superior and Ladies of it: that they should consent to relinquish their right to the property adjoining to the Cathedral of the HOLY CROSS ,and accept as an equivalent the sum of eight thousand Dollars; and with this sum or so much of it as might be required, that they should purchase the farm of ten acres situate on Ploughed-Hill, west of Bunker-Hill, and that they should improve the same for an appropriate Convent. He stated to them further-more that the above farm could be had for the sum of 3300 Dollars, which was deemed a moderate price by competent judges, as it possessed, besides a convenient country-dwelling house, a good Barn, and all the necessary outhouses.—The Superior having consulted her religious Sisters—they unanimously agreed to accept the proposal. The farm was accordingly purchased, and possession given by the former Proprietor; and the Ursulines removed to the same on the 17th of July, 1826, after having resided 6 years and six months in Boston. Two small wings had been added to the building, after the purchase, to render it more convenient. Here, they opened their school for a limited number of scholars. The following year the new Convent-building was commenced, and on the 21st of November, a part of it was so far completed, that they were able to take possession of it. Since that period two new purchases of land were made adjoining to the original one, which afforded them, all together, an area of twenty three or four acres. Early in the following spring they issued a new Prospectus and opened [125] their school to female children of all denominations of Christians, who eagerly embraced the opportunity afforded them, and flocked to it in considerable numbers.

The Building is situated on the summit of the mount, now called Mount Benedict; and although considerably elevated above the country immediately surrounding it, the ascent to it is so gradual on the side of Boston, that it is scarcely perceptible. The prospect from it on every side for beauty and extent is unrivalled in any country. In front you see Boston with its beautiful State house and Dome towering over all other buildings, and its capacious harbour, with the varied scenery about it of Vessels perpetually entering and departing from it; of Islands covered with rich verdure, and others surmounted with fortifications. Between lies Charlestown with the United States Navy Yard, Bunker and Breed's hills, on the latter of which stands the Obelisk (still unfinished) to mark the spot where Warren fell. A little to the left may be seen from the same position the villages of the towns of Chelsea and of Malden connected with Charlestown by two bridges over the Mystick River, and the beautiful hills rising in that direction with a gentle slope; and again a little to the right you have, still from the same position a clear and perfect view of the town of Roxbury, of Brookline, and of the beautiful azure hills which skirt the horison at a distance in the direction of Dorchester, and, still nearer to you, of East Cambridge with Charles river, and the bridges connecting it with Boston.—Again, if you look from the rear of the Building your eye will range over Cambridge, Medford and Malden with the verdant fields and highly cultivated country lying between them, adorned with innumerable country seats and Cottages, gardens, Orchards, rich meadows, and all the variety of both town and country, with the Middlesex Canal winding around the different hills, and leaving the Convent lands on its way to mingle its waters with those of Charles river. On this side the view is again intercepted only by the distant hills which rise higher and higher as they recede, until they are so blended [126] with the pale blue of the distant clouds as scarcely to be distinguished from them. Nothing can equal the beauty of the setting sun in this quarter.

The whole of this interesting spot is laid out with an eye to the object to which it is appropriated. A large garden tastefully arranged occupies the rear of the Building, while extensive gravel walks shaded with select forest trees consisting of the Elm, the Horse-chestnut, and the Sycammore afford a large and spacious playground in front. The parts adjacent to the Canal, already mentioned, are appropriated to meadow, or are cultivated for culinary purposes. The south side, which is of steep descent, is distributed into a number of artificial falls, where a vineyard of the choicest grapes is planted **en Espalier** affording, at the same time, most delightful walks. In short, every advantage has been taken, under the direction of the Bishop, of the situation, naturally beautiful, to make it one of the most lovely and agreable spots in the vicinity of Boston.

The next object which the Bishop had in view, was to enlarge the Cathedral of the Holy Cross, as far as the Lot of ground on which it was erected, would admit of, in order to render it as capacious as possible for the accommodation of the Congregation, now grown to a considerable number, and at the same time, to give greater extent to the sanctuary for the admission of the Candidates to the ministry of the Church, as well as of the children serving at the altar—a measure the more necessary to be adopted, as the Church of the HOLY CROSS had become the Cathedral of the Diocess, and in its original construction, had not been designed for that purpose. A plan of the alteration and enlargement was drawn by Bishop Fenwick, which was presented to the Congregation and accepted. According to this plan the gable end only of the original Church was to be removed, and a new building to be erected, 72 feet in width and nearly forty in length so as to unite with the former one and make one entire, compact edifice of nearly 120 feet in the entire length, including Sacristies in the rear of the Altar, by sixty in its narrowest, and 72 feet in its widest part. This arrangement was the more called [127] for, as, besides its other advantages, it would afford ample space in the Basement story under the Church for two spacious and convenient School-rooms, the one for Boys, and the other for Girls, which had long been a **desideration** in the congregation.

A subscription was immediately opened to carry into effect the above design when the members of the congregation came forward with their well known liberality and contributed generously towards defraying the expense of the undertaking. The work was commenced in the summer of 1827, and completed the following year. As the Cathedral now stands, it is one of the largest and most beautiful Churches in Boston and is capable of containing three thousand persons, having three Altars, and three spacious galleries. Its central situation in the City and the respectability of its neighbourhood will always ensure it a preference among Catholics, even when other churches come to be hereafter erected.

As soon as the addition to the Cathedral was completed the Bishop commenced opening the schools in the apartments below. These were divided into two rooms of equal size; the one for boys, and the other for girls. The former were superintended by the young Candidates for the ecclesiastical state, generally four in number; and the latter by one or more mistresses selected from the congregation. As the object was to diffuse the benefits of a good education as extensively as possible, and at the same time to secure a moderate support to the respective teachers, the price of tuition was put at $8 annually in each department. About one hundred children are there educated in all the useful branches who have generally evinced at the stated examinations proofs of great industry and improvement.

In addition to the above the children of the congregation are assembled twice on every Sunday before Mass and Vespers, as well as on wednesday and saturday evenings to recite their catechism in their respective Classes. The [128] number of children usually attending on these occasions avarage from two to three hundred, male and female.

The Bishop having arranged these matters in the principal Church and congregation of the Diocess, began next to turn his attention to the other parts of it. Accordingly, after administering the holy sacrament of confirmation, in the Cathedral, to 99 children, on Pentecost Sunday, the greater part of whom were admitted to their first communion on the same day, he left Boston on the 31st of May, accompanied by the Rev. Virgil H. Barber,* and commended his visitation at Claremont, New Hampshire.

*The first time Bishop Fenwick saw the Rev. Virgil H. Barber, and became acquainted with him, was in the City of New York in the year 1816. The Bishop was then administrator of that Diocess, **Sede vacante, and M.** Barber besides being Pastor of an Episcopal Church occupied the situation of Principal in an Academy in the upper part of the State, about fifteen miles from Utica. It was in one of his visits to the city of New-

York, he took occasion to call on the Reverend Administrator, and to enter into conversation with him upon the subject of religion. He was open and candid in his remarks, and seemed to manifest a sincere desire to know the truth. The Reverend Administrator was equally free on his side, and took some pains to satisfy him in his inquiries, and to explain to him the real doctrines of the Catholic Church, satisfied that if he could but remove the prejudices of his education, he should find but little difficulty to convince him of the truth of the Catholic religion. In the course of the conversation, the administrator learnt who he was, and the situation he held. He became, accordingly more anxious to gain him over to the truth.—After some time spent in discussing various matters M. Barbour manifested a desire to retire; but requested at the same time permission to be allowed another interview at some future day, which was readily assented to. The administrator took the opportunity of putting into his hands several books which he requested him to read in the mean time; and on his return, should he find any passage in them that required explanation, he would with pleasure give it—earnestly intreated him to pursue his investigation, assuring him, that if he was sincere in it, of which he did not entertain the least doubt, God, the Father of light, would un-[129]doubtedly lead him on to the truth; and recommended to him to have frequent recourse to him by prayer. All which he promised and took an affectionate leave.

Some months elapsed before he returned, he having shortly after set out upon his journey home, where he remained wholly engrossed by the cares of his Academy. That he had, in the interim, many debates with himself in the inquiry he was making, and to struggle hard against the power of habit, no one can doubt who has any knowledge of the human heart, and the prodigeous hold, which habit, backed by strong prejudice, takes upon it. M. Barbour had besides many reasons of a worldly nature, which have no small influence upon the generality of mankind, for remaining in the religion (the Episcopal) in which he then was. He was the Principal of a flourishing academy; which bid fair, in process of time, to become a college, agreably to the law then in force in New York, relative to the establishment of Colleges. He was also the Pastor of a congregation, which two situations secured to him a handsome living. His prospects, especially in the academy had induced him to make a purchase of land immediately in the neighbourhood, which, though not really very valuable at that time, would become so, if, he continued to manage the Institution of which he was Principal. Add to all this the claims of his wife and five small children upon him whose support required his active exertions. On the other hand all was dark and uncertain, as to this life—If he embraced what might prove to be the true religion, he should certainly lose [130] his present situation, as well in the Academy as in the Church, and would he obtain as an equivalent? Nothing certain. Not even had a promise of any thing been made to him. Should he then go and lose by the step he was taking a certainty for an uncertainty, and expose his wife and children to beggary and want? Human and worldly prudence naturally forbade it. He was, besides, not quite sure that the Catholic Church was the only true Church, although every thing, as far as he had yet gone into the inquiry, seemed to prove it; yet, it might not be;—other Churches might also be true Churches; and among these, his own. Why therefore, should he, by a precipitate step, jeopardize his family? Could he not remain as he was, until he should realize at least a sufficiency for the support and education of his children? And if hereafter he should be perfectly convinced, after a full investigation, that the Catholic Church is the mistress and mother of all other Churches, the true Church and the only true Church,—why, he could then embrace it without hasarding his worldly prospects.—

These and such like were his thoughts during this interval; and upon ten thousand individuals they might have had their influence, whom if they did not wholly withdraw from the inquiry might, at least, have had the effect to interupt and postpone it. But M. Barbour was not so easily to be turned aside. He had read and learnt enough to know, that the religion of which he was a minister, was not a sure one to lead to heaven;—he had read enough and learnt enough to have the strongest doubts of its truth. This was enough for him, who, in the sincerity of his heart, sought the truth, to persevere, and not to stop until he should have found it; and having found it to embrace it, whatever might be the consequence to his worldly prospects.

He accordingly took another journey to New York. The administrator recognized him as soon as he entered his room, greeted him in the most cordial manner, and inquired affectionately after his [131] health and that of his family. After a few moments of desultory conversation, the former subject was revewed [sic] and much ground in religious controversy was travelled over in the course of a few hours. M. Barber in the course of the conversation, admitted, that the Protestant religion could not be defended,—and seemed greatly at a loss what to do. The situation of his family seemed to rush again into his mind—and the awkward predicament in which they would be placed. "Trust," said the administrator guessing at what passed within him,—"Trust your affairs to the management of a beneficent Providence. Embrace the truth, now that you have found it, and leave the rest to God. He has led you on to make this inquiry, he has followed and directed you step by step;—and now that you yield yourself up to his grace, he will abandon you! No, believe me, you were never more sure of subsistence." "What shall I then do"? he replied. "First embrace the Catholic religion," said the administrator; then, go back to your academy,—resign your situation in the Episcopal Church; and if your academy alone will not afford you and your family maintenance, wind up its affairs, as soon as you conveniently can, and come to New York. I shall, in the mean time, use my best endeavours to procure you scholars; so that as soon as you arrive, you may open a new school in the

City, which, I doubt not, will prove far more flourishing, in the course of time, than the one you will forsake."—"Well, I submit;" was his reply,—"I am ready to make my recantation whenever you may think fit, and do whatever else you shall prescribe."

A few days after, he made his recantation, read the Profession of Catholic faith—was baptized (sub conditione) made a general confession of his whole life, and was regularly received by the administrator into the [132] communion of the Catholic Church. Upon this he immediately returned home, where he set about arranging his affairs;—informed his Congregation of the change he had undergone in his religious sentiments, since he saw them last;—and bid them a final adieu. As he had anticipated, so it happened with him. His Parishioners immediately turned against him; soon deprived him, by their interference, of the situation he held in the school; and finally carried their persecution against him even to the compelling him to sacrifice, by a forced sale, the land he had recently purchased, but for which he had not wholly paid, and which in consequence was sold to great disadvantage.

Not very long after these proceedings, the administrator received a letter from M. Barbour, in which he acquainted him with what had happened, since his return home, and informed him, moreover, of his arrangements and final determination to leave that part of the country, and accept of his invitation to New-York. The administrator lost no time in replying to his letter, and telling him, that all was ready for him;—that a house was procured in a central situation;—that scholars were promised;—and (what bid fair to be of considerable service to him), that the good feelings of the Catholics were all enlisted in his favour. M. Barbour shortly after arrived bringing with him his wife and interesting little children, five in number, viz: one Boy and four girls. The administrator received them with kindly arms, gave them lodging in his own house, until he had seen all things properly arranged, as far at least as circumstances would admit, in their future abode, and considered that as one of the happiest days of his life in which he had received and entertained a family who had sacrificed their all for conscience sake.

M. Barbour having moved into his own house immediately opened his school, when a number of children, many [133] of whom of the most respectable families, flocked to him for instruction. Nor did he neglect in the mean time, to prosecute his study of religion. He was well aware, that though he was now a Catholic; yet, he had much to learn before he should be fully acquainted with all the principles and practises of the Church. His first care was to bring over his good Lady into that way which he now knew to be the true one, and to cause all his children to be baptized, like himself (sub conditione.) It was not long before Mrs. Barber also presented herself to be received. Naturally pious she had offered little or no resistance to the abundance of divine grace. It was now, truly, an enviable family, and almighty God seemed to delight in blessing them in a signal manner.

For some time things continued in this state, the school progressing and receiving daily a new accession of scholars from the high opinion parents began to entertain of the talents of the Teacher and his long experience in the art of instructing. His attention, however, was not wholly engrossed by his school; his leisure hours were principally taken up in studying and instructing himself in the science of the saints. He had scarcely made, together with his wife, his first communion when he began to aspire already to a high state of perfection, viz: that of devoting and consecrating himself entirely to the service of his Maker. He thought the Almighty had a further claim upon him, by having, through his infinite mercy, brought him to the knowledge of himself and his true Church; and required something more of him than simply to edify his neighbour in the state of Layman. He was aware that great obstacles lay in his way, which seemed to forbid him to foster even a thought of the kind; but then he knew also that he who inspired him with the thought, could (if such were indeed his holy will) easily [134] remove these seeming obstacles, and enable him to accomplish the object. Before he opened the subject to any one, he spoke with his wife, and consulted her thereupon. God had already prepared her by his holy grace. The reading of the **Lives of the Saints**, and the heroick examples of so many blessed servants of God in all ages had already filled her with a noble ardour to emulate their virtues. She readily assents to all, and is equally anxious to carry it into effect so laudable a design, if prudently practicable. She knows not whether such a thing is allowed in the Catholic Church as the separation of man and wife, for the purpose of enabling the former to enter into holy orders. She takes the first opportunity to consult the administrator on the subject, assuring him at the same time, "that if the matter can be accomplished with justice to the children, she is every way desirous of it." The administrator is perfectly astonished—he knows not how to view the matter; or what advice to impart. Upon her pressing him to say "whether he knew or had read of any example of the kind in the Church; or whether the Church approved of such acts of consecration to God"? He replied in the affirmative, stating that he had read of several instances of the kind, and especially of Lord and Lady Warner two distinguished persons in England, of whom both had been brought up Protestants; but who afterwards were converted to the true faith, and afterwards, by mutual consent were separated, when the husband studied and became a Priest in the Society of Jesus; and the wife took the veil in a Convent on the Continent. They had, moreover, two young daughters to be provided for but these, previous to their separation, they had placed, for their education, in a Convent, in the Low-countrie, having taken care to appoint proper guardians for them, and surrendered their whole estate for their provision, as soon as they should become of age, or in case they should not, like their pious parents, have a call from God and take to religion. But the Almighty [135] so disposed all things, that at a proper age they both took the veil and entered into a convent at Dunkirk. The administrator informed her, furthermore, that the Church never prevented married persons from consecrating themselves to God in holy religion, if it were done with mutual consent, and if proper provision were made for their children, and they should be well taken care of, in case God had blessed them with any. But for the present he dissuaded her from thinking of the matter, principally on account of her children, who had no other means of support than their parents, and who, if a separation were now to take place, would necessarily suffer; and therefore, a separation under such circumstances, no matter for how laudable a motive, could in no manner be justified.

On the arrival of the new Bishop of New York, (Dr. Connelly) the administrator was recalled by his religious Superior to George Town College. At his departure, which took place after the Easter Holidays, he recommended in the strongest terms M. Barbour and Family to the Bishop, beseeching him to have an eye to them, and not to suffer them to be neglected. The administrator, obliged to obey the call of his Superior, regretted nothing so much on leaving a City where he had lived the last nine years, and which had been his first mission after ordination, as his being compelled to desert a family, whose welfare he had so much at heart, and whose interests he was afraid would not now be so well attended to. A perfect stranger in the place, under a Bishop who was equally so, without a friend and with a growing family, without resources and with many cares, having nothing to depend upon but his school, which in a City like New York is always so precarious, the administrator felt greatly for him. He had it no longer in his power, as he thought, to do any thing more for [136] them;—he could, therefore, only recommend them to God, and to Him whom he had established in his place, the Father and protector of the poor. But the Almighty had resources which the administrator knew nothing of, and ways and means, too, of applying them, which he could not foresee. How admirable is the providence of God! And how wisely does he dispose all things, to bring about the object he has particularly in view! Had the administrator been left in New York, in all probability M. Barbour would have continued there also; and had he not been recalled by his Superior to George Town, he would never have found the means of providing for and educating the children of that worthy man, and thereby, of furthering the plan, he had, in common with his virtuous and amiable wife, so dear at heart. But by his recall all was accomplished.

But a few weeks had elapsed after the departure of the administrator (for so we must still call him for the sake of the narritive) and his arrival at the College, when he received a letter from M. Barber recalling his attention to the former subject of conversation and inquiring whether something could not be done for him in George Town towards the accomplishment of his wishes. The administrator held as yet no situation or office in the College, but he possessed some influence with the rector of it, the Rev. John Grassi, as well as with the Archbishop (Dr. L. Neale) who, at this time resided at the Visitation Convent in George Town. Knowing the great desire, which both M. Barber and his good Lady had to consecrate themselves to God in holy religion, and aware of the obstacle in the way by their having five small children to provide for, and willing to serve him in the best of his power, he began to reflect and consider how he might best dispose of these helpless children; and whether some arrangement might not be made in their behalf so as to leave their parents quite free and unincumbered. [137] With this view he first called upon the President of the College, and laid open to him the whole business, stating the situation of M. Barbour and that of his family, his conversion to the Catholic faith, as well as the conversion of his wife, and their great desire to separate for the sole purpose of entering into religion etc.;—that above all things he was most anxious to be united to the Society of Jesus, of which he had heard and read so so much and whose holy Institute he admired; and pressed him in the most earnest manner to favour his design by admitting him as a Novice, and his little Son as a pupil into the College to remain there until completely educated. The Rector struck at the heroism of M. Barbour in the generous sacrifice he was about to make of himself to God,—and glad at the opportunity here afforded him to exhibit to the eyes of a profane world so striking an instance of the power of divine grace, immediately gave his consent, and authorised the administrator to make the same known to him as soon as convenient. Having succeeded thus far, he next proceeded to the Convent of the Visitation, to confer with his Grace, the Archbishop about Mrs. Barbour and her other children, viz: the four remaining daughters. Here he expected quite an unfavourable answer; but he still trusted in God. The Convent had been but just established—its number was, nevertheless great, and its income small, scarcely sufficient for the support of those already admitted into it as members. Besides, the number he intended to petition for, was too great even were the convent in far better circumstances, viz: a mother and her four children. But, no matter; he resolved to try and to persevere. He accordingly entered the archbishop's apartment, and immediately introduced the subject. He spoke of the great charity he would confer by [138] receiving them into the Convent, and how likely such a step would draw upon an infant institution—dwelt a good deal upon the merits of Mrs. Barbour, her piety, her desire of perfection, her talents and acquirements, and how useful a person possessing these accomplishments might prove in an establishment, whose object in a great measure is to educate female children. The administrator finally concluded with assuring him that he entertained no doubt but that God would hereafter amply compensate for any expences the house might incur on their account.

The archbishop during the whole time seemed to listen with much attention. On the one side his benevolent disposition inclined him to open the Convent to her; on the other his prudence dissuaded him from it. The absolute want of funds on her part to defray any portion of the expence of the children appeared to weigh very much upon him. He wished not to impose a heavier burthen upon the good Ladies of the Convent than they could conveniently bear. "Really," said he at length, "I am much at a loss to know what to do in this matter. I fear it will be impossible to admit her—not precisely herself; for, we might compass that—but her children, What shall we do with them"? "Educate them," replied the administrator. "Aye, aye," he rejoined, "that is easily enough said; but who is to support them in the mean time, and defray all the expences of their education"? **"Deus providebit.** God will provide. The widow of Sarephta was in but indifferent circumstances, when the prophet Elias called upon her for a little bread;—scarcely had she a handful of meal at the time; yet, she made him, at his request, a cake of that meal; and the consequence was a great blessing upon her; for, **from that day,** says the scripture, **the pot of meal wasted not** in her house. And will God," added the administrator, "bless less the charity bestowed by the [139] children of his own election, than he did that bestowed by a gentile woman"? "Well, well," answered the archbishop somewhat hastily,—"we shall see. Be it so—Be it so.—I cannot, however, consent to take the Infant she has;" (the administrator had given him, in the course of the conversation, the ages as nearly as he could recollect of all the children) "what should we do with that? We could not employ a nurse; besides, it is contrary to the rule of the convent to receive one so young." "As to that," replied the administrator, "the poor little creature shall not want a home when the others are provided for. My Mother shall take charge of her and shall nurse her as if she were her own. But at a proper age, you will receive her also into the school of the Convent"? "Very well," he replied.—Thus was this important matter settled, greatly to the joy of the administrator, as well as to the credit of the good Archbishop and the Rector of the College.

The administrator gave immediate information of the result of what had passed to M. Barbour, and invited him to lose no time in coming on. Accordingly, in a few weeks, he arrived with his whole family—was received in the College hall by the Reverend Rector, Dr. Grassi, by the Professors, and by the administrator, who all expressed the liveliest joy upon the occasion. After some days rest from the fatigue of their journey, the pious Couple were taken to the College Chapel where the archbishop in the presence of a number of individuals, both Clergy and secular, pronounced the Divorse, having first ascertained of themselves individually their full consent thereto. He gave an eloquent admonition on the occasion which drew tears from the eyes of many who were present; and concluded by recommending to them to continue faithful to the grace of the Lord, and to persevere in that perfect path which he had traced out to them. They were then dismissed. [140] M. Barbour was conducted to the room which had been prepared for him; his little son was taken into the College; Mrs. Barbour, with three of her daughters, were conducted to the Visitation Convent; and little Josephine was cordially received by the administrator's mother.

In the course of a few months, the Rev. Mr. Grassi, having occasion to go to Italy, resigned his situation in the College, when the administrator was nominated Rector in his stead. It was determined in Council that M. Barbour with three of the more promising Scholastics should accompany him, in order that he might have an opportunity of seeing Catholic countries, and especially Rome; and that they might complete their education in the Jesuit's college there. In a short time they set sail, and after a prosperous navigation they all reached Italy in safety. On landing they immediately repaired to Rome, where they were received, in the most friendly manner, by the Fathers of the Society, and not less kindly by the then Sovereign Pontif[f], Pius, VII. to whom they were presented by one of the Fathers.

M. Barbour, after an absence of nearly a year during which time he principally lodged at the Jesuit's College at Rome, returned to this country and commenced his studies in Theology in the College at George Town, which he prosecuted with ardour until December 1822, when he was sent by his Superiour (for he had already been admitted to his vows and received into the Society) to Boston, where he was ordained Priest on the 3d of December, the feast of St. Francis Xaverius, to whom he always professed a particular devotion, by Dr. Cheverus, Bishop of Boston. Mrs. Barbour had some time before this taken the Veil in the Visitation Convent in George Town, D.C. where she still continues an example of patience, of humility, of obedience and of every religious virtue, enjoying the happiness of seeing all her daughters (little Josephine included) successively improving in virtue, knowledge and of every polite accomplishment. The eldest took the veil in the Ursuline Convent in Boston; the two [141] next succeeding, one in the Ursuline Convent in Quebec and the other in that at **Trois Rivieres** in Canada. Last of all, little Josephine has taken the veil in the Visitation Convent at Kaskaskias. The Son, now grown into manhood, after having completed his studies at George Town College, has been sent to Rome to enjoy the superior advantages to be enjoyed there in the Theological department—where he still is—to come forth shortly a worthy disciple of Ignatius.

The conversion of the Rev. Virgil H. Barbour was not without producing the happiest results, as it led the way to the conversion of the Rev. Dr. Keeley, Episcopal clergyman, Rector of St. George's Chapel, New-York, and of George Ironside, a member, also, of the Episcopal Church, both of whom the administrator

[129] On the day after his arrival, which was a sunday, the Bishop celebrated Mass, and administered the sacrament of confirmation to twenty one individuals, male and female, after having previously addressed them on this sacrament, and the dispositions for worthily receiving it. The little Church was crowded to excess. The greater part of those who were present, on this occasion, were Protestants from the Church on the opposite side of the Village, which they had left completely deserted, to the very great dissatisfaction of their Minister. From the impossibility of all being able to enter into the Catholic Church, many occupied [130] the rooms below and above, of the house adjoining, and strove to catch, through the doors and windows, a view of what was passing; while a still greater number lined the street and occupied the ground next to the side of the Church, unable [131] to approach nearer in consequence of the crowd. The anxiety of the Protestants of this neighborhood to observe the ceremony on this occasion will not surprise, when it is recollected, that the Rev. Daniel Barbour, Father [132] of the Rev. Virgil H. Barbour, also become a Catholic, was formerly Pastor of this very neighbourhood, and of the Episcopal Church over the way;—that [133] it was only a few years, since the Catholic religion was first introduced here;—that, before that period, the grossest ignorance prevailed in the town of Claremont, [134] in regard to the real tenets of Catholics, and the strongest prejudices existed; and that, even now, altho much care had been taken by their Pastor to undeceive them, a disposition still prevailed among the greater part, not by any means [135] favourable to the growth of Catholicity.

The Bishop, after the morning service was over, continued in the Church until the Vespers were sung. The Rev. Mr. Barber at the conclusion of these, [136] addressed the congregation in an excellent discourse on the great principles of Catholicity, which was the more appropriate, as there were so many of other denominations present, who listened to it with great attention. The people, after this, returned to their homes.

[137] The Catholic congregation of Claremont is now pretty large. It consists chiefly of converts to the faith, who reside in this, and some of the adjacent [138] towns. There are but very few who dwell in the immediate vicinity of the Church. The Rev. M. Barbour, encouraged by some of the

had the happiness to receive into the pale of the Catholic Church, about the same time. It paved the way, also, to the conversion of his aged Father, the Rev. Daniel Barbour, an Episcopal Clergyman in the town of Claremont, New Hampshire, of Rev. Calvin White of Connecticut and of many others.

[142] The Rev. Virgil H. Barber, after having been ordained Priest, as mentioned above, (by the hands of Dr. Cheverus), was sent to Claremont, N[ew] Hampshire, by the order of his Superior, where he began to labour towards the conversion of Protestants in and about that neighbourhood. With the aid of his Father and the charitable contributions of the Clergy and Laity in Canada, he laid the foundation of and soon raised the neat little Brick-Church which distinguishes that section of the country. In order to secure a subsistence without being a burden to his little flock, he opened a Classical School, which soon attracted a number of scholars, from different parts of the country.[10]

more prominent among the inhabitants of the town of Windsor, had it in contemplation [139] to remove his school to, what he deemed, a more attractive situation on **Ascutney** Mountain, beyond the Connecticut river; but the Bishop, having examined the Site, and weighed the matter in his mind, advised [140] him against the measure. The establishment of a school in such a situation as this, would necessarily be attended with many disadvantages, and it would be quite doubtful whether it would meet with encouragement.—The Bishop [141] spent three days at Claremont during which time he visited several of the principal Catholic converts, and exhorted them to perseverance in the holy faith they had embraced. (He returned to Boston on the following thursday).

In the course of this year (1826) two Priests arrived in Boston, and offered their services to the Bishop, viz: the Rev. John Mahoney[21] and the Rev. Charles Ffrench,[22] the former from Maryland, and the latter from the British Province of New Brunswick. As they both produced highly favourable **Exeats** from the Bishops, under whom they had respectively last served, with other letters of approbation, the Bishop accepted their services. The Rev. Mr. Mahoney he sent to Salem, and the Rev. Mr. Ffrench to Eastport, Maine, having recommended to him, at the same time, to erect, as soon as possible, a Church in that town, and attend in a particular manner to the Passamaquoddy Indians, in that neighbourhood.

The Bishop having ascertained that this tribe as well as that at Old Town on the Penobscot river, had [142] been left without a Pastor for a considerable time, became greatly concerned for them. Nor were they alone left destitute; he had learnt that a great number of Catholics were also scattered in various parts of that State, who called loudly for the visit of a Clergyman. To meet the wants of as many of these as possible, the Bishop directed the Rev. Mr. Barber, who could best be spared for such a mission, to make an excursion, during the fall of this year, and to visit all such places, in order to afford the Catholics in them an opportunity of receiving the sacraments, and especially to prepare them for the grace of confirmation which it was his intention to confer the ensuing summer. In a few weeks the Rev. Mr. Barber, having made the necessary arrangements, set out upon this mission, and did not return until the 11th of December. He gave the most flattering account of his reception every where as well by the Catholics, as by persons of other denominations—dwelt particularly on the favourable prospects at Dover, N[ew] Hampshire, spoke of the great desire, manifested by all classes, to have a Catholic Church erected there, and of their willingness to contribute generously towards it. He spent also some time with each of the tribes of Indians, and was delighted with their sincere piety, and their unbounded attachment to their holy religion. He reported in fine the ardent desire which each of them had to have a Priest reside with them as formerly, and their willingness to bear even the whole burden of his support, sooner than to be left without one.

[143] On the third Sunday of Advent, (December 17th 1826) the Bishop proclaimed the Jubilee, by order of his Holiness, throughout his diocess, as he deemed this the fittest and most convenient time to the major part of the Catholics. During the solemn High-Mass, which was celebrated by the Bishop, immediately after the Gospel, he caused the Brief of his Holiness, Leo XII. to be read to a crowded audience, wherein he had extended the jubilee, celebrated in Rome, during the last year, to the whole world; and also, his own Mandate on the subject, with the particular regulations relative thereto. In the same document it was announced, that, during the succeeding eight days, a Spiritual retreat would be given in the Cathedral to prepare the congregation for the grace of the Jubilee at which all the members of it were exhorted to attend.—In the afternoon of the same day, immediately after Vespers, the **Veni Creator** was sung by the Choir; after which the Bishop ascended the Pulpit and addressed an elaborate discourse to the people on the nature of Indulgences—the true doctrine of the Catholic Church relative thereto, and their great advantages, and concluded with exhorting them all in the most earnest manner to profit by the favourable opportunity now offered of sanctifying their souls—and of testifying their gratitude to God for so signal a display of his mercy towards them. The Church was immensely crowded—and he was listened to with the most marked attention.—The regulations were again read; after which the people were informed, that three Confessors would be in constant attendance in the Church during the eight days until ten O'Clock at night, for the convenience of those, who should wish to recur to their ministry, viz: the Bishop, the Rev. Mr. Byrne[23] and the Rev. Mr. Mahoney—that on each of the days morning prayers would be publickly recited, a meditation would be given, three Masses would be celebrated and a discourse would be delivered—that the Church would be left open the entire day; and in the evening at 6 O'Clock a solemn **Miserere** would be sung; after which, a long Prayer would be recited in which all the intentions for gaining the indulgence would be included—then an exhortation would be given—then a number of pious canticles would be sung—and the exer-[144]cises of the day would be concluded with the Benediction of the Blessed Sacrament.

Such was the order of the exercises during the eight days of the retreat. Never was the Church better attended than it was during the whole of this time. The confessionals were constantly crowded at the hours allotted for confession—on each of the days, and at every Mass, numbers were admitted to holy communion—in short, the entire congregation seemed to be completely renovated. It was computed at the end of the Jubilee that not fewer than twelve hundred persons received communion on this happy occasion. The number of confessions heard during the same period must, consequently, have been far greater, as among the communicants many of the children were not included.

On the 25th of December, Christmass-Day, the exercises of the Retreat were concluded. On this day the Bishop celebrated Mass pontifically. The Rev. Mr. Byrne, although worn down by the continual labours of the preceding week, delivered, at the Gospel, a discourse to the people, which was well received. In the afternoon, the Bishop officiated at Vespers, again pontifically;—and, after the **Magnificat,** ascended the Pulpit, and addressed the people on the subject of alms-deeds; after which, a collection was taken up in behalf of the poor. The concourse of people during the entire day was very great; it was impossible, in fact, that the Cathedral could have been more crowded, than on this occasion.

The number of Baptisms performed this year (1826) in the Cathedral amounted to 413;—The number of marriages celebrated during the same period, to 86.

During the entire year, the Bishop had scarcely a moment to himself; for having no other Priest than the Rev. Mr. Byrne to assist him in the Cathedral. (the Rev. Mr. Mahoney of Salem having attended only during the exercises of the jubilee) he was obliged to take an equal share in all the parochial duties of the Church, in catechising the children, in preaching every Sunday and Holiday, in performing the baptisms, celebrating the marriages, attending at the Confessionals, in visiting the sick, and assisting at interments. Independantly of these laborious duties, he had also taken a Class of young Theologians, whom he instructed daily in theology, in the hope, that one day or another, they would be able to take also a part in the [145] ministry, and become useful and active Collabourers in the Lord's Vineyard. In this he was not disappointed as the sequel will shew.

CHAPTER VII

THE EVENTS OF 1827

In the following year (1827) he commenced his visitation of the eastern section of his Diocess. Having administered the holy sacrament of confirmation, again in the Cathedral, to 86 persons, and having left the Rev. Messrs. Byrne and Mahoney to do duty in Boston during his absence, he embarked the 10th of July, on board the Steam-boat **legislator,** bound for Portland. General Wool, of the United States army, and a number of respectable gentlemen had also taken passage in the same Boat. The following abstract, taken from the journal kept by the Bishop in this visitation, will not, we trust, be unacceptable to many of our readers.

"Left the Wharf at 4 O'Clock A.M. In the forepart of the day, our passage through the harbour to the sea was sufficiently pleasant—the weather was clear and the prospect delightful. But about noon a thick fog came on which completely deprived us of all view of the shore, and rendered our navigation disagreable and even dangerous. The same continuing at the approach of night, the Captain deemed it prudent to cast anchor until the following day.

July 11th. Weighed anchor at a very early hour, and proceeded on our voyage, the fog still extremely dense. At six breakers were discovered at a very short distance a-head. Great alarm and confusion on board. The Captain in his perplexity gave no orders. The presence of mind of a passenger, who had formerly been master of a vessel, saved us from destruction. He directed the Engineer instantly to put back ship, which order was promptly executed. It was soon ascertained, that the rocks, which had caused us so much danger, formed a part of Boon-Island. At 10 O'Clock A.M. we reached Portland. Left the **Legislator,** and went on board the **Patent,** Captain

Cramm. After an hour's delay in taking in wood, put off from the shore and stood for Belfast. On the approach of night again cast anchor in consequence of the fog.

[146] **July 12th.** Proceeded on our voyage. Arrived at Belfast, at 1 O'Clock P.M. Went on shore, while the Boat was taking in wood, to inquire on what day and at what hour the stage usually left Belfast for Bangor. At 3 O'Clock the Boat started for Castine—arrived there at 8 O'Clock, and remained there the whole night still beset by the fog.

July 13th. Left Castine at 4 O'Clock A.M.—At 1 O'Clock touched at Cramberry Island to take in a new supply of wood. Went on shore with General Wool, Mr. Brown, agent for the Steam-boat, and some others. Admired the great quantity of Cod fish spread out to dry on this Island, a place of great resort for fishermen—Saw upwards of thirty sail of Boats standing in and out, and nearly a third of that number already moored and discharging their Cargoes. Weather clear and bright. After a short delay proceeded again on our voyage, with the coast in sight. At night the fog set in again; but at this time, we had got too far out to sea to apprehend any danger from land.

July 14th. Arose and went on deck a little after 4 O'Clock—The first object which presented itself was the Light-house at the entrance into Passamaquoddy Bay. The fog was still dense and it was only at intervals any object could be descried. The Captain as he drew near caused his bell to be rung, which was immediately answered from the great Bell of the Lighthouse. All the passengers crowded the deck as we approached the entrance; the fog cleared away as the Sun arose, which afforded a delightful view of the scenerary [sic] around. Reached Lubeck at 8 O'Clock—stopped for a moment to take in a passenger, and continued on to Eastport where we finally arrived at 10 O'Clock. Took breakfast and went on shore.

Had scarcely landed when I saw a number of Indians of both sexes of the Passamaquoddy tribe who had just left their Canoes and were going up to one of the stores to trade.[24] A perfect stranger in this town I accosted one of the Indians and requested him to shew me the way. He paid no attention to my request and proceed[ed] on. I then addressed myself to another whom I perceived just crossing the street. He stopped for a while—looked stedfastly at me, then shook his head and left me. I soon recollected that I had seen at Boston, the year before, an Indian of this [147] tribe, whose name was Socco-Bason. (James Vincent) I made up to a group of Indians, and inquired whether he had come to town. One of them answered in broken english and informed me that he had—and would go and look for him. He returned soon after with Socco-Bason, who immediately recognized me. The news of my arrival soon spread through the town. I informed Socco-

Bason that my intention was to repair to Pleasant-Point, their Village, without delay and wished him to acquaint his brethren with it. He promised me to notify them and stated that he would himself shortly return home, and in the afternoon come again with several canoes to conduct me to it. He then accompanied me to the house of Mr. Jeremiah Kelly, a respectable Catholic of East-Port, where I found the Rev. Mr. Ffrench, whom I had sent to this town the preceding year. After making some inquiry into the state of religion at Eastport, and the adjoining country, I requested him to accompany me to Pleasant-Point whither it was my intention to proceed immediately, in order to assist me in preparing the Indians and their children for the sacraments of confirmation and the Eucharist. In the afternoon, as it had been arranged, the Indians, who were to conduct me to their village arrived, in four bark-canoes with the Lieutenant Governor at their head. They were dressed in the full costume of their nation and in their gayest apparel. On entering the Parlour each of them alternately advanced and kissed my hand respectfully; and after a short conversation invited me to repair to their canoes. The afternoon was pleasant, and we set out. The distance from East-Port to Pleasant-Point does not exceed six or seven miles. On reaching the wharf I was invited to take my seat in the middle of a large and beautiful Canoe which was paddled by Socco-Bason in front and another Indian in rear. Rev. Mr. Ffrench with two Indians occupied another Canoe. Our baggage was conveyed in the two remaining ones which followed behind. We had scarcely put off from shore, when each of the Indians struck fire and lighted his pipe, a matter, it would seem, quite indispensa-[148]ble with them; for so great is their attachment to the Pipe, they would sooner on some occasions, as they acknowledged to me, go without their dinner. When we had reached a point of land from which their village could be seen, a salute was fired with their Carabines, which was answered from the village by a discharge as well of carabines as of a Six-Pounder which they had mounted for purposes of ceremony. A flag, bearing a red cross on a white ground, was also hoisted. This firing continued without intermission until the Canoes reached the shore. On arriving the whole population flocked to the landing with the Governor, a venerable old man, at their head, to welcome me. He addressed me in tolerably good french, which he must have learnt in Canada, and expressed the liveliest joy at seeing once more a Bishop before he died. He knelt down, and received my blessing, which I also gave to all the others who had equally placed themselves on their knees to receive it.

From the landing we proceeded to the Church where after offering up a prayer, I expressed to them my happiness at being among them for the purpose of affording them the benefits of their religion—that I had visited them expressly, in order to become acquainted with them, and see with my own eyes their present condition, with a view to better it, if in my power. I then caused all the children above eight years of age, as well as those among the adults, who had not yet been confirmed, to be paraded before me; and inquiry to be made how many among them were sufficiently instructed to be admitted to the sacrament of confirmation. I had already been apprised that the Rev. Mr. Ffrench had made frequent visits during two of the last months and had during this time taken some pains to instruct them. I accordingly directed him to assist me in hearing the confessions of all those whom he should deem sufficiently instructed, and in otherwise prepairing them for confirmation, which I intended to confer the following day.

I then left the Church and repaired to my lodgings. These were assigned me in a small wooden building at a short distance from the Church, which was of better construction than the ordinary habitations of the Indians, although of mean appearance. I had two chambers on the ground floor, one of which was used as [149] a kitchen. The village is situate on a tongue of land which juts with the Bay, and consists of rude cabins built of unplaned pineboards, with an opening at top or at one of the ends for the smoke to escape. Every family possesses one of these Cabins and scarcely ever spends a winter in them; for at the approach of cold weather, the Indians take care to withdraw into the interior of the forest, where they may have plenty of wood for their fires; for this reason their habitations are constructed rather for the summer than for the winter. The abbé Romagné, a worthy french ecclesiastick, had been the last tenant of the house which I now occupied. He had laboured, during many years, and with great success, in this arduous mission, and had left it with the sole view of returning to France, where he hoped to alleviate his great infirmities. I had not the pleasure of knowing him; but his attention to these poor Indians, and the happy fruit of his apostolick labours are yet quite visible, and have given me great cause to regret his departure, especially as his experience would have been of essential service to me in the government and instruction of this portion of my flock. He had left the mission but a few years before I was appointed to take charge of the Diocess, regretted by all.

Sunday, July 15th. Said Mass in the Indian Church, at 8 O'Clock; all the Passamaquoddies were present. At 11 O'Clock a solemn procession was formed to the Church which was composed of the whole Tribe. As soon as it began to move, preceded by the Cross-bearer, the Indians, who followed in it, intoned a hymn in their own language which was sung with enthusiasm by all the others. When it had arrived at the Church, the Rev. Mr. Ffrench began the **Asperges;** Mass was afterwards sung according to the notes of

M. **Dumont** in his **Missa regia,** with a precision which would have done honour to many of the Choirs of Europe. A number of Protestants from East-Port, and the adjacent country were present, attracted by the arrival of the Bishop. [150] They conducted themselves with great propriety in the Church; indeed, the behaviour of the Indians themselves in the house of God, was well calculated to inspire respect, for they never look either to the right or to the left while there, and during the whole time of the celebration of the divine mysteries, they appear absorbed in the contemplation of what passes before them at the altar. At the end of Mass I delivered a discourse to the Protestants present, in which I expounded the principal mysteries of our holy religion and pointed out its superior excellence over other religions. The leading points of my discourse I caused to be interpreted to the Indians who did not understand English I afterwards addressed myself particularly to the young Indians and those adults who were about to be confirmed, and endeavoured to impress upon them tne dispositions essentially requisite to receive this sacrament worthily; and at length proceeded to administer this sacrament to all those who were sufficiently instructed and prepared to receive it; several of them had already been admitted to holy communion at the early mass in the morning. After the solemn Benediction which I gave them at the conclusion, we left the Church in the same order in which we had come, and returned to the Village. In the afternoon, at 4 O'Clock Vespers were sung in which the Indians acquitted themselves fully as well as in the forenoon, thanks to the good Missionary, their former Pastor, who had so well instructed them. After Vespers they recited ordinary prayers for the evening, and then retired quietly to their Cabins. The Rev. Mr. Ffrench remained in the Church, in order to hear the confessions of those who were preparing for their first communion.

July 16th. Again said Mass at 8 O'Clock, after which I administered the holy sacrament of confirmation to other Indians, young and old, who all gave evidence of a sincere devotion. After this we repaired in procession to the Burying-ground, where I performed the usual service over the graves of those who had departed this life since the last visit of a Priest. In the course of this day I received a visit from a Calvinist minister, by the name of K***[25] who informed me that he was sent to [151] this village by the Governour and Council of the State of Maine, in the capacity of School-Master to the young Indians, and that he received a salary as such from them as well as from the government of the United States. I soon saw through the game this man was playing, and penetrated the object he had principally in view in coming to this village. However, I said nothing more to him at this time, than express the hope that he would not interfere with the religion of the Indians. He replied that he neither had meddled, nor should meddle with it. I then informed him that it was my intention to visit his school the following day in order to satisfy myself as to the progress of the children under his care. The Rev. M. Ffrench was not present at this conversation. A short time after K* * *. had left me, he returned from the Church; and having informed him of the visit of this Calvinist Minister, he immediately acquainted me with what he had known of his conduct towards the Indians, and especially of his **Report** published at Cambridge, and addressed to a Society of Calvinist Missionaries, of which he is a member, in which he considers himself not only as a School-Master under the pay of government, but also as a Missionary sent among the Passamaquoddies under the pay of this same Society. I was astonished at the coolness with which he had, a moment before, persisted in assuring me that he acted only in the capacity of a School-master, and did not at all meddle with religion. I accordingly resolved to take further information on this subject, and not to lose sight of him.

After breakfast I went to the Council-hall of the Indians. This was an oblong room, constructed with rough boards, in which the men generally held their meetings when they deliberated on the affairs of the Tribe. On entering, I found the men already assembled and seated on the ground strewed with leaves and the tender branches of the Spruce. They all arose to salute me at my entrance, and conducted me to a Seat somewhat elevated, covered also with spruce and near to that of the aged Governor. I inquired into the state of their affairs, examined their papers, their treaties with the Government, and other of their transactions of a public nature. They urged [152] me to send them a Priest who should reside among them. I acquainted them with my situation in this repect; that at present this was impossible, as I had none to spare; but that I hoped the following year to have it in my power to send them one who should take special care of the instruction of their children for whom I felt much concerned—that I was pained to see that the Governor and Council of the State of Maine had sent them a Calvinist Minister, who was a stranger, and an enemy to their religion, to take the charge of their children in this important matter—that most assuredly they would not have done so, had a Catholick Priest lived among them and charged himself with their education, especially as it was neither the policy nor the intention of the Government to interfere in religious matters, which was bound to protect all alike. I informed them, moreover, that, for the present, the Rev. Mr. Ffrench, who was stationed at East-Port, should be directed to visit them often, attend to their spiritual wants, and afford, at the same time, such instruction to their Children as circumstances would allow. The Indians appeared very well satisfied, and promised to conduct themselves in a satisfactory manner towards the

Priest whom I should send to be their spiritual Father. I then gave them my
benediction, which they received on their knees, and withdrew from the
Council-chamber. After this I went from Cabin to Cabin, and visited each
family in the Village informing myself of their health and respective situation. In the afternoon I was invited to be present at a diversion, which is a
great favourite with them, called the game at Hurley, in which I had an opportunity of witnessing their surprising strength and agility, which exceeded any thing I had seen before. This exercize lasted about two hours.
They perspired copiously during the whole time. All who took an active
part in this diversion were full grown men; the married men on one side,
and the young and unmarried, in equal number, on the other. The day was
carried by the former as I had anticipated. These being older and more
vigorous, had acquired from long habit, greater skill and dexterity in the
management of the play. I was next invited to be present at their dance. I
accepted the invitation the more readily as I was curious to learn as [153]
much of their manners and customs as possible. This dance took place in
their Council-chamber as it was the only spacious apartment they had in
the village. As soon as night had set in they all met together in it, both men
and women, dressed in their most gaudy apparel. The room was well
lighted.

After having remained seated for some time in profound silence, they
arose and walked, at first, leisurely around a kind of theatre which had
been constructed in the middle of the hall, in a single file, the men in advance and the women following. The principal singer was at the head of all;
he held in his hand a horn which contained a few pebbles mixed with small
shot, which he occasionally struck against his arm, and this produced a rat-
tling noise which he accompanied with his voice, as he beat the time. When
he became animated he jumped and sprung forward crying with a loud
voice, which all who followed in the dance imitated. As it continued, so it
became more and more animated—they were thrown into a violent per-
spiration; and thus they continued to go around the theatre always jumping
and hallowing. Yet, the greatest order and decency reigned throughout the
entire dance. The step of the men was generally long and slow; that of the
women short and quick; but all was done in time according to measure. As
great uniformity prevailed in the whole of their movements, I withdrew at
the end of a half hour, convinced I had seen enough to have a correct idea of
their dance, and satisfied that the whole was conducted with the greatest
decency and decorum.

July 17th. Said Mass at 7 O'Clock; all the Indians assisted at it. I again
gave confirmation to those who had hitherto not been able to prepare for it,
and among others to the son of an Indian named Stanislaus. So great was

the desire of this good Indian to have his son confirmed, although confined to his bed at home by a violent fever, he, with the aid of some of his friends, conveyed the bed with the youth, aged 16, lying thereon, to the Church in the midst of the ceremony. His ardent zeal greatly edified me; but I was fearful that such an exertion with the exposure might prove finally prejudicial to the youth. He had, however, received the [154] last sacraments the evening before, and was well disposed: I confirmed him with the others to the very great joy of his Father. After breakfast which consisted in the ordinary diet of the Indians, I took the Census of the tribe, and found that the entire population amounted to 450 souls. About 15 or 20 individuals were said to be absent at this time.

The hour appointed for the examination of the children under the direction of K* * *. having arrived, I repaired to the school, accompanied by the Rev. Mr. Ffrench. K* * *. was already there with 14 or 15 children of both sexes. I inquired how long he had been employed as school-master among the Indians? He informed me that he had been, if I mistake not, about three years. I had then conceived hopes that the children had made some progress; but what was my surprise, after having examined them, to find that there was not one individual among them who could spell even a word of two syllables, and but a very small number who could even recite their letters. It was evident that K* * * had been sent hither for the purpose of receiving the double salary of Missionary of the Calvinist Missionary Society, and of School-Master of the Government of Maine as well as of the United States, and that the whole was a piece of imposition practised with a view to obtain a kind of retreat which the Sect had procured him; for he had been dismissed by the congregation of Portland where he had formerly exercised his ministry. A man of this character was certainly highly dangerous to the simple and uneducated Indians. I had learnt moreover that he had occasionally distributed presents among the most influential of the Tribe. I had, however, no means of applying a remedy to the evil, having no Priest to station there to counteract his designs.

Having examined the children in the presence of Rev. Mr. Ffrench and found that they knew absolutely nothing, I turned to the Calvinist Minister K* * *. and asked him whether his services might not in future be dispensed with, seeing the little progress which the Children had made? I then drew out of my pocket the report of his ministerial labours among the Passamaquoddy Indians, drawn up by himself and sent to the Calvinist Missionary society, in which he had styled himself, not a school-[155]master, but **Missionary**. I asked him whether or not he had attended and prayed over some of the Indians, when dying, as he had stated in his report? Whether, on other occasions he had not also exercised among them the functions of a

Minister?—And, in fine, whether his **Report** agreed with what he had stated on a former occasion, viz: that he had never interfered with them in matters of religion? The sight of the Pamphlet confounded him, obliging him to acknowledge that he had lied, and during the first moments he knew not what reply to make. At length, he gave me to understand, "that, in truth, he was considered a missionary by the Calvinist Society, and in this capacity he was obliged to give in **a report** in which he must appear to have laboured as a Minister, in order to receive his salary; but that in reality he had never exercised any ministerial function among the Indians, and that he never would meddle with religion among them." Such are the men who are generally employed by the Missionary and Bible Societies to send them **faithful** reports of the state of the countries to which they are sent, and which these Societies afterwards scatter in every direction. An infinity of these **Reports** are to be found in Boston. We have them from the Sandwich Isles in the Pacifick, from Malta, from Greece, from the Archipelago, from Smyrna, from Constantinople, the East Indies, and sundry other places. They are commonly drawn up in the form of letters; they are generally filled with the most abominable and manifest falsehoods. Nevertheless, they are read with great avidity by the common Classes, and circulate through the United States. Large sums of money are collected for the support of these Missionaries, who always take care to render to their employers regular accounts of their surprising success in the conversion of the natives and even of Catholics, but which are sure to be contradicted by the Captains of Vessels and others arriving from the same places.[26]

In the afternoon I visited again the Indians in their Cabins, and spent a little longer time with them, especially with the old and infirm. I went also to see the sick youth whom [156] I had confirmed in the morning, and whom I found extremely low, his fever having considerably increased. I conversed a short time with him, and found him in the happiest disposition. As he had received all the last sacraments, I had nothing more to do than to exhort him to submit with patience and resignation to the will of God.

July 18th. Said Mass at 6 O'Clock. The whole Tribe attended as usual. Those Indians, who composed the Choir, sang during the whole time of the celebration a number of hymns in their own tongue. I addressed them a short discourse through an Interpretor—"exhorted them to be faithful in their duty to God, to their neighbour and to themselves, and especially to remain constantly attached to their holy religion, and to live in union and charity with one another. I informed them that it was my intention to leave them today, in order to go to their Brethren, the Penobscots, for whom I felt the same solicitude, and requested them to offer up their prayers to God for the success of my voyage." Having finished the discourse, a woman who had committed a scandalous fault, and for which, agreably to the custom prevailing among the Indians, she had been condemned to kneel outside of the door of the Church during the divine office for three months, was this day admitted again into the Church by special favour in consequence of her sincere repentance, although the time had not yet wholly expired.—After Breakfast, I again convened the Indians—bid them a last Adieu—gave them my blessing, and set out for East-Port in the same manner in which I had come, accompanied by the Rev. Mr. Ffrench. We arrived after a few hours. Went immediately to Mr. Kelly's where the Rev. Mr. Ffrench had his apartments. After Dinner took a walk through the town for the purpose of selecting a Lot of land for the site of a future Church. The Catholics here were few in number and these in general very poor; but they expressed great anxiety to have a small Church erected in which they might assemble on Sundays to hear the word of God. Accordingly to favour their views as much as possible I selected a spot of ground which I recommended to them to purchase as soon as they should find themselves able, and encouraged them to open a subscription immediately for this object. On my return to Mr. Kelly's, was waited upon by [157] three of the principal men of the Town, all of whom were Protestants, and requested by them to preach. They informed me that the people of East-Port were desirous of hearing me, and as the Catholics had as yet no Church, they offered me one of theirs. I accepted their invitation and offer and left it to them to appoint the day and hour. They appointed the following day at 8 O'Clock P.M.

July 19th. Said Mass in Mr. Kelly's parlour, the same having been previously fitted up for the purpose. Many of the Indians from Pleasant Point attended besides the Catholics of the town. After Mass gave a short exhortation and administered the sacrament of confirmation to about 18 or 20 individuals, some of whom were from St. Andrew's on the British side of the Bay. At 8 O'Clock, according to promise, repaired to the Unitarian Church, accompanied by Rev. Mr. Ffrench. A great concourse of people had already assembled, consisting mostly of Protestants. The service was opened with prayer by the Rev. Mr. Ffrench, after which I delivered a discourse which lasted about an hour. The people present conducted themselves in an orderly manner and listened with great attention. Both before and after sermon a number of select hymns were sung by the Choir.

July 20th. Returned the visits received the preceding day. At 5 O'Clock went on board the Steam Boat, **Patent,** Captain Cram, where I found my former fellow passenger, General Wool, likewise on his return. The Rev. Mr. Ffrench having to visit a sick Catholic at Lubeck, accompanied me thus far. and took his leave.

July 21st. Arrived at Castine at 8 O'Clock P.M. Went on shore to inquire whether any conveyance could be had to Bangor from this place. Found there was no stage; nor could a horse and Chaise be procured. Returned to the Steam-Boat, and proceeded in her as far as Belfast. Arrived there at midnight, and took lodging at Appleton's Hotel.

July 22d (Sunday). Could not celebrate Mass. Read the divine Office. After breakfast, inquired whether there were any Catholics in this town?— Was informed there were none. Took a walk to the lower part of the town to see whether [158] I could discover any. Was unsuccessful; returned to the Hotel and employed myself in reciting the divine Office until Dinner. After dinner took another walk to the upper part of the town—had not proceeded far, when I met an Irish woman coming into town from the country with a child in her arms. Stopped her and inquired "whether she were not a Catholic"? After surveing [sic] me cautiously with her eyes some moments, she answered, "she was." I then asked her "whither she was going"? She said "to Mr. McGann's."—"Would she conduct me to his house"? She said, "No;" for, what had **the like of me** to do at Mr. McGann's? I stated to her that I desired very much to see him, as well as all the other Catholics in town. "Surely," she replied, "you were not going to his house when I first saw you; why therefore do you wish to go to it now"? "In order to give him and the other Catholics a little good advice on the Sabbath day," said I. "Maybe, then, you are a Minister"? said she, looking archly at me. "I am," I replied. "Then, I can tell you," said she, turning abruptly off, "neither he, nor his family, want to see **the like of you**." At this time it began to rain. I opened my Umbrella, and held it over her and her child, following her as she walked on, determined not to lose the opportunity of seeing as many of the Catholics as possible, before I left town, and of ascertaining their number. We had not proceeded far in this way, when she stopped abruptly, and said: "Surely, it is not to McGann's I am going now; why therefore do you follow me"? "Because you told me awhile ago, it was thither you were going." "Why then, I am going to another place now," said she. "It is no matter, I shall follow you until you shew me where McGann lives." "Well, he lives down there," she replied, pointing to a house near to one of the wharves of the village. I immediately went thither. On entering a room of this house I beheld on every side but objects of poverty and wretchedness—a sick woman groaning in a corner of the room; two other women, with very poor clothing, seated on the floor, eight or ten sickly children huddled around, and only one man, and he also poorly clad. I soon learnt from him that he and another had just arrived at Belfast with their families—that they had been able to get but little work since their arrival—that almost all of [159] them had been, and some of them

were still sick—and that they were perishing for the want of the necessaries of life. Seeing so much misery I immediately informed him who I
was, gave him money, and directed him to go out without delay, and
purchase tea, sugar, bread, butter, and milk, if he could find it, at that hour
of the day,—and that afterwards I should enable him to procure other
provisions. As he went out, I called to him to purchase, also, some ginger-
bread for the children, who appeared very hungry. After this I approached
the bed where the poor sick woman lay, and spoke to her in a manner suited
to her present circumstances, and at the same time informed her that I
should leave her and return in a couple of hours to hear her confession as
well as the confessions of all the others in the house. The poor woman was
greatly overjoyed and with abundance of tears expressed her gratitude to
God for having sent her a Priest at so critical a time in a foreign land. In a
short time the man returned with the tea, sugar and other things sent for. I
caused the tea to be immediately prepared and given to the sick woman. I
next distributed the ginger-bread among the children. A total change immediately ensued. Gloom and almost despair were succeeded by joy and
hope. I then acquainted them with the nature of the country into which they
had just arrived, the favourable prospects it held out to the sober and
industrious—and concluded by observing to them "that in my opinion
Whitefield would be a far more suitable country for them, as a number of
their countrymen had already taken farms there, and were doing well." I
requested them, as I was about to withdraw, "to give notice to other
Catholics who might be in town, that I should return in a couple of hours to
this house, for the purpose of giving them an opportunity of going to their
confessions; for," added I, "it is important that you should make a good
beginning in this country of your adoption; and besides, you know not, when
you may enjoy another opportunity of seeing a Priest."

About this time, the woman whom I had met in the upper part of the
town, came in. As soon as she had entered and seated herself, staring all
the time wildly at me: "There," said I jokingly, "is an Irish woman and a
Catholick, [160] who, when asked by a stranger, to shew the way to a
friend's house, refused to do it! She cannot be a true born Catholic." "And
surely it was, because I thought it was no good you were after," she
replied, continuing still to gaze around. "Whist! Whist!" said one of the
women present, "mind,—it is to the Bishop you are speaking all this
while." I could not forbear laughing at the peculiar tone in which this was
expressed, in which they all joined. The poor woman seemed much dis-
concerted for a while; but when I assured her that I viewed her conduct on
that occasion as an act of prudence on her part, and that I commended her
for it, she soon recovered her spirits. "No, No;" said she, "it is not for the

like of me to behave amiss to my own Clergy when I know them."—Upon this I left the room and returned to the Hotel, greatly pleased with the discovery I had made. After an interval of two hours, or thereabouts, I returned, according to promise, to McGan's, where I found a pretty good number assembled. I gave them an exhortation and afterwards heard all their confessions. In conclusion, I recommended to them to be particularly careful of their conduct, attentive to the duty, which they owed to God, and observant of his holy law. At parting, I gave them more money to supply their more pressing necessities, and was particularly happy to see the good effects the tea had already produced upon the sick woman; for, she was soon able to move about a little, and exhibited in her appearance a great alteration for the better. I gave them all my blessing, took leave of them and departed.

July 23d. Left Appleton's Hotel at 10 O'Clock in the Mail stage for Bangor. The distance is 32 miles. On this route after leaving the half-way house, as it is called, I was very near being precipitated, coach and all, into a deep ravine, while descending a steep hill, in consequence of one of the horses becoming unmanageable.—Arrived at Bangor about 6 O'Clock P.M. Inquired for Mr. Call, the Indian Agent. Found him at the stage Tavern— expressed to him my desire to proceed on without delay to Old Town, distant 12 miles. He informed me that the stage would not leave Bangor for the above place before the ensuing morning, that it would be difficult to procure [161] a conveyance at this hour; but that if I would consent to wait until the following day, he would accompany me thither. I acceded to his proposal.

July 24th. Left Bangor for Old Town, after breakfast, in the Stage. Mr. Call not having been able to get ready at the hour of departure promised to follow on in a Chaise. Arrived at Old Town at 12 O'Clock—dined. During dinner Mr. Call arrived; and immediately crossed the river to the Island where the Indians reside, to apprize them of my arrival and make arrangements for my reception. When all things were prepared he returned and invited me into a Canoe. Landed on the Island amidst the firing of Carabines and the loud report of another Six-Pounder. A flag similar to the one at Pleasant Point was at the same time hoisted. The Indians received me drawn up in a double row on the beach, the men in front, and the women in the rear. They all knelt down and received my benediction. After conversing for some moments with one or two whose countenances I had recognised having seen them at Boston I proceeded to the Church where, after prayer, I addressed them in a short discourse, and went to the house prepared for my lodgings.

July 25th. I opened the mission with a solemn High-Mass, at which all the Indians assisted. The Choir here also acquitted itself in a manner highly satisfactory. I was really astonished to find among them so many individuals who had retained the Chant of the Church notwithstanding the great length of time this tribe had been without a Priest; for during the last five years a Priest had visited them only at long intervals and for a short time each. The same evening I commenced hearing their confessions which were protracted until late at night. I found that the young men could all recite their prayers, and that the Parents had been as faithful in instructing their children here as they had been at Pleasant-Point.

July 26th. Again celebrated a solemn High-Mass; afterwards repaired to the Burying-ground followed by the whole Tribe where I went through the ceremonies and recited [162] the prayers prescribed by the Church over those who had died since the last visit of a Priest. After Breakfast I again set about hearing confessions, in which I was interupted for some moments by Mr. Call, the Indian Agent, who introduced two persons to me, one of whom was a Unitarian Minister. I returned to the Confessional where I remained until the hour of dinner. While at dinner some Indians came in and entered into conversation with me. Hearing the name of one of them mentioned, I recalled to mind what a merchant in Bangor had told me of his unfair dealing in trade. I availed myself of this opportunity to speak to him about it. "Sabbatis," said I, "I have heard a complaint against you at Bangor, in which I have been told that in skinning your Beaver, you always leave a good deal of the flesh of the animal adhering to the skin, in order to make it weigh the more."—"That is true," he replied; but as long as the white men continue to sell me meat with large bones in it, I shall continue to sell them Beaver-skins with the flesh remaining on them." I could not forbear smiling at this idea of Indian justice, in which all seemed to agree. After dinner I returned to the confessional and continued there till 10 O'Clock at night.

July 28th. Said low-Mass. The Indians during it sang some hymns and canticles in their own tongue. Admitted about 20 to communion of the more advanced in years. After Breakfast resumed hearing confessions—continued until 2 O'Clock P.M. Dined. After dinner recommenced hearing confessions and continued until 11 O'Clock P.M. So great was the desire of being heard in confession among both great and small, that I was allowed scarcely any respite, having no Priest with me, and the whole duty, consequently devolving on me alone.

July 29th. (Sunday) Recommenced hearing confessions at a very early hour, and continued until 10 O'Clock A.M.—Found upon examination that I had heard as many as 120, eighty of whom were to be confirmed. Began to prepare for solemn High-Mass. An immense concourse of people, attracted partly by curiosity and partly by sinister motives, had already crossed the river and begun to encompass the house in which I was. [163] Some of these had gone even so far as to enter my apartment uninvited, whilst others pulled down the curtains of the windows, and thrust their heads through the opening to my very great annoyance and inconvenience. These people consisted chiefly of the lowest class of society—their usual occupation was lumbering—their habits were gross and their manners uncouth. Religion they had none of any kind. They had been brought up, however, with strong prejudices against the Catholic. Occasionally individuals among them would use harsh expressions, such as—that unless free access to the house were given them they would enter it by force;—and if others would unite with them they would proceed to pull it down. At this time I was occupied in taking a list of the names of those who were to be confirmed, and of those who were to be admitted to holy communion. Hearing the expressions above mentioned, I arose and advanced to the window, from which I addressed the Banditts without. My words were those of remonstrance. They appeared to feel ashamed of their conduct and walked away. But these were scarcely gone when others succeeded; and the same scene was renewed. Thus harassed, I continued writing. When the list was made out, I sent word to the Indians to assemble at the door of my Cabbin, (for, the humble dwelling in which I lodged scarcely deserved a better name,) and at the same time gave directions, that no one should be suffered to enter the Church, until the Indians should move to it in procession. I began to apprehend that these uncouth woodmen might force their way into and preoccupy it to the exclusion of the Indians. My orders were speedily obeyed. In a short time the whole Tribe was assembled and in waiting, each one dressed in his best attire. A Procession was soon formed. The Children preceded by a Cross-Bearer marched first—after these the Men—then the women walking two and two; after these came the Choir of Chanters. At a small distance behind, I followed, dressed in Rochet and Surplice, and wearing the Mitre and Crozier. On my right was the Governor of the Tribe, holding the Card of confirmation before his breast; and on my left, the Lieutenant Governor, holding an Umbrella. It was now about 11 O'Clock [164] and the weather was uncommonly warm. We proceeded slowly as the Chanters intoned a solemn hymn in their native tongue. When I first saw the crowd of people in every direction, and knowing well their general character I became in some degree apprehensive that some disorder might be occasioned by them in the course of the procession. But whether awed by its imposing solemnity, and the beautiful order maintained in it, or whether restrained by some other motive, they observed during the whole time it lasted, the strictest silence. Neither did any of them attempt to close in upon the ranks, nor attempt to fill up the space before—but they all kept off at a respectful distance, and seemed rather filled with admiration, than inclined to disturb. Thus we continued to move slowly through the main street of the Camp. As we approached the Church the lines divided and formed an avenue, down which I passed, whilst all knelt, into the great door of the Church. This was soon filled by the Indians. Three Door-keepers immediately stationed themselves at the door to keep out strangers. Their task soon became an arduous one, from the extreme desire of all to obtain admittance. They, however, maintained their ground. Some little noise was made, and some sharp words were exchanged; but no great disorder ensued.—On entering the Church I proceeded to baptize seven children. This duty being discharged I commenced High-Mass. Never did I experience greater heat than on this occasion. The weather was excessively warm; but in addition to this, I had to encounter all the heat produced by a crowded congregation in a small Church, every window and door of which was closed; for, the Indians would not suffer any of them to be opened through fear of insults from the rabble without. During Mass I gave communion to 70 or 80 Individuals, who evinced sincere piety and fervour. At the end of Mass, I gave a short exhortation to those about to be confirmed; after which I proceeded to administer the sacrament of confirmation to 82 persons, the greater part of whom were children. The ceremony was long and fatiguing, and the weather continued intensely hot. As soon as the whole was concluded I withdrew from the Church to my apartments where I had scarcely arrived when a deputation was sent to me by the Lumberers described above, requesting me [165] to give them a discourse. I sent word to them, that, if they would go home quietly and return to the Church at 5 O'Clock in the evening, I would then address them. On receiving this word they immediately dispersed.

3 O'Clock P.M. Dined—but had scarcely any appetite in consequence of the great heat and fatigue in the forenoon. After dinner lay for an half hour on my Pallet—arose, took my Breviary with a chair and retired to the shade of the house, and began to read my Vespers. Some of the Lumberers who continued still to lounge and hanker about the premises, seeing me out of doors came around and gazed at me as if I had been a Bear or some strange wild Beast. I said nothing to them but let them quietly gaze their fill,—and continued to read my Breviary. After they had gazed a short time they left me, apparently fully satisfied with the extent of their observations. At 5 O'Clock P.M. I sent an Indian, whose name was Michel Louis and who acted as Sacristan, to give notice through the Camp that it was time for Vespers. This he did by hallowing, there being no Bell to the

Church. I also gave directions that the Lumberers and other strangers should at this time be admitted into the Church, as I had promised to preached [sic] to them. At the hour appointed and when all had assembled, I went up to the Altar and intoned Vespers. The order of the divine service was the same time as is usual in the Catholic Church in the afternoon. The Psalms were all sung with the hymn of the **Magnificat.** When these were finished I turned to the People, and addressed them. I have often been obliged in the course of my ministry to chide and to reprove for ill conduct; but never on any occasion were my feelings wound up to a greater pitch than on the present. The mean, unmannerly disgraceful behaviour of these Lumberers during the whole forenoon was still present to my mind. I contrasted their behaviour with that of the Indians, and inquired which of the two gave the greater proofs of civilization? I continued to address them for about an half hour during which I said many things respecting the religion of the Indians which must have left an impression upon their minds very different from that which they had brought with them into the Church. They remained all the time as if they had been chained down. Not an individual [166] stirred until I had concluded. The effect of the discourse could be easily perceived. Even the Indians, though they did not comprehend a single word of it, were astonished; for, they withdrew from the Church, when the service was over, confounded and ashamed; nor did they stop, as they had been always accustomed to do before, to ramble and saunter about the Camp; but went directly to their Boats and passed over to the other shore. "Father." said an Indian to me, after I had retired to my room, "what did you say to make these bad white men go away so soon?" "Why, Louis," said I, "I told them it was an invariable practice with me, whenever I wished to find out who had good sense and a good religion, to look at their behaviour, and I told them that according to this rule, I found the Indians had far more sense and a far better religion than they." the Indians had far more sense and a far better religion than they." "Father, that is true," replied the Indian, and seemed greatly to enjoy it.

At 7 O'Clock recommenced hearing confessions, and continued until 10— heard nearly 30. Just as I had concluded for the night, a little Indian Boy, about 12 years old, came to me to complain, that after I had given him leave to make his first communion in the morning, as he approached the Altar, his Uncle had drawn him back, and would not let him go to the holy table. He seemed greatly affected, and wept bitterly. I immediately inquired into the matter, and found that his Uncle had acted in this manner upon the supposition that this Boy had not received leave to communicate. I explained the matter to him, heard his confession anew, and promised to give him communion at Mass the following morning. He departed quite overjoyed.

July 30th. Heard some more confessions this morning. After this celebrated Mass—admitted the little boy, spoken of above, to communion with 30 others—was greatly pleased with their piety. After Breakfast married a couple of Indians, with an Interpretor. Went through the whole Camp and visited every family. At 12 dined. At 1 O'Clock called a general meeting of the Indians in their large hall, to take my leave of them. They entered the hall with every expression of sorrow and grief on their countenances. When seated I addressed them, through an Interpretor, a short discourse informing them, that the time [167] was now come for me to depart, and to commit them to the care of their good Father who is in heaven—promised to see them again as soon as I could—and hoped when I came again I should bring a Priest with me to leave with them—informed them, moreover, that I should as I passed through Portland, call upon the Governor of Maine (Mr. Lincoln) and try to prevail on him to use his influence with the government to better their condition—warned them against disposing of any more of their lands—stated that it was the wish of some speculators to drive them back still farther into the interior of the country; but that this could not be done agreably to their treaty, without their consent—and this, as they valued their wives and little ones, they should never give.—After I had concluded, there was a pause for some moments; after which the Indian governor arose and expressed in a few words his own and his people's acknowledgements for the favour I had conferred upon by visiting and affording them the comforts of religion. He promised on the part of all to adhere strictly to my advice, and stated farther that he could not express in words the happiness which the word I had dropped, had imparted to all, viz: the promise of visiting them again, and of bringing with me besides a Priest whom I should leave with them. He then resumed his seat. After sitting for a moment longer in deep silence, and observing tears beginning to flow, I rose up and walked towards the landing. My trunk had already been conveyed and placed in a Canoe. They all followed closely and crowded around me. I walked on silently to the beach when I turned about and gave my blessing to all. I then stepped into the Canoe, and made a sign to the Sacristan who had accompanied me to put off from the shore. At this instant the Six Pounder was fired which was succeeded by a constant discharge of Carabines till the Canoe had reached the opposite shore. This was lined with Lumberers and other men employed in the numerous adjacent saw-mills in Old Town, some, nay, the greater part of whom were the very individuals, I had addressed in so pointed a manner the day before. They immediately made way and opened a Lane for me on landing, and [168] I passed with my Sacristan, through the middle of them without their having uttered a single word. When the Indians from the Island saw me land, about forty or fifty of them, both men and women, immediately took to their canoes and followed me. This movement was observed by the good young Indians who had accompanied me with the Sacristan, and whose heart was already full. "Father," said he to me, with eyes swimming in tears, my heart is sick." This he expressed with a most sorrowful countenance. "Here," said I to him, and at the same time taking out a half-dollar piece and presenting it to him,—"here, take this and you will be better." "No, no;" he replied shaking his head, "Father, I am not sick for that, but for your going away from us." "Take it, nevertheless," said I, "and keep it to remember me." The poor fellow took it, but at the same time wept bitterly.

I proceeded to the tavern, whence the Stage was to depart for Bangor. I had scarcely seated myself to wait for the Stage when a crowd of Indians rushed into the room and completely filled it. The half savage, rough and unprincipled Lumberers of the town, observing this, could not account for these demonstrations of attachment and respect. They crowded around and looked on with the air of people wrapped in wonder. On ordinary occasions they shewed no regard for the Indians, not even common civility; but, on this, they paid them every respect. If an Indian wished to move through the crowd of white people, they instantly gave way and made an opening for him. I thought I could perceive in this conduct, that they began to entertain a far more favourable opinion both of them and of their religion. About half past two, the Bangor Stage drove up to the door, and a call was made for the passengers. Unwilling to go through another parting scene, I simply bowed to the Indians, waved my hand and briskly entered the Stage. On driving from the door, when at some distance, I could still observe them looking on, which, I am persuaded they continued to do, as long as the Stage was in sight.—Poor, good, simple, harmless People!—Adieu! And may God protect and defend you against the semi-barbarous white people by whom you are surrounded! Hitherto, you have been sheltered by him—and, I trust, he will not yet abandon you!—Arrived in Bangor about 5 O'Clock P.M. Went immediately [169] to Mr. Call, the Indian Agent,—stated to him the highly improper conduct of the Lumberers on Sunday, and touched upon several other matters of a particular nature to which I directed his attention. He expressed his regret that indisposition had prevented him from having been present, as being a Magistrate, he could easily have prevented every intrusion. He promised faithfully to look into what I had represented to him, and as far as it depended on him, should apply a remedy.

July 31st. Left Bangor for Belfast in the Mail Stage, or rather in a light Waggon which carried the Mail, the Carriage formerly used for this purpose, having broken down the preceding day precisely in the same place where, in my journey up, I had been exposed to so much danger. Arrived at

Belfast at 11 O'Clock A.M. Got immediately into another Stage and continued my journey through Camden, Thomastown etc. and arrived at the Stage Hotel in Waldoboro at 6 O'Clock P.M. Spent the night there.

August 1st. Rose at 4 O'Clock—again took the Stage and arrived at the Mansion of the amiable and respectable Mr. Kavenagh at New Castle at 7 O'Clock. Took breakfast—then went with Mr. Edward Kavenagh, eldest Son of the former, to visit the Catholic Church in this place. Found it a neat, well finished decent Brick Building and well worthy of its principal Founder, his respectable Father. It is situate on an eminence within sight of his house and not more than a few hundred yards from it. A better situation for a Church could not have been found. It has a few acres attached to it, besides a decent burying ground. I was truly charmed with the spot, and only regretted that the number of Catholics was so small that the Rev. Mr. Ryan,[27] their Pastor, could not devote more of his time to them from his more numerous congregation at Whitefield, than one sunday in every month. Disappointed at not finding the above Reverend Gentleman at New Castle on my arrival, and anxious to see him as soon as possible for the purpose of making arrangements for confirmation in his respective congregations I set out at 4 O'Clock P.M., accompanied by young Mr. Kavenagh, for Whitefield. Met the Rev. Mr. Ryan [170] on the road, on his way to New Castle, about five miles from Whitefield. He returned and accompanied us to his lodgings. Arrived there at 7 O'Clock P.M. The weather was exceedingly warm the whole afternoon; and as we had performed our journey facing the Sun the entire way, the heat was more sensibly felt. Immediately on my arrival drank a cup of cold water—felt very unwell a little after it; but said nothing. At supper drank a cup of tea; yet did not feel better. At the usual time of retiring, went to bed. During the night experienced a fever—slept none. Arose in the morning with all the feelings of one about to encounter a serious illness. Could take no breakfast—took, however, a cup of tea; but eat [sic] nothing. Was anxious to conceal, lest I should give trouble to the worthy family at whose house Rev. Mr. Ryan lodged. Proposed to him a walk to the Church, which was a mile back on the public road. As soon as arrived, went to the Sacristy, took a chair, sat down and leaned my head against the wall—felt very ill. As he saw no disposition in me to look at the Church at that moment, he expressed a desire to absent himself for a while, stating that he had business with his brother. I requested him to go—that I should await his return there. He immediately left me while I continued leaning my head against the wall in a reclined posture in the Chair, still feeling very ill. In this posture I continued, varying it a little, till the return of Rev. Mr. Ryan, which was four hours afterwards. He roused me from my slumber by telling me it was the hour of dinner. Told him I was ready to return to the house though still felt very ill. Reached the house—the dinner was on the table—sat down—took a few mouthfulls; but experienced no appetite. After sitting a half hour with the family proposed to return to the Church—arrived—took my former position in the chair, and leaned my head against the wall. Rev. Mr. Ryan thinking I was inclined to sleep, again left me to myself and took a walk to his farm. I continued in this posture till towards evening, when I thought it incumbent on me to try at least to recite my Breviary. Took the Book and recited **Matins and Lauds** for the day, which I had not yet read. I then laid down the book, my head aching very much and sought a little repose. In a little while I again took up the book, and continued to recite until I had finished the whole. Walked into the little Orchard back [171] of the Church—soon returned to my chair in the Sacristy where I continued until Rev. Mr. Ryan came in, and informed me it was time to return to the house. Went down—took tea—conversed a little after it—retired to bed with my head still oppressed.

August 3d. Rose from bed something better—had slept well during the night—recited a part of my Breviary and sat down to Breakfast with a tolerable appetite. Afterwards walked to the Church with Rev. Mr. Ryan— took a view of it and went over the premises.—The Catholic Church in Whitefield is a framed building finished in the usual style of such buildings in country places—is of sufficient size to contain a pretty numerous congregation. Situate on a hill in front of the main rode it commands an extensive prospect. The country around can scarcely be said to be properly settled—the population is as yet thin and scattered. Here and there a farm house may be seen surrounded by forests of spruce and pine trees, with just a sufficiency of cleared land, to enable the Proprietor to live. A few years ago the whole country hereabouts was a wilderness. Much, therefore, has been done since it first began to be settled. The Church has ten acres of land surrounding it, one third only of which is cleared. On this a young orchard is planted. One of the greatest acquisitions here as an excellent spring of water. Passed the whole day in the Church.

August 4th. Felt considerably better today—no longer any apprehension of sickness, the fever having entirely left me. Passed the day again in the Church.

August 5th. (Sunday,) Celebrated early Mass—Took breakfast and returned immediately to the Church. During the solemn Mass at 11 O'Clock preached to a crowded audience. After Mass gave confirmation to about 20 individuals, the major part of whom had come from a great distance. When the service of the forenoon was over repaired to the Vestry where I remained about a half hour, while the people remained either in the Church or walked about the garden; for it is usual here as in country places generally, to give Vespers before the Congregation are dismissed. On the return of Rev. Mr. Ryan from his lodgings immediately commenced Vespers. These were sung with some English hymns. After the **Magnificat** I gave an exhortation [172] which was listened to with great attention; and afterwards gave confirmation to five or six more. During the whole service the Church was crowded. Of these several were Protestants or persons professing no faith. The number of confirmations on this occasion compared with the extent of the Congregation was small. This arose from the short notice which had been given of my intention to visit Whitefield this summer, and the great distance which many lived from the Church, and who had not received information that this sacrament was to be administed on this Sunday.

August 6th. After breakfast set out on my return to New Castle, accompanied by Rev. Mr. Ryan, the weather still excessively warm. Arrived at Mr. Kavenagh's at 12 O'Clock. Dined and paid some visits.

August 7th. Dined with Lawyer Smith a very intelligent and worthy man. In the evening visited Mr. Cotterel another of the principal Founders of the Church at New Castle. On my return was informed by the Rev. Mr. Ryan that as the chief part of his Congregation in this quarter resided at Bristol, a town twelve miles off, it would be impossible for him to assemble them unless I waited until Sunday; and that even in that case, he should not have time to prepare them for confirmation with so short a notice. In consequence of this, concluded to take the stage and continue my route to Portland.

August 8th. Left New-Castle at 6 O'Clock A.M. passed through Wiscasset, Bath etc. and arrived at Portland at 6 O'Clock P.M. Put up at the stage Hotel not being acquainted with any Catholic family in the town. In the course of the evening learnt that a Mr. O'Connor, a very decent man resided in it—Called on him to make my arrival known.

August 9th. Having understood that the Catholics were in the habit of assembling every Sunday in order to recite their prayers together and read spiritual books, went to visit the room hired by them for this purpose. This was an Upper-chamber in a house adjoining the **Museum**. It had a very poor appearance, and bespoke the poverty of the Catholics of this place— reminded me of the Upper-Chamber spoken of in the Acts of the Apostles— nevertheless, informed the two Catholics that accompanied me that I should celebrate Mass and give confirmation in it on the ensuing Sunday. Requested them in the mean time to have [173] it well swept and the altar decently arranged by that day. Paid a visit to the Governor (Enoch Lincoln). Conversed with him for a considerable time on the subject of the Penobscot and Passamaquoddy Indians. Exposed to him the real situation of these Indians and claimed his protection and that of the State in their behalf. Had the satisfaction to find him an intelligent man and one every way disposed to see their just rights maintained against the Harpies by whom they were beset.

August 10th. At the invitation of Mr. O'Connor removed my lodgings from the Hotel to his house. Walked through the town and took a general view of it—was greatly pleased with the prospect from the **Observatory** and with the neat appearance of the buildings of the town. Lamented that the Catholics did not yet enjoy a place of public worship of their own—hoped that they would not be long without one. Ascertained from Mr. O'Connor that the actual population of Catholics [amounted] to about one hundred and twenty.

August 11th In the afternoon of this day went to the hall hired by the Catholics, and heard the confessions of those preparing for confirmation till late in the evening.

August 12th (Sunday.) Went at an early hour to the Upper-Chamber—heard confessions till 10 O'Clock—then began to prepare for the celebration of Mass. The room was soon filled, probably to the number of 160 persons. Celebrated Mass; at the end of which preached and gave confirmation to 13 persons. At the conclusion of the ceremony addressed the Catholics again, and recommended to them to make a collection among themselves monthly, and to apply the proceeds towards the purchase of a Lot of ground—that when this was once obtained, it would be easy to find funds to erect a Church thereon. I also enjoined them to continue to assemble every Sunday for the purpose of devotion, and that as soon as possible I should send them a Priest to attend them. In the afternoon gave them Vespers, (for there were none who understood how to chant them) recited some prayers, and again preached to them. The day was excessively warm—and having had the whole duty to perform, felt, when all was over, exceedingly fatigued. At the end of divine service took a walk with Mr. Thomas Murphy, [174] lately arrived from Boston, Mr. O'Connor, and some other Catholics, to view a Lot of ground in the upper part of the town. Was pleased with its situation—thought it a good location for a Church—Recommended to the Catholics to purchase it as soon as they should have it in their power.

August 13th. Left Portland at 4 O'Clock A.M. for Saco—arrived there at 7 O'Clock—stopped at the Stage Hotel and took breakfast. Went in quest of the house of Dr. Henry Greene—was received cordially by him and invited to take lodgings in his house. Was informed by him that Mr. Tucker and himself were the only two individuals professing the Catholic faith in the town, with the exception of three or four Irish families lately come into it. In the course of the afternoon took a ride through the town with Dr.

Greene's Brother—Learnt from his conversation that he was an Episcopalian; but was still open to conviction. Expressed to him my hope that he would give the subject an attentive examination—stated that it was a matter of extreme importance to be in the right way to heaven—and was confident that if he sought it with sincerity he would find it.

August 14th. Was informed by Dr. Greene that a number of Individuals of various Denominations had sent him to request [me] to preach to them the following day in the Hall used by the Episcopalians for divine service. Inquired of him whether he thought it would be attended with any good effect? He answered.he thought it would—that the minds of many of that town were not yet made up to embrace any particular religion—that they felt as favourably disposed towards the Catholic as any other, and that it might, at least be the means of instilling into them a spirit of inquiry, which might be attended with happy results. I accordingly consented to preach and authorised them to make it generally known. In the afternoon rode with him to visit the harbour of Saco, and on my return baptized his youngest child.

August 15th (Feast of the Assumption.) Celebrated Mass in Dr. H. Greene's Parlour—gave communion to and confirmed him and three other individuals. Was told it was the first Mass ever celebrated in Saco. He expressed his joy that this event had taken place in his house, and only regretted that his brother Convert Mr. [175] Tucker, who was on business in Boston, was not present. In the afternoon took tea at the house of Dr. Greene's Father in law—and immediately after proceeded to the Episcopalian Hall to deliver a discourse according to promise. Found the place crowded to excess. After reciting a prayer, a hymn was sung, accompanied by the organ. I then addressed them for about an hour on the great truths of religion, and was listened to during the whole time with the greatest attention. At the end of the discourse another hymn was sung when the meeting was dissolved.

August 16th. At 10 O'Clock set out for Dover. Arrived at 6 O'Clock P.M. Took lodgings at a respectable Hotel, not being acquainted with a single individual in the town; or knowing where to find any of the few Catholics residing in it. On taking up a News paper was greatly aflicted to learn the death of Sr. Mary Austin, one of the Religious of the Ursuline Convent at Mount Benedict in Charlestown.

August 17th. After breakfast took a walk in the hope of finding some Catholic to whom I might communicate the news of my arrival. Could find none; they were all engaged in the extensive Factory of this town, into which admittance could not be obtained without a Ticket. Returned to the Hotel and addressed a note through the Post Office to Mr. Scanlan, a

Catholic with whom I had corresponded, without being personally acquainted. In a couple of hours afterwards he called on me. Made him many inquiries concerning the Catholics of this town, their number, condition, employment etc. To all which he replied very satisfactorily. After some time was invited by him to see the Factory—spent the greatest part of the morning in going through it—was introduced to the Catholics employed there. Returned home—had scarcely dined when the same gentleman returned with a Chaise, inviting me to take a ride to the Great Falls to see the Factories there, observing that there were a number of Catholics also employed in them to whom he wished to give information of my arrival, in order that they [176] might come and hear Mass on the following sunday. The distance was only 5 or 6 miles. On reaching the place was struck at the great enterprise of the Company; for the Factories here seemed to me to exceed even those at Dover. In addition to the manufacture of Cotton, they carry on also an extensive manufacture of wollen [sic] cloths and even a superior kind of carpeting. Returned to Dover at 7 O'Clock.

August 18th. Called a meeting of the Catholics to determine where I should say Mass on Sunday, for the hired apartment where they usually assembled on the Lord's day was too far from the centre of the town to be convenient. It was agreed that the house of Mr. Burns would best answer for the purpose. Arrangements were accordingly made in it.

August 19th (Sunday.) Repaired to Mr. Burns' house at an early hour—immediately commenced hearing confessions—continued until 10 O'Clock. At this hour the Catholics assembled. These amounted to 40 or 50. Celebrated Mass and gave communion to but few—confirmation to two. After Mass preached to them. In the afternoon gave vespers. These were sung by some of the women accompanied by some of the men. After reciting a prayer preached again—in conclusion, recommended to them to subscribe something monthly towards the purchase of a Lot of ground for a Church. After service a subscription was immediately opened when 25 obligated themselves to pay each one Dollar per month till the object should be attained. Was pleased with the spirit manifested on this occasion. Promised to send them a Priest as soon as it should be in my power. Gave them my Benediction and departed.

August 20th Left Dover for Boston at 7 O'Clock in the morning—reached Boston at half past 6, after an absence of nearly six weeks.[28]

The Bishop on his return to Boston was greatly pleased to find that all things had been conducted with due order and regularity in his absence—that no part of the duties had been omitted by the Reverend Clergymen in the Cathedral and that their health notwithstanding their great labour as well [177] as the health of the Catholics in general in the City had continued good. He immediately resumed his part of the labour of the ministry in Boston, and directed the Rev. Mr. Mahoney to return to Salem; and having ascertained that there were fifty Catholics (adults) residing at Lowell, a manufactoring town 25 miles from Boston, and that twenty one of these had families, he authorized him to extend his mission to this town also and to visit it once at least in every month. He, at the same time, addressed a letter to the Rev. Mr. Ffrench at Eastport in which he informed him of the destitute condition of the Catholics at Portland and Dover, and directed him, as soon as he conveniently could, to visit them and use all his endeavours to have a Church erected at each of the above places—he stated to him furthermore the favourable disposition of the Catholics in them and their great desire to have these objects accomplished.

On the 21st of December this year (1827) the Bishop confered the order of **Subdeacon** upon the following gentlemen, having already admitted them to the minor orders, viz: James Fitton,[29] William Wiley, [30] William Tyler, [31] John Smyth[32] and james Rooney; on the 22d the same were advanced to the order of **Deacon**; and on the 23d they were ordained Priests, with the exception of William Tyler who had not yet attained the age required by the Canons of the Church. All the above received ordination for this Diocess, except the Rev. James Rooney, who was ordained at the special request and recommendation of the Rt. Rev. Dr. Conwell, for the Diocess of Philadelphia.

The number of Baptisms performed this year (1827) in the Cathedral of the Holy Cross amounted to

The number of Marriages in the same, to............[37]

CHAPTER VIII

THE EVENTS OF 1828

In the early part of this year (january 2d) the Rev. Robert D. Woodley arrived and offered his services to the Bishop for the Diocess of Boston. This Reverend Gentleman had been [178] ordained Priest by Bishop England of Charleston, S.C.; but the Climate of Carolina not having agreed with his constitution, he was under the necessity, after a short residence, of soliciting his **Exeat** for the preservation of his health, and of removing to a more northern habitude. The Bishop, having examined his letters and found them favourable, accepted his services. He immediately appointed him to take charge of the mission of Providence and Pawtucket, and instructed him at the same time to extend his visits occasionally to Newport, Fall-River and Taunton. At this time the catholic population of Pawtucket amounted to about 100 souls; of Providence to scarcely 50; of Taunton to about the same number; of Fall-River to about 20; and of New-Port to scarcely that number.[33]

The Rev. Mr. Barber having been recalled this year by his Religious Superior in George Town, arrived in Boston on the 24th of February on his way thither. The Bishop was exceedingly grieved to see him leave his Diocess especially at a time when his services seemed to be most wanted, and when he had no one whom he could send to supply his place. He was well aware of the wants of the Society in Maryland; yet he could not but entertain the hope that by addressing a line to the Rev. F. Dzierozinski, at this time Superior of the Society, he might be able to obtain his services a little longer. He accordingly wrote to him, a few days after, a pressing letter on the subject and begged him to allow him to return and remain in the

221

Diocess at least until it should be in his power to provide a successor. He stated to him, moreover, that it had been his intention to send him as a missionary among the Penobscot Indians, who had so long and so loudly called for a Priest; but that if he persisted in his removal, it would be utterly out of his power to provide for the spiritual wants of that long neglected tribe. He hoped therefore he would not deprive him of his services at this time. The Reverénd Superior, on learning the true situation of things and especially the destitute condition of the Indians immediately acceded to his wishes. The Rev. Mr. Barber in consequence returned to Boston after a short delay in George Town, and on the 26th of May, set out upon his mission among the Penobscot Indians. On the 29th of [179] the same month, the Rev. John Smyth, who had been lately ordained, left Boston for **Pleasant Point,** to commence his ministry among the Passamaquoddy Tribe. He had not, however, been long there, when symptoms of insanity began to manifest themselves so clearly, that it became absolutely necessary to withdraw him from that mission. After some ineffectual efforts on the part of the physician to restore him, it was finally deemed proper that he should be sent to his native country, in the hope, that the society of his near relatives and friends might accomplish what could not be effected in Boston. He accordingly sailed for Ireland in the care of a friend on the 27th of August, after having been only seven months ordained Priest. The Rev. James Fitton was sent to supply his place at Passamaquoddy.

The Bishop became every day more and more sensible of the want of Priests in his Diocess. He saw clearly the necessity of having some Ecclesiastical Seminary in which candidates for the Priesthood might be received and from which he might draw in process of time such as should be qualified for the Ministry. To establish an Institution of this kind in his own Diocess was at present wholly impracticable. He had neither the funds to construct the necessary buildings, nor the Professors such an Institution would require to be properly and usefully conducted. In this emergency he turned his eyes towards Canada in the hope of finding in the Sulpician College at Montreal and their Ecclesiastical Seminary appended to it a fit nursery for his Diocess. Having been himself partly educated under the Sulpicians, he had seen the true Ecclesiastical spirit which prevailed among their Clergy and had also frequently had occasion to admire their superior learning and talents. He could not, therefore, but feel a partiality in their favour; and if some arrangement could be made by which the education of his Candidates could be accomplished, and the expense thereof could be properly met, he was resolved to give it the preference. To ascertain this, he resolved to repair to Montreal, and to visit their establishment in person. This he was enabled to effect in the course of this summer. [180]

The following is an abstract of the notes taken by him during this excursion.

June 24th 1828. Left Boston at 6 O'Clock in the morning, in the Stage for Whitehall, having in company two Boys destined for the Church whom I intended to place in the Montreal College, A.A. and N. O'Brien the former 16 years old, the latter 10.—Arrived at Whitehall on the third day after our departure, for Breakfast. As the St. John's Steam-boat did not leave this place till after dinner took a walk with the Boys to see what was remarkable in the town. The first thing which attracted notice were the splendid Locks at the termination of the Canal, which connects the waters of the Hudson with Lake Champlain. Boats are here lifted 31 feet before they are brought on a level with the water in the Canal. The scenery around is bold and romantick. The rocks rise perpendicularly from the stream to a considerable height. Spent some time in looking at the Boats as they ascended and descended. The village seems to be a place of some business, and a complete thoroughfare during the summer months. It possesses besides an academy, a Church, a bridge and a decent Hotel. Dined at 1 O'Clock, and immediately after went on board the Steamboat. This being the first time the Boys had ever traveled by this mode of conveyance, they were greatly amused. Reached Burlington towards the close of evening, and stopped for a half hour—then proceeded on to St. Johns.

June 28th [sic] Arrived at St. John's in time for Breakfast—soon perceived that we were in Canada from the french language being spoken by all. The Collector of the Port came on board, and demanded to see my trunk opened—was just opening it for inspection when he said "that will do, Sir," and passed on. My baggage was then taken on shore, and conveyed to the nearest tavern where we breakfasted.

The town of St. John is situate near the head of Lake Champlain, which is navigable thus far for Vessels of some burden. Here the river commences which forms the outlet into the St. Laurence. A beautiful bridge unites the town with the opposite country. The buildings are generally built in the french style and are mostly of stone.—The streets are unpaved, and in wet weather extreme-[181]ly dirty. A neat Catholic Church was just building at no great distance from the tavern; but had not sufficient time to examine it. Took the stage for Laprairie distant 18 miles over a level country—saw, as we advanced, to the left extensive and beautiful wheat fields, which announced a fertile country—observed on this road the houses of the farmers to be everywhere small; and their barns large. These are constructed with very steep roofs, a precaution highly necessary in a country in which the winters are severe and the snows frequent. Arrived at La Prairie, a town on the St. Laurence, at 12 O'Clock. Called on the Curé and presented him my respects. Found him to be an intelligent and worthy man, and highly respected;—was pleased with the appearance of the town, and especially of the Parish Church—regretted I could not examine it for the want of time. Had a view of Montreal; but could distinguish nothing in particular, the distance being nine miles. The St. Laurence here is very wide. At 1 O'Clock went on board the Ferry Boat, and was soon after landed at Montreal. Repaired immediately to the Seminary—inquired for the Superior, the Rev. Mr. Roux—was informed he was in Europe—asked to see the Curé d'Office, the Rev. Mr. Le Saulnier—was told he was sick, and in the infirmary, and could not be seen. Not knowing the name of any other Reverend Gentleman was at a loss what to do, when a Clergyman, in Cassock and surplice, having overheard me inquiring for the Rev. Mr. Le Saulnier, came up and informed me he would conduct me to him. Found him, as stated, in the Infirmary with the Rev. Mr. Hubert, another aged and venerable Priest, who was equally an Invalid. On giving him my name was received by him with the greatest politeness and attention. He took the earliest moment to apprise me of the custom prevailing in Canada for the Clergy to wear their Soutanes, even in the street, and recommended to me to put on mine. Having complied with this laudable custom, I was immediately introduced, one by one, to the Reverend Gentlemen of the Seminary, viz: Rev. Messrs. Malard, Dufresne, Humbert, Sauvage, Satin, Conte, [182] St. Pierre, Bonin, Phelan and Gabourie, with whom I soon became familiar.

June 28th. Said Mass at the Convent of the Hotel-Dieu. After Mass breakfasted in their Parlour—then visited the whole establishment, especially the new part. Found it very extensive and every thing in the best order—an institution calculated to do immense good by the care and attention which are here bestowed upon the sick. Could not but admire the charity of these good Nuns, who received into their hospital the sick of all denominations, and shewed equal attention to them all,—and who, in spite of their constant labours, appeared always cheerful, always happy. Conversed with Madame La Pailleur, the most aged of this community, who had been over 50 years in the Convent, and who by her ingenious contrivance in establishing a Bakery at a time of great distress, had afforded ample support to the whole Convent.

On my way back to the Seminary called in to see the new Parish Church now erecting—was struck with the grandour and magnificence of the design. It covers a space of thirty four thousand, three hundred and twenty square feet—measuring 260 feet in length, without including the sacristies, 132 in width, and 60 in height to the eves. It has besides two square towers, not yet completed in front. The structure is wholly Gothick. The roof is covered with tin, which at this distance from the sea is not liable to rust.

Saw, on entering the Building, a number of workmen still employed about it, and among these soon recognized Signor L'Ange Pinovi, an Italian artist, whom I had known at New York some years ago. The interior of the edifice corresponds well with the exterior in grandour and beauty. A double row of columns, painted to represent marble, supports the roof and two side Galleries, also double, which, though contrary to the rules of Gothick Architecture, has nevertheless a pleasing effect. It is supposed the entire cost of this magestick Church, when finished, will exceed two hundred thousand pounds. It certainly reflects the highest honour on the Sulpician Clergy of the City, and affords equal evidence of the piety of their worthy parishioners, the good people of Montreal.

On leaving this splendid edifice, I repaired immediately to the College with my two Boys, accompanied by one of the Reverend [183] Clergy with the view of visiting the Establishment and of becoming acquainted with the President and Professors of it. Was introduced to the learned and venerable M. Roque its present Director, and to the Rev. M. Quibilier one of its principal Professors, who had the kindness to accompany me through it. Was greatly pleased with the extent and distribution of the Building the beautiful order which reigned throughout, and every other thing connected with it. Congratulated my Boys upon the advantages they were to reap from so beautiful an Establishment—recommended to them to profit by them—and do their best to please and to edify all, especially their Professors, by their good conduct.

June 29th (Sunday) Said Mass in the Parish Church, at an early hour during which was assisted by one of the Reverend Gentlemen of the Seminary. Several Canticles were sung by the little children belonging to the public school under the patronage of the Rev. Messrs. of St. Sulpice. Breakfasted and prepared for High-Mass, this being Sunday. At the appointed hour repaired to the Exercise Room with the Reverend Gentlemen of the Seminary where the **Veni Sancte Spiritus** was recited—afterwards proceeded to the Church through the Corridores repeating the psalm **Miserere**. When arrived at the Sanctuary was shewn the place in which I was to hear mass—this was on the right as you face the high-altar where the Superior of the Seminary was usually stationed. The Mass was sung beautifully by the Rev. M. Quiblier who officiated on this day, assisted by a Deacon and Subdeacon, Acolytes, Master of ceremonies, and all the requisites of a Mass of the first class. The discourse was pronounced by the Rev. Mr. Roque, President of the College. It was a Panygerick on the Apostles, Sts. Peter and Paul. Though Extemporaneus it was a substantial and interesting one, and gave me a high opinion of the Superior talents and learning of the venerable Preacher. Greatly admired the order and regularity in which the ceremonies were conducted.—Was requested in the afternoon to give the **Salut** to the Religious of the Hotel-Dieu convent. Although it rained exceedingly hard, [184] was unwilling to disappoint those good Ladies, went thither, accompanied by Rev. Mr. Coute, Procurator of the Seminary and performed the ceremony. The Chapel of these good Nuns is small, yet beautiful and neat—their Altar Vestments are truly elegant. Among the Religious who sang during the Benediction distinguished a voice that was truly peculiar, strong, shrill and masculine and which resembled more the voice of a Boy than that of a female. The piece sung by her was **O Jesu Deus magne** in which she acquitted herself with equal piety and taste. After the **Salut** was presented to the Community whom I complimented upon the enlargement of their establishment (for it had received considerable additions of late) and consequently of their sphere of usefulness. It was founded by Madame de Bullion in 1644.

June 30th Said Mass at the Convent of the **Soeurs de la Congregation de Notre Dame.** This splendid establishment owes its foundation to Dlle. Marguerite Bourgeois and has for its principal object the education of female children. A number of these assisted at the Mass which I celebrated, and sung during the divine service a variety of choice canticles in very good taste.—Breakfasted and visited their schools—was greatly pleased with the specimens which they shewed me of their drawing and writing. This Institution is one of the most popular in Canada; for independantly of the instruction which these good Sisters afford to female children at the Convent, they have besides a number of missions in other parts of the Province where they are regularly catechised and instructed. At the invitation of the Rev. Mr. Sauvage went in the afternoon to visit the farm on the Island which belongs to these Sisters; and afterwards to see the Locks on the Canal which far surpassed in beauty and solidity those at Whitehall.

July 1st Said Mass in the Convent of the **Grey-Sisters.** After Mass was invited to take breakfast in a large apartment at the house in which the Community also breakfasted. Was afterwards conducted through the entire Establishment, which embraces the general Hospital for the sick-poor and invalids. It was founded in the year 1753, [185] by Madame Veuve Youville. Saw in it besides a great number of old and infirm men and women, many poor and neglected orphans who are here taken care of and instructed by these truly charitable Sisters. The greatest cleanliness and order were visible throughout. The Chapel connected with this institution is highly ornamented and so situated that even the sick and infirm can almost at all times assist at the divine office performed in it. The Rev. Mr. Satin was the Clergyman who attended, while I celebrated Mass in it. There was here also a choir of little children who sang the praises of their heavenly father in very pretty style during its celebration. Was greatly pleased with the Grey Sisters, so called from the colour of the habit worn by them;— received a pressing invitation to visit them again before I left town.

July 2d Said Mass at the Parish Church. After breakfast paid a visit to the Church of **St. jacques.** The Co-adjutor Bishop, Monseigneur Lartigue, had caused this to be erected about four years ago in the suburbs of the town together with a large adjoining building which serves as his dwelling and as a Seminary for young Ecclesiastics. Both are large and well constructed edifices. The Church being recently erected is yet without decoration. The Right Reverend Prelate was absent on a visitation. Could not therefore pay him my respects; but was kindly shewn the Church and house by the Rev. M. Prince, the Superior in his absence. The Seminary consists at present of eleven Divines, who seemed promising and pious young men. The Rev. Mr. McMahon, one of the Bishop's chaplains was extremely kind. While visiting the Garden observed an elderly man in a Franciscan's habit—inquired who he was? Was told he was one of the last of the old **Recollets** whose order had been suppressed by the British Government on their taking possession of Canada. He was permitted to live in the Seminary by the Right Reverend Co-adjutor, and was supported by him. The good old man appeared cheerful and happy. He was not in Priest's orders. After surveying the Episcopal Premises took my leave promising to return and repeat my visit in a week, at which time I [186] was told the Bishop would be at home.

This being the day on which all the Reverend Gentlemen both of the Seminary and College spend the day at their country Seat a little out of the City, I was invited on my return from the Co-adjutors to join them. Accordingly got into one of their **Calesthes,** which, by the bye, is not one of the most agreable ways in the world of travelling, took my seat along side of the Rev. M. Conte, and set off for the mountain, at the base of which on a gentle declivity their Villa is situated. To enable me to see the Farm which belongs to the Seminary and which is adjacent to the Canal, the driver of the Calesche was ordered to take a circuitous route. We reached the Villa about 10 O'Clock. The Reverend Gentlemen had already assembled, and were amusing themselves, some in the grand Saloon and others in walking in the garden and Park. Three or four Curés of the adjoining Parishes were likewise there. After viewing the house and garden was conducted to the Park through the middle of which a little Canal had been dug for the sake of ornament which was filled with fresh water from the mountain, and in the center of which a Jet d'eau played very prettily. The sides of the Canal were lined with rows of Linden Trees which afforded a delightful walk. The whole is beautifully arranged and tastefully laid out. The Villa of the College adjoins that of the Seminary. Being near and hearing the College Boys loud in their sports in the grove I walked over to them and was greatly amused by their diversions. They appeared fully to enjoy themselves. They were attended by the Rev. M. Roque, their venerable President, the Rev. Mr. Quiblier and all the Professors and Prefects of the Establishment, who generally joined and took part in their sports. The number of the students assembled did not appear fewer than 120. The College is attended likewise by a number of Day-Scholars; but none of these were allowed to mix or recreate with the other children—a salutary provision; consequently none of these were to be seen at the Villa. In the midst of our walk we were summoned to dinner—returned to the Seminary Villa and sat down to a plentiful dinner. The company was large, and the conversation during dinner [187] was both cheerful and instructive. In the evening returned to the Seminary and prepared for my journey to Quebec.—Embarked the same evening at 8 O'Clock—was accompanied to the Steam-boat by three or four of the Reverend Gentlemen of the Seminary and two of the Curés who had dined with us at the Villa. My two Boys also came to bid farewell. Although they knew that I should soon see them again, they could not however bear feeling a depression of spirits on being left alone in a strange country whose language they did not understand. Got under way about 10 O'Clock—found on board some of my Boston acquaintance viz Dr. Kirkland, former President of Harvard College, and Lady. The Doctor appeared to enjoy no better health than he did at Boston.

July 3d Rose from bed and went on deck—found that we had not yet reached **Trois Rivieres,** a considerable village nearly half way to Quebec. The country on each side of the St. Laurence appeared beautiful. Every four or five miles brought us in sight of a Village on each of the banks, with the Parish Church and steeple towering far above the other buildings, whose cross was seen glittering in the sun. At 10 O'Clock arrived at **Trois Rivieres,** so called from three Rivers which join their currents here, and fall into the St. Laurence. It is much resorted to by the Indians, who, by means of these rivers come hither and trade with the inhabitants in various kinds of furs and skins. Saw great numbers of them on shore from the deck of the steamboat. As the Boat had stopped merely to take in wood, and the delay was to be only a half hour would not land and contented myself with viewing the more prominent buildings with a Spy-Glass. Saw two, whose external appearance pleased me much;—these were the Parish Church, and the Ursuline Convent, founded in 1677 by M. de St. Vallier, Bishop of Quebec for the education of young females and the benefit of the sick Poor. Both appeared to be very fine buildings. Continued our route, and although the wind towards evening blew directly ahead, had the good fortune to arrive at Quebec about 6 O'Clock in the evening. Landed immediately and

directed the [188] Porter to take my baggage to the Seminary—had to ascend a steep and high hill to reach this, and to wind my way through a narrow and crooked street. The first individual, whom I saw on arriving was
the Rev. Mr. McMahon, who had stopped a few days at Boston on his way to
Quebec from St. Johns, New Brunswick. With this Reverend Gentleman I
was acquainted. He immediately conducted me to the Parlour and introduced me to the Rev. Mr. Demers, Superior of the Seminary, and to the
other Reverend Clergy, inmates of the house. The aged and respectable
Bishop of Quebec, Dr. Panet, was absent on a visitation; but his worthy Co-
adjutor, Dr. Sinai, was at home and being soon informed of my arrival,
gave me a cordial reception. Among the Reverend Clergy to whom I was introduced I was happy to see the Rev. Mr. Holmes, a native of my Diocess,
who for a number of years had resided in this Seminary, and had here taken
orders. He was at this time Professor of Natural Philosophy in the College
connected with it.

July 4th Said Mass at the Hotel-Dieu Convent—after which was introduced to the Rev. M. Desjardins, one of the most amiable and best of
men, chaplain to this Community, and by him was made acquainted with
the Lady Superior and some of her religious. Breakfasted in their little
Parlour during which was asked many questions about Boston, and the Ursuline Establishment there. Having hastily satisfied their inquiries
repaired to the Ursuline Convent to deliver my commissions from their
Sisters in Boston. Was received by the Lady Superiour, Mére Sr. Monique,
and the former Superiour Meré St. Henrie with great politeness. Inquired
for the two daughters of the Rev. Mr. Barber, one of whom I knew was
already admitted a Novice in this Establishment,—and was extremely
pleased to see them both happy and well. In a short time the Rev. Mr.
Daulé their venerable Chaplain came in and requested me to celebrate
Mass in their Chapel the following day; which I promised. After spending a
good part of the morning in conversation with these good Religious took my
leave and returned to the Seminary. Took this opportunity to see this
beautiful establishment, conducted by the Rev. Mr. Holmes. Found it, upon
examination, to be far more extensive than I had imagined.

[189] It is situated in the upper town and adjoins the rear of the Cathedral.
The building is an immense superstructure of stone in the form of a parallellogram having three sides of more than 210 feet in length, forty in width
and three stories in height; to this is added recently a wing of four stories
on the northeast of 150 feet in length and of considerable depth. It is encircled by a large garden, walled in, covering in the whole about 7 acres,
and extending to the Ramparts. All the necessary convenient apartments
are comprised in the building, adapted both for the recitations of the pupils
and the residence of the Professors. The course of instruction is subdivided

into the **Grand** and **Petit Seminaire,** the former for the higher, and the latter for the lower studies. This institution appears well supported. It was founded as early as the year 1663. It was originally designed for the education of Ecclesiastics; but is now open for the reception of all who comply with its terms and regulations. The Chapel is a plain neat edifice, and contains a number of excellent paintings. There is a Museum attached also to the Seminary which contains a variety of natural curiosities. The view from the garden, near the ramparts, is one of the most commanding in the city, and affords a delightful prospect of the River and of the adjacent country.

In the afternoon took a walk, at the invitation of the Rev. Mr. McMahon, and Mr. Cannon, a very respectable Irish gentleman, to view the fortifications and Cape Diamond, the view from which is the most splendid I ever beheld. The following delineation by Colonel Bouchette is so accurately descriptive of it that I cannot forbear transcribing it.

"Whoever views the environs of Quebec with a mind and taste capable of receiving impressions thro' the medium of the eyes will acknowledge, that as a whole the prospect is peculiarly grand—and that if taken in detail every part of it pleases by the gradual unfolding of its picturesque beauties. Towards Beauport, Charlebourg and Lorette the view is diversified with every trait that can render a landscape rich, full and complete. The foreground shews the River St. Charles meandering for some miles [190] through a fertile valley, embellished by a succession of objects, that diffuse great animation over the whole scene. The three villages with their respective Churches, and many handsome detached houses in the vicinity, seated on gently rising eminences, form so many distinct objects—the intervals between which display many of the most strongly marked specimens of forest scenery combined with a wide spread appearance of fertility and good cultivation. As the prospect recedes, the land rises in gradation, height over height, with primeval covered weeds, until the whole is terminated by a lofty ridge of mountains. Turning towards the basin, which is about two miles across the scene is enlivened by the variety of ships entering or leaving the port. On the right, Point Levi with its Church and groupe of white houses and several other Promontories clothed with trees, and in front, the western end of the island of Orleans, present an interesting and agreable subject to the observer. On the plains of Abraham, from the precipice that overlooks the timber grounds, the St. Laurence is seen rolling its magestic wave, studded with sails from the stately ship to the humble Pilot boat—and the opposite bank extending up the river is highly cultivated; and the houses thickly strewed by the main road, from this height and distance, have the appearance of an almost interupted village.

The country to the southward rises by a gentle ascent, and the whole view, which is richly embellished by water, woodland and cultivation, is bounded by remote and lofty mountains, softening shade by shade until they meet into air. Hence the summer scenery of the environs of Quebec vies in beauty variety and magnificence, sublimity, and the naturally harmonized combination of all these prominent features, with the most splendid that has been portrayed in Europe, or any other part of the world."

Quebec is situate between the rivers St. Charles and St. Laurence on a tongue of land formed at their confluence. A straight line drawn from one river to the other at the Barrier on the south and west is something more than a mile in length—and the whole wall is two miles and three quarters in circuit—but including the Citadel, the Esplanade, the different large gar- |191|dens, and other vacant spaces, a considerable portion of the area within the fortification remains unoccupied for buildings. The City is divided into the upper and lower town. That part which is within the walls is called the upper town, and can be approached solely by five gates. The Citadel is a stupendous fortress and circumscribes the whole area on the highest part of Cape Diamond. It perfectly commands the City and river St. Laurence. The height here from the river is 345 feet. The plains of Abraham, so remarkable in history, lie back of the St. Louis Suburbs. It was here that General Wolfe was killed. The examination of the many interesting objects both within and without the fortifications took up the whole of the afternoon. Towards the close of evening returned to the City highly gratified, and took tea at the hospitable mansion of Mr. Cannon— after which returned to the Seminary.

July 5th Said Mass at the Ursuline Chapel, assisted by the Rev. Mr. Daulé. The little children of the academy connected with the Convent sang a variety of hymns during the celebration. Breakfasted in the little Parlour, and afterwards went through the whole establishment, accompanied by the Rev. Messrs. Desjardins and Daulé and visited in succession the Chapel, Choir, Novitiate, Community, Refectory, Schools etc.

This beautiful Convent occupies a large space—is surrounded by a high barrier of stone, and comprises an excellent and fertile garden—the whole area includes about seven acres. It was founded by Madame De la Peltrie, in 1639, a very short time after the first settlement of the City, expressly to promote female education. The edifice, which is built of stone, is two stories high, forming a square of nearly 114 feet in length, and as many in breadth, being of ample capacity and convenience to accommodate the residents—but the outside combines no attraction; its interior, however, is neat and well distributed. The Chapel is nearly 100 feet in length, and fifty in width—the interior of which is highly decorated. The Altars are exquisitely ornamented, and the emblematic figure on the roof gives a light and airy appearance to the whole. [192] The paintings are numerous and valuable—spent a considerable time in viewing them. The dinner hour of the Religious having arrived, expressed my thanks to them for their extreme kindness and attention, and withdrew to the apartments of the Rev. Mr. Daulé, where refreshments were prepared of which I partook, not being able to dine, having previously engaged to take dinner with the Governor in chief, Earl Dalhousie, at 6 O'Clock.—Returned to the Seminary, and was there waited on by Valliere de St. Réal, Esq., and by my good friend and former School fellow, Lieutenant Col. Duchesnay—was greatly rejoiced at meeting with the latter, not having seen him for the last twenty five years, or since the time we were children together in College. At his earnest solicitation agreed to postpone my departure until tuesday the 8th on purpose to have the pleasure of dining with him and his amiable family. At 6 P.M. accompanied by the Rt. Rev. Co-adjutor, dined with his Excellency, the Governor in chief in company with his principal Officers, and Sir James Kempt, Governor of Nova Scotia and New Brunswick, who happened to have just arrived from Halifax, on special business. Became here acquainted with Chief justice Sewale, a learned and very clever man, and his brother in law, a Mr. Smith. Left the table at 9 O'Clock and returned to the Seminary.

July 6th (Sunday.) Said Mass again at the Hotel-Dieu. After breakfast returned to the Seminary and proceeded with the Reverend Clergy to the Cathedral in order to be present at the High Mass. This was celebrated by the Rev. P. McMahon, and the ceremonies on the occasion were similar to those I had seen at Montreal. There was no sermon, in consequence, as I was told, of the unusual length of the Prône.

The Cathedral stands in the upper town immediately in front of the Market-place. It is a massive, unornamented and spacious stone building— measuring 210 feet in length, and 108 in width. The spire from having been erected on the South side of the edifice, gives to the front view an ungrateful [sic] appearance. The Church is in other respects [193] disproportionately high and greatly defective in geometrical delineation. From the vestibule, the body of the interior is subdivided into equal proportions; and on the north and south are two spacious aisles. At the termination of the nave is the grand Altar in the middle of the Elipse constituting the sanctuary, the walls of which are ornamented with representations and figures commingled with various other graphical emblems. It possesses several paintings of great beauty and value.

After dinner set out with the Rev. Mr. Parant, director of the College, to assist at Vespers in the Church of St. Roch in the lower town, lately erected by the venerable Bishop Plessis, and which was for a long time the great object of his concern. His heart is here kept in a tomb under one of the Altars. The evening service consisted of the Litanies of the Blessed Virgin which were chaunted, and a sermon which was preached by one of the Chaplains. Adjoining the Church is a large building erected by the same Prelate for the purpose of a Seminary; but which as yet is only occupied by the two Chaplains. The Church itself is still in an unfinished state, the founder not having lived to see it completed.

July 7th Said Mass at the General Hospital, which is under the direction of a Community of religious Ladies. After Mass breakfasted and went through the establishment accompanied by the Rev. Messrs. Parant and Bedard. This beautiful establishment is situated a mile west of the fortifications, on the banks of the river St. Charles, and was founded in the year 1693, by Mr. de St. Vallier, Bishop of Quebec expressly to relieve invalids and persons afflicted by disease. It is a spacious structure—a parallellogram of nearly equal sides, 228 feet in length and 33 in depth—and on the south west a wing projects more than 120 feet by 50 broad. The uncircumscribed principle upon which the Institution was founded, necessarily introduces a great number of patients, so that it is ordinarily occupied by the children of sorrow, in all its diversified exhibitions. To super-[194]intend the Hospital there are, besides the Lady Superiour, of the Convent, about forty five or fifty Professed Nuns, all of whom are amply accommodated, and also sufficient and convenient apartments for their varied avocations. The comfortable economy of this Hospital is very regular, and all possible alleviation is tendered to the disconsolate, pained and enfeebled inmates. Attached to the Convent is a neat and convenient Church.

After having surveyed the entire establishment, was conducted into a spacious and magnificent hall where the Nuns were all assembled. Here we conversed together for some time; and afterwards was shewn into the Choir, the centre of which was occupied by a very handsome Pianno. At my solicitation two of the Religious performed several sacred pieces with great judgment and taste. I was truly astonished at their skill. They accompanied each piece with their voices with equal taste. Remained a considerable time in this apartment listening to the music, and admiring the paintings from which I had also a good view of the interior of the Chapel which is highly ornamented. The Bell for dinner reminded us that it was time to depart—took leave of the good Ladies, and returned to meet the Rev. Mr. Desjardins at the Hotel-Dieu. Immediately set off with him to visit the celebrated falls of Montmorency, distant about 7 miles from Quebec.—Roads very bad in consequence of late rains—very much washed. Passed through Beauport from which village a delightful view is had of the

City, which appears to great advantage from this place. On arriving found the river at the brink of the Falls to be about 60 feet broad. There is a continued declivity in the stream for some distance above, which adds much to the velocity of the water in its descent. A large rock is seen about the middle of the bed—with this exception the whole is one compact sheet of foam, which is discharged, almost perpendicularly, at the depth, it is said, of nearly 240 feet into a reservoir among the rocks below. The sound was deafening. A mill is erected near the falls from the upper windows of which a good view was had. After some time, passed through the mill, and proceeded along the brow of the hill until we came in full face of the Cataract. Here the view was [195] magnificent—and could we have descended to the bottom it would have been still better. But this we could not effect with any degree of safety. From none of the positions in fact taken by us did the fall appear to be as great as it is said, viz: 240 feet. This, however, might have been owing to the great quantity of spray which was continually thrown up from below, and which had the effect to diminish the distance to the eye. After some time spent in contemplating this stupendous wonder of nature, superior to Niagara in the greatness of the fall, and only inferior to it in quantity of water returned to the Hotel-Dieu highly gratified—found the Rev. Mr. Daulé already there awaiting us—took a **lunch** prepared by the good nuns—afterwards went through and visited the whole establishment.

The Hotel-Dieu of Quebec was founded in the year 1637 by Madame La Duchesse d'Aiguillon for the sick Poor. It includes a large portion of the northern part of the interior of the City—commencing from the gate of the burial ground on Couillard Street and extending to Palace Street, with a wall on the north, parallel to the fortifications; the whole space covering about 12 acres. It is a capacious edifice, the longest portion of which extends nearly 390 feet by 51 in depth, and three stories high. On the northwest side from the centre, a range is erected two stories high, 150 feet in length and nearly as many feet broad, plain and unadorned. This wing is appropriated to Patients; the upper story of which is occupied by the Females. All proper attendance both from the Nuns and Physicians with every necessary comfort, is gratuitously administered.

The religious reside in the Convent part and in general number about 40 Professed. The regularity and neatness with which the establishment is conducted, and the solace of the wretched who find comfort in this hospitable mansion are highly exemplary.

The Chapel is a plain building, and is adorned with several paintings, some of which are original. One painting I was shewn by my venerable friend, the Chaplain which merits notice, not for the skill of the artist, but for the subject. [196] as illustrative of the perils and sufferings of the early Missionaries in Canada.—"In the winter of the year 1649, the Indians assailed the Church of the Jesuit Missionaries at **Trois Rivieres**. The society at that period numbered seven members. Two made their escape, one of whom was subsequently found in the woods, congealed in the attitude of prayer, and the other was discovered prostrate, frozen on the ice of one of the rivers."

"The Rev. Pere Daniel and his brother were shot as they fled out of the Church then in flames. Another of the Society Father jogues was mutilated by the loss of his fingers in succession; and with his wrists fettered, kneeling down, was butchered by two of the Indians, who cleaved his head with their battle axes."

"The venerable Father Breboeuf, and a young Missionary, by the name of Lallemand, were reserved for still more excruciating and protracted tortures. They were tied to two stakes, separated by a short distance. The junior was literally burnt piecemeal, by the application of ignited pine sticks, successively brought into immediate contact with the various parts of the body, the most distant from the vitals. In the intensity of his corporeal agonies, just before the mortal frame succumed to the ingenious and infuriated malevolence and cruelty of the savages, he addressed the venerable Breboeuf—"ah! Father, I have scarcely a grain of faith left." To which his aged fellow sufferer magnanimously replied—"One grain of true faith in Christ, my Son, is enough to remove all this mountain of anguish and misery." The senior Priest had long endeavoured to gain these savages, but in vain. They astonished him by saying:—"You have come a long distance, you tell us, to baptize us in cold water—we will baptize you with hot water."

"To execute their inhuman and horrid scheme, they fastened a cross pole between the stakes to which the two Priests were bound, and hung on their large pots to boil the water. A refinement of almost unparalleled merciless infliction was superadded. They strung on an Iron hoop or ring several axe heads and placed them in the fire; when the axes were red-hot, they cast the ring over Father Breboeuf's head, so that thus [197] suspended, his breast and shoulders were corroded by the heated axes, to his inexpressible torment. When the water was ready, two of the Indians with large shears cut off huge pieces of flesh, and made other deep incisions in the arms, legs etc. to the very bones—as soon as a number of these gashes were made in various parts of the frame, one of the Savages poured a kettle of scalding water over the agonized Breboeuf; and thus in a continual alteration of relentless butchery and scalding, combined with triumphant yellings at their novel mode of baptism, they ceased not their successive tortures, until life being extinct, the remains of their victims were transferred to be consumed in the same fire."

After having conversed a short time with the good ladies of this charitable Institution, took leave of them and went to the lodgings of the Right Reverend Co-adjutor, Dr. Signai, and thence to Lt. Col. Ducesnay's where we dined agreably to promise. The company at dinner was select and respectable.

July 8th Said Mass at the Church of the Congregation Nuns in the lower town—afterwards breakfasted and visited their school. The number of Sisters here is only four. Their Chapel is small, and badly situated being very near a market, and in a very noisy part of the town—could hear from the Altar, with little attention, what was said in the street. Dined at the Seminary in company with the Right Reverend Coadjutor and the Reverend Superior and Professors. Paid a parting visit to the good Ursulines, and took their commissions for their Sisters in Boston. The remaining part of the afternoon was spent in visiting the Armory, which is said to contain 15,000 stand of arms. They are kept in a state of admirable cleanliness and polish, in constant repair, and are always ready to be issued, should any emergency require the equipment of the militia.

In passing and repassing the west side of the Market place in the upper town, as I had frequent occasion, while visiting the different religious establishments of this interesting City, my eyes were frequently arested by a splendid IHS, in gilt letters, inscribed [198] over the main entrance into a magnificent stone Edifice, surrounded by a high and extensive wall—inquired what building that was? Was told that it was formerly the College of the Jesuits, which was seized by order of Government some years back, and converted into Barracks for soldiers;—and which are still employed for that base and unworthy purpose! Poor, injured Society of Jesus! How hast thou been traduced—how hast thou been persecuted by the world in every clime! But, it is a satisfaction to know that the disciple is not above the Master, and that thus the Lord of all was himself treated! This was then the house out of which so many apostolic men issued in their day to carry the gospel to all the savage tribes of North America, and who by their enlightened zeal and their truly exemplary conduct brought so many of them into the one fold and under the one Shepherd! This was the house to which the martyred Rasles was wont to resort annually for his spiritual renovation, and from which he again and again returned with new energy and vigour to edify, and to teach the Abenakis tribes of Maine how to live as Christians,—and how to endure their many hardships and privations, by his own example! Yes, this house—this sacred Edifice, to which Canada in particular owes so much—in which the highest and most heroic virtues were daily inculcated and practised—in which the praises of God were so often sung,—this house is now converted by government into a common receptacle for soldiers! And how is this? Are there no Jesuits tolerated in England? Yes, the splendid establishment of Stonyhearse is wholly Jesuit. Again, are there no Jesuits tolerated even in oppressed Ireland? Yes, even in that persecuted and oppressed country, the College of Clongows-wood is purely a Jesuit Institution. And in Canada, another portion of the same Empire, the magnificent building, formerly a Jesuit College is converted, and by the same Government, too, into Barracks for Soldiers!—What inconsistency! O shame! where is thy blush! People of Canada!—has no remonstrance been ever made? No protest been issued?

I would not enter it—the opportunity was offered; yet I would not avail myself of it. I would not visit the interior of a house polluted by sacreledge and crime—and where in lieu of the praises of God my ears might be stunned by the blasphemies of a [199] wicked and licentious soldiery. I beheld its exterior—that was enough for the present. It is a magnificent quadrangular edifice measuring 225 feet by 201, encircled by a wall which extends on the north through the whole length of Fabrique Street, and more than 600 feet on St. Ann's Street. The Area inclosed and which is now appropriated for idle parades and the exercise of the troops, was formerly a garden and parterre much admired for their horticultural beauty and elegance.

Supped at the Seminary and immeately after went on board of the Steam-Boat for Montreal—was accompanied to the wharf by several of the Reverend Professors of the Seminary and College, greatly pleased with my visit to Quebec. Embarked with the Rev. Mr. Gauvreau, and the Rev. Mr. Derome, the former intending to stop at **Trois Rivieres,** and the latter to continue on to Montreal. They both appeared to be worthy and respectable Clergymen.

July 9th Arrived at **Trois Rivieres,** about noon. As the Boat was to stop here for the space of a half hour to take in wood, ventured to go ashore for the purpose of visiting the Curé of the place, and his Church—and if I should still have time, also the Ursuline Convent. But in this last was greatly disappointed. Had just time to take a rapid view of the interiour of the Church, when the Steam-Boat bell summoned us on board. Remarked, however, that the Church was a handsome neat Edifice, and not so overloaded with Gold Leaf as the Churches in Canada usually are. The Curé was kind and polite. Continued our route—reached Sorrel at 6 O'Clock. While taking in wood the Rev. Mr. Kelly, Curé of this village came on board, and invited us ashore—was obliged to decline on account of the shortness of time allowed—had seen him at Montreal and was sorry I could not avail myself of his kind invitation.

July 10th Arrived at Montreal about 7 O'Clock A.M. Found the Servant of the Seminary waiting for me on shore to take my baggage. Went to the Seminary—was rejoiced to find that the Bishop of New York, Dr. Dubois was there. Conversed with him for some moments when word was brought [200] us from the Rev. Mr. Lesaulnier that the Reverend Gentlemen of the Seminary would be happy to see us at the Country-Seat. Recollected that this was one of the days when the Clergy all dined there. Set off immediately, and found them mostly assembled, and engaged in their usual recreations—Took a walk over to the College Villa. Was soon discovered by my two Boys who immediately ran to me quite overjoyed. I was glad to see them in the Uniform of the College, and admitted as Inmates into it. They seemed quite pleased, and only regretted they did not know the language of the Country, nor how to converse with the other students. It was not long before we were joined by the Bishop of New York, the Rev. Mr. Roque, the President, and the Rev. Mr. Quiblier. After some conversation returned to the Seminary Villa—found the dinner on the table and all the Priests assembled. Never spent a more agreable time in conversation. The Bishop of New York soon withdrew as he had to leave Montreal that evening. After tarrying some time at the Villa returned to the Seminary.

July 11th Said Mass at the Hotel-Dieu, and breakfasted in the Apothecary room of the Establishment. The good Religious were just on the point of entering into their new Building. Returned to the Seminary. Called for paper and pencil—went into the garden and commenced a sketch of the side view of the new Parish Church wishing to exhibit the size and style of this magnificent structure to some friends in Boston. At 11 O'Clock set out in company with the Rev. Mr. Lesaulnier for St. Jacques where, at the invitation of the Right Reverend Bishop of Telmesse we were to dine. The Bishop received us with great kindness, shewed us his premises and entertained us with his agreable conversation—His Seminarians dined with us in the same room, but at a different table. After dinner returned to the Seminary, and finished my drawing.

July 12th Said Mass at the Convent of the Sisters of the Congregation—Breakfasted in the Community Room in which I had the pleasure of seeing again the Sisters all assembled. Conversed some time with them, and returned to the Seminary. [201] Spent the morning chiefly in arranging my little matters and preparing for my departure—was happy to find on my table a couple of Chalices, a pair of cruets and some other things for the Altar, a present from the good M. Le Saulnier which was the more acceptable as they were much wanted in my Diocess and could not be easily procured. Dined at the Seminary—after dinner proceeded to the College with Rev. Mr. Phelan to see my Boys for the last time, and to pay the advance for their education—Walked into the garden where they soon observed and came to me. Saw the Rev. Mr. Roque and made my arrangements with him for the year—informed him that in a short time I hoped to be able to put a number of others under his direction—as the want of Priests in my Diocess was great and the only means I had to procure them was to educate them. Took my leave and returned to the Seminary. On my way back called in to see the **Recollet** Church lately purchased by the Seminary of M. Grant into whose hands it had fallen after it had been seized by the Government. The Purchase was made exclusively for the benefit of the Irish Catholics. Found the Church old and not very large; but was capable of being greatly improved by additions, which, in time, would undoubtedly be attended to.

July 13th (Sunday.) Said Mass in the Parish Church—breakfasted in the Seminary—Assisted at the High-Mass which was celebrated by the venerable President of the College. His voice was so melodious and just that at first could not persuade myself it was the voice of the venerable M. Roque whose hairs had been bleached by the frosts of more than seventy winters, but of some younger Clergyman. It was nevertheless himself— Listened to him with much satisfaction. The sermon was delivered by the Rev. Mr. Sauvage. Both the matter and the manner of his delivery pleased me much. The **Pain beni** was served as usual, which ceremony prevails throughout [202] all lower Canada. Dined at the Seminary—After dinner took an affectionate leave of all the Reverend Gentlemen whose kindness and attention during my stay with them I shall never forget; and also of my two Boys, who took care to be on the spot at my departure. Repaired to the Boat accompanied by the Rev. Messrs. Sauvage and Satin, who had the politeness to cross the river with me to **Laprairie**. On landing waited on the Curé, who had just finished Vespers. Took a hasty view of the Church and of the school under the direction of the good Sisters of the Congregation. In a short time the Carriage arrived promised by the good Curé of St. Philip to take me to his house on my way to St. John's. Bade a last farewell to the Reverend Gentlemen who had accompanied me thus far and of the worthy Curé of **Laprairie** and set out for the Rev. M. Pigeon's at St. Philip accompanied by his brother. Arrived there after an hour or two, and was received by him with great kindness and cordiality. As a token of his respect he caused the Bells of his Church to be rung on my approach, which drew together a number of his Parishioners, who received my benediction. Found at his house Rev. Mr. Derome who had travelled with me from Quebec. After a little while repaired to his Church which was near at hand and was greatly surprised to see so neat and beautiful an Edivice in a Country Parish. Found that the Reverend Curé was a lover of music and also a very ingenious artist; for he had by his own skill fitted up and so adapted a hand Organ as to be able to perform upon it and with it to go through the entire service of Gregorian music used in his Church. Greatly admired his ingenuity in being able to adapt to sacred purposes what otherwise would have been perfectly useless. Wrote my name, at the invitation of Rev. M. Pigeon, on his **Album,** as one of the many, who had enjoyed the hospitality of this worthy Curé, and continued my journey towards St. John's. At 6 O'Clock I reached the parish of **L'accadie,** and was hospitably received by the Rev. Mr. Paquin, the Curé and his Vicar the Rev. M. Caron. The Rev. Mr. Paquin was at this time in ill health, and seemed to labour under a great depression of spirits, although to a super-[203]ficial observer, he would appear in perfect health. Took a hasty repast—visited his Church and sacristy, which I found beautiful and well furnished, and drove on to St. John's, having changed my Carriage, the Reverend Curé of L'accadie having insisted on my taking his and sending the Rev. M. Pigeon's back. Reached St. John's at 9 O'Clock and immediately went on board the Steam Boat which was to start the following morning for Burlington at 4 O'Clock.

July 14th Rose in the morning—went on Deck and found that we were close upon **Isle aux noix.** Looked for a retired part of the Boat, and sat down to read my Breviary. Had hardly finished when I observed near the Passengers Cabin a Clergyman in Sutanne—could not make out who it was. In a little while he came up and introduced himself as the Rev. M. Mignault of Chambly. I immediately recognized him having formerly seen him at New York when on a visit from Halifax. He informed me that the Bishop of New York had been at his house a few days before, and had requested him to join him at Platsburg and that he was now on his way thither. Rejoiced in his company, and only regretted that he had not farther to go. About 10 O'Clock we reached Platsburg. The Vessel stopped merely long enough to land the Passengers for this village. Saw the Bishop of New York on shore who beckoned to me to land, but could not do so without losing my passage. Rev. Mr. Mignault here joined the Bishop while the Boat proceeded on to Burlington where we arrived at 2 O'Clock P.M. Went to the Hotel to dine— learnt there that there would be no stage for Boston before the following morning. Dined, and after dinner took a horse and Chaise with a Mr. Trask of Cape Ann who was one of my fellow passengers for the purpose of taking a ride through the village, and beholding the many beautiful prospects from it. Was greatly pleased with the views it afforded, especially that from the heights near the College.

July 15th Left Burlington at 4 O'Clock A.M. Dined at Montpelier at 12 O'Clock and arrived to pass the night at Royalton. Our company in the

Stage was very agreable consisting of Mr. [204] Trask, already mentioned, and his two Daughters, a Mr. Fisk, merchant of Boston, two young gentlemen, merchants of New York, who had been at the Springs, and were now returning home, via Boston which they had never seen. Our route during the fore part of the day lay along the Banks of the Onion River one of the prettiest and most romantick little streams I had ever seen. The country around was bold and mountenous—the road, however, was excellent; so that our journey this day was very pleasant.

July 16th Left Ro[y]alton at 4 O'Clock A.M. On our setting out it rained hard, and the weather was besides extremely warm. In addition to this, having taken in three more passengers and being obliged to keep the curtains of the Stage down, could not but feel greatly incommoded. On arriving at Woodstock, however the weather cleared up, and two of our supernumerary passengers left us. At this town we breakfasted. Resumed our journey and arrived at Windsor. Here we divided—one half of our company, viz: Mr. Trask, his two daughters, and Mr. Fisk took the Stage that travelled to Northampton, wishing to see that country; while the two New York Merchants and myself continued on direct to Boston. Our two stages kept in view for seven miles as we descended the opposite sides of the Connecticut River, during which we often saluted one another with handkerchiefs. Dined at Newport, and passed the night at Francis-town.

July 17th Left Francis Town at 4 O'Clock the day setting in fair and pleasant, and reached Boston at 5 O'Clock P.M.—Found the Clergy in good health, and the Church prosperous.

July 18th Repaired to the Convent on Mount Benedict to celebrate Mass and to deliver the commissions with which I had been charged by the good Nuns of Montreal and Quebec. Found the Ursulines also in good health, their school increasing, and all things in a prosperous state. Satisfied the good Religious in all their inquiries about Canada."

In the course of this year three Churches were commenced, viz: at Dover in New Hampshire; at Portland in Maine; and also, at Eastport, in Maine. The situation chosen for each of [205] them was highly eligible, and the Lots of ground abundantly ample. Although the number of Catholics in the town of Saco, Maine, was yet small, the Bishop thought it adviseable to purchase a Lot of ground also in a central part of this town for a future Church, in the hope that the time was not far distant when one might be erected. The same was done at Newport, Rhode Island. On this Lot, however, a School house had been previously erected in which a small number of Catholics might be conveniently accommodated on Sundays, until a proper Church could be erected. In Providence, the Catholics assembled for divine worship in a large hall which had been hired for the purpose.

On the Feast of the Assumption of this year, (1828) the Bishop repaired to the Ursuline Convent of Mount Benedict, in Charlestown, for the purpose of giving the Religious Veil to Sister Mary Benedict, daughter of the Rev. Virgil H. Barber, whose two years of Noviceship had expired this day. He commenced the ceremony at 7 O'Clock in the Chapel of the Convent, in which a number of respectable Protestant Ladies had assembled, with the consent of the Superior, they having expressed a great desire to be present at it, and in the presence also of the Children of the School, who sang a number of beautiful hymns on the occasion, which they accompanied with various musical Instruments. The ceremony was solemn, and drew tears from the eyes of almost every stranger present, who were struck with admiration at the heroism of this amiable and highly accomplished young Lady in thus renouncing the vanities of the world, and devoting herself to God alone. The Bishop addressed an elaborate discourse to the persons present, having taken for his text these appropriate words of the Gospel: "Mary hath chosen the better part which shall not be taken from her," which was listened to with great attention. Thus was another member added to this interesting little Community, which now consisted of four professed Nuns, two Lay-Sisters, and two Novices.

[206] The number of Catholics in Charlestown and Lichmere's Point having greatly increased, the Bishop became exceedingly anxious to have a Church erected in some central situation, which might accommodate the inhabitants of both places. He accordingly called a meeting of them, on the 25th of August, and made the following proposition: viz: To open a subscription for the purpose of raising an immediate sum of $6000—to divide the subscribers into three classes, 1st, 2d, and 3d, consisting of twenty in each class—and to require of each of the subscribers of the first class $150; of those of the second $100; and of those of the third $50; these sums to be paid immediately on subscription. On the completion of the Church, the persons so subscribing, alone to be allowed the priviledge of bidding on the Pews, when offered for sale, for choice, and in payment of the purchase, to be credited with the sums subscribed, and respectively paid in by them. It was supposed that the surplus money which would be raised on the day of sale on the Pews, by the Subscribers bidding against one another for choice of situation, would, with the original sum paid in, be amply sufficient to purchase the land and complete the Church.

The proposition, after little discussion, was approved and accepted—the Bishop was requested to draw a plan of the proposed Church—and a Committee was appointed to select a convenient spot of Ground in Charlestown, some where in the vicinity of the Bridge leading from the above town to Lichmere's Point, which was requested to report as early as possible.

On the 7th day of September a new meeting of the Catholics of Charlestown and Lichmere Point was called, which met in the School-room of the Cathedral in Boston. At this meeting the Bishop presented the Plan of the contemplated Church which was highly approved. According to this plan the Church was to be a plain brick Edifice of the Dorick Order—measuring eighty feet in length, and forty five feet in width, with Galleries on the sides and over the entrance, and two [207] square towers to ornament the front of the building. The report of the Committee was at the same time made, which ascertained that there was a Lot of ground for sale, on Richmond Street, at the rate of fifteen cents per square foot, which they thought was advantageously situated, and which measured one hundred and sixty feet deep by 75 feet in front—they accordingly recommended the immediate purchase of it, as land in general was rising, and they thought so convenient a piece of land could not easily be procured within the same vicinity. The report was approved and adopted. In conformity to the above, the land was purchased, and a Deed was taken of it, which is recorded in Middlesex, in the Registry of Deeds, Book 284, page 110. Contracts for the Building were immediately after entered into, and the same was commenced. The subscriptions were also soon filled—so that every thing announced a successful and speedy issue.

Having accomplished this important business the Bishop was anxious to see Providence, and learn the prospects there; he accordingly set off accompanied by the Rev. Mr Tyler, on the 13th of September, and arrived in that City the same day—saw the Rev. Mr. Woodley, and made arrangements with him for the order of divine service on the following day. On the 14th after having celebrated Mass in a private apartment, as there was no Catholic Church yet erected in Providence, he repaired to Mechanick's hall opposite the Market, a room capable of containing 500 individuals, and in which nearly that number had assembled, to assist at mass celebrated by the Rev. Mr Woodley; during which, at the Gospel, he addressed the Catholics present on the great truths of religion, and gave confirmation to five individuals. In the afternoon the Rev. Mr. Tyler also preached to a crouded audience, among which were a great number of Protestants. On the 15th he left Providence for Pawtucket, a small village within five miles of the above City. Here he received a donation of a beautiful Lot of land for a Church from David Wilkinson, Esq. As this village was a growing one and the number of Ca-[208]tholics in it was already considerable, he was greatly rejoiced at this acquisition in the hope of soon having it in his power to erect a Church upon it. It is beautifully situated on the Rhode Island side of the village, and commands a very pretty view of the surrounding country. Having recommended to the Rev. Mr. Woodley to institute a subscription among the Catholics with a view to carry the above object into effect as speedily as possible, he returned to Boston.

On the 3d of October, agreeably to public notice, he proceeded to Charlestown to perform the interesting ceremony of laying the corner stone of the first Catholic Church ever erected in this town. He left Boston accompanied by the Rev. Messrs. Wiley, Tyler, Mahoney and Woodly, and repaired to the house of Mr. Robertson, a Protestant gentleman who lived convenient to the ground, and who had kindly offered his house to them to prepare for the ceremony. A temporary altar, and a large cross had been already erected on the Lot, and every other necessary arrangement had been made. As soon as dressed, the Bishop in his Rochet and Cope, with the Clergy in their Cassocks and Surplices, and the Accolythes as usually vested when attending about the altar, walked in procession to the Spot, preceded by the Cross-bearer. A large concourse of people of all Denominations had already assembled on the ground to witness the ceremony, among whom the greatest order prevailed. The ceremony was performed in a solemn manner to the great edification of the Catholics who assisted in great number. Under the Corner Stone, which consisted of a huge block of granite, a copper Plate about a foot square was laid bearing the following inscription:

D. O. M.
Auspice Mariâ
hunc Lapidem angularem
posuit Benedictus Episcopus Bostoniensis secundus
Die tertiâ Octobris A.D. MDCCCXXVIII.

At the conclusion of the ceremony the Bishop addressed a discourse to the people, and afterwards gave his benediction. [209] The procession was then again formed, and returned in the same manner to the house of Mr. Robertson, and thence to Boston.

On the 25th of October he again left Boston accompanied by the Rev. Mr. Tyler for Lowell. On getting out of the Stage he sent to inquire whether the Rev. Mr. Mahoney had arrived from Salem, and if so, to request him to come to his lodgings. Shortly after he made his appearance, when all things were arranged for divine service the following morning.

On Sunday (the 26th) the Bishop repaired to the School house (which by the permission of Kirke Boote, Esq. the Catholics were allowed to use on Sundays) early in the morning caused an altar to be arranged and celebrated Mass which was served by the Rev. Mr. Tyler. At 10 O'Clock a large concourse of people assembled consisting of both Catholics and Protestants which crowded the room to that degree that it was with difficulty the Bishop could get to the altar. He, however made his way through the multitude with the other Clergy. The Rev. Mr. Mahoney soon after commenced Mass, and the divine service proceeded. The Bishop preached at the Gospel upon the Love of God which attracted great attention. At 2 O'Clock Vespers were recited, as there was no Choir, and the Rosary was said, after which the Rev. Mr. Mahoney preached. The Bishop having dined with Kirk Boote, Esq. took this opportunity to represent to him the poverty of the Catholics in this new but growing town, and the benefits that would result to society at large, if they could have a Church to assemble in on Sundays—that in their present poverty it would be impossible for them to pay the usual price of a Lot, and afterwards undergo also the expence of a building of sufficient size to accommodate them;—he hoped, therefore, that the Company, of which he was Agent, would take this into their consideration, and make them a present of a suitable Lot of Ground—he did not doubt but that the Catholics, small as their Body was, would be able to effect in a short time the other object. Mr. Boote was kind enough to promise to use his influence with the Gentlemen of the Company—and did not doubt but that they would give a Lot. The follow-[210]ing day, the Bishop left Lowell and returned to Boston.

On the 31st of October he again left Boston for Newport, Rhode Island, in the Stage—distance 72 miles. he arrived towards the close of evening and found the Rev. Mr. Woodly waiting to receive him. Visited the following morning (All Saints) the Lot and School-house and celebrated Mass in it— the number of people assembled was very small. On surveying the Premises he was greatly disappointed. He found the Lot extremely small for the sum given for it, and the building old and much decayed. There was, however, one redeeming quality, the situation was highly eligible. He, therefore concluded to recommend the purchase, as early as possible, of the next Lot to it, that a sufficient space might be obtained for a future Church.

The following day being Sunday, after having celebrated Mass, he addressed the congregation from the Gospel of the day, and before he concluded directed his discourse more particularly to those who were about to be confirmed—and afterwards administered the holy sacrament of confirmation to eleven persons. The concourse of persons was so great that scarcely one third of the number present could obtain admittance into the room, and were consequently obliged to remain without doors. The weather, however, was mild and agreable. After divine service he called a special meeting of the Catholics, and earnestly recommended to them the object alluded to above;—and on the 3d of November returned to Boston.

On his arrival he learnt with great pleasure that the Church in Eastport; Maine, was already covered in, and so far advanced in other respects that divine service could be performed it; also, that the Church in Portland, Maine, was equally advanced; and the one in Dover, Ṅ.H. was nearly completed. He felt highly satisfied with the exertions of the Rev. Mr. Ffrench, and particularly pleased at the speedy prospect of having the good Catholics in those respective places accommodated. He only regretted his inability to supply them all as yet with proper and efficient Clergymen; but, this he hoped to be able to [211] do before very long.

The following will shew the number and the stations of the Clergymen doing duty in this Diocess at the close of this year:

1. The Rt. Rev. Bishop Fenwick in Boston, assisted by the Rev. Messrs. Byrne and Wiley;

2. The Rev. Virgil H. Barber, Indian Old Town, on the Penobscot; charged also with the mission at Claremont, N[ew] Hampshire.

3. The Rev. James Fitton, Pleasant Point, Passamaquoddy, Maine.

4. The Rev. Charles Ffrench, Portland, Maine; also charged with the missions of Dover N.H., Saco, Me. and Eastport, Me.

5. The Rev. Dennis Ryan, Whitefield, Maine; also charged with New Castle, and Gardiner, Me.

6. The Rev. Robert D. Woodley, Providence, R.I.—also, charged with the mission at Newport and Pawtucket, Rhode Island.

The number of Baptisms performed in the Cathedral during this year (1828) amounted to...........

The number of Marriages to.............[37]

CHAPTER IX

THE EVENTS OF 1829

In the commencement of this year the Rev. Mr. Byrne having asked and obtained permission to visit Ireland, his native country, sailed from Boston in the **Boston** Packet for Liverpool on the 31st of January. In consequence of his absence the Bishop was obliged to recall the Rev. Mr. Fitton from Pleasant Point, and station him in Boston. Thus were the Passamaquoddy Indians left again without a Pastor.

The Ursuline Convent sustained another heavy loss on the 7th of April, this year, in the death of Sister Mary Frances, after a lingering illness of nearly six months. This was the second death which had occurred in this Community since its removal from Boston—and never was a Religious more lamented, or, whose loss was more regretted; pious, amiable, intelligent and accomplished, she had acquired the esteem and [212] affection of all. Her funeral took place the following day at which the Bishop presided, assisted by the Rev. Messrs. Fitton and Wiley. A solemn service was performed—after which the Corpse was removed from the Choir, and borne in procession to the Tomb, at the bottom of the Garden, accompanied by the Religious and all the Children of the School in tears, where the last rites were performed.

The Rev. William Tyler, who had been ordained a Deacon on the 22nd of December, 1827, and whose ordination to the Priesthood had been postponed, in consequence of his not having at that time attained the age prescribed by the Canons, was, this year, ordained Priest. The holy Order was conferred upon him in the Cathedral of the HOLY CROSS by the Bishop, during the solemnity of the holy Sacrifice of Mass, assisted by the Rev. Messrs. Wiley and Fitton, on Sunday, the 3d of May. On the 4th he celebrated his first Mass, assisted by the Rev. Mr. Fitton.

247

The new Church in Charlestown having been completed, was on Sunday, the 10th of May, dedicated to God under the patronage of his blessed mother. As this was the first Catholic Church which had ever been erected in this town an immense concourse of people of all denominations assembled to witness the ceremony. After the usual blessing, as prescribed by the Roman Ritual, was gone through, the Rev. Mr. Tyler celebrated solemn High Mass, assisted by the Rev. Messrs. Fitton and Wiley as Deacon and Subdeacon, during which at the Gospel, the Bishop addressed a discourse which lasted an hour, to the people, in which he took a general view of the establishment of religion, and the progress of the Catholic Church in every age. He was listened to with marked attention during the whole. The Choir was conducted by Mongr. Mallet, who by his superior performance upon the fine new organ, with which the Church was provided, contributed in no small degree to the solemnity of the Service. In the afternoon Vespers were chaunted, after which another discourse was delivered by the Rev. Mr. Fitton, when the Bishop concluded the Office of the day with a solemn benediction. The Church of St. Mary is a plain neat edifice, built perfectly conformable to the plan presented by [213] the Bishop, and is capable of containing a thousand persons.

On the 12th Inst. a solemn service was performed in the Cathedral for the repose of the soul of Leo XII. in which the Bishop officiated pontifically, assisted by the Rev. Messrs. Tyler and Wiley, as Deacon and Subdeacon, and by several other Clergymen. The usual ceremony of the Absolution was scarcely over, when news was received of the election of a new Pope, under the name of Pius VIII.

On Pentecost Sunday, (june 7th) he again celebrated Mass Pontifically, and administered the holy sacrament of confirmation to 115 persons a number of whom were converts, and the greater part had made their first communion on the same day; and on Sunday, the 21st Inst. he again administered the same holy sacrament, in Salem, to four individuals, one of whom was a convert to the Church from the Baptist religion.

On the 1st of july he presided at the examination of the young Ladies at the Ursuline Convent, previous to the vacation. It was the third day of the examination, and the one appointed for the distribution of rewards. The large Hall of the Convent was beautifully fitted up for the purpose, and highly decorated. Two Thrones were erected on a square Platform at each extremity of the hall, the one destined for the Bishop—the other for the two young Ladies, who had particularly distinguished themselves during the last year, by their proficiency in study, as well as by their generally good conduct. This last was surmounted by a splendid Baldaquino of white Satin, and was highly ornamented. At the termination of the exercises of the day, which consisted partly of recitations, and partly of performances of vocal and instrumental music, the compositions both in Poetry and Prose, of the young Ladies, as well in English as in French, together with various specimens of their writing, and needlework, were exhibited. Miss Mead of Charlestown was then led to the throne of the Bishop, and presented to him by the Superior, as the young Lady, who had merited the highest Prize in the Senior Class. He received her with great attention, and having complimented [214] her upon her progress in study, and the great satisfaction which she had given to her teachers, all the while standing he advanced towards her and placed a wreath of white roses upon her head. He did the same to Miss Maria Fay, daughter of Judge Fay of Cambridge-Port, who had also merited the highest prize in the junior class. They were then both conducted to and seated upon the beautiful throne which had been previously prepared for them. After this, Premiums were distributed among several of the young Ladies, who had also distinguished themselves in some particular branches in their prospective classes. An original Ode was next sung in honour of the two Queens, in which all the young Ladies joined—and after a number of airs had been performed as well on the Harp as on the Piano, they were all conducted to the dining apartment, where they sat down to a splendid dinner. Never did children appear more gratified, or more contented and happy than they did on this day. The Bishop seemed also well pleased, and, previous to his departure from the Convent, took occasion to congratulate the good Ladies upon the great improvement he had witnessed of their children, and to express the peculiar satisfaction which their respective performances had this day afforded him.[34]

The Bishop having received information from Mr. Deodat Taylor, a Convert, in Hartford, Connecticut, that the Episcopalians having nearly completed their new Church in that City, were anxious to dispose of their old one, and only required the sum of $500 for the same, on the express condition, however, that it should be moved to some other Lot—and that they were willing also to dispose of their Organ for the sum of $400. As he had long had a desire to establish the Catholic religion in this central City of Connecticut, he resolved to set out immediately and learn in person the exact situation of things there. He accordingly left Boston on the 9th Inst. at 10 O'Clock P.M. in the Mail Stage, and having travelled all night, arrived in that City the following day at 2 O'Clock P.M. and took up his Lodgings in the City Hotel. In the course of the afternoon he called on Mr. Deodat Taylor and his Brother Francis, and [215] with them went to examine the premises—and after thorough examination he felt fully satisfied that the Building proposed to be sold was well worth the money—and if a Lot of land could be purchased at no great distance from its present site it would prove a valuable acquisition to the Catholics. He therefore instructed Mr. Taylor to conclude the purchase on the above terms; but previously to ascertain fully whether the Lot of land nearly opposite on the brow of the hill could in like manner be procured, at a reasonable rate. In the course of a few hours all was accomplished—a handsome new site was obtained, and the Church was purchased, to be delivered up in the month of November ensuing.

On the following Sunday, (the 12th Inst.) he celebrated Mass in a private room, at which all the Catholics in Hartford attended. These did not amount to more than a couple of dozzen. He gave them a short exhortation on the Gospel of the day, and recommended to them in a particular manner to live in peace and union among themselves, and on all occasions to edify the people by whom they were surrounded by their good conduct.

In the evening at 6 O'Clock he repaired to the State House, and in the principal Hall, which had been previously obtained, delivered a discourse to a crowded audience consisting of all denominations of Christians, the subject of which was, the forgetfulness of man in relation to the duties which he owed to God. He was happy to learn afterwards that the manner in which he treated it was calculated to produce a happy effect upon many who were present.

In the course of the two following days he was waited upon by a number of the inhabitants of the town who requested to be informed of the peculiar doctrines of the Catholic Church, and the grounds of the same. He took some pains to satisfy their inquiries, and devoted the entire of the evenings of each of them to this object.

On the 15th at 2 O'Clock in the morning, he took the mail-[216]Stage, and arrived in Boston at 6 O'Clock the same evening highly pleased with Hartford, and the prospect of his soon having a neat and respectable Church there.

On the 19th Inst. the Bishop celebrated Mass in the Cathedral of the Holy Cross, in Pontificals, during which he promoted the Rev. Bernard O'Cavenah to the Priesthood; after which he gave him in charge the mission of Hartford, and directed him to visit also occasionally New Haven and Middletown.[35]

The Catholics of Claremont, N.H. having been some time without a resident Pastor he directed the Rev. Mr. Fitton, who could best be spared in present circumstances to pay them a visit. He left Boston on the 20th and arrived there on the 21st and having spent a month among them, returned to Boston.

The Bishop having learnt that a number of Catholics were employed in and around Sandwich, a manufacturing town in Massachusetts, sent on the 4th of September the Rev. Mr. Tyler to afford them the consolations of their religion. He reported on his return that the whole of the number, who could be assembled for divine service, did not exceed 20.

On Sunday (the 6th of the same month,) the Bishop again celebrated Mass in the Cathedral, in Pontificals, during which he promoted the Rev. Thomas J. O'Flaherty to the Priesthood on which occasion the Rev. Charles Ffrench delivered to an overflowing Congregation a very impressive discourse on the occasion, which drew tears from the eyes of many.[36] In the afternoon of the same day the Bishop also preached from the Gospel of the Sunday.

The Archbishop of Baltimore having summoned a Provincial Council to meet in Baltimore on the 4th of October, the Bishop made all the necessary dispositions in Boston to enable him to assist at it. The following is an abstract of the journal which he kept during his absence from home on that occasion.

[217] **September 22d** "Left Boston in the Stage for Providence at 5 O'Clock in the morning for the purpose of repairing to Baltimore to assist at the Provincial Council to be held there on the 4th of October. The day was beautiful. Arrived in Providence at 11 O'Clock—hastened on board the Steam-Boat—Reached New York the following morning at 7 O'Clock.

Sept. 23d Visited the Rev. Dr. Power—learnt from him that the Bishop of New York, the Rt. Rev. Dr. Dubois, had left the country in the Packet for Havre, but the week before, with the intention of going to Rome, at the invitation of the Prefect of the Propaganda. Was greatly surprised at this, especially as the assembling of the Council was so near at hand, and the presence of the Bishop of so important a Diocess as that of New York, was so necessary at it. Learnt moreover that previous to his departure, he had authorized the Rt. Rev. Dr. David, Co-adjutor to the Bishop of Kentucky, to represent him in his absence.

Sept. 24th Left New York in the Steam Boat for Philadelphia—arrived there at 6 O'Clock P.M. Took lodgings at Mr. Joseph Snyders at his special invitation.

Sept. 25th Left Philadelphia in the Union Line, and reached Baltimore at 7 O'Clock P.M.—Paid a visit to the Archbishop was informed by him that the Bishop of Kentucky, Dr. Flaget, and the Bishop of St. Louis, Missouri, Dr. Rosati, were the only Bishops yet arrived;—that the Bishop of Charleston, Dr. England, he understood was at Mount St. Mary's and would arrive in a few days—and that Dr. Fenwick of Ohio, was then in Washington, and in a day or two would also be in Baltimore accompanied by Dr. Matthews, administrator of the Diocess of Philadelphia.

Sept. 26th Went to the Archbishop's—breakfasted with him. After Breakfast took a walk to the Seminary of St. Sulpice in company with the archbishop—was there introduced to Bishops Flaget and Rosati. The Bishop [218] of Kentucky had long been known to the Bishop of Boston, he having, in his childhood, been long under his tuition in the College of George Town. Was exceedingly rejoiced to see his old Master in excellent health, and apparently in as good spirits and vigour as he was in 1799—and also to become acquainted with the good Bishop of St. Louis.

Sept. 27th (Sunday) Said early Mass in St. Peter's Church the Cradle of Catholicity in Baltimore. Breakfasted with the Archbishop, and afterwards assisted at the High-Mass celebrated in the Cathedral—the Rev. Roger Smith preached. Dined with the Archbishop—assisted at Vespers, after which took lodgings at Mr. Basil S. Elder's at his pressing invitation and that of his amiable and pious Family.

Sept. 28th Waited upon the Archbishop—was notified that a meeting of such Bishops as were then in Baltimore would take place the following morning to arrange the different Officers preparatory to the Council.

Sept. 29th The following Bishops, being all that were then in Baltimore, assembled at the Archbishop's, viz: the Most Rev. Dr. Whitfield, Archbishop of Baltimore; Rt. Rev. Dr. Flaget, Bishop of Bardstown, Kentucky; Rt. Rev. Dr. Rosati, Bishop of St. Louis, Missouri; and Rt. Rev. B. Fenwick, Bishop of Boston. At this meeting the Archbishop appointed the Bishop of Boston to the office of Promotor to the Council, and proposed the various points to be discussed in it. Dined with the Archbishop—during dinner, Dr. Fenwick, Bishop of Cincinnati arrived accompanied by the Very Rev. William Matthews, Pastor of St. Patrick's, Washington City, and Administrator of the Diocese of Philadelphia.

Sept. 30th The Rt. Rev. Dr. England, Bishop of Charleston, S.C. arrived. The Bishops having now all assembled, the following Sunday was appointed for the opening of the Council. It was proposed and decided, that on each of the days during the ensuing week the Bishops should celebrate High-mass in turn, and that the Bishop of Charleston, and the Bishop of Boston should alternately preach during [219] the same.

October 1st The Bishops held a private Session—and appointed their respective Theologians. The Bishop of Bardstown, Dr. Flaget, appointed the Rev. Patrick Kenrick; the Bishop of Charleston, Dr. England, the Rev. Simon Bruté; the Bishop of Cincinnati, Dr. Fenwick, the Rev. Lewis Debarth; the Bishop of St. Louis, Dr. Rosati, the Rev. M. Jeanjean; the Bishop of Boston, Dr. B. Fenwick, the Rev. Anth. Blanc; the Very Reverend Administrator of Philadelphia, Dr. Matthews, the Rev. M. Wheeler;—Besides these the Archbishop, Dr. Whitfield having expressed a wish that the Superiors of the Religious Orders and Communities, as well as the Reverend Doctors of Divinity connected with the Cathedral should likewise be present, the same was approved of by all the Bishops. Accordingly, the following respectable Divines were notified to assist, viz: the Rev. Francis Dzierozinski, Superior of the Jesuits; the Rev. M. Carrere, Visitor of the Sulpicians; the Rev. John Tessier, late Superior of the same; the Rev. L.R. Deluol, Superior of the same; and the Rev. Dr. Damphoux. In consequence of the absence of the Bishop of New York, and the indisposition of the Rt. Rev. Bishop David, his representative, at the solicitation of the Bishop of Charleston, the Very Rev. Dr. Power, one of the Vicar generals of New York was likewise notified to attend. After this, the Rev. Dr. Damphoux, was appointed secretary to the Council, and the Rev. P. Kenrick of Kentucky, assistant Secretary. Things having been thus arranged, all the Theologians were notified to attend the Cathedral on the Saturday following, between the hours of 9 and 12 A.M.—The Bishops today by special invitation were invited to dine at Mr. Basil S. Elder's.

October 2d Wrote letters and returned a number of visits.

October 3d Celebrated Mass in St. Peter's—at 9 O'Clock attended the first congregation of Divines in the Cathedral, with the other Bishops, at which the first discussion took place.

October 4th (Sunday) The Provincial Council [220] opened today with the celebration of a solemn High-Mass by the Archbishop, at which all the Bishops assisted richly habited each with a Cope and Mitre, and arranged three on a side together with about 40 Priests dressed in Chasubles. The Music in the Choir was truly sublime and calculated to produce a happy effect. The Cathedral was crowded to excess. At the conclusion of the Mass the Bishop of Charleston ascended the Pulpit, and in his usual happy manner delivered a beautiful discourse on the benefits which were likely to arise from the Council now assembled, and towards the close gave a full explanation of the ceremony of the **Pallium** about to be conferred upon Dr. Whitfield, the Archbishop. When the sermon was concluded, the Bishop of Boston advanced to the High Altar, and having taken his seat in front of it, delivered the **Pallium** to the Archbishop, who knelt before him to receive it, according to the Roman Pontifical. After this, the Psalm and usual prayers were chaunted for the opening of the Council.—The whole did not conclude till after 3 O'Clock P.M. At 5, the Vespers were sung during which the Bishops occupied the same place in the Sanctuary as in the forenoon, as well as the other Clergy. After the **Magnificat,** the Bishop of Boston delivered a discourse which was succeeded by the Benediction of the Blessed Sacrament, when the Service was concluded quite late in the evening.

Oct. 5th The Rt. Rev. Bishop of Bardstown being the oldest Bishop, celebrated High Mass this day at 7 O'Clock. After mass the Bishop of Charleston preached. Then followed the prayers and Psalm, as specified by the Pontifical. These being concluded, the Bishops assembled in the Archbishop's Sacristy dressed in Surplice and Rochet, and accompanied by their secretaries where the business of the Council was entered upon. They dined at 1 O'Clock and at 3 P.M. They assembled again, at this time in the sanctuary of the Cathedral, with their respective Divines accompanied also by the Superiors of Orders and the Doctors of Divinity of the Cathedral, in a Congregation to discuss together the points which were to be submitted to the judgment of the Bishops the following day. Such was the order of things to be observed during the continuance of the Council. The Congregation closed its sitting at 7 O'Clock P.M.

[221] **October 6th** The Rt. Rev. Bishop of Charleston celebrated High Mass, and the Rt. Rev. Bishop of Boston preached. The Psalm and Prayers followed as on yesterday. The meeting of the Bishops then took place which continued till 1 O'Clock—In the afternoon the Congregation was extended to 7 O'Clock.

Oct. 7th The Rt. Rev. Bishop of Cincinnati celebrated Mass, and the Rt. Rev. Bishop of Charleston preached—The Forenoon and Afternoon were afterwards employed, as above.

Oct. 8th The Rt. Rev. Bishop of St. Louis celebrated Mass, and the Rt. Rev. Bishop of Boston preached—The day was afterwards employed as above.

Oct. 9th The Rt. Rev. Bishop of Boston celebrated Mass—no sermon—the Rt. Rev. Bishops having decided to discontinue them in order to allow more time for the business of the Council. The rest of the day employed as before.

Oct. 10th The Rt. Rev. Bishop of Bardstown celebrated Mass in lieu of the Very Reverend Administrator of Philadelphia. The day employed as above.

Oct. 11th (Sunday) The Right Reverend Bishops assisted at the Solemn Mass celebrated in the Cathedral, in Cope and Mitre, as on the previous Sunday. The Rt. Rev. Dr. England preached in the forenoon and the Rev. P. Kenrick in the afternoon.

Oct. 12th During this week, the solemn High-Masses were discontinued, the Bishops having desired to assemble at an earlier hour for deliberation with a view to expedite the business of the forenoon. In the afternoon the Congregations were held as before.

Oct. 13th The Bishop of Charleston was appointed to draw up the common Pastoral, after the Bishops had agreed upon the topics.

Oct. 14th The Decrees were read in the Council, and translated.

Oct. 16th The Rt. Rev. Dr. Rosati, Bishop of St. Louis, was appointed to draw up the Letter to the Cardinal Secretary, which was to accompany the Decrees.

Oct. 17th The unfinished business was taken up and disposed of. Arrangements were made for bringing the Council to [222] a close.

Oct. 18th (Sunday) A solemn High Mass was this day celebrated by the Most Reverend Archbishop. The ceremonies the same as at the opening of the Council. At the Gospel the Bishop of Charleston preached a Charity Sermon in behalf of the Orphan Asylum in Baltimore under the direction of the Sisters of Charity. At the end of the Mass, the Psalms and Prayers were recited for the closing of the Council. The Decrees were then read and publickly signed by the Bishops, a table had been placed for this purpose in the middle of the Sanctuary. After this the Bishops embraced one another, when the Council was concluded. The Cathedral was immensely crowded during the morning service of this day which lasted during several hours.

Oct. 19th (Sunday) The Bishops this day by previous arrangement left Baltimore, at 8 O'Clock A.M. to pay a visit to the Hon. Charles Carroll of Carrolton, at his Manor, fifteen miles from Baltimore on the Frederick Town road. At Ellicot's Mills, or a little beyond, it was observed that the Iron which bound one of the hind-wheels had broken and fallen off, and the Carriage in consequence was not in a condition to proceed. They were accordingly obliged to dismount and to continue the remainder of the journey on foot, about 4 miles. Fortunately the Chaise of Mr. Carroll was just passing. This Dr. England being lame and unable to walk was persuaded to mount. In a short time all arrived at the mansion of this last Signer of American Independance, and were introduced to him and the rest of his family. The aged Patriot, though in his 96th year, appeared to enjoy perfect health, and to be full of life. The Bishops in the course of the forenoon conversed severally with him, and had full opportunity of witnessing the surprising retentiveness of his memory, and how perfectly he retained his mental faculties. Dinner was served at 1 O'Clock after which all returned to Baltimore.

October 20th Dined at St. Mary's College. Besides the Bishops, many of the Clergy, who had assisted at the Council, and who had not yet left Baltimore on their return home, [223] were also present at dinner. At the invitation of the President took this opportunity after dinner to visit this beautiful Sulpician Establishment.

NOTES TO INTRODUCTION

[1]Robert H. Lord, John E. Sexton and Edward T. Harrington, **History of the Archdiocese of Boston In the Various Stages of Its Development, 1604 to 1943** (3 vols.; Boston: Pilot Publishing Company, 1945), II, 385. Hereafter cited as **Hist. Arch. Bost.**

[2]Orestes Brownson, "The Right Reverend Benedict Joseph Fenwick, Second Bishop of the Diocese of Boston," **Brownson's Quarterly Review,** III (Oct., 1846), 526f. Quoted in **Hist. Arch. Bost.**, II, 275.

[3]Fenwick to his brother, George Fenwick, S.J., Dec. 8, 1842. Fordham University Archives, 213 G 5.

[4]**Hist. Arch. Bost.**, II, 376.

NOTES TO TEXT

[1]The words "whose son has since apostatized from the faith and become an Episcopal Clergyman in the town of Newton" were written by Fenwick and then crossed out.

[2]The original of this letter was in French. In his **Bibliographia Catholica Americana** (N.Y.: Catholic Publication House, 1872), p. 224, Finotti gave the date of this letter as May 29th.

[3]Prior to leaving Boston, de la Poterie made a nuisance of himself by trying to interest the Cardinal Prefect of Propaganda in constituting New England a separate Vicariate Apostolic, by repeatedly accusing Archbishop Carroll of seeking to reestablish the Jesuits, by disrupting the Midnight Mass at Christmas by trying to officiate and heaping abuse on his successor, Father Rousselet, when he could not. Repudiated publicly by the Catholics of Boston, he returned to France, took the constitutional oath, and became something of a revolutionary firebrand. After the Concordat he regularized his status in the Church and served thereafter in various dioceses. As late as 1824-25 he was serving in a small parish near Chateau-Gontiers. See **Hist. Arch, Bost.**, I, 407-420.

[4]The tactlessness of Thayer in demanding complete authority over the Catholic congregation in Boston caused a falling out with Fr. Rousselet and a short-lived schism between the French and Irish Catholics. See **Hist. Arch. Bost.**, I, 425-453.

[5]This narrative paraphrases and condenses Thayer's **An Account of the Conversion of the Rev. Mr. John Thayer** (5th ed.; Baltimore: Wm. Goddard, 1788).

[6]Papal infallibility was not defined as dogma until the promulgation of the decree **Pastor aeternus** on July 18, 1870.

[7]Fr. Nagot, first Rector of St. Mary's Seminary in Baltimore.

[8]The advertisement appeared in the **Columbian Centinel**. The controversial exchanges of Fr. Thayer and his antagonists generally appeared in the **Essex Journal** and were reprinted in the **Salem Gazette** and Boston's **Argus**. In describing these

controversies, Fenwick had reference to versions later published in pamphlet and book form by Fr. Thayer, and would paste whole sections of these into his manuscript. See Thayer's **Controversy between the Rev. John Thayer, Catholic Missionary of Boston, and the Rev. George Leslie, Pastor of a Church in Washington, N.H.** (Georgetown 'Potomack': Alexander Doyle, 1791); **Idem.** (Philadelphia: Richard Folwell, 1795); **The Controversial Writings of John Thayer** (Boston, 1793); and **The Catholic Controversy, maintained in the Periodical Publications of Boston, New Salem, and other Towns of the U.S. of America, against the calumnious objections and false imputations of the Rev. George Leslie, Pastor of a church in Warrington, N.H.** (Dublin: R. Coyne, 1809).

[9]Rev. George Lessley was born in Ireland in 1727. Having graduated from Harvard in 1748, he became minister in the Ipswich, Massachusetts area in 1749 and conducted a boarding-school there after 1752. In 1780 he moved to Washington, N.H. He died in 1810. **Hist. Arch. Bost.,** I, 465-467, 470-473, 475.

[10]If Fenwick's identification was correct (for the newspaper controversialist used only the initials "J.G.") this may have been the John Gardiner who was representative of Pownalboro, Maine, in the Massachusetts legislature. Born in Boston in 1739, he had been educated at the University of Glasgow and the Inner Temple, practised law in the British Isles, was Chief Justice of New York in 1766, Attorney-General of St. Christopher, West Indies, in 1768, and returned to Boston in 1783. His reputation as a wit and outspoken commentator on public questions is compatible with the style of the communications to the newspaper. Gardiner died in a shipwreck off Cape Ann in 1793. See **DAB.**

[11]Thayer here refers to Belknap's **Discourse intended to Commemorate the Discovery of America by Christopher Columbus.** The "Perez" referred to in Thayer's note was Fray Juan Perez, who arranged Columbus' audience with Queen Isabella.

[12]Fenwick has here copied, with only minor alterations, the obituary notice which appeared in **New England Galaxy and Masonic Magazine,** Sept. 25, 1818, and was signed "L". It was copied in the **Boston Commercial Gazette,** Sept. 28, 1818 and **Columbian Centinel,** Sept. 28, 1818.

[13]Thayer remained in Kentucky despite his anti-slavery views and intemperate zeal until 1803, when he went to Limerick, Ireland, as a missionary until his death in 1815. **Hist. Arch. Bost.,** I, 513-517, 524, 542-543, 602-603, 669, 677-683; **DAB.**

[14]Fenwick has here copied, with only minor alterations, Samuel L. Knapp's "Memoir of Bishop Cheverus," **Boston Monthly Magazine,** I (June, 1825), 2-22.

[15]This concludes the quotation from Knapp's article.

[16]The item in question is "Lettre du P. de la Chasse, Superieur Général des Missions de la Nouvelle France au Pere * * * de la Même Compagnie. Sur la mort du P. Rasles. A Quebec, le 29 octobre 1724." For a discussion of weaknesses in this and other French accounts of Rasles' assassination, see Arthur J. Riley, **Catholicism in New England to 1788** (Washington, D.C.: Catholic University of America Press, 1936), pp. 200ff.

[17]This enumeration leaves out of account Rev. Patrick Byrne, who had been sent on a missionary trip to Vermont.

[18]This begins another lengthy extract from Knapp's "Memoir of Bishop Cheverus".

[19]This concludes the quotation from Knapp's article.

[20]Family quarrels led to the closing of Rev. Barber's school in 1828. For some

years thereafter, he conducted a mission to the Penobscot Indians in Maine. He died at Georgetown College, where he was teaching, in 1847. **Hist. Arch., Bost., II, 59-64, 78, 81-82; Who Was Who in America.**

[21]Born in County Kerry, Ireland, in 1781, John Mahony had previously preached in Maryland and Virginia. In 1826 he became the first pastor of St. Mary's Church in Salem, Massachusetts and was pastor in Lowell, Massachusetts after 1831. **Hist. Arch. Bost., II, 45, 52, 55, 143, 145.**

[22]Charles Dominic Ffrench was born in County Galway, Ireland, in 1775. After ministries in Ireland and Canada, he joined the Diocese of New York in 1817. After coming to Boston in 1826, he labored in Maine and New Hampshire for some years. He left the diocese in 1839 and returned in 1846 to establish Immaculate Conception Parish in Lawrence, Massachusetts. He died in 1851. See his autobiographical accounts, **A Short Memoir, with Some Documents, in Vindication of the Charges Made by Malicious Persons against the Character of the Rev. Charles Ffrench, Addressed to the Roman Catholics of British America and the United States** (St. John, New Brunswick, 1822), and "The Conversion of Charles Ffrench to the Catholic Church," photostat in the Dominican College, Washington, D.C., transcript in the Archives of the Archdiocese of Boston. See also **Hist. Arch. Bost., I,** 745; **II,** 45-48, 51, 58, 67, 68-71, 149, 161, 275, 528-529, 531, 620; **DAB.**

[23]Patrick Byrne came from Kilkenny, Ireland, as a student in 1818 and was ordained priest in 1820. During Cheverus' episcopate, he labored among the Indians and in Vermont. Under Fenwick, he served briefly at Holy Cross Cathedral before becoming the first pastor of St. Mary's in the North End of Boston. He died in 1844, shortly after becoming the first resident pastor in New Bedford, Massachusetts. **Hist. Arch. Bost., I,** 700, 719, 736, 738, 809; **II,** 31, 55, 57, 72, 84-85, 105, 267, 284, 296; **III,** 7, 9.

[24]This section of the narrative appeared, with some alterations, in **Annales de l'association de la propagation de la foi,** V (1831), 451ff.

[25]Born in 1761, Elijah Kellogg was, after service in the revolutionary army, graduated from Dartmouth in 1785 and ordained a Congregational minister in 1788. Dismissed by his parish in Portland, Maine, in 1811, he led a secessionist congregation until 1821. From that time until his death in 1842, he held no settled position. **Hist. Arch. Bost., II,** 72-81, 157.

[26]Fenwick's initiatives led to a struggle between Kellogg and Roman Catholic clergy which led to Kellogg's abandoning his efforts among the Passamaquoddies in 1830. **Hist. Arch. Bost., II,** 72-81.

[27]Dennis Ryan arrived in Boston as a prisoner of war in 1814. Ordained in 1817, he was sent to Maine in the following year and carried on his apostolate there with brief interruptions until 1840, when he left the diocese. When he died in Lockport, Illinois, in 1852, he was reputed to be the third oldest priest in the United States. **Hist. Arch. Bost., I,** 675, 698-699, 735; **II,** 31, 65, 150, 151, 267, 282, 304.

[28]Here ends the section which appeared in **Annales de la propagation de la foi.**

[29]James Fitton was born in Boston in 1805 and attended Rev. Virgil Barber's school at Claremont, N.H. Immediately after his ordination, he was sent on missionary journeys to Maine and Vermont and then became in 1830 the second resident priest in Hartford, Connecticut. To conduct his apostolate in central and western Massachusetts, he moved in 1836 to Worcester, where he purchased and deeded to Fenwick the land for Holy Cross College. After a few years of service in the newly-established Diocese of Hartford, he became in 1855 pastor of the Church of the Most

Holy Redeemer in Boston and remained there until his death in 1881. See autobiographical information in his **Sketches of the Establishment of the Church in New England** (Boston: P. Donahoe, 1872). See also **Hist. Arch. Bost.**, II, 42-43, 48, 79, 100-101, 105, 166-169, 171-178, 285-286, 290, 323-324, 333, 342, 347, 469, 471, 511-513, 619, 763; III, 9, 25, 146, 257, 263, 264; **DAB.**

[30]An orphan who insisted upon converting to Catholicism, William Wiley pursued an apostolate in Salem, Massachusetts, and Boston until going to Taunton and Fall River in 1837. He was pastor in Providence, Rhode Island, from 1842 until his return to East Boston in 1851. He died in 1855. **Hist. Arch. Bost.**, Il, 42-44, 48, 143, 145-146, 149, 165, 171, 272, 282, 285, 510-512; III, 9.

[31]A cousin of Rev. Virgil Barber, William Tyler was born in 1806. After his ordina- tion he undertook a variety of tasks, including a stint at Benedicta, the Irish farm- ing community in Maine. In 1844 he became bishop of the new Diocese of Hartford, Conneticut, the first native New Englander raised to the episcopacy. He died in 1849. **Hist. Arch. Bost.**, I, 750; II, 42-44-45, 49, 89, 155, 161, 293-294, 306, 402; **Who Was Who in America.**

[32]John Smith was assigned to minister to the Passamaquoddy Indians, but suf- fered a nervous breakdown within a year and returned to his native Ireland. **Hist. Arch. Bost.**, II, 48, 78.

[33]Robert D. Woodley was sent to Rhode Island and Connecticut. Providing inept at dealing with Irish congregations, he was recalled to the Cathedral parish. He left the diocese in 1830 to enter the Jesuit order and died in Maryland in 1857. **Hist. Arch. Bost.**, II, 49, 51, 85-91, 94, 98, 161.

[34]The Ursuline Convent was burned by a Nativist mob in 1834.

[35]Bernard O'Cavanaugh was the first resident pastor in Hartford, Connecticut. He left the diocese in 1831 and, after service in Cincinnati, Detroit and Europe, returned in 1845 to pursue an apostolate in western Massachusetts. **Hist. Arch. Bost.**, II, 49, 98, 101, 168, 286, 333, 550, 551, 622.

[36]Born in County Kerry, Ireland, Thomas J. O'Flaherty was a physician before entering the priesthood. He became Vicar General of the diocese in 1830 and as- sisted in editing the diocesan newspaper briefly before setting out for Ireland in 1833. After his return to the diocese in 1840 he was at St. Mary's in the North End of Boston until a power struggle with his co-pastor raised the specter of Trusteeism. Sent to St. Mary's in Salem, Massachusetts, in 1842, he died in 1846. **Hist. Arch. Bost.**, II, 45, 58, 90, 198-200, 267, 273-274, 301-306, 342, 347; III, 9.

[37]Bishop Fenwick left this item for later completion.

VITA

Joseph M. McCarthy pursued his studies at St. John's Seminary and Boston Col- lege, where he received the doctorate in history and philosophy of education. Now Associate Professor of Education in Suffolk University, Boston, Massachusetts, he is the author of **Humanistic Emphases in the Educational Thought of Vincent of Beauvais** (Leiden and Cologne: E.J. Brill, 1976), as well as three other books and numerous scholarly articles on historical subjects.

INDEX

U.S. Catholic Historical Society

ADDITIONAL   TITLES   FROM   THE   MONOGRAPH   SERIES:

William Harper Bennett
CATHOLIC FOOTSTEPS IN OLD NEW
A Chronicle of Catholicity in the City of New York from 1524 to 1808

This long out of print volume provides a readable and useful account of the early history of Catholicism in New York, from the founding of New Amsterdam to the early federal period, and is recommended to all who seek a clear, well written chronicle of this period. In the context of life in the colonial and early federal periods the author details the lives of many important figures who had a direct influence on the manner of Catholic life, including Father Jogues, Bishop Carroll, Governor Dongan, and Dominick Lynch.
"Vigorous in style, and never dull...it is to be cordially commended for its intrinsic merit and for its loyal tribute to the Church."
THE CATHOLIC WORLD

"Nowhere else can (this material) be made so readily and practically available ...The volume...makes a most serviceable and attractive contribution to our local historical records."
AMERICA

Monograph No. 28   499p.   Cloth $8.00
ISBN: 0-930060-08-3   LC: 77-359169

Rev. Clarence E. Walworth
THE OXFORD MOVEMENT IN AMERICA
Glimpses of Life in an Anglican Seminary
Reprinted from the edition of 1895, with an Introduction by David N.O'Brien and a Commentary by James H. Smylie

The Oxford Movement in America was an event of signal importance in American Catholic history as it was in the history of the Episcopal Church. This volume by Clarence Walworth, one of the first Paulists, is the only work by a Catholic on the American phase of the Oxford Movement, and is an excellent introduction to the subject. It also contains an interesting account of Cardinal Newman just prior to his conversion.

The new introduction and commentary analyze Walworth's own place in the Movement. This work should stimulate reflection on the crucial questions of history, religion, and culture which remain as alive for this generation as they were a century ago.
Monograph No. 30   175p.   Cloth $7.50
ISBN: 0-930060-10-5   LC:.77-150436

Reverend Michael J. DeVito, Ph.D.
THE NEW YORK REVIEW (1905-1908)
An in-depth study of a scholarly journal that has always been suspected of having had ties with the Modernist crisis in America.

The New York Review, America's first Catholic scientific theological journal was founded during the peak years of the Modernist movement. Published from 1905 to 1908 by the professors of St. Joseph's Seminary, Dunwoodie, New York, it "silently but mysteriously" ceased publication with the promulgation of Pope Pius X's encyclical which condemned the movement. This detailed examination of the New York Review thoroughly probes its editorial policy, concept of church, relationship to modernism, and openness to scientific methods in treating theology and the Bible.

Many central figures of the Modernist crisis in America had close ties with the editors of the Review, articles appeared in its pages which involved principles of eccles-iastical reform, and exhibited a strong tendency towards sympathy with the Modernists. Father DeVito explores the theological controversy, its place in American church history, and the long-standing thesis that the Review was suppressed or condemned by the Holy See, and its Sulpicion founders censured for their views.

Monograph No. 34   342p. Illustrated   Cloth $13.95
ISBN: 0-930060-14-8   LC: 77-75637

Sr. Mary Christine Taylor, SSJ
"NORTH COUNTRY"
A History of the Foundations of Catholicism in Northern New York

"A valuable account of the institutional development of an American diocese"
CATHOLIC HISTORICAL REVIEW

"A scholarly study that is noteworthy for its comprehensive approach and thorough analysis. This book will appeal to the scholar and the student, but all northern New Yorkers will find much to reward individual interests."
NORTH COUNTRY CATHOLIC

"North Country" traces the growth of Catholicism in northern New York from the time of the early Iroquois Missions. The book follows the trail first blazed by the Indian missionaries and later revived by immigrant settlers in Jefferson, Lewis, Franklin, Clinton and St. Lawrence counties; the present diocese of Ogdensburg. The author examines the harsh poverty of the parishes, nationalistic rivalries of French and Irish Catholics, the dearth of clergy, and a bigoted opposition that transformed scattered Catholic settlements into a thriving unified diocese.

Monograph No. 32   450p.   Cloth $12.00
ISBN: 0-930060-12-1   LC: 77-359034

Martin J. Becker, Ph.D.
ALBANY
A History of Catholic Life in the Diocese of Albany, 1609-1864

"Contributes to a more sophisticated understanding of Catholicism in upstate New York, and the conflicts which pitted various groups of laity against pastors and diocessan officials. The author's tale of the development of a diocese and region encompassing 28 counties and over 28,000 square miles in 1847 is painstakingly researched and documented. It sketches the growth of Catholicism from the arrival of the Jesuit missionaries through the 1860's, drawing upon an impressive body of archival and manuscript material. A valuable compendium of hitherto scattered information. It attempts to survey the development of the entire diocese."

CATHOLIC HISTORICAL REVIEW

Albany is a scholarly reconstruction of the circumstances of daily life for Catholics in upstate New York before the Civil War. The author describes how Catholics lived the faith, the immigration to the region and its economic activities. The number of Catholics in the area and their ethnic divisions are studied. Chapters cover the specific problems and successes of the parishes in Troy, Oswego, Utica and Carthage. Dr. Becker carefully develops his subject to illustrate why the Catholic Church prospered in spite of Protestant nativism and Catholic poverty, ethnic cleavage and Lay trusteeism.

"Presents a fresh educational glimpse of the people who were the roots of the Albany Diocese."

THE EVANGELIST

"It is refreshing to find an historian who is sensitive to the geographical influencees of historical events."

NORTH COUNTRY CATHOLIC

Monograph No. 31   244p.   Cloth $13.75
ISBN: 0-930060-11-3   LC: 77-359170

James Addison White
THE FOUNDING OF CLIFF HAVEN
Early Years of the Catholic Summer School of America

The Catholic Summer School of America was the Catholic adaptation of the Chautauqua. The School constituted an unprecedented cooperative attempt on part of cleric and lay leaders to draw closer bonds of cultural and spiritual unity within a rapidly-expanding Catholic communion at a time when such work was of vital importance. This book covers the formative years of the CSSA, 1892-1905, when Catholics gathered each year to hear lectures and participate in a recreation program.

Monograph No. 24   105p.   Cloth $5.00
ISBN: 0-930060-06-7   LC: 53-1915